# THE COLLECTED COURSES OF THE ACADEMY OF EUROPEAN LAW

*Series Editors*

PROFESSOR LOÏC AZOULAI,

PROFESSOR MARISE CREMONA,

PROFESSOR FRANCESCO FRANCIONI

*European University Institute, Florence*

*Assistant Editor*

ANNY BREMNER

*European University Institute, Florence*


# VOLUME XXII/1

# The Cultural Dimension of Human Rights

# THE COLLECTED COURSES OF THE ACADEMY OF EUROPEAN LAW

*Edited by*
Professor Loïc Azoulai,
Professor Marise Cremona, and Professor Francesco Francioni

*Assistant Editor*
Anny Bremner

Each year the Academy of European Law in Florence, Italy, invites a group of outstanding lecturers to teach at its summer courses on Human Rights law and European Union law.
A 'general course' is given in each of the two fields by a distinguished scholar or practitioner, who examines the field as a whole through a particular thematic, conceptual, or philosophical lens, or looks at a theme in the context of the overall body of law. In addition, a series of 'specialized courses' brings together a group of highly qualified scholars to explore and analyse a specific theme in relation to Human Rights law and EU law.
The Academy's mission, to produce scholarly analyses which are at the cutting edge of these two fields, is achieved through the publication of this series, the Collected Courses of the Academy of European Law.

# The Cultural Dimension of Human Rights

Edited by
ANA FILIPA VRDOLJAK

OXFORD
UNIVERSITY PRESS

# OXFORD
UNIVERSITY PRESS

Great Clarendon Street, Oxford, OX2 6DP,
United Kingdom

Oxford University Press is a department of the University of Oxford.
It furthers the University's objective of excellence in research, scholarship,
and education by publishing worldwide. Oxford is a registered trade mark of
Oxford University Press in the UK and in certain other countries

Published in the United States of America by Oxford University Press
198 Madison Avenue, New York, NY 10016, United States of America

British Library Cataloguing in Publication Data
Data available

Library of Congress Control Number: 2013943835

ISBN 978-0-19-964212-0

Printed and bound in Great Britain by
CPI Group (UK) Ltd, Croydon, CR0 4YY

# *Acknowledgments*

This collection of essays emerged from a series of lectures delivered as part of the Academy of European Law's annual human rights law summer school held at the European University Institute, Florence. A setting and city steeped in the preoccupations of culture and humanism which run through this volume. Francesco Francioni's determination to make culture the theme of the 2011 summer school provided a forum for lecturers and students from every corner of the globe to engage in challenging and animated discussions in a spirit of collegiality and intellectual rigour for which the EUI is renowned. This lecture series, and the many that have preceded it and those that will no doubt follow in the decades to come, are only made possible through the tireless work and extraordinary commitment of Anny Bremner, Joyce Davies, Francesco Francioni, Marise Cremona, and Loïc Azoulai at the Academy of European Law, and the enthusiasm of the summer school participants themselves. I am also grateful for the contributions made by the individual lecturers, Yvonne Donders, Federico Lenzerini, Gaetano Pentassuglia, Olivier Roy, and Siegfried Weissner, and those who generously accepted my subsequent invitation to prepare contributions, Pasquale Annicchino, Evangelia Psychogiopoulou, and Tania Voon. Each has added to the richness of this collection.

We are all indebted to the meticulous editorial assistance provided by researchers at the EUI, Wim Muller and Valentina Spiga. Special thanks are due to the ever patient, generous, and joyous Anny Bremner, the assistant editor of this series, and Natasha Flemming, Clare Kennedy and Alex Flach at Oxford University Press.

This book is dedicated to Florence, long may its humanist flame burn, and to the Academy of European Law, long may it be a forum for dialogue and deliberation.

Ana Filipa Vrdoljak
*Sydney*

# Contents

# Table of Cases

# Tables of Instruments

# Notes on Contributors

**Pasquale Annicchino** is a Research Fellow at the Robert Schuman Centre for Advanced Studies at the European University Institute. He received his PhD in Law from the University of Siena where he also graduated in law summa cum laude in December 2006. In 2007 he was a Visiting Scholar at the Centre for Law and Religion of the Emory University Law School in Atlanta (United States). In 2009 he specialized (LLM) in European Public Law at University College London (United Kingdom), where he also served as Editor in Chief of the *UCL Human Rights Review*. Pasquale is also a fellow in Constitutional Law and Comparative Constitutional Law in the Department of Political Science of the University of Salerno. He serves as Book Review editor for *Religion and Human Rights: An International Journal* and is a member of the Editorial Board of *Quaderni di Diritto e Politica Ecclesiastica* published by Il Mulino. His main interests lie in the areas of legal theory, law and religion, EU law, religion, and politics.

**Yvonne Donders** is Professor of International Human Rights and Cultural Diversity and Executive Director of the Amsterdam Center for International Law at the Faculty of Law of the University of Amsterdam. She graduated from Utrecht University in international relations and obtained her PhD at the Law Faculty of Maastricht University on cultural human rights and the right to cultural identity. Her research interests include public international law, international human rights law, in particular economic, social and cultural rights, and human rights and cultural diversity. Yvonne Donders worked from March 2011 to October 2012 as project manager (one day per week detachment) at the Netherlands Institute for Human Rights (College voor de Rechten van de Mens), assisting the transformation of the Equal Treatment Commission to the NHRI. Previously Yvonne Donders worked as Programme Specialist on Economic, Social and Cultural Rights in the Division of Human Rights and Struggle against Discrimination of UNESCO's Secretariat in Paris. She is currently a member of the National Commission for UNESCO, member of the European Expert Network on Culture (EENC), member of the Board of the Royal Netherlands Society of International Law and Chair of the Dutch United Nations Association (Nederlandse Vereniging voor de Verenigde Naties, NVVN).

**Federico Lenzerini** is Professor of International Law and European Union Law at the University of Siena (Italy). He is also Professor in the LLM programme in Intercultural Human Rights at St Thomas University School of Law, Miami (FL), USA. He has been Consultant to UNESCO (Paris) and Counsel to the Italian Ministry of Foreign Affairs for international negotiations related to cultural heritage. He has been Rapporteur of the Committee on the Rights of Indigenous Peoples and a member of the Biotechnology Committee of the International Law Association, and is currently a member of the Committee on Cultural Heritage Law of the same Association. His fields of research include human rights law, culture and cultural heritage, asylum and refugee law, international trade law, rights of indigenous peoples.

**Gaetano Pentassuglia**, PhD, is currently a Reader in International Law and Human Rights, Director of LLM Studies, and Director of the Human Rights and International Law Unit at the University of Liverpool Law School. He has taught at prestigious universities in Europe and North America. More recently, he was a Fernand Braudel Senior Fellow at the European University Institute, Italy, and a Visiting Professor at the University of Toronto. He is the author of numerous leading works in the area of international law, particularly human rights, minority and indigenous rights, including *Minority Groups and Judicial Discourse in International Law* (2009), and *Minorities in International Law* (2002).

**Evangelia Psychogiopoulou** is a lawyer and research fellow at the Hellenic Foundation for European and Foreign Policy (ELIAMEP), Athens, Greece. A graduate of the Faculty of Law of the Kapodistrian University of Athens, she holds a DEA in EU law from Paris I University, a master of research degree in law from the European University Institute (Florence, Italy), and a PhD in Law from the same university. Her main areas of research include EU cultural and media policies and human rights protection. She has held research and management positions at the Academy of European Law (Florence, Italy), the Directorate General Education and Culture of the European Commission and UNESCO. Her articles have appeared in *European Foreign Affairs Review, European Law Journal, European Law Review, Legal Issues of Economic Integration and European State Aid Law Quarterly*, among others. Her recent publications include *The Integration of Cultural Considerations in EU Law and Policies* (2008), *The European Court of Human Rights and the Rights of Marginalised Individuals and Minorities in National Context* (ed) (2010), and *Understanding Media Policies: A European Perspective* (ed) (2012).

**Olivier Roy** is presently Professor at the European University Institute (Florence), where he heads the Mediterranean programme at the Robert Schuman Centre for Advanced Studies. Professor Roy received an 'Agrégation de Philosophie' and a PhD in Political Science (Sciences-Po, Paris). He has been a Senior Researcher at the French National Center for Scientific Research (since 1985), Professor at the Ecole des Hautes Etudes en Sciences Sociales (since 2003), and visiting professor at Berkeley University (2008/09). He headed the OSCE's Mission for Tajikistan (1993–94) and was a Consultant for the UN Office of the Coordinator for Afghanistan (1988). His field works include studies on Afghanistan, Political Islam, Middle East, Islam in the West and comparative religions. He is the author of *Holy Ignorance* (2010), *Globalized Islam* (2004), and *The Failure of Political Islam* (1994). He currently heads a major project, 'ReligioWest', which is investigating the 'formatting' of religions in the West.

**Ana Filipa Vrdoljak** is Professor of Law and Associate Dean (Research), Faculty of Law, University of Technology, Sydney. She is the author of *International Law, Museums and the Return of Cultural Objects* (2006) and co-editor with Federico Lenzerini of *International Law for Common Goods: Normative Perspectives on Human Rights, Culture and Nature* (2013). She is co-General Editor, with Francesco Francioni, of the new Oxford University Press book series entitled *Cultural Heritage Law and Policy* and Advisory Board member for the *International Journal of Cultural Property*. She is a member of the International Law Association's Cultural Heritage Law Committee and Secretary of the International Cultural Property Society (US). Professor Vrdoljak has been Marie Curie Fellow and Jean Monnet Fellow, in the Department of Law, European University Institute, Florence. She holds a Doctor of Philosophy (in Law) from the University of Sydney.

**Tania Voon** is Professor and Associate Dean (Research) at Melbourne Law School, The University of Melbourne. She is a former Legal Officer of the WTO Appellate Body Secretariat and has previously practised law with Mallesons Stephen Jaques (now King & Wood Mallesons) and the Australian Government Solicitor. Tania has also taught law at Georgetown University, the University of Western Ontario, the Australian National University, Monash University, and Bond University. Tania undertook her Master of

Laws at Harvard Law School and her PhD in Law at the University of Cambridge. She has published widely in the areas of public international law and international economic law. She is the author of *Cultural Products and the World Trade Organization* (2007) and a member of the Indicative List of Governmental and Non-Governmental Panelists for resolving WTO disputes. Tania has provided expert advice and training to entities such as the Australian Department of Foreign Affairs and Trade, the WTO, the World Health Organization, Telstra, and the McCabe Centre for Law and Cancer.

**Siegfried Wiessner** is Professor of Law at St Thomas University School of Law and the Founder and Director of its LLM and JSD programmes in Intercultural Human Rights. He holds a law degree (1977) as well as a Dr iur (1989) from the University of Tübingen and an LLM from Yale University (1982). He is the Editor-in-Chief of Martinus Nijhoff's 'Studies in Intercultural Human Rights'. In 2009, he was a Fernand Braudel Senior Fellow at the European University Institute in Florence, Italy. From 2007 to 2010, he was a member of the Executive Council of The American Society of International Law. From 2008 to 2012, he served as the Chair of the International Law Association's Committee on the Rights of Indigenous Peoples. Professor Weissner has published widely in the fields of constitutional law, international law, human rights, international indigenous law, the law of armed conflict, arbitration, space law, and refugee law. He is co-author, with Michael Reisman, of *International Law in Contemporary Perspective* (2004) and is the author of *Die Funktion der Staatsangehörigkeit* (1989), on the function of nationality.

# Introduction

*Ana Filipa Vrdoljak*

The manifestations of culture are ever present and cultures themselves are diverse. These characteristics have rendered culture a difficult fit for international law. It has either largely ignored culture, as is typified by the underdevelopment of cultural rights, or has promoted its exclusivity, as exemplified in the rules governing state succession or state immunity. As understandings of culture have evolved in recent decades beyond the realms of so-called high culture to encompass culture as ways of life there has been a shift in emphasis from national cultures to cultural diversity within and across states. This has entailed a push to more fully articulate cultural rights within human rights law. A renewed academic focus on this area of international human rights law has thus grown, in particular, with the evolution of Article 15 of the International Covenant of Economic, Social and Cultural Rights (ICESCR) (the right to participate in cultural life) and Article 27 of the International Covenant on Civil and Political Rights (ICCPR) (Minorities). While fundamentally important to the theme of this volume—*the cultural dimension of human rights*—it is not its driving force. Instead, the intersections between culture and human rights are shown to have engaged some of the most heated and controversial debates across international law and theory, broadly testing their boundaries and fostering their evolution in response to these challenges.

Despite the diversity of contributions to this volume, they are clearly tied by one unifying thread—that culture is understood, protected, and promoted not only for its physical manifestations. Rather, it is the relationship of culture to people, individually or in groups, and the diversity of these relationships which is being protected and promoted; hence, the overlap between culture and human rights.

The significance in this shift in outlook that has occurred in international law in the last half century is clearly evident in its interaction with states, the international community and individuals. For states, where Article 15 ICESCR was previously defined as the right to participate in national cultural life and Article 27 ICCPR was drafted on the premise that the state would determine the existence of minorities within its territory, they are today required to report on positive measures they have implemented to enable minorities and indigenous peoples to maintain and develop their distinct cultural identities. For the international community, where previously the importance of culture and its manifestations was promoted largely on the basis of its role in the arts and sciences, today its promotion is based on its importance in ensuring the contribution of all peoples to the cultural heritage of humanity. For the individual, where cultural rights were interpreted to harmonize with civil and political rights designed to foster their integration within the state, today there is a greater cognizance in human rights law that we carry within us a multiplicity of identities, whether they be cultural, religious, or other communal affiliations, and equally defining, immutable characteristics like gender, ethnicity, age, sexual orientation, or disabilities. The shift and its impact should not be over-stated. The preeminence of the state and the scaffolding created for it by modern international law has not dissolved. But what this volume seeks to do is at the very least register how this shift is occurring.

The two contributions in Part I provide an overview of the tensions between culture and human rights in law from a political and social theory perspective and legal perspective. They serve as a backdrop for the remaining discussions con-tained in this volume. Both chapters focus on the interplay of religion, culture, and human rights in defining relations between individuals and groups within states and the broader international community. They take a wider historical view and hit similar thematic notes of contention, narrowing in on questions of compro-mise and consensus.

In *Human Rights between Religions, Cultures and Universality*, Olivier Roy and Pasquale Annicchino focus on the questions and concerns raised by contemporary societies which expose the tensions and clashes between human rights, cultures, and religions. They explore how the totalizing and universalizing mythology of each renders this conflict inevitable and necessary. Yet they point out that that which brings them into conflict—that they occupy the same space (relations between individuals, groups, and society) and employ the same strategies (norma-tive source)—is also a possible ground for consensus and their compatibility. They examine the intersection between human rights, Christianity, and secularism in Western societies through time, noting that the link made between human rights and secularization has received push back from religious conservatives and from those opposing the imposition of a supranational system of values and norms. Those in the latter camp who reject the universality of human rights law either adopt a relativist view which embraces an anthropological notion of culture and argue that it is a product of one particular (Western) cultural tradition; or con-versely, hold the view that universal values can only be formulated by a divine being and are above individual will. Roy and Annicchino observe that both posi-tions and their various manifestations today are highly politicized, as reflected in the response of certain religious or religiously dominated states to the Convention on the Elimination of Discrimination Against Women (CEDAW) and the United Nations resolutions on sexual orientation and gender identity. Yet, they note that migration and the resultant cultural and religious diversity have required secular countries themselves to revisit and re-evaluate the relationship between religion, culture, and human rights within their states. Human rights are used to impose a set of common values internally within a state and externally it has led to a loss of state sovereignty through the judicialization of international relations. Roy and Annicchino argue that a consensus on human rights is not possible for political reasons and, in any case, these debates are irrelevant. Rather, the current discon-nection of religions from culture has allowed religious groups to engage new tools to respond to changes in the contemporary political sphere. This has led diverse religious and cultural groups towards a 'common paradigm of legal norms and principles', which will result in a 'common political culture, but not a common secularization process'.

My chapter, *Liberty, Equality, Diversity: States, Cultures, and International Law* covers similar terrain from an international law perspective. I explore how culture is engaged by contemporary international law, particularly human rights law. As with Roy and Annicchino, the state remains my central focus as its relations with individuals and groups are defined and refined through law and rights discourse. A structure based on the remodelled republican cry of *liberté, égalité, fraternité* highlights the various strategies employed over almost 400 years, from tolerance, non-discrimination, and solidarity, to address relations between majority and minority groups within societies, whether that affiliation be religious or cultural. The first and most narrow phase arose with the move to reconfigure relations between the church and state, through the adoption of official tolerance and acceptance of religious pluralism, and the articulation of the right to religious freedom. These and related freedoms (like freedom of expression, association, assembly) defined relations between the state and the individual but also between the individual and other individuals within society. These freedoms were limited so that their enjoyment did not harm others or offend public morals. This template was extended to encompass cultural groups and the notion of non-discrimination. Strict equality between individuals could not feasibly be attained through civil and political rights alone. It had to encompass the cultural realm and ensure that public resources and spaces were available to all groups and individuals. Non-discrimination has been pivotal in the breakdown of segregation between groups within states and to ensuring the participation of all individuals in political processes regardless of their religious, cultural, or racial affiliation. Yet, conversely, the right to culture was no longer simply defined as a right to a culture (usually the national culture), but a right to one's own culture. There was an opening up of the numerical breadth of participation and depth in the diversity of views and values. Cultural diversity is promoted in contemporary international law not because of the principle of equality but because it is viewed as a common good of the international community. Yet, there is awareness that diversity is only sustainable with the recognition that cultures and religions are not static, homogeneous, or apolitical and there is a vital need to ensure effective participation and dialogue within groups themselves. Such processes would lead to consensus on the core values of a common culture in which the majority and minorities can co-exist.

Part II contains contributions which extrapolate the influence on international law of two distinct groups, minorities and indigenous peoples, which have pursued recognition of collective cultural rights through human rights law. Both chapters speak to the evolutionary potential of human rights law in responding to such claims.

In *Protecting Minority Groups through Human Rights Courts: The Interpretive Role of European and Inter-American Jurisprudence*, Gaetano Pentassuglia compares and contrasts the jurisprudence of the European Court of Human Rights (ECtHR) and the Inter-American Court of Human Rights (I/ACtHR) concerning cases brought by minorities and indigenous peoples respectively. In his detailed account,

Pentassuglia initially reviews how recognition of collective rights has influenced the substantive and procedural aspects of each jurisdiction. Under the European Convention, this has been driven by the principle of non-discrimination and claims by minorities. Under the American Convention, it is propelled by claims by indigenous peoples and positive obligations concerning land rights. Pentassuglia details how the European jurisprudence is driven by the principle of 'special vigilance' in respect of racial discrimination. So while the ECtHR usually promotes negative obligations, it is prepared to circumscribe state discretion through positive obligations in order to promote pluralism. By contrast, the American Court works from the starting point of a framework of positive obligations arising under the ACHR which limit state sovereignty. Pentassuglia argues that despite this divergence in approaches there is a convergence on procedural aspects which recognizes the collective characteristic of these actions. He also notes that both Courts are open to developments beyond their own jurisdictions in human rights law relating to minorities and indigenous peoples. But again, the European Court has shown itself to date to be more reticent and cautious than its American counterpart. A telling example of this difference is typified in their respective stances on self-identification. Where the ECtHR has indicated that subjective determination by the group itself was not enough (while indicating that it would exercise a degree of oversight over the state's margin of appreciation concerning internal definitions and recognition mechanisms), the I/ACtHR has adopted a more fluid interpretation revolving around historical links to land. Pentassuglia makes the telling point that the jurisprudence of both Courts is important not so much for these definitional aspects but because of the malleability of the judicial readings of human rights law which renders it responsive to the claims of groups made vulnerable because of their group identity. He rightly suggests that the divergent judicial responses are inevitable with distinct instruments and the socio-political contexts of the states parties, but equally that increased convergence is likely in the future as supranational and domestic courts open themselves up to developments in other jurisdictions.

Siegfried Wiessner, in his chapter entitled *Culture and the Rights of Indigenous Peoples*, explores the cultural rights claims of indigenous peoples through various international law instruments, not only human rights treaties. He explores in depth why and how these claims have been instrumental in transforming our understanding of the relationship between land, culture and identity, and between cultural rights and other human rights. Indigenous peoples' claims centre on preserving and promoting their unique collective cultural identities which have been further hewn in recent centuries by losses visited upon them by foreign and colonial occupation. Weissner shows that by framing their actions within human rights discourse, indigenous peoples have effectively challenged the existing parameters concerning cultural rights and collective rights. They have always made clear that their claims concerning culture are intimately tied to other rights, including to land, to life, and to self-determination. It is an approach exposed not only by Weissner but also by Pentassuglia. The centrality and interconnectedness of culture with other human rights, rather than its siloing, is significant not only in more fully appreciating indigenous claims but also for better understanding the role of culture in the field more generally for all. As Weissner ably details, this way of understanding the culture is reflected in the various strategies used by indigenous peoples seeking recognition and realization of these rights across a range of international law instruments—not only human rights treaties. The culmination of these efforts to date has been the 2007 UN Declaration on the Rights of Indigenous Peoples, which he shows is already having a symbiotic impact upon the development of customary international law concerning the interface between culture and human rights.

Part III focuses upon ways in which cultural rights can be realized beyond specialist human rights law frameworks. Both contributions consider the interplay between culture, human rights, and international law within the context of legal frameworks governing trade between states. The ability and indeed suitability of specialist legal regimes governing trade or investment disputes in addressing human rights violations remains a focus of intense intellectual debate. For our purposes, this debate is further intensified because it covers a category of human rights which has often been sidelined. These are important contributions because they build on the characteristic highlighted by Weissner concerning the creativity and breadth of strategies deployed to protect culture and promote cultural rights.

In her chapter entitled *The European Union and Cultural Rights*, Evangelia Psychogiopoulou explores how the European Union facilitates the protection and promotion of these rights through the cultural dimension of other human rights, including civil, political, economic, and social rights and non-discrimination, and through its mandate in respect of religious, cultural, and linguistic diversity under the latest iteration of its constitutive treaty. The European project was not about human rights when it started; its focus was and remains the common market. However, with the 1992 Maastricht Treaty and its reference to the European Convention of Human Rights and more recently the Charter of Fundamental Rights which was rendered binding with the 2009 Lisbon Treaty, human rights has come to the fore. But not cultural rights per se. Key provisions of the ECHR and Charter have been interpreted by the ECtHR and European Court of Justice (ECJ) respectively in support of a cultural dimension. Also, the ECJ has indicated that international treaties like the Universal Declaration of Human Rights, the International Covenant on Civil and Political Rights, and the International Covenant on Economic, Social and Cultural Rights as well as other multilateral human rights treaties to which member states are signatories, point the way for the protection of human rights under EU law. The Charter also provides specifically for cultural diversity not only as it pertains to national cultures but also to peoples, that is, within member states. However, as Psychogiopoulou points out, its power is negatively conferred, with no positive rights articulated in respect of individuals or groups. She explains that not only is the Charter found wanting in its lack of substantive provisions specifically covering cultural rights, but its limited enforcement regime is likewise problematic as the focus yet again remains on other human rights. Under the powers granted to the EU concerning culture, the primary responsibility for cultural matters remains with member states. However, the EU is required to respect and promote cultural diversity in its actions under its constitutive treaties. The EU's negotiation and promotion of the ratification of the UNESCO Convention on the Protection and Promotion of the Diversity of Cultural Expressions, is the leading example in this arena. It is telling that this instrument morphed substantially from an initiative centred on the articulation of cultural rights to a treaty designed to promote cultural diversity through the circulation of cultural goods and services. Psychogiopoulou highlights how efforts by the EU internally through initiatives in the field of equality, citizenship, and immigration policies have had a distinct and explicit cultural dimension to their design and operation. She ends on a positive note explaining that the EU cultural policy endeavours to promote cultural engagement and cross-cultural dialogue across and within member states through financial assistance.

Tania Voon's contribution, entitled _Culture, Human Rights and the WTO_, considers the continuing limited response of the WTO to cultural rights across its treaties. This is to be expected because unlike the European Union which has evolved into a regional organization covering concerns beyond trade, the WTO remains a specialist legal regime with an ever-expanding membership. Indeed, as Voon points out, it is the growth in the diversity of its membership which has necessarily brought questions of culture to the fore, though not cultural rights. This underdevelopment, she suggests, may in part be explained by member states' reluctance to venture beyond WTO law to other fields of international law, like human rights law, when resolving disputes. Voon explores the impact of culture on WTO law through two case studies: cultural products and food safety. She notes that the question of cultural products has been an ongoing source of tension between the United States and the European Union which has often proved intractable. Instead, what has transpired is the relocation of this contestation to another forum, namely, UNESCO and its adoption of the Cultural Diversity Convention. The United States and the European Union have also clashed in the area of food technology and safety regulation. The lengthy history of such contests, particularly concerning genetic modification, reveals a cultural divide between Europe, favouring less intervention and manipulation of food, and the United States, which is more open to taking up new food technologies. Voon queries whether the WTO rules favouring science-based findings and trade liberalization betray the organization's own cultural bias. The most obvious intersection between culture, human rights, and trade in this context is the regulation of intellectual property rights and its impact on cultural rights. The right to participate in cultural life (Article 15 ICESCR) explicitly recognizes the rights flowing to the creators of scientific, literary, and artistic works from intellectual property regimes. The boundaries of this right are being pushed by indigenous peoples towards greater recognition of collective cultural rights through their efforts to have intellectual property protect traditional knowledge. Voon explains that the WTO's Agreement on Trade-Related Aspects of Intellectual Property Rights (TRIPS Agreement) and its coverage of 'geographical indicators' likewise has the potential to protect and preserve cultures and ways of life associated with traditional methods of food and wine production encompassed by this provision. Yet, she observes that all these interventions into the WTO framework are limited. Despite some analysis by UN human rights bodies concerning the impact of the WTO and particularly the TRIPS Agreement on cultural and property rights, the WTO itself rarely contemplates the interplay of its rules with human rights norms. Voon suggests it is this reluctance to go beyond the regime's framework which has stymied its ability to address areas relating to culture and human rights, like traditional knowledge and genetic resources.

Part IV covers procedural aspects rather than substantive aspects of the intersection between culture, human rights, and international law. Yet, as was noted by other contributors to this volume, the procedural components are intrinsic and vital; both for using culture as a vehicle for hindering human rights, and as a mode for the effective realization of reparations in the face of gross violations of the human rights of individuals or communities.

Yvonne Donders in her chapter entitled *Cultural Pluralism in International Human Rights Law: The Role of Reservations* provides a detailed analysis of the reservations and responses to those reservations entered in respect of CEDAW. This becomes a case study for the use of reservations as a mode of cultural pluralism, that is, a vehicle for the realization of cultural diversity. But it is also important because it serves to highlight that culture can be used by states to justify reading down or avoiding human rights obligations altogether in respect of vulnerable individuals and groups. Donders outlines the debate concerning the special nature of human rights treaties as going beyond contractual agreements between states to agreements on common norms and behaviour of a state towards individuals within it. This distinguishing characteristic has had a knock-on effect in how reservations are interpreted in respect of such treaties, including whether international monitoring bodies, and not just other states parties, can assess the reservation's compatibility with the object and purpose of the treaty; and whether they can then sever the offending reservation from the remaining obligations of the relevant state party. Donders' case study of the CEDAW reservations centres on the use of culture as a source of justification, which is invariably attached to substantive rather than procedural treaty provisions. Her survey reveals that most reservations pertain to justifications based on incompatibility of the Convention with Islamic law and Sharia. These are either blanket reservations covering the treaty generally or are attached to specific provisions (usually concerning equality between men and women). She notes that other states have made reservations on cultural or religious grounds which point to cultural pluralism within states and not just between states. Responses to these reservations by other states parties to the Convention range from challenging the relevant countries' commitment to the instrument, objecting because the reservation is deemed contrary to its object and purpose, or objecting to a provision of a fundamental nature. The majority of states parties did not object to these reservations. Those that did clearly indicated that they viewed the reserving state as being bound, but without the benefit of the reservation. Donders, however, notes that perhaps the most effective mechanism for states to withdraw or strictly define the operation of such reservations is through the work of the Committee on the Elimination of Discrimination Against Women, which has required states to justify and detail the operation of such reservations in their state reports. She concludes that while such reservations enable states parties to human rights instruments to reflect the cultural pluralism between them, current international law has clearly stated that cultural diversity cannot be used to circumvent human rights obligations. Donders' chapter exposes that, unlike race, discrimination on grounds of gender continues to be justified on the grounds of religion or culture.

It is apt that this volume finishes with Federico Lenzerini's contribution entitled *Suppressing and Remedying Offences against Culture* which traverses a range of fields of international law to provide his own formulation of a framework for crimes against culture as an extension of the protection and promotion of cultural rights. It is not just the physical manifestations of cultures that are being protected but their intrinsic importance to the identity of individuals and the communities to which they may belong. His interpretation of culture is broadly defined in keeping with the developments in human rights law outlined by Pentassuglia and Weissner and the panoply of multilateral instruments adopted for the protection of cultural heritage during armed conflict and peacetime. The first category of offences against culture he elaborates are those where cultural heritage is destroyed in pursuit of a purpose which is legal. This includes military necessity during armed conflict or damage arising from exploitation of natural resources which results in serious violations of human rights, including cultural rights of individuals or a community. The second category encompasses acts which have an unlawful purpose, such as where the cultural heritage is deliberately targeted for destruction or damage and impacts upon humanity generally, or a particular community or an individual. The third and final category of offences against culture encompasses acts which target the cultural heritage of a religious, cultural, or ethnic group, as a collective, on a discriminatory basis, and which most recently is exemplified in the jurisprudence arising from the ad hoc International Criminal Tribunal for the former Yugoslavia. Lenzerini correctly observes that most specialist cultural heritage treaties, save the 1954 Hague Convention for the Protection of Cultural Property during Armed Conflict and the 1972 World Heritage Convention, provide little in the way of obligations which would prevent or suppress such acts. For these reasons, he points to the recent jurisprudence in international criminal tribunals and regional human rights courts as offering a means of holding perpetrators of such acts to account and providing remedies for victims. However, he concludes that the specific nature of such crimes requires a long-term view which promotes mechanisms for reconciliation between victims and perpetrators and between diverse religious and cultural groups to prevent the occurrence or recurrence of such acts in the future. This chapter's focus is procedural and particularly concentrates on enforcement mechanisms. But as with Donder's contribution before it, Lenzerini's work serves to highlight that even in the apparently innocuous realm of procedure, culture and the effective realization of cultural rights is playing a fundamental role in the shaping of existing international law norms.

This volume provides a taster of the responses by international law, and particularly human rights law, to some of the thorniest, perennial, and sadly, sometimes violent confrontations and contestations fuelled by culture in relations between individuals, groups, and the state in international society. These interventions and the changes that they herald may appear frustratingly modest and interminably incremental to some; and revolutionary or ill-conceived to others. It is nonetheless evident that a tide of change is occurring. This speaks to the plethora of challenges that culture brings forth, and the malleability or otherwise of international law to respond to them.

# PART I

# 1

# Human Rights between Religions, Cultures, and Universality[*]

*Olivier Roy and Pasquale Annicchino*

## 1. Introduction

Human rights are traditionally understood as a set of universal, inalienable, and individual rights. Almost by definition, they are supposed to be applicable everywhere and anytime, not to depend on a specific political system or culture, and to have value even in political systems, cultures, or societies that do not make any reference to them or even explicitly reject their centrality.[1] Nevertheless, it is clear that human rights have a history and a genealogy: they have been slowly established and defined in a precise historical and cultural context, mainly in England and the United States, in the wake of the Enlightenment (we might also consider a more ancient and complex genealogy, like for instance the writ of *habeas corpus*).[2] Beside the different roots that are possible to trace, we can say that there is an underlying anthropology of human rights, or more precisely, that human rights theory presupposes a certain anthropological definition of the human being: a 'self' who possesses its body, its thoughts, and is in a contracting relationship with other free

[*] The authors acknowledge travel and research funding from the ReligioWest project based at the Robert Schuman Centre for Advanced Studies (EUI) and financed by the European Research Council.

[1] This is true also for the legal instruments that have listed the basic categories of human rights. As Thomas Franck has argued: 'The Universal Declaration of Human Rights and the several ensuing legal treaties setting out civil, women, ethnic groups, and religions, were meant to create a global safety net of rights applicable to all persons, everywhere. Although these legal instruments allow some restrictions in time of national emergency, they brook no cultural exceptionalism.' See Franck, 'Are Human Rights Universal?', 80 *Foreign Affairs* (2001) 191 at 193.

[2] As Mary Ann Glendon has pointed out: 'The British Bill of Rights of 1689, the U.S. Declaration of Independence of 1776, and the French Declaration of the Rights of Man and Citizen of 1789 were born out of struggles to overthrow autocratic rule and to establish governments based on the consent of the governed. They proclaimed that all men were born free and equal and that the purpose of government was to protect man's natural liberties. They gave rise to the modern language of rights'. See M.A. Glendon, *A World Made New: Eleanor Roosevelt and the Universal Declaration of Human Rights* (2001) xvii.

selves. '*Possessive individualism*' is at the core of this vision of human rights, what-ever extension or interpretation we give to this term.[3]

The social bind is thus a consequence of the will or action of the self; hence the centrality of the theory of the social contract in the philosophical construction of human rights theory. It goes with a rejection of the conception of a holistic soci-ety, and even of a religion where God is supposed to be the supreme norm. The political sphere is therefore understood not as the expression of a transcendental power, nor even the embodiment of a holistic society, but rather as a space ruled by law, which is in fact a set of rules of the game, enabling individual citizens to enjoy their rights without infringing upon those of others; constraints do not come from a great '*Other*' (God, the Sovereign, the 'We'), but from the need for rules of the game agreed in the name of the public good by the citizens themselves. The compatibility of the theory of human rights with religions (which set an absolute truth and/or the will of God as source of norms), or with cultures (which translate into an all-encompassing set of basic norms that define a holistic society, assigning their place to individual human beings), as we will argue, is clearly the big issue concerning their generalization.

## 2. Human Rights and the Secularization of Christian Theology

Human rights are traditionally understood as ignoring religion and to be purely based on secular grounds, not necessarily opposing religions, but putting on them the onus of proving that they are human rights compatible.[4] The debate is in fact more complex: in many cases, both proponents and opponents of the theory of the universality of human rights underline the close relationship between human rights

---

[3] The term was coined by C.B. MacPherson, *The Political Theory of Possessive Individualism: Hobbes to Locke* (1962); for a critical approach see Balibar, 'Possessive Individualism Reversed: From Locke to Derrida', 9 *Constellations* (2002) 299. It is also true that other authors assert that human rights have profound religious origins. See M.J. Perry, *The Idea of Human Rights: Four Inquiries* (1998). Another definition useful to capture this aspect of the 'rights discourse' has been created by Mary Ann Glendon. Criticizing the current American dialect of rights talk, she refers to the '*Lone Rights-Bearer*': 'The eighteenth-century rights of life, liberty, and property, as Karl Marx was the first to note, are pre-eminently rights of separated, independent, individuals. The liberty vaunted by revo-lutionaries in France and North America, he wrote, was the freedom of "man regarded as an isolated monad, withdrawn into himself." It was "founded... upon the separation of man from man"; indeed, it was the very "right of such separation." Nowhere, however, is that separation so pronounced as in the rights discourse of the United States, where "liberty," and "equality" did not rub shoulders with "fraternity," and where, at the end of the nineteenth century, the essence of the right to life would be reconceptualized as "the right to be let alone." ' See M.A. Glendon, *Rights Talk: The Impoverishment of Political Discourse* (1991) 47–8.

[4] For a general perspective, see Kiper, 'Do Human Rights Have Religious Foundations?', 7 *Religion and Human Rights* (2012) 109. The point is also made by Zachary Calo: 'The emergence of human rights not only involved a borrowing from religion, but a supersessionist move against religion. Human rights norms became an alternative theology that advanced a totalizing account of the human person and the person's place within the cosmos. Theological claims were thus not only excluded from the idea of human rights, but deemed antithetical to their realization. Human rights became, in Elie [Wiesel]'s phrase, the "secular religion" of the modern world.' See Calo, 'Religion, Human Rights, and Post-Secular Legal Theory', 85 *St John's Law Review* (2011) 495 at 501.

and Christian theology. They see human rights as a secularization of Christian theological concepts, which in a sense make human rights Western on two counts: as a product of Christianity (hence being religiously Western), and as a product of secularization (hence culturally Western), and thus at odds with any purely religious world vision, including Christianity as faith, as well as with any non-Western culture. As John Witte, Jr has argued: 'The modern human rights movement was thus born out of desperation in the aftermath of World War II. It was an attempt to find a world faith to fill a spiritual void. It was an attempt to harvest from the traditions of Christianity and the Enlightenment the rudimentary elements of a new faith and a new law that would unite a badly broken world order.'[5] The anthropology underlying human rights theory is itself a cultural byproduct of the secularization of Christianity. To this extent, Western political culture could in fact to a great extent be defined as the secularization of Christianity.[6]

The Christian sources of the concept of human rights are obvious; we can characterize this Christian anthropology through the following criteria: a human being is defined by an autonomous individual soul that is not under the control of the state or society, both entitled only to control the body; a '*for intérieur*' (inner core, heart of hearts) that can deliberate for itself, the sacred nature of the body as a template of the divine creation; the equal dignity (in God, not in society) of all human beings; and free will.[7] A theological school of thought, from Augustine to Ockham, considers God's will to be above good and evil, or more exactly as defining what good and evil are: in this sense individual will (which reflects God's will) is not bound by a 'natural good', by the law of nature or by social constraints, but sets its own limits in the interaction with others. However, even the opposite concept of 'natural law' of Aquinas (although it condones an unequal social order) may prefigure the concept of universal rights.[8] Within Christianity, the Catholic Church has always tried to inscribe human rights in a larger theological framework, which, while recognizing the 'sacredness' of the human body and person, subordinates rights to higher duties and norms (God's will).[9]

[5] See Witte, Jr, 'Law, Religion and Human Rights', 28 *Columbia Human Rights Law Review* (1996) 1 at 9.

[6] This can be defined as the most relevant difference between the Western and non-Western understanding of rights. As John Witte, Jr has argued: 'Many non-Western traditions, particularly those of Islamic, Hindu, Buddhist, Taoist, and Traditional stock, cannot conceive of, nor accept, a system of rights that excludes religion. Religion is for these traditions inextricably integrated into every facet of life. Religious rights are, for them, an inherent part of rights of speech, press, assembly, and other individual rights as well as ethnic, cultural, linguistic, and similar associational rights. No system of rights that ignores or deprecates this cardinal place of religion can be respected or adopted', Witte, Jr (1996) 12.

[7] See J. Witte, Jr and F.S. Alexander (eds), *Christianity and Human Rights: An Introduction* (2010).

[8] On these debates, see Milbank, 'Against Human Rights: Liberty in the Western Tradition', 1 *Oxford Journal of Law and Religion* (2012) 203.

[9] *See* H. Joas, *The Sacredness of the Person: A New Genealogy of Human Rights* (2013).

## 3. The Separation of Human Rights Theory from Christianity

The separation of the theory of human rights from Christianity supposes its 'secularization', that is, its disconnection from a transcendental order and its connection with an absolute and abstract self, the human being as an end in itself. This explains why the secularization of the public and political sphere is often presented by various proponents of human rights as a prerequisite, making religious freedom a mere consequence of human rights, and hence depriving religion of its founding role or centrality in society. This paradigmatic change, where religion is no longer at the centre but at the periphery, creates tension between human rights theory and many conservative Christians, but also stirs criticism from other religions: they cannot accept this privileged link between human rights and secularization.

Nevertheless, in many cases, what is at the core of the various human rights (the human being as a free subject) is culturally, anthropologically, or theologically perceived as '*Western*'. From this standpoint, many criticisms of the supposed universality of human rights are undertaken by different opponents. This Christian religious-turned-cultural origin has been advanced by various quarters which oppose the expansion of human rights theory into some sort of universal supranational legal system of norms and values that could be opposed to or imposed upon any governments, countries, and societies: authoritarian secular regimes (China, Singapore), religious leaders (from Muslim clerics to the Catholic Church), Marxist thinkers (Alain Badiou), or even multiculturalist militants. The issue for them is either to bluntly reject the concept, or to push for limitations (on issues like abortion or contraception), or to recast the human rights theory into a religiously acceptable framework (for instance an 'Islamic declaration of human rights').[10]

## 4. Opponents of the Universality of Human Rights

We may classify opponents of the universality of the human rights in two categories. The first is relativist and insists on the cultural roots of any system of values (among them human rights), a critique that can be framed from two different angles: by defining human rights either as the exclusive product of a Western culture (democracy as merely a Western value), or as more general values that can be expressed differently in every cultural system (democracy as being achieved in respecting the priority of communal identities).[11] The second category is universalist, but

---

[10]  This is for instance the case with the Cairo Declaration on Human Rights in Islam, adopted by the Organization of the Islamic Conference in Cairo in 1990, where it is possible to find an overview of the Islamic point of view on human rights and where *sharia* is the only source of rights.

[11]  A classical example would be the Taliban in Afghanistan. As T.M. Franck has clearly argued: 'The Taliban may brandish national sovereignty as a shield, but they also see themselves as militant guardians of a religion and culture that should be exempted from a "Western" system of human rights that is inimical to Islam as they practice it.... In taking a stand against global human rights, the Taliban have made common cause not with the tired nationalist defenders of state sovereignty, but with a powerful and growing subset of cultural exceptionalists. These include some traditional indigenous

considers that norms have been set outside this earthly world, by a transcendental God, and that no human rights declaration may ignore or transgress divine norms; in this case, too, there are two ways of positioning oneself towards the issue: discarding human rights as a profane or even pagan construction, because it replaces God with the human being as the source of norms (which is the position of the Salafists), or by opposing against secular human rights the 'true' rights that should be understood in a more general religious framework and come with limits and duties (which is the underlying logic of the Cairo Declaration of Human Rights in Islam).

The relativist rejection of universal human rights brings forth the anthropological concept of culture: cultures are defined, following the anthropological *doxa* of the mid-twentieth century (from Franz Boas to Claude Lévi-Strauss) as homogeneous, coherent, all-encompassing, based on different sets of rules, norms, values, but intrinsically equal in dignity.[12] For instance, the primacy given in 'confucianist' societies to the community versus the individual, the emphasis on arranged marriages in Indian society, polygamy and the veil in Muslim societies, and honour killings and female circumcision in other cultures, are not evaluated on a 'value scale' in terms of being more or less against individual rights (and specifically 'women's rights'), but as part of a coherent system aiming at ensuring exchanges, circulation, and stability. Culture is not a truth. Rather, it is a regulating system, an habitus, a legacy.

On the contrary, religions, and more specifically monotheistic religions, define a transcendental norm, which is above individual will and rights and is not negotiable (this is exactly the way the Catholic Church is presently presenting its demands to political leaders: abortion, gay marriage, and other similar topics cannot be debated in terms of 'human rights', but in terms of life or death for abortion, and in terms of the reliance on a natural model of anthropology, mainly through the lens of sexual—and not gender—division). Religion is the universal truth: God's rules may or may not be interpreted in terms of values, and may hence be slightly adaptable to the dominant culture, but in any case, human rights are subordinated to human duties, or interpreted in terms of 'limits' (see, for instance, the debate on decency and women in Islam: the dignity of women is called upon to limit freedom even if it is sometimes recast in modern human rights terms—'my veil is my choice'). The Church may also accept the 'two kingdoms' theory, letting the secular society establish rules and norms, but not giving up the idea of a superior set of values and norms.[13] This gives way to a complex array of compromises, protests,

---

tribes, theocratic national regimes, fundamentalists of many religions, and surprisingly, a mixed bag of Western intellectuals who deplore the emphasis placed by modern human rights rhetoric on individual autonomy. Although these exceptionalists have little else in common, they share an antipathy for the whole human rights system . . . The exceptionalists view this system as corrosive of social cohesion and a solvent of community, eroding the social customs and traditions that become unsustainable once the individual ceases to be subordinate to the group.' See Franck (2001) 195.

[12] See C. Lévi-Strauss, *Race et Histoire: Suivi de l'Œuvre de Claude Lévi-Strauss* (1967).

[13] This was clearly stated in the recent written submission by bishop Michael Nazir-Ali of the Anglican Church in the case of *Eweida and Others v United Kingdom*, ECHR (2013) (App Nos 48420/10, 59842/10, 51671/10, and 36516/10), judgment of 15 January 2013, before the European Court of Human Rights: 'The abuse of human rights by secular Governments in Central and Eastern

and exemptions. For instance, one may cite the conscience clause for doctors, or the request to be granted exceptions in providing health care that may include contraception, the general clashes between the principle of autonomy of religious groups, and anti-discrimination norms.[14] In the end, the debate is, and has always been, heavily politically charged.[15]

Let us examine some examples: when the Universal Declaration of Human Rights was approved by the United Nations in 1948, the communist countries abstained, as did Saudi Arabia and South Africa, though for different reasons (the communists opposed a lack of 'real rights' versus bourgeois formal rights, South Africa opposed the rejection of race discrimination, and Saudi Arabia considered *sharia* as the only universal norm).[16] At the Beijing World Conference on Women (September 1995) the Convention on the Elimination of All Forms of Discrimination against Women (CEDAW, entered into force in 1981) was rejected both by some religious groups and authoritarian regimes: 11 Islamic countries introduced reservations to Article 16 and the Vatican City State did not ratify it.

Massive immigration into Western Europe brought a new debate on the universality of human rights: should migrants be forced to adopt Western norms and values or could some exceptions be made in the name of multiculturalism? And, if so, how should such rights be qualified: as cultural exceptionalism or religious freedom? Should the veil be seen as a rejection of gender equality or as an individual religious right?[17] In dealing with immigrants, the issue of the universality

Europe is all too recent; the new Human Rights agenda must respect Judeo Christian values if it is not to become another inhuman ideology imposing restrictions on individuals. There is a deep fear in the United Kingdom that the Human Rights agenda is becoming set against human rights; and seeking to remove Judaeo Christian values from the public square.' See Written submission on behalf of Bishop Michael Nazir-Ali (intervener), *Nadia Eweida and Shirley Chaplin v United Kingdom*, ECtHR, App Nos 48420/10, 59842/10 at 7.

[14] For instance, the European Court of Human Rights in a recent judgment ruled that clergy (and lay employees) of the Romanian Orthodox Church have a right to unionize notwithstanding the objections of the Church hierarchy. See *Sindicatul 'Păstorul cel Bun' v Romania*, ECHR (2012) App No 2330/09, judgment of 31 January 2012. For a general perspective, see Annicchino, 'Osservazioni sul conflitto tra il principio di autonomia dei gruppi religiosi ed altri diritti fondamentali: a proposito di alcune recenti pronunce della Corte Suprema degli Stati Uniti e della Corte europea dei diritti dell'uomo', *Quaderni di diritto e politica ecclesiastica* (2013).

[15] As Mary Ann Glendon recounts, part of the debate involves also the role of NGOs and their particular interests: 'The UN and the governments of major powers are surrounded by—and their agencies are often symbiotically intertwined with—a host of nongovernmental organizations...to the extent that human rights become the instrument of this or that nation or interest group bent on universalizing its own agenda, the charge of cultural imperialism must be taken seriously', Glendon (2001) 229.

[16] The differences among the different countries were clear to the drafters of the Universal Declaration of Human Rights, which in fact used a very vague language. As Mary Ann Glendon has argued: 'The open texture of the Declaration was not only a consequence of political compromise on controversial issues. It also reflected the framers' desire for a document of broad application that would endure through changing times. They established a "common standard of achievement" that could be interpreted and implemented in a legitimate variety of ways', Glendon (2001) 191.

[17] There has been an important debate on this topic, fostered also by important decisions of the European Court of Human Rights. See, for instance, the case *Leyla Şahin v Turkey*, ECHR (2004) App No 44774/98, judgment of 29 June 2004, and subsequent Grand Chamber judgment of 10 November 2005.

of human rights is recast in terms of multiculturalism more than religious freedom: for instance, is female circumcision an issue of cultural perception or an infringement upon women's rights? The same goes for arranged marriages, often confused with forced marriages. Could different values be taken into consideration by courts in judging migrants, for instance by accepting the battering of women by their husbands in the name of cultural and/or religious differences?[18] A debate ensued for almost ten years in Ontario where the project to establish a private 'Islamic arbitration court' was opposed by feminist uproar.[19] Once again, the debate on human rights mixed two different terms of reference: culture understood as a transmitted set of values referring to implicit social traditions and religion understood as a chosen faith referring to explicit divine norms. While in traditional societies the difference between culture as defined by anthropology, and religion as defined by theology, is not obvious because the religious norms maintain social relevance, this is no longer the case when secularization or immigration bring about a disconnect between religious norms and the dominant secular culture.[20] More recently, church-state tensions have been arising again in Europe, in Israel, and in the United States under the Obama administration, in the wake of the conservative backlash on social issues driven by the Catholic Church and the evangelicals (on abortion, gay marriage, and the call for exemption for the Church from some labour laws or national regulations—for instance the obligation to pay for contraception in social insurance) and by the Haredim in Israel (on gender separation and women's visibility in the public sphere).

Historically, the issue of human rights also played an important role in undermining the Soviet Union, after the signing of the Final Act of the Conference on Security and Cooperation in Europe in Helsinki in 1975. Later, ensuring the protection of human rights became a basic principle of the doctrine of the legitimacy to wage a military intervention for an 'altruist reason', or 'humanitarian intervention' (Yugoslavia, Kosovo), which, during the 1990s, transformed into a push for democratization (the idea being that only democratic countries could implement human rights). The group dubbed 'neo-conservatives' around President G.W. Bush explicitly championed the universality of human rights in order to call for military intervention: they made democratization a goal of war for the military intervention in Iraq in 2003 beyond the destruction of the so-called 'weapons of mass destruction'.[21] Even if the military intervention in Afghanistan in 2001 was motivated by the hunt for Al Qaeda, it was largely framed in terms of human rights: freeing the Afghan women from the Taliban yoke. Paradoxically or not, these interventions

---

[18] This happened in Germany, where Judge Christa Datz-Winter ruled that a German woman of Moroccan descent would not be granted a divorce because she and her husband came from a 'Moroccan cultural environment in which it is not uncommon for a man to exert a right of corporal punishment over his wife'. Connoly, 'German judge invokes Qur'an to deny abused wife a divorce', *The Guardian*, 23 March 2007.

[19] For a summary of the case and reactions to it, see the report of the Law Society of Upper Canada, 24 June 2004, available at <http://www.lsuc.on.ca/media/convjune04_gov_relations.pdf> (accessed 17 June 2013).

[20] See, in general, O. Roy, *Holy Ignorance: When Religion and Culture Part Ways* (2010).

[21] See J. Vaïsse, *Neoconservatism: The Biography of a Movement* (2010).

were seen by their opponents as the apex of US imperialism, leading to an ambivalent attitude towards the enemies of the United States (branding the Taliban as
legitimate nationalists fighting a foreign invasion). Interestingly enough, advocacy
for expanding human rights shifted from the left to a certain part of the right.
An example of this process can be seen in the effort that many religious conservatives expend in lobbying for the establishment of the United States Commission
on International Religious Freedom,[22] now seen as a model also by the European
Union for its External Action Service.[23]

More recently, the establishment of an International Criminal Court has completed this reading of political events and violence in terms of human rights, but
not without negative side-effects: suing former activists, political leaders, or military commanders for having violated human rights might prevent processes of
conciliation and local peace processes by complicating the reconciliation process in
the aftermath of a civil war. This stress on democratization and human rights has
been deemed hypocritical in many quarters, from independent NGOs to authoritarian regimes (China, Singapore), who often counterattack by using culturalist rhetoric: confucianism and Asian culture allegedly stress communal ties over
individual rights. Another cultural argument is that democratization in certain
contexts would lead to anarchy or to a religious dictatorship, an argument used by
many who think that the Arab Spring would turn into an Arab Winter, due to the
victory of the Islamist parties.

## 5. The Use of Human Rights

Human rights have thus been used at two levels: internally, to homogenize a society under a set of common norms, imposed if not shared (hence the idea that
human rights could be seen more as cultural identity markers rather than a universal set of norms—a fact that could explain the use of a human rights rhetoric by
populist or far-rightist parties when opposing Muslim migrants); and externally,
with the aim of replacing the very basis of international relations since the Treaty
of Westphalia (agreements between sovereign and competing national states, constituting the 'realist school' in international relations), working towards a kind of
judicialization of international and political relations, where the state is no longer
sovereign, either in itself (it can be indicted) or because it has ceased to be the
sole referee for its subjects and citizens who can appeal against it.[24] The concept
of an autonomous international court is, by definition, linked to the recognition

---

[22]  See A.D. Hertzke, *Freeing God's Children: The Unlikely Alliance for Global Human Rights* (2004).

[23]  See K. Thames, 'Making Freedom of Religion of Belief a True EU Priority', EUI Working Paper
RSCAS 2012/41 (July 2012), available at <http://www.eui.eu/Projects/ReligioWest/Documents/
workingpaper/RSCAS2012-41.pdf> (accessed 17 June 2013).

[24]  There is a growing literature on the role of the courts in international relations and international
politics. Among this, see Slaughter, 'A Global Community of Courts', 44 *Harvard International Law
Journal* (2003) 191; A.-M. Slaughter, *A New World Order* (2004). For a critical perspective, see E.A.
Posner, *The Perils of Global Legalism* (2009).

of universal legal norms and therefore, among them, human rights. We seem to reach here a conundrum about the universalization of human rights. Either one should wait to achieve some global consensus on the definition of human rights, which seems difficult, not so much for theoretical as for political reasons: there are so many vested interests that as long as democracy does not become the universal political regime, there is no chance that authoritarian leaders or religious leaders will agree on a compromise that deprives them of their status of value makers (or implementers). Or, alternatively, one should accept that there can be no consensus on final norms and values (what Rawls calls the '*Good*') and then accept the concept of multiculturalism, making human rights just a Western identity marker.[25]

Many North American thinkers (John Rawls, Charles Taylor) have endeavoured to find a form of compromise that does not assume an agreement on the contents of values: reasonable accommodation (Taylor) or Justice versus Good (Rawls). In *Political Liberalism*,[26] Rawls debates the issue of how to handle a society where groups totally disagree on what is the highest good, specifically of course religious communities; in this case, the just means treating all citizens with fairness, without debating about the highest good. Interestingly enough, some Islamist thinkers try to do the same, by defining for instance a 'minority *fiqh*' (an adaptation of Muslim law for Muslims living in a Western context, a term used by Sheikh Qaradawi).[27] In fact, the Islamic thinkers who choose this path pick some traditional legal concepts (like the '*millet*' which in the Ottoman tradition defines ethno-religious minorities of 'people of the Book', mainly referring to Jews and Christians, but now extended to any religion, and even to 'secularists') to reinterpret them in multiculturalist terms (where for instance political citizenship can go hand in hand with a special dispensatory exception concerning family law or religious practices, like in India). In a word, the idea is to promote coexistence as a good in itself, finding common ground on the smallest common denominator, but keeping the *absolute 'Good'* outside the compromise. This is probably what Tariq Ramadan meant when he called for a 'moratorium' on *hudud* punishments (stoning for adultery, for instance): the religious community could not reject a norm seen as unacceptable by the others, but pledges not to implement it.[28] The Catholic Church, for instance, does not call upon its followers to attack clinics which perform abortions, but asks not to be obliged to pay for contraception in the health plans for its employees. All these endeavours have in common the idea that there are different systems of norms, but that a sort of accommodation can be found which allows different groups to coexist in the same polity, and to disagree on many other issues.

Recent conflicts show that such accommodations are not easy to reach: a local German court banned circumcision for underage boys in 2012, precisely in the

---

[25] On the relationships between secularism and multiculturalism, see Modood, '2011 *Paul Hanly Furfey Lecture*: Is There a Crisis of Secularism in Western Europe?', 73 *Sociology of Religion* (2012) 130.

[26] J. Rawls, *Political Liberalism* (1993).

[27] He used the term the title of his famous book: *Fi fiqh al-aqalliyat al-Muslimah: Hayat al-Muslimin wasat al-mujtamaat al-ukhra* [*About the Muslim minority fiqh: the life of Muslims amidst foreign societies*] (2001).

[28] Television debate between Tariq Ramadan and Nicolas Sarkozy, *France 2*, 21 November 2003.

name of their right to bodily integrity, and interestingly enough, of religious freedom (here the freedom not to have a religion imposed upon them before being able to make a free choice).[29] A protest movement in France followed the disclosure that *halal* and *kosher* meat were on the market without being branded as such,[30] while secular residents in Montreal opposed the installation of an *erouv* (a tiny and almost invisible thread around a neighbourhood) by Jewish orthodox followers who wanted to create a symbolic 'private' space for the Shabbat.[31] In the two latter cases, the religious communities used the same arguments than the Italian government used in the *Lautsi* case concerning crucifixes in classrooms:[32] because the religious sign has a general secular meaning, non-believers should be indifferent to it. However, this argument does not work: secularists in fact do care about religious symbols and this is why they often bring cases to courts.

## 6. Theoretical Paradigm and Sociological Praxis

What we are contesting here is not the richness and validity of such debates, but their relevance. It supposes that there is a great variety in the way to define the 'common bind', a different conception of polity and citizenship at work. In fact, the mistake is to think that one should first find a theoretical common paradigm and then live together, which supposes that political participation is intrinsically linked to a political culture, itself based on a political anthropology. If that were true, the simple concept of a political revolution would be unthinkable. The same issue is at work with the concept of secularization: either secularization goes along with the decline of the centrality of religion in the public sphere (and in this case secularization is a silent revolution), or secularization is an avatar of a specific religion; which allows conceiving a persistent trend in the history of Europe. Except that to think of Europe as a continuity is a circular definition, which ignores precisely the 'revolutions' in its midst, from the Reformation to the French Revolution.

---

[29] See 'German Court bans circumcision of young boys', Reuters, 27 June 2012, available at <http://www.reuters.com/article/2012/06/27/us-germany-circumcision-idUSBRE85Q19Y20120627> (accessed 17 June 2013).

[30] Willsher, 'France's Muslims hit back at Nicolas Sarkozy's policy on halal meat', *The Guardian*, 10 March 2012, available at: <http://www.guardian.co.uk/world/2012/mar/10/nicolas-sarkozy-halal-meat-france-election> (accessed 17 June 2013).

[31] Germain, 'La religion dans l'espace public en context multiethnique: des accommodements raisonnables au zonage', *Plan Canada*, 11 January 2010, available at <http://www.inrs.ca/sites/default/files/u62/PlanCanada_AnnickGermain_f.pdf> (accessed 17 June 2013).

[32] *Lautsi and Others v Italy*, ECHR (2011) App No 30814/06, judgments of 3 November 2009 and 18 March 2011 (GC). See Annicchino, 'Tra margine di apprezzamento e neutralità: il caso "Lautsi" e i nuovi equilibri della tutela europea della libertà religiosa', in R. Mazzola (ed), *Diritto e religione in Europa. Rapporto sulla giurisprudenza della Corte europea dei diritti dell'uomo in materia di libertà religiosa* (2012) 179. See also Annicchino, 'Winning the Battle by Losing the War: The Lautsi Case and the Holy Alliance between American Conservative Evangelicals, the Russian Orthodox Church and the Vatican to Reshape European Identity', 6 *Religion and Human Rights* (2011) 213.

The same issue applies to the perception of Islam as a political culture where there is no separation between religion and politics.[33] This is true in the way Islam has been constructed as a political ideology,[34] it is not true (or more exactly not relevant) if we consider history and politics in the Muslim world. A political anthropology is a post-hoc intellectual rationalization, but it does not help to understand changes, and there are changes.

The only way to leave the conundrum of the contradiction between the cultural genealogy of human rights and the need to define a universal set of legal and political norms is to rethink the link between culture and political anthropology. It is true that human rights are not just a set of rules to organize the coexistence of citizens. They do suppose a certain conception of what a human being is, in a word, a common political anthropology. However, we must consider that contemporary societies are experiencing an 'anthropological change', linked to the globalization process. We are not saying that the Internet is bringing a new anthropology, but the use of the Internet and social networks is certainly going along with such demographic and cultural changes, towards a greater individualization, a reduction of the extended family to a nuclear one, a decrease in fertility rate, a growing trend towards horizontal communications and networking between 'peers', in opposition to a patriarchal hierarchy.[35] The debate on citizenship in the wake of the Arab Spring is precisely about the predominance of the individual identity over the collective. It is not about secularism (an optical illusion in the West), but about the freedom to be religious the way the believer wants to be. In a word, there is a new political culture that is compatible with democracy but should not be confused with 'liberalism' or 'secularism'. The big mistake is to consider that in order to make a religious culture compatible with democracy, there should be a preliminary reformation and liberalization of the theological sphere, some sort of a 'reset' button, that would then allow the religious referential to condone such concepts as individual freedom, freedom of speech, freedom to change religion, secularism, and atheism. It is precisely because religions are disconnecting themselves from cultures that they can find new tools to manage a change in a political sphere, which, in fact, also mirrors the changes in religiosity.[36] The emphasis on individual faith, personal choice (even when it takes the form of becoming a 'born again'), and even fundamentalism (which always goes with an endeavour to make

---

[33] See O. Roy, *Secularism Confronts Islam* (2009).

[34] For instance, the judges of the European Court of Human Rights in the judgment *Refah Partisi (the Welfare Party) and Others v Turkey* wrote: 'the Court considers that sharia, which faithfully reflects the dogmas and divine rules laid down by religion, is stable and invariable. Principles such as pluralism in the political sphere or the constant evolution of public freedoms have no place in it. . . . It is difficult to declare one's respect for democracy and human rights while at the same time supporting a regime based on sharia, which clearly diverges from Convention values, its rules on the legal status of women and the way it intervenes in all spheres of private and public life in accordance with religious precepts.' *Refah Partisi (the Welfare Party) and Others v Turkey*, ECHR (2001), App Nos 41340/98, 41342/98, 41343/98, and 41344/98, judgment of 31 July 2001, para 72.

[35] See C. Merlini and O. Roy (eds), *Arab Society in Revolt. The West's Mediterranean Challenge* (2012).

[36] See Roy (2010) 30.

the religious norm explicit and visible, and consequently, even if inadvertently, debatable) are pushing towards a common political anthropology. A consequence of the process we have tried to describe is that we can already observe a process of formatting of norms and values coming from different cultures and religions into a common paradigm of legal norms and principles. The process began in the nineteenth century, when the Ottoman state published the '*Mejelle*', the law of the Empire, where *sharia* is codified under legal western paradigms. Under these paradigms *sharia* is positive law, thereby losing its autonomy. It is also a written code imposed on judges who lost their autonomy and a classification between criminal law, trade law, and civil law is made where *sharia* principles are just an element of the law. In a complex dialogic process of conflicts, compromises, and reformulation, we can witness how this trend is being pursued. For instance, a concept that seems to be the most opposed to human rights, blasphemy, has been recast by religious actors, following the 'Rushdie affair'[37] into the concept of 'defamation of religions', which is not necessarily agreed on by liberal secularists, but is at least intellectually compatible with the concept of human rights. Often, courts, judging on religious issues, advance concepts like tort or *pretium doloris* to deal with the reference to faith and religious norms not recognized by state law, for instance to forbid an advertisement campaign mocking religious symbols, as in France,[38] or to fine a Jewish orthodox husband refusing to grant his divorced wife a '*get*' or right to marry again.

## 7. Conclusion

The recasting of religious norms into a secular paradigm cannot satisfy the most fundamentalist groups, but they have then no choice other than to take responsibility for their separateness from the dominant society. Religious norms, because they ceased to be cultural, are paradoxically more adapted to the process of formatting into a common legal paradigm, ending in a separation between the different spheres (religious and political), which means a political secularization, not to be confused with a cultural secularization. We are certainly heading towards a common political culture, but not a common secularization process, which explains why our age seems to be more religious, which is an optical illusion.

In this sense, the universality of human rights can be conceived beyond the specific heritage of Western culture, as a fast-track process (taking some decades instead of centuries) of recasting of different cultural systems of values along a

---

[37] We refer here to the violent reaction of some Muslims to the publication of the book *The Satanic Verses* by Salman Rushdie and the relative political and judicial developments.

[38] On 10 March 2005, the Paris Tribunal de Grande Instance ordered the end of an advertising campaign by the publicist Marithé et François Girbaud. They had used the Leonardo da Vinci painting *The Last Supper*, replacing the Apostles by half-naked young women. The Court considered that this was an insult to the 'sensitivity' of Catholics. The judge stated that the poster was an '*acte d'intrusion agressive et gratuite dans le tréfonds des croyances intimes*'. The Court of Cassation reversed the decision.

common paradigm (individualization, gender equality), under a complex array of conflicts, pressures, internal dynamics (democratization), compromises, and effects of globalization. However, the price to be paid, everywhere including in Europe, is the sudden surge of a feeling of deculturation and uprootedness, leading towards a populist quest for 'identity', which constitutes an explicit rejection of any form of universalism.

# 2

# Liberty, Equality, Diversity: States, Cultures, and International Law

*Ana Filipa Vrdoljak*

## 1. Introduction

Territorial boundaries of present-day states rarely accord with the cultural affiliations of their inhabitants. International boundaries demarcate vertically the physical and political realm of the state. Despite the oft-concerted assimilationist policies and practices of national authorities, they have been unable to weaken (or have inadvertently strengthened) the horizontal, relational ties which bind cultural and religious groups.[1] It is at the interface of international borders that there is usually heightened confrontation and contestation between the political and cultural, vertical and horizontal understandings of space. Despite the efforts of early twentieth-century statesmen to square territorial boundaries with cultural groupings, there was a realization that this task could (and should) never been fully implemented. Instead, international law, and more specifically human rights law, has been deployed in achieving a workable equilibrium for that which cannot be realized as a reality on the ground.

This chapter explores how culture is addressed by contemporary international law, with particular reference to human rights law norms. With the rise of the modern, secular state in Europe, human rights have largely remained a vehicle for defining relations between the state and individuals. Civil and political rights which dominated the first articulations of human rights underpinned the new vertical demarcations of the state, its realm and its citizens. Yet, concomitantly, the international community recognized and afforded protection (to varying degrees and with increasing consistency) to the multiple, existing, and persistent relations between individuals arising from religious, cultural, and linguistic affiliation which run horizontally across the newly imposed ties of citizenship. The ensuing battleground is one of the rise of the modern state accompanied by human rights and the ongoing plight to achieve a workable and sustainable resolution between existing

---

[1] R. Muir, *Modern Political Geography* (1975) 119.

and newly evolving understandings of common identities—'the We between the I and the All'—from the religious to the secular, the national to multicultural, and back again.[2] Human rights law has been pivotal in defining conflicting rights claims between groups, individuals, and the state in which they are located.

In examining how contemporary human rights law has been challenged by and adapted to the stresses and strains of relations between states and their inhabitants over claims of culture, I adopt a structure which is a riff on the national motto of an archetypal secular state: liberty, equality, diversity. The first part covering freedom focuses on the rise of the modern state and its conscious reimagining of ties with its citizens through the promotion of tolerance and a secular, national identity. The shift is explored through the prisms of the freedom of religion, the right to participate in (national) cultural life, and the limitations on freedom of expression including prohibition of hate speech and domestic blasphemy laws. The second part on equality centres on the relationship between the state, the group, and its individuals by moving beyond the strictures of tolerance to the fostering of non-discrimination not only in respect of civil and political rights but cultural rights also. This transformation of the right to *a* culture to the right to one's *own* culture is examined through the right to self-identification, non-discrimination, and minority protections and cultural rights in international law. The third and final part concentrates on the embrace of cultural diversity by the international community as a common good. The promotion of diversity is examined at the state level through the implementation of cultural pluralism, at the international level through the sanctioning of voluntary isolation and secession of groups, and at the group level, through the protection of individual human rights and equality.

## 2. Liberty

Conceptions of fundamental freedoms have been intrinsic to legal and political theoretical understandings of the relationship between the modern state and its inhabitants since the emergence of the secular state from the ashes of relentless civil and continental religious fratricide in Europe. Sectarianism is not the exclusive preserve of this region and the responses to it carry resonance for those experiencing conflicts beyond its boundaries. This first part explores three notions of freedom: the separation of church and state and the recognition of religious freedom; the relationship between the right to participate in cultural life and national culture; and finally, balancing freedoms, and the right to freedom of expression, hate speech, and blasphemy laws. These freedoms and the limitations attached to their enjoyment illustrate the strictures of toleration as a means of calibrating relations between the majority and minority within a state.[3]

---

[2] Allott, 'On First Understanding Plato's *Republic*', 22 *EJIL* (2011) 1165 at 1168.
[3] J. Raz, *Ethics in the Public Domain: Essays in the Morality of Law and Politics* (1994) 155–76.

## A. The right to freedom of religion or beliefs

The matrix which defines the contours and limits of the right to freedom of religion or beliefs serves as an important template for international law responses to the right to culture. The corollaries, and overlap, between cultural and religious ties have been made in human rights law, particularly in respect of minorities. Not least because balancing the interests of minorities and majorities, the distinction between the public and private spheres, and the promotion of tolerance and pluralism, continue to be grappled with by democratic societies.

The reconfiguration of relations between church and state and between the state and individuals defined the peace settlement which ended the Thirty Years War across continental Europe.[4] The Treaty of Westphalia of 1648, often viewed as the starting point of modern international law, recognized state sovereignty and national self-determination, which enabled sovereigns to decide the religious affiliation of their states. Conversely, for communities which were effectively rendered religious minorities as a result of the peace settlement, the treaties recognized the right of freedom of religion in the private and equal rights in public life regardless of religious affiliation.

On the back of these guarantees at the supranational level, the movement towards separation of church and state and religious tolerance gained momentum at the national level, that is, within states. As people redefined their relations with each other and the state, these evolving constitutional arrangements formally enumerated individual rights which included the right to freedom of religion. For example, the English Bill of Rights of 1689 and related legislation represented both an assertion of national self-determination through its reaffirmation of the Church of England as the official church and tolerance of other Protestant groups (but not the Catholic Church), and early articulation of individual rights defining relations between the sovereign and subjects. John Locke, in his *Letters Concerning Toleration* (1689–92), argued that the pursuit of religious uniformity rather than tolerating diversity created greater social unrest and obtaining religious uniformity through violence was not desirable.[5] Drawing on these developments, the French and US drafters of their respective bills of rights also promoted religious tolerance and recognized the right to freedom of religion. The *Déclaration des droits de l'homme et du citoyen* adopted on 26 August 1789 provides in Article 10: 'No one shall be disquieted on account of his opinions, including his religious views, provided their manifestation does not disturb the public order established by law.' The French drew inspiration from the writings and advocacy of Voltaire on religious tolerance and the separation

---

[4] Peace Treaty between the Holy Roman Emperor and the King of France and their respective Allies (Treaty of Münster), 24 October 1648, 1 CTS 271, Arts XLIX ('the Liberty of the Exercise of Religion...') and XXVIII ('...who shall demand it, shall have the free Exercise of their Religion, as well in publick Churches at the appointed Hours, as in private in their own Houses, or in others chosen for this purpose...').

[5] J. Locke, *Locke on Toleration*, R. Vernon (ed) (Cambridge, 2010).

of church and state. In his 1763 essay *A Treatise on Toleration*, Voltaire wrote by way of analogy:

[Y]ou know that each province of Italy has their own dialect, and that people do not speak at Venice or Bergamo the same way they speak at Florence. The Academy of Crusca near Florence has fixed the language; its dictionary is a rule which one dare not depart from.... [B]ut do you believe that the consul of the Academy...could in conscience cut the tongues out of all the Venetians and all the Bergamese who persist in speaking their dialect?[6]

In September 1789, the First Amendment to the US Constitution proposed by Congress provided that the state would 'make no law respecting an establishment of religion, or prohibiting the free exercise thereof' and tied to this guarantee was freedom of speech, the press, and peaceful assembly. As explained below, present-day formulations of the right to freedom of religion or beliefs in international human rights law owe much to these early supranational and national examples.

While there had been several earlier attempts to guarantee religious freedom to minorities, it was not formulated as a universally applicable right in international law until the adoption of several international and regional human rights instruments after the Second World War. The Universal Declaration of Human Rights (UDHR),[7] in Article 18, provides that

Everyone has the right to freedom of thought, conscience and religion; this right includes freedom to change his religion or belief, and freedom, either alone or in community with others and in public or private, to manifest his religion or belief in teaching, practice, worship and observance.

Like the Treaty of Westphalia, the UDHR recognizes the private and public, individual and communal dimensions of this right. This right was translated into binding form by Article 18 of the International Covenant on Civil and Political Rights (ICCPR).[8] As well as replicating Article 18 UDHR, the ICCPR also provides that individuals shall be free from coercion in making such a choice, that the right to manifest one's religion or beliefs is subject only to those limits 'prescribed by law and...necessary to protect public safety, order, health or morals or the

---

[6] Voltaire, *Letters Concerning the English Nation* (1733); and *Treatise on Toleration* (1763). Reproduced in Voltaire, *Treatise on Tolerance*, S. Harvey (ed), (2000):

*[V]ous savez que chaque province d'Italie a son jargon, et qu'on ne parle point à Venise et à Bergame comme à Florence. L'Académie de la Crusca a fixé la langue; son dictionnaire est une règle dont on ne doit pas s'écarter...mais croyez-vous que le consul de l'Académie...auraient pu en conscience faire couper la langue à tous les Vénitiens et à tous les Bergamasques qui auraient persisté dans leur patois?*

[7] Universal Declaration of Human Rights, GA Res 217A (III), 10 December 1948, UN Doc A/810 at 71.

[8] International Covenant on Civil and Political Rights, 16 December 1966, entered into force 23 March 1976, 999 UNTS 171. See also Art 9, European Convention for the Protection of Human Rights and Fundamental Freedoms (ECHR), 4 November 1950, entered into force 3 September 1953, ETS 5; Art 10, Charter of Fundamental Rights of the European Union, 7 December 2000, OJ 2000 C 364/01; Art 12 American Convention on Human Rights (ACHR), 22 November 1969, entered into force 18 July 1978, OASTS No. 36, 1144 UNTS 123; Art 8, African Charter on Human and Peoples' Rights (ACHPR), 27 June 1981, entered into force 21 October 1986, OAU Doc CAB/LEG/67/3, rev 5, 21 ILM [1982] 58.

fundamental rights and freedoms of others', and right of parents or legal guardians of children to 'ensure the religious and moral education of their children in conformity with their own convictions'. As explained below, each of these elements is relevant not only to religious affiliation but cultural affiliation.

The UN Human Rights Committee (HRC), which monitors the implementation of the ICCPR, has noted in its General Comment on Article 18 that the protection afforded by 'right to freedom of thought, conscience and religions (which includes the freedom to hold beliefs)', known as *forum internum*, extends to holding 'theistic, non-theistic, atheistic beliefs, and the right not to profess any belief or religion'.[9] However, the European Court of Human Rights (ECtHR) has indicated the protection only covers 'views that attain a certain level of cogency, seriousness, cohesion, and importance'.[10] The HRC describes the right as 'far-reaching and profound' and it cannot be derogated from, even during states of emergency. No limitation is permitted on freedom of thought, conscience or the freedom to hold or adopt a religion or belief. Like the right to hold an opinion without interference, this freedom is protected unconditionally. This is reinforced by Article 18 UDHR stipulating that the right includes the freedom to change one's religion or belief. This wording is weaker in Article 18 ICCPR, which provides only for 'freedom to have or to adopt', modified in response to Muslim states objections that their domestic, religious based, laws prohibit conversion from Islam.[11] Nonetheless, the Committee has confirmed the 'freedom to choose a religion or belief, including the right to replace one's current religion or belief with another or to adopt atheistic views, as well as the right to retain one's religion or belief'.[12] The African Commission on Human and Peoples' Rights has found that persecution of non-Muslim communities to force their conversion to Islam is a violation of the African Charter.[13] The prohibition of coercion, inserted in respect to state action but also motivated by fear of proselytizing, extends not only to physical force or penal sanctions but encompasses 'policies or practices having the same intention or effect, such as, for example, those restricting access to education, medical care, employment' and the holding of public office.[14] Further to this, the HRC has found that 'measures restricting eligibility for government services to members of the predominant religion or giving economic privileges to them or imposing special

[9] HRC, *General Comment No 22: The right to freedom of thought, conscience and religion (Art 18)*, 30 July 1993, UN Doc CCPR/C/21/Rev.1/Add.4, para 2.

[10] *Eweida and Others v United Kingdom*, ECHR (2013) App No 48420/10, judgment of 15 January 2013, para 81.

[11] See UN Doc A/C.3/5/SR(1050–1), 288–367, and UN Doc A/C.3/15/SR(1960), 1021–6.

[12] HRC, *General Comment No 22*, para 5.

[13] *Amnesty International and Others v Sudan*, ACHPR, Comm Nos 48/90, 50/91, 52/91, 89/93, not dated, paras 74 and 76; and *Free Legal Assistance Group and Others v Zaire*, ACHPR, Comm Nos 25/89, 47/90, 56/91, 100/93, not dated, para 45.

[14] *Amnesty International*, paras 74 and 76 and *Free Legal Assistance Group and Others*, para 45. See *Loren Laroye Riebe Star and Ors v Mexico*, I/ACHR (1999) Case 11.610, Report No 49/99, 13 April 1999.

restrictions on the practice of other faiths' is contrary to non-discrimination and equal treatment under the International Covenant.[15]

The right to manifest one's belief or religion is held 'either individually or in community with others and in public or private'.[16] The European Court has affirmed that this collective aspect of the right is a crucial component of the guarantee and drawn a link between the right to freedom of religion or beliefs (Article 9) and freedom of association (Article 11 ECHR).[17] It held that:

The right to manifest one's religion collectively, presupposes that believers may associate freely, without arbitrary interference from the State. The autonomy of religious communities is in fact indispensable to pluralism in a democratic society and is thus an issue at the very heart of the protection afforded by Article 9.[18]

Further, the Court noted that a group's fundamental activities can only be carried out if it possesses legal personality, which would enable it to legally protect the community, its members and property.[19] By the same token, the European Court has also stressed that the right is enjoyed not only in public with those who share one's religion or beliefs, but also alone and in private.[20]

By contrast to *forum internum*, the right to manifest one's religion or beliefs can be subject to limitations under defined circumstances, which are stricter and narrower

[15] HRC, *General Comment No 22*, para 9. See also para 10.

[16] The HRC has stated, in *General Comment No 22*, para 4, that this right to manifest includes: 'The freedom to manifest religion or belief in worship, observance, practice and teaching encompasses a broad range of acts. The concept of worship extends to ritual and ceremonial acts giving direct expression to belief, as well as various practices integral to such acts, including the building of places of worship, the use of ritual formulae and objects, the display of symbols and the observance of holidays and days of rest. The observance and practice of religion or belief may include not only ceremonial acts but also such customs as the observance of dietary regulations, the wearing of distinctive clothing or headcoverings, participation in rituals associated with certain stages of life, and the use of a particular language customarily spoken by a group. In addition, the practice and teaching of religion or belief includes acts integral to the conduct by religious groups of their basic affairs, such as the freedom to choose their religious leaders, priests and teachers, the freedom to establish seminaries or religious schools and the freedom to prepare and distribute religious texts or publications.' See also Art 6, Declaration on the Elimination of All Forms of Intolerance and of Discrimination Based on Religion or Belief, GA Res 36/55, 25 November 1981, UN Doc A/36/68.

[17] *X v United Kingdom*, ECHR (1981) App No 8160/78, 22 DR 27 at 34. While the ICCPR only permits complaints by individuals, the ECHR allows for complaints by groups: see *Metropolitan Church of Bessarabia and Ors v Moldova*, ECHR (2001) App No 45701/99, judgment of 13 December 2001 at 51, para 1; and *Canea Catholic Church v Greece*, ECHR (1997) Reports 1997-VIII, judgment of 16 December 1997.

[18] *Metropolitan Church of Bessarabia and Ors v Moldova*, ECHR (2001) App No 45701/99, judgment of 13 December 2001, para 18. See also *Free Legal Assistance Group v Zaire*, ACHPR, Comm Nos 25/89, 47/90, 56/91, 100/93, October 1995, para 4, which held that the right includes assembling for the purpose of the religion or beliefs and establishing places of worship for this purpose.

[19] *Metropolitan Church of Bessarabia and Ors v Moldova*, ECHR (2001) App No 45701/99, judgment of 13 December 2001, para 18. In this case, the religious community, having been refused registration and legal personality, was unable to bring legal proceedings to protect its assets which were crucial for conducting services and other aspects of worship: see paras 105 and 129.

[20] *Kokkinakis v Greece*, ECHR (1993) Series A, No 260-A, App No14307/88, judgment of 25 May 1993, para 31.

than those set down for other human rights.[21] The European Court has noted that this is because the right is:

[O]ne of the most vital elements that go to make up the identity of believers and their conception of life, but it is also a precious asset for atheists, agnostics, sceptics and the unconcerned. The pluralism indissoluble for a democratic society, which has been dearly won over centuries, depends on it.[22]

Any limitations must be prescribed by law and be necessary for the protection of 'public safety, order, health or morals, or the fundamental freedoms of others'.[23] Purposes beyond this, like national security, are not permissible. The limitations can only be applied for the purposes set down in law and must be directly related and proportionate to the specific purpose. They must not be imposed for a discriminatory purpose nor applied discriminatorily.[24] The European Court has paid special concern to the impact of restrictions in a diverse society and in particular minorities within it. Consequently, it has found in determining whether a restriction on religious worship or observance is proportionate to a legitimate aim, it would examine it with 'very strict scrutiny' and when considering the margin of appreciation it would 'have regard to what is at stake, namely the need to secure true religious pluralism, an inherent feature of the notion of a democratic society'.[25] In *Serif v Greece*, the Court held that '[t]he role of the authorities ... is not to remove the cause of the tensions by eliminating pluralism, but to ensure that the competing groups *tolerate* each other'.[26]

The restriction on the manifestation of religion or beliefs based on public order and the rights of others came under the spotlight in a series of cases before the European Court of Human Rights concerning the wearing of headscarves by Muslim women in the public education system in states promoting secularism. In *Şahin v Turkey*,[27] a medical student at an Istanbul university, and *Dogru v France*,[28] an 11-year-old student in a French state secondary school, alleged violations of

---

[21] Article 18(3) ICCPR; Art 9(2) ECHR; Art 12(3) ACHR; and Art 8 ACHPR. See *Centre for Minority Rights Development and Minority Rights Group (on behalf of Endorois Welfare Council) v Kenya*, ACHPR, Comm No 276/03, 4 February 2010, para 173: 'The African Commission is of the view that the limitations placed on the State's duties to protect rights should be viewed in light of the underlying sentiments of the African Charter.'

[22] *Kokkinakis v Greece*, para 31.

[23] The HRC has stated, in *General Comment No 22*, para 8, in respect of limitations grounded on public morals that 'the concept of morals derives from many social, philosophical and religious traditions; consequently, limitations on the freedom to manifest a religion or belief for the purpose of protecting morals must be based on principles not deriving exclusively from a single tradition.'

[24] HRC, *General Comment No 22*, para 8.

[25] *Manoussakis and Ors v Greece*, ECHR (1996) App No 18748/91, judgment of 26 September 1996, para 44.

[26] ECHR (1999) App No 38178/97, judgment of 14 December 1999, para 53 (emphasis added). See Raz (1994) 156 concerning the liberal notions of tolerance, freedom and the Harm Principle.

[27] *Şahin v Turkey*, ECHR (2005) App No 44774/98, judgment of 10 November 2005.

[28] *Dogru v France*, ECHR (2008) App No 27058/05, judgment of 4 December 2008.

their rights to manifest their religion under Article 9 ECHR. In *Dogru*, the Court affirmed again that:

[I]n a democratic society, in which several religions coexist within one and the same population, it may be necessary to place restrictions on this freedom in order to reconcile the interests of the various groups and ensure that everyone's beliefs are respected. It has frequently emphasised the State's role as the neutral and impartial organiser of the exercise of various religions, faiths and beliefs, and stated that this role is conducive to public order, religious harmony and tolerance in a democratic society. It also considers that the State's duty of neutrality and impartiality is incompatible with any power on the State's part to assess the legitimacy of religious beliefs and that it requires the State to ensure mutual tolerance between opposing groups. Pluralism and democracy must also be based on dialogue and a spirit of compromise necessarily entailing various concessions on the part of individuals which are justified in order to maintain and promote the ideals and values of a democratic society.[29]

The Court found that the banning of the headscarf and the subsequent expulsion of the student was a prima facie restriction on the exercise of the right to freedom of religion.

The respondent state would be in violation of the Convention if the restriction did not come within the requirements laid down in the Convention, that is, it was prescribed by law, directed towards one or more of the legitimate aims set down in Article 9 ECHR and was 'necessary in a democratic society' to achieve these aims.[30] The Court had held earlier in *Şahin* that the provision does not 'protect every act motivated or inspired by a religion or belief and does not always guarantee the right to behave in a manner governed by a religious belief'.[31] Accordingly, in *Dogru* it found that France could limit the wearing of a headscarf because of the margin of appreciation left to member state to negotiate the relations between church and state which underpin religious freedom.[32] It found that the ensuing interference to the freedom arising from the policy of secularism was 'justified as a matter of principle and proportionate' to this aim and therefore permitted under the Convention.[33]

The distinction between the private and public sphere is further enlivened concerning the right to freedom of religion or belief in respect of the 'freedom' of parents and legal guardians 'to ensure the religious and moral education of their children in conformity with their own convictions' (Article 18(4) ICCPR).[34] This

[29] *Dogru v France*, para 48. See also *Şahin v Turkey*, paras 106 and 107.
[30] *Dogru v France*, para 48.  [31] *Şahin v Turkey*, paras 105 and 212.
[32] *Dogru v France*, para 72.
[33] *Dogru v France*, para 72. In respect of the US First Amendment: see *City of Boerne v Flores, Archbishop of San Antonio et al*, 521 US 507 (1997); and *Wallace v Jaffree*, 472 US 38 (1985).
[34] See also Art 26(3) UDHR; Art 13(3) ICESCR; concerning parental choice, children's education and specifically in respect of religious instruction: Protocol 1, Art 2 ECHR and Art 12(4) ACHR. This issue also engages the right to privacy and family life. In *Case 'Relating to Certain Aspects of the Laws on the Use of Languages in Education in Belgium' v Belgium*, ECHR (1968) Series A, No 6, App No 1474/62, judgment of 23 July 1968, at 7, the Court found that the decision by the parents to send their children to a French-language school because it was not available in their district did not constitute an interference with right to family life, in effect affirming that the state may determine

right is reinforced by the wording of the right to education in Article 26(3) UDHR ('parents have a prior right to choose the kind of education that shall be given to their children') and Article 2 Protocol 1 ECHR ('[T]he State shall respect the right of parents to ensure such education and teaching in conformity with their own religious and philosophical convictions'). The HRC has stated that public school curricula may provide instruction in the general history of religions and ethics provided 'it is given in a neutral and objective way'.[35] It added that public education which includes instruction in a particular religion or belief will contravene Article 18(4) ICCPR unless non-discriminatory exemptions or alternatives are in place to accommodate the wishes of parents or legal guardians.[36]

In *Lautsi and Others v Italy*,[37] the European Court considered an application brought by a mother whose children attended a public school in which crucifixes were affixed in the classroom and who argued that this was contrary to her beliefs, those she wished to impart to her children, and the principle of secularism adopted by the respondent state. The Grand Chamber held that Article 8 ECHR and Article 2 Protocol No 1:

[Did] not prevent States from imparting through teaching or education information or knowledge of a directly or indirectly religious or philosophical kind. It does not even permit parents to object to the integration of such teaching or education in the school curriculum.

On the other hand, as its aim is to safeguard the possibility of pluralism in education, it requires the State, in exercising its functions with regard to education and teaching, to take care that information or knowledge included in the curriculum is conveyed in an objective, critical and pluralistic manner, enabling pupils to develop a critical mind particularly with regard to religion in a calm atmosphere free of any proselytism. The State is forbidden to pursue an aim of indoctrination that might be considered as not respecting parents' religious and philosophical convictions. That is the limit that the States must not exceed.[38]

The Court found that this fell within the state's margin of appreciation even though the crucifix was a symbol of majoritarian religion of the country, it came to represent a tradition of democracy and tolerance and it was this tradition and meaning being promoted by the respondent state.[39] Despite the prominent display, the Court found that the respondent was neutral. There was insufficient evidence of indoctrination because it was deemed a 'passive' symbol (unlike the wearing of a headscarf by a teacher), and there was nothing to suggest the authorities were

---

the official languages which are used in instruction in public schools. However, Judge Maridakis noted: 'Private and family life would be violated if the authorities intervened to force a person to shape that life in a way that departed from his traditions and thus from the spirit that by virtue of blood ties predominate in relations between parents and their children and between members of the same family in general.' However, he found that this had not occurred in this case.

[35] HRC, *Hartikainen v Finland*, Comm No 40/1978, 9 April 1981, UN Doc A/36/40 (1981) at 147, para 10.4.

[36] HRC, *General Comment No 22*, para 6.

[37] *Lautsi and Others v Italy*, ECHR (2011) App No 30814/06, judgment of 18 March 2011.

[38] *Lautsi and Others v Italy*, para 62. See also *Kjeldsen, Busk Madsen and Pedersen v Denmark*, ECHR (1976) App Nos 5095/71, 5920/72, 5926/72, judgment of 7 December 1976 at 53.

[39] *Lautsi and Others v Italy*, paras 67 and 68.

intolerant of students who professed another religion, or no religion, or held non-religious philosophical views.[40] The applicant mother was not prevented from guiding her children pursuant to her own philosophical convictions.[41] Indeed, the European Court and Commission have repeatedly indicated that if an individual can take action to circumvent the limitation of his or her right to freedom of religion or beliefs, no interference to the right exists, and the respondent does not need to justify the restriction.[42]

## B. Right to participate in (national) cultural life

The unravelling of horizontal ties based on religious facilitation with the rise of the modern, secular state left a vacuum which had to be filled. In order to ensure their stability and viability, deliberate strategies by states were adopted to fill this void through the creation of 'imagined communities' bounded by manufactured affiliations based on a national cultural identity.[43] The secular state utilized new technologies (such as the printing press) and systems of knowledge to demarcate and systematize its domain, its territory, its populace. Standardization brought with it a single national language promoted through books, newspapers, and public education. Census and maps had a similar influence on the notion of nationality and flattened or eradicated existing spatial and physical conceptions of communities based on religion, ethnicity, culture, or language. The processes involved in the manufacture of a unified national identity worked not only to replace the void at the supranational level left with the demise of the church, it also worked to concertedly and deliberately remove the diverse, competing ties at the subnational level. These were all to be assimilated into the national cultural identity in order that individuals were able to fully realize their rights as citizens.

It is not surprising then that when it was first articulated, the right to participate in cultural life was resolutely defined by participation in the *national* cultural life and designed to foster relations between the state and its citizens. The right to participate in the cultural life of the community was incorporated into Article 27 UDHR and subsequently rearticulated in Article 15 of the International Covenant on Economic, Social and Cultural Rights (ICESCR).[44] This right has until recently been strictly limited to participation in the 'national culture' by the individual right holder. The *travaux* of Article 27(1) UDHR reveal that the drafters were preoccupied with the participation and enjoyment by the wider population of culture manifestations confined ordinarily to a small élite. Culture was defined narrowly

---

[40] *Lautsi and Others v Italy*, paras 71–4. Cf *Dahlab v Switzerland*, ECHR (2001) App No 42393/98, judgment of 15 February 2001 (GC).

[41] *Lautsi and Others v Italy*, para 75. See also Concurring Opinion of Judge Rozakis (with Judge Vajic) finding that 'the duties of the State have largely shifted from concerns of the parents to concerns of the society at large, thus reducing the extent of the parents' ability to determine, outside the home, the kind of education that their children receive.'

[42] *Eweida and Ors v United Kingdom*, para 83.

[43] B. Anderson, *Imagined Communities: Reflections on the Origin and Spread of Nationalism* (2nd edn, Verso, 1991).

[44] GA Res 2200A(XXI), 16 December 1966, entered into force 3 January 1976.

as 'high' culture including museums, libraries, and theatres.[45] While the UDHR is a non-binding declaration, this human right's later inclusion in the ICESCR renders it legally binding on states parties. Also, the inclusion of Article 27 in the UDHR meant that the right was to be enjoyed by every human being and it was a right equal to and indivisible from all other rights contained in the Declaration.[46]

However, UNESCO had presented a preliminary draft Article 15 which required states parties to 'encourage[e] the free cultural development of racial and linguistic minorities'.[47] The Committee of Experts called by UNESCO to elaborate upon this right observed that a distinction needed to be made 'between different types of communities, to which any given individual may belong at one and the same [time]...[and which] may run counter to, or at least differ considerably from, those of the national community'.[48] UNESCO's recommendation to include the words 'to take part in the cultural life of the communities to which he belongs', was eventually defeated.[49] The focus of the international community remained resolutely on the 'national' community until the late twentieth century.

This interpretation of the right to culture—that is national culture—reinforced the position of some liberal theorists who promote the right to *a* culture and not necessarily the right to one's *own* culture on the basis that cultural context is crucial to enable an individual to exercise free choice. As the United Nations Development Programme noted:

Cultural liberty is about expanding individual choices, not about preserving values and practices as an end in itself with blind allegiance to tradition. Culture is not a frozen set of values and practices. It is constantly recreated as people question, adapt and redefine their values and practices to changing realities and exchange of ideas.... Those making demands for cultural accommodation should also abide by democratic principles and the objectives of human freedom and human rights.[50]

This rationale for the right to culture impacts significantly upon implementation and its relationship to other human rights. In essence, for some liberal theorists, it is only within a cultural context that we are able to fully assess and choose between available life choices, and the right to culture is a mechanism by which individuals can realize freedom of expression, thought, assembly, and association.[51] Consequently, such a rationale protects the right to a cultural affiliation but does not seek to afford protection to a particular culture; it does not view the granting of privileges to minority cultures in the face of possible assimilation of the majority culture as necessary.[52] This interpretation is examined with reference to the right

[45] Y.M. Donders, *Towards a Right to Cultural Identity?* (2002), 139; O'Keefe, 'The "Right to Take Part in Cultural Life" under Article 15 of the ICESCR', 47 *ICLQ* (1998) 904.

[46] UNESCO Doc UNESCO/DG/188, 6 October 1952.

[47] UN Doc E/CN.4/541.          [48] UNESCO Doc UNESCO/CUA/42, at 17.

[49] UN Doc A/C.3/SR.797, at 178; UN Doc A/C.3/SR.799, 190–1.

[50] United Nations Development Programme, Human Development Report 2004: Cultural Liberty in Today's Diverse World (2004) 4.

[51] W. Kymlicka, *Liberalism, Community and Culture* (1989).

[52] Margalit and Halbertal, 'Liberalism and the Right to Culture', 61 *Social Research* (1994) 491 at 502–4.

to freedom of expression, a right which has been linked to the right to freedom of religion or beliefs and the right to culture since their earliest formulations.

## C. Freedom of expression, hate speech, and blasphemy laws

Freedom of expression has been described as a cornerstone of a democratic society.[53] The African Commission on Human and Peoples' Rights has stated that this right is 'vital to an individual's personal development, his political consciousness and participation in the conduct of public affairs in his country'.[54] The European Court of Human Rights has held that it 'constitutes one of the essential foundations of a democratic society and one of the basic conditions for its progress and for each individual's self-fulfilment'.[55] Although freedom of expression is viewed as a fundamental right attached to individuals, it carries little meaning unless there is recognition of a communal or collective context. Therefore, it is also considered critical for cultural (or religious) minorities. For example, the right to freedom of expression was recognized as such in the interwar minority treaties which protected communities in newly created states in Central and Eastern Europe.[56] This right was universalized with its inclusion as Article 19 UDHR, which provides for the imparting and receiving of information and ideas without interference and across territorial boundaries.[57] This latter extension is significant for minorities straddling frontiers or removed from their kin-state. However, human rights bodies have been reluctant to sanction it as a guarantee for the use of one's mother language in public spaces. The Human Rights Committee has confirmed that while a state party is permitted to choose an official national language, it cannot restrict the use of other languages in the private sphere.[58] The European Court in an application concerning the education of children in Turkish-controlled northern Cyprus which had been regulated by specialist international agreements incorporating guarantees for mother tongue tuition, found that education led in the Turkish or English languages did not fulfil the 'legitimate wish to educate their children in accordance with their cultural and ethnic tradition'.[59] But this is a rare example. Generally speaking, human rights bodies have been reluctant to endorse the extension of the right to freedom of expression to encompass the guaranteed protection of the use of mother tongue languages in public places.

---

[53] HRC, *General Comment No 34: Article 19: Freedoms of Opinion and Expression*, 12 September 2011, UN Doc CCPR/C/GC/34, para 13; *Marques v Angola*, ACHPR Comm No 1128/2002, 29 March 2005.
[54] *Media Rights Agenda and Others v Nigeria*, ACHPR Comm Nos 105/93, 128/94, 130/94, 152/92, not dated.
[55] *Arslan v Turkey*, ECHR (1999) App No 23462/94, judgment of 8 July 1999, para 44(i).
[56] See, eg Art 7 Treaty of Peace of St Germain-en-Laye, 10 September 1919, entered into force 8 November 1921, BFSP 112, at 317; 14 (supp) *AJIL* (1920) 1 at 77, provided: 'No restriction shall be imposed on the free use by any Czecho-Slovak national of any language in private intercourse, in commerce, in religion, in the press or publication of any kind, or at public meetings.'
[57] See Art 19 UDHR; Art 19 ICCPR; Art 10 ECHR; Art 9 ACHPR; and Art 13 ACHR.
[58] HRC, *Singer v Canada*, 26 July 1994, UN Doc CCPR/C/51/D/455/1991 (1994).
[59] *Cyprus v Turkey*, ECHR (2001) App No 25781/94, judgment of 10 May 2001, paras 274–9.

As was shown in respect of the right to freedom of religion or beliefs, freedoms guaranteed under human rights law are not without limitations, both those contained within the definition of the human right itself and those imposed by courts called upon to balance competing rights and freedoms. The right to freedom of expression is also circumscribed.[60] However, how these restrictions are interpreted and these conflicts resolved, points to the nature of the right and what it is designed to protect. The European Court has found that the freedom of expression

is applicable not only to 'information' or 'ideas' that are favourably received or regarded as inoffensive or as a matter of indifference, but also to those that offend, shock or disturb the State or any sector of the population. Such are the demands of that pluralism, tolerance and broadmindedness without which there is no 'democratic society'. This means, amongst other things, that every 'formality', 'condition', 'restriction' or 'penalty' imposed in this sphere must be proportionate to the legitimate aim pursued.[61]

Nevertheless, as a result of interreligious strife and its impact on peace and stability, even this broad interpretation of tolerance has its limitation, and the human rights instruments explicitly prohibit so-called hate speech.[62] Article 20 ICCPR provides that religious expressions or activities which promote religious hatred or incite religious intolerance must be prohibited by law by states parties.[63] The HRC has indicated that a state of emergency cannot be used as a justification by a state party for engaging in actions contrary to Article 20.[64] The provision is considered by the Committee to fall within the limitations prescribed by Article 19 on freedom of expression, but as *lex specialis*. It requires states parties to prohibit by law such speech and acts as being contrary to public policy and to 'provide an appropriate sanction in case of violation'.[65] The HRC has found hate speech by individuals to be contrary to the right to freedom of expression and dismissed complaints contesting the criminalization of persons who have denied the Holocaust as a historical event, as well as concerning the prohibition of using telephone messages to disseminate anti-Semitic views.[66] Similarly, the European Court of Human Rights, in *Hizb Ut-Tahrir and Others v Germany*, dismissed an application concerning the

---

[60]  See Art 19(3) ICCPR; Art 10(2) ECHR; and Art 13(2) ACHR.

[61]  *Handyside v United Kingdom*, ECHR (1976) Series A, No 24 para 49. Also in *Arslan v Turkey*, para 44: 'it is applicable not only to "information" or "ideas" that are favourably received or regarded as inoffensive or as a matter of indifference, but also to those that offend, shock or disturb. Such are the demands of that pluralism, tolerance and broadmindness without which there is no "democratic society".'

[62]  See Raz, 'Free Expression and Personal Identification', 11 *Oxford Journal of Legal Studies* (1991) 303 at 320; and Waldron, 'Dignity and Defamation: The Visibility of Hate', 123 *Harvard Law Review* (2010) 1569.

[63]  See HRC, *General Comment No 22*, para 7; and HRC, *General Comment No 11: Prohibition of propaganda for war and inciting national, racial or religious hatred (Art 20)*, 29 September 1983, para 19; and Art 13(5) ACHPR.

[64]  HRC, *General Comment No 29: States of Emergency (Art. 14)*, 31 August 2001, UN Doc CCPR/C/21/Rev.1/Add.11, para 13(e).

[65]  HRC, *General Comment No 11*.

[66]  HRC, *Faurisson v France*, 8 November 1996, UN Doc CCPR/C/58/D/550/1993; and *J.R.T. and W.G. Party v Canada*, Comm No 104/1981, 6 April 1983, UN Doc CCPR/C/OP/2, 25. Cf HRC, *General Comment No 34, Article 19: Freedom of opinion and expression*, 21 July 2011, para 49.

prohibition of an Islamic association which promoted the overthrow of non-Islamic governments and found that the ECHR did not protect acts which were designed to destroy rights and freedoms set down in the Convention.[67] The Committee on the Elimination of Racial Discrimination has stated that the prohibition of hate speech protects non-citizens.[68]

As detailed in Part 3 below, general and specialist human rights instruments which enunciate cultural rights reaffirm that such rights cannot be used to justify violations of other human rights norms and fundamental freedoms. The Committee on Economic, Social and Cultural Rights (CESCR) has observed that a state may need to impose limitations on the right to participate in cultural life especially in respect of 'negative' practices which infringe other human rights.[69] These limitations must pursue a 'legitimate aim', be 'compatible' with the right and 'strictly necessary for promotion of the general welfare in a democratic society', and proportionate (that is, the least restrictive measures for attaining the ends).[70] The CESCR has noted that states adopting such measures must also consider other rights related to participation in cultural life including the right to privacy, freedom of thought, conscience, or religion, to freedom of opinion and expression, to peaceful assembly, and to freedom of association.[71] Conversely, the HRC has indicated that any restriction on freedom of expression is a 'serious curtailment of human rights' and therefore must be provided for by law; however, it is incompatible with the ICCPR that the restriction be sanctioned by 'traditional, religious or other such customary law'.[72]

The provisos to the right to freedom of expression contained in Articles 19(3) and 20 ICCPR cannot be used by a state party to justify blasphemy laws or prohibition of displays which are viewed as disrespectful of a religion or belief. The ongoing debate around Human Rights Council resolutions on Combating Defamation of Religions promoted by the Organization of Islamic Conference and domestic blasphemy laws encapsulate this intersection between the rights of a group, in this case a religious group, and individual fundamental freedoms.[73] The HRC has

---

[67] ECHR (2012) App No 31098/08, decision of 19 June 2012. See also *Ivanov v Russia*, ECHR (2007) App No 35222/04, decision of 20 February 2007 (concerning conviction for incitement to ethnic, racial, or religious hatred); and *Garaudy v France*, ECHR (2003) App No 65831/01, decision of 24 June 2003 (concerning conviction for disputing the existence of crimes against humanity, defamation in public of a group of persons, and incitement to racial hatred). See, generally, Recommendation R 97(20) of the Committee of Ministers of the Council of Europe on hate speech; Recommendation 1805 (2007) of the Parliamentary Assembly of the Council of Europe on blasphemy, religious insults, and hate speech against persons on grounds of their religion; Venice Commission Study 406/2006 on blasphemy, religious insults, and incitement to religious hatred; General Policy Recommendation No 7 of the European Commission against Racism and Intolerance (ECRI) on national legislation to combat racism and discrimination. See also Waldron (2010). Cf Dworkin, 'Foreword', in I. Hare and J. Weinstein (eds), *Extreme Speech and Democracy* (2009) v.

[68] CERD, *General Recommendation No 30: Discrimination against non-citizens*, 1 October 1994, paras 11 and 12.

[69] UN Doc E/C.12/GC/21, para 19.     [70] Article 4 ICESCR.

[71] UN Doc E/C.12/GC/21, para 19.     [72] HRC, *General Comment No 34*, para 24.

[73] HRC resolutions 2000/84, 26 April 2000 (Defamation of religions) to the latest 22/L.40, 22 March 2013 (Combating intolerance, negative stereotyping and stigmatization of, and discrimination, incitement to violence and violence against, persons based on religion or belief); Report of the

observed that such prohibitions and blasphemy laws are incompatible with the ICCPR except where they are designed to prevent incitement to war or ethnic or religious discrimination or hostility.[74] It has indicated that such laws cannot be used to discriminate for or against a religion or its adherents or between believers or non-believers, nor can it be a vehicle for preventing or punishing 'criticism of religious leaders or commentary on religious doctrine and tenets of faith'.[75]

# 3. Equality

The bills of rights which accompanied the rise of modern secular states and human rights which define contemporary international law are headlined by the principle of equality. The 1789 *Déclaration des droit de l'homme* commences in Article 1 with: 'Men are born and remain free and equal in rights'. The US Declaration of Independence of 1776 likewise provides that 'all men are created equal' and that they are endowed with inalienable rights, among them liberty. Inspired by these documents, the Universal Declaration of Human Rights adopted by the international community in 1948 commences with the words: 'Whereas recognition of the inherent dignity and of the equal and inalienable rights of all members of the human family is the foundation of freedom, justice and peace in the world'.[76] These various pronouncements reflect this continual deliberation in political and legal thought since the Enlightenment concerning the link between equality and freedom, the tensions arising between them, and their possible resolution.

Part 2 examined how the promotion of liberty and nondiscrimination on grounds of race, religion, culture, or language extended and moved beyond conceptions of tolerance and the emphasis on civil and political rights in the public sphere. Strict equality not only permits minorities to establish and control their own institutions but means that public institutions and spaces are to be enjoyed by all individuals and are no longer confined to the majority.[77] This Part concentrates on the relationship between the state, the group, and individual members of the group. Its structure follows the formulation of guarantees provided in the interwar minority treaties, a framework which has undergone a revival in the post-cold war period. First, there is an overview of the concept of self-identification and the role of the state and group in determining its membership. Then, there is an exploration of the role of non-discrimination in the protection of minorities

---

UN High Commissioner for Human Rights on the implementation of Human Rights Council resolution 10/22 entitled 'Combating defamation of religions', 11 January 2010, UN Doc A/HRC/2010; and HRC, *Ahmad and Abdol-Hamid v Denmark*, 1 April 2008, Decision on admissibility, UN Doc CCPR/C/92/D/1487/2006.

[74] HRC, *General Comment No 34*, para 48. See HRC, Concluding Observation on the United Kingdom of Great Britain and Northern Ireland, 27 March 2000, UN Doc CCPR/C/79/Add.119, para 15; and HRC, Concluding Observations on Kuwait, 27 July 2000, UN Doc CCPR/CO/69/KWT, para 20.

[75] *General Comment No 34*, para 48.       [76] First recital, Preamble, UDHR.

[77] Raz (1994) 158.

through an exploration of case law on education and minority children from the interwar period to the present day.[78] Finally, I return to the right to participate in cultural life as it is presently being interpreted, how this harmonizes with the revived minority rights regime, and the promotion of the right to participate in one's *own* culture.

## A. Group affiliation and self-identification

The relationship between the state, the cultural (religious or linguistic) group and its individual members in law has raised 'starting gate' issues since the first formulations of minority guarantees in international law in the early twentieth century. As these guarantees often arose with the recognition of new states or the reconfiguration of the territorial boundaries of existing states, the international community enabled some individuals to choose their nationality.[79] This had the twin effect of permitting individuals to determine which state they wished to belong to, but also ensured that they were not rendered stateless and would be afforded the rights and protections of citizenship. Whilst the right to hold and change one's nationality is contained in Article 15 UDHR, subsequent international and regional human rights instruments are either silent or more qualified.[80] Nationality and citizenship remains a starting gate issue as it is clear that certain human rights (particularly certain civil and political rights and guarantees of equality before the law) are quarantined to nationals; however, human rights bodies have indicated repeatedly that cultural rights can be enjoyed by non-nationals and nationals, alike.[81]

The relationship between the state and the religious, cultural or linguistic communities is likewise tempered by the question of who defines the group. Although there have been repeated attempts to define what constitutes a minority

---

[78] Article 29(1)(c) Convention on the Rights of the Child (CRC), 20 November 1989, entered into force 2 September 1990, 1577 UNTS 3, provides 'the aim of education of the child is: the development of respect for the child's parents, his or her own cultural identity, languages and values, for the national values of the country in which the child is living, the country from which have originate, and for the civilizations different from his or her own'. See also Committee on the Rights of the Child, *General Comment No 11, Indigenous Children and their Rights under the Convention*, 12 February 2009, para 56.

[79] Articles 3 to 6, Treaty between the Principal Allied and Associated Powers and Poland, 28 June 1919, 225 CTS 412 (Peace Treaty with Poland) were the first such provisions and they became the model of subsequent minority protections imposed on other states seeking recognition or entry into the League of Nations.

[80] See Art 5(d)(iii) International Convention on the Elimination of All Forms of Racial Discrimination (CERD), 7 March 1966, entered into force 4 January 1969, 660 UNTS 195. Cf Art 20 ACHR; Art 4(a), (c), European Convention on Nationality, 6 November 1997, entered into force 1 March 2000, ETS 166; and Art 6 UN Declaration on the Rights of Indigenous Peoples (UNDRIP), GA Res 61/295, 13 September 2007.

[81] CERD, *General Recommendation No 30*, para 37 ('Take the necessary measures to prevent practices that deny non-citizens their cultural identity, such as legal or de facto requirements that non-citizens change their name in order to obtain citizenship, and to take measures to enable non-citizens to preserve and develop their culture'); and Human Rights Committee, *General Comment No 23: Rights of Minorities (Art 27)*, UN Doc HRI/GEN/1/Rev.1, 38 (1994), para 5.2. Cf *Advisory Opinion on the Acquisition of Polish Nationality*, 1923 PCIJ Series B, No 7 at 15ff; and Framework Convention on National Minorities (FCNM), 1 February 1995, entered into force 1 February 1998, ETS 157.

in international law, there is no agreed legal definition.[82] However, international tribunals have emphasized that the existence of a minority is determined by 'fact not law';[83] and it is not a state or states who determine whether they exist or not within their territory. Yet, in an effort to limit the reach of the protection of Article 27 ICCPR, several states during its drafting insisted on the inclusion of the words '[i]n those states in which ethnic, religious or linguistic minorities exist'.[84] Similarly, when ratifying the International Covenant, France attached a 'declaration' concerning Article 27 in which it maintained that minorities did not exist in the state because its constitution ensures equality before the law, without distinction as to origin, gender, or religion.[85] However, like the Permanent Court of International Justice (PCIJ) before it, the HRC does not accept that France does not have minorities on its territory:

[T]he mere fact that equal rights are granted to all individuals and that all individuals are equal before the law does not preclude the existence in fact of minorities in a country, and their entitlement to the enjoyment of their culture, the practice of their religion or the use of their language in community with other members of their group.[86]

Accordingly, in its *General Comment No 23 (Article 27 ICCPR)*, the Committee provides that the existence of a minority within 'a given state party does not depend upon a decision by that state party but requires to be established by objective criteria'.[87] Likewise, the ILO Convention concerning Indigenous and Tribal Peoples in Independent Countries provides that self-identification is the fundamental criterion for establishing the existence of an indigenous people, with no need for official state recognition.[88] To permit states to define or determine the existence of a minority or indigenous community would effectively render such legal protection illusory.

This jurisprudence in respect of the right to nationality and existence of a minority group is complemented by rights pertaining to self-identification by the individual to the group and by the group of the individual. The UN Minorities Declaration provides under Article 3(2) that there shall be 'no disadvantage . . . for any person belonging to a minority as a consequence of the exercise or non-exercise

---

[82] See *Greco-Bulgarian 'Communities' case*, 1930 PCIJ Series B, No 17 at 21; and Special Rapporteur of the Sub-Commission on the Prevention of Discrimination and Protection of Minorities, Study of the Rights of Persons Belonging to Ethnic, Religious and Linguistic Minorities, F. Capotorti, June 1977, UN Doc E/CN.4/Sub.2/384/Rev.1, paras 28–81.

[83] *Rights of Minorities in Upper Silesia (Minority Schools)*, 1928 PCIJ Series A, No 15, 18 at 29.

[84] See UN Doc A/C.3/SR.1104, para 23.

[85] See HRC, *T.K. v France*, HRC, Decision on Admissibility, 8 November 1989, UN Doc CCPR/C/37/D/220/1987; *M.K. v France*, Decision on Admissibility, 18 December 1989, UN Doc CCPR/C/37/D/222/1987; and *S.G. v France*, Decision on Admissibility, 1 November 1991, UN Doc CCPR/C/43/D/347/1988 at 8, see separate opinion of R. Higgins.

[86] HRC, Concluding Remarks of the Human Rights Committee: France, 8 April 1997, UN Doc CCPR/C/79/Add.80, para 24.

[87] HRC, i, para 5.2. See also HRC, *Lovelace v Canada*, Comm No 24/1977, 30 July 1981, para 14, UN Doc A/36/40 (1981), 166 and *Kitok v Sweden*, Comm No 197/1985, 27 July 1988, UN Doc A/43/40 (1988), 221, para 9.7.

[88] Article 1(2) ILO Convention No 169 (1989) concerning Indigenous and Tribal Peoples in Independent Countries, 27 June 1989, entered into force 5 September 1991, 1650 UNTS 383.

of rights set forth in the present Declaration'.[89] The provision also applies at least 'moral duties' on 'agencies of the minority group', with states parties obliged to prohibit minorities from taking measures which impose rules on persons who do not wish to be part of the minority nor exercise their related rights.[90] Similarly, *General Comment No 21* defines it as a 'freedom' and it is in effect the ultimate freedom which attaches to an individual, that is, the right to exit the group. The CESCR has noted that '[t]he decision by a person whether or not to exercise the right take part in cultural life individually, or in association with others, is a cultural choice and, as such, should be recognized, respected, and protected on the basis of equality.'[91]

The HRC has held that this was a right of special importance for indigenous peoples, individually and collectively.[92] It is augmented by Article 9 of the UN Declaration on the Rights of Indigenous Peoples (UNDRIP) which provides that indigenous peoples and individuals have the right to belong to an indigenous community in accordance with the community's traditions and customs.[93] Discrimination is not permitted in respect of the exercise of this right. Also, under Article 33, indigenous peoples have a right to 'determine their own identity or membership in accordance with their customs and traditions'. This does not impact upon the right of indigenous persons to obtain the citizenship of their relevant state.

Yet, conflicts may arise between the collective and individual rights to self-identification. In *Lovelace v Canada*, the Human Rights Committee found the state in violation of Article 27 ICCPR because the relevant national legislation had stripped the complainant of her Indian status following her marriage to a non-Indian, which continued even after the relationship ended, and meant that she was prevented from returning to her tribal land. The Committee accepted the 'need to define the category of peoples entitled to live on a reserve, for such purposes as . . . preservation of the identity of its people'.[94] However, it concluded that the denial of Ms Lovelace's right to access her culture and language 'in community with other members' of her group was not 'reasonable or necessary' in order to achieve this aim.[95]

---

[89] Its commentary states that this provision prohibits states from imposing an ethnic identity on individuals through sanctions against those that refuse to form part of that group, as occurred during Apartheid in South Africa: UN Doc /CN.4/Sub.2/AC.5/2005/2, para 54.

[90] UN Doc /CN.4/Sub.2/AC.5/2005/2, para 54.

[91] CESCR, General Comment No 21 Right of everyone to take part in cultural life, 21 December 2009, UN Doc E/C.12/GC/21, para 6.

[92] CESCR, *General Comment No 21*, para 7. See also CERD, *General Recommendation No 8: Identification of a particular racial or ethnic group, Art 1*, 22 August 1990 (self-identification of the individual); and CERD, *General Recommendation No 27: Discrimination against Roma*, 16 August 2000, para 3 ('To respect the wishes of Roma as to the designation they want to be given and the group to which they want to belong').

[93] UN Declaration on the Rights of Indigenous Peoples (UNDRIP), GA Res 61/295, 13 September 2007.

[94] *Lovelace v Canada*, para 15.    [95] *Lovelace v Canada*, paras 15 and 17.

## B. Non-discrimination

Provisions at the international level covering minorities have at the very least included guarantees of non-discrimination relating to equality in law and equality in fact. The framework established by interwar minority treaties contained these two understandings of equality. The principle of equality in law and non-discrimination as to civil and political rights is explored with reference to education of minority children. The principle of equality in fact and non-discrimination as to cultural rights specifically will be detailed in the subsequent section covering Article 15 ICESCR and Article 27 ICCPR.

As noted above, the Treaty of Westphalia guaranteed to religious minorities that they would enjoy equal rights to public life regardless of their religious affiliation. This guarantee of non-discrimination and equality in law was extended to cover religious, cultural, and linguistic groups in the interwar minority treaties. The protection was universalized in the second half of the twentieth century with its inclusion in the UDHR and rendered binding with the ICCPR and specialist instruments like the Convention on the Elimination of All Forms of Racial Discrimination (CERD).[96] Applying the principle of non-discrimination, members of the minority as nationals of the relevant state were entitled to equality before the law and enjoyment of same civil and political rights as other nationals, without distinction as to race, language, or religion.[97] The PCIJ found the intended purpose of this arm of the minority provisions was to 'ensure that nationals belonging to racial, religious or linguistic minorities [were] placed in every respect on a footing of perfect equality with other nationals of the State'.[98] Furthermore, it held that these provisions were designed to 'prevent any unfavourable treatment, and not to grant a special regime of privileged treatment'; consequently they were of 'a purely negative character in that they were confined to a prohibition of any discrimination'.[99]

However, the interwar minority guarantees also provided that these communities should enjoy equal rights 'both in law and in fact' to establish, control, and manage their own charitable, religious, and social institutions, schools and other educational establishments, with the right to use their own language and to exercise their religion freely without interference by the national authorities, 'provided that the interest of public order [was] safeguarded'.[100] When interpreting this provision

---

[96] International Convention on the Elimination of All Forms of Racial Discrimination (CERD), 7 March 1966, entered into force 4 January 1969, 660 UNTS 195.

[97] *Rights of Minorities in Upper Silesia (Minority Schools)*, 18. See also Arts 2, 7, and 8, Peace Treaty with Poland; and *Treatment of Polish Nationals and other Persons of Polish Origin or Speech in the Danzig Territory*, 1932 PCIJ Series A/B, No 44 at 28 and 39.

[98] *Rights of Minorities in Upper Silesia (Minority Schools)*, 17.

[99] *Rights of Minorities in Upper Silesia (Minority Schools)*, 17.

[100] Article 9, Peace Treaty with Poland. See also CERD, *General Recommendation No 32: The meaning and scope of special measures in the International Covenant on the Elimination of All Forms of Racial Discrimination*, 24 September 2009, UN Doc CERD/C/GC/32, para 6: 'The Convention is based on the principles of the dignity and equality of all human beings. The principle of equality underpinned by the Convention combines formal equality before the law with equal protection of the law, with substantive or de facto equality in the enjoyment and exercise of human rights as the aim to be achieved by the faithful implementation of its principles.'

in the *Minority Schools in Albania* case, the Permanent Court observed that its purpose was 'to ensure for the minority elements suitable means for the preservation of their racial peculiarities, their traditions and their national characteristics'.[101] In this case, Albania had argued that it had met its obligations under the minority provision when it ordered the closure of all private schools and the attendance of children at public schools because the arrangement applied to all children in the state. In rejecting the respondent state's arguments, the Court held:

Equality in law precludes discrimination of any kind; whereas equality in fact may involve the necessity of different treatment in order to attain a result which establishes an equilibrium between different situations.

It is easy to imagine cases in which equality of treatment of the majority and of the minority, whose situation and requirements are different, would result in inequality in fact.... The equality between members of the majority and of the minority must be an effective, genuine equality...[102]

Accordingly, the Court found that the institutions listed were 'indispensable' in ensuring that the minority enjoyed equal treatment to the majority 'not only in law but also in fact'. It observed that the schools' closure and replacement with government institutions removed this equal treatment because it 'deprive[d] the minority of the institutions appropriate to its needs, whereas the majority would continue to have them supplied in the institutions created by the State'. It concluded that rather than creating a special privilege for the minority, the guarantee was designed to make sure the majority was not privileged when compared to the minority.[103] Therefore, the respondent state was under a positive obligation to ensure the realization of these rights. In territories where the minority made up a 'considerable proportion of...nationals', it was required to provide instruction in the minority language in the public education system and an equitable share of public funds to the communities to realize these goals.[104]

The ultimate purpose of the interwar minority guarantees was the subject of considerable contemporary debate. On the one hand, it was clear that the drafters did not intend to create 'states within states' by granting national groups political autonomy but to prohibit discrimination between citizens on the basis of their religion, language, or race.[105] For this reason, they referred throughout to 'members of minorities' and not simply 'minorities'.[106] This position was adopted by the dissenting judges in *Minority Schools in Albania*, who insisted that the Court interpret the provision according to existing precedents.[107] They observed that the

---

[101] *Minority Schools in Albania*, 1935 PCIJ Series A/B, No 64, 4 at 17.

[102] *Minority Schools in Albania*, 1935 PCIJ Series A/B, No 64, 4 at 18–21.

[103] *Minority Schools in Albania*, 1935 PCIJ Series A/B, No 64, 4 at 18–21

[104] *Minority Schools in Albania*, 1935 PCIJ Series A/B, No 64, 4 at 22. See also *Greco-Bulgarian 'Communities'*, 1930 PCIJ Series B, No17 at 33.

[105] Calderwood, 'The Protection of Minorities by the League of Nations', 2 *Geneva Research Information Committee Special Studies* (1931) 17 at 21. See Report of M. de Mello-Franco, 9 December 1925, LNOJ, 7th year (February 1926) 141.

[106] Calderwood (1931) 17 at 21. See Report of M. de Mello-Franco, 141.

[107] *Minority Schools in Albania*, 32 (Sir C. Hurst, Count Rostworowski, and M. Negulesco).

*travaux préparatoires* did not indicate any intention on the part of the drafters
to provide 'an unconditional right to the minority to maintain institutions and
schools'; rather the object was to prohibit 'discrimination, i.e. differential treatment' and recognize 'a right for the minority equal to that enjoyed by the majority'.[108] Conversely, the majority found the framework was designed to protect the
minority's cultural identity within the state but with its members 'living peaceably
alongside that population and co-operating amicably with it'.[109] They observed
that twin arms of the minority guarantees were directed toward the same purpose.

[I]ndeed [they were] closely interlocked, for there would be no true equality between a
majority and a minority if the latter were deprived of its own institutions, and were consequently compelled to renounce that which constitutes the very essence of its being as a
minority.[110]

As Calderwood pointed out, the interwar minority treaties 'if they [did] not establish the minorities as collectives, confer[ed] rights that [could] only be enjoyed by
individuals acting together'.[111] They were adopted to ensure these communities'
cultural autonomy in the shadow of the dominant culture.[112]

Under the League's successor, the United Nations, the protection of minorities would take on the interpretation of minority judgment in *Minority Schools in
Albania*, as it fell within the human rights framework and almost exclusively, initially, under the principle of non-discrimination. A stated purpose of the new international body was 'promoting and encouraging respect for human rights and for
fundamental freedoms for all without distinction as to race, sex, language, or religion'.[113] In the lead-up to the UDHR, the UN Sub-Commission on the Prevention
of Discrimination and Protection of Minorities and UN Secretary-General distinguished between non-discrimination provisions and a regime of minority
protection.[114] The latter option confronted the problem in a direct, positive manner, by stipulating the establishment of educational and cultural institutions for
non-dominant groups, and implied a permanent set of arrangements to protect
the culture, language, and religion of the community.[115] The Sub-Commission
prepared a draft provision which largely replicated the interwar minority guarantees, but would have been of universal application.[116] The draft provision was not
included in the final text of the UDHR.

The Universal Declaration does not contain explicit protection for minorities
but does provide for the principle of non-discrimination.[117] During its negotiation,
states with significant migrant and indigenous populations championed individual

---

[108] *Minority Schools in Albania*, 26 and 29.      [109] *Minority Schools in Albania*, 19.
[110] *Minority Schools in Albania*, 19.      [111] Calderwood (1931) 20.
[112] See *Greco-Bulgarian 'Communities'* (note 104).
[113] Article 1, Charter of the United Nations, 26 June 1945, entered into force 24 October 1945,
UNCIO XV, 335; amendments by GA Resolutions in UNTS 557.
[114] UN Doc E/CN.4/Sub.2/8, 29 October 1947.
[115] See Capotorti, 'The Protection of Minorities under Multilateral Agreements on Human Rights',
2 *Italian Yearbook of International Law* (1976) 3.
[116] UN Doc A/CN.4/AC.1/3.      [117] Articles 2 and 7 UDHR.

human rights over the revival of minority guarantees.[118] They argued that the equal and effective realization of human rights norms for individuals would safeguard the identity of the members of minority groups.[119] In addition, they maintained that cultural rights in the form of collective rights could threaten the unity and the stability of their existing, national structures.[120] In response to such arguments, Hersch Lauterpacht recalled the reasoning of the Permanent Court. He countered that the cultural unity of the state must not trump the rights of minorities and thereby deny the equality intended by the principle of non-discrimination, which they championed.[121]

Yet, non-discrimination has played an important role in circumstances where the state segregated groups on the grounds of race, language, or religion. The application of the principle of non-discrimination in respect of racial segregation of public education was addressed by the US Supreme Court in *Brown v Board of Education of Topeka, Shawnee County et al.*[122] The case involved a class action brought by coloured children in Kansas, South Carolina, Virginia, and Delaware who sought but were denied admission to public schools attended by white children because of laws permitting or requiring segregation. The lower courts had found that there was equality between coloured and white schools in respect of the tangible aspects of 'buildings, curricula, qualifications, and salaries of teachers'. However, Chief Justice Warren observed that:

We must consider public education in the light of its full development and its present place in American life throughout the Nation. Only in this way can it be determined if segregation in public schools deprives these plaintiffs of the equal protection of the laws. Today, education is perhaps the most important function of state and local governments.... It is the very foundation of good citizenship. Today it is a principal instrument in awakening the child in cultural values, in preparing him for later professional training, and in helping him to adjust normally to his environment. In these days, it is doubtful that any child may reasonably be expected to succeed in life if he is denied the opportunity of an education. Such an opportunity, where the state has undertaken to provide it, is a right which must be made available to all on equal terms.[123]

The Supreme Court found that racial segregation in public education had a detrimental effect on coloured children, that is 'greater when it has the sanction of the law; for the policy of separating the races is usually interpreted as denoting the inferiority of the negro group', and which adversely affects the child's motivation

---

[118] See UN Doc A/C.3/SR.162, 723.

[119] Some contemporary legal scholars argue that non-discrimination (Art 26 ICCPR), freedom of association (Arts 21 and 22 ICCPR), the right to take part in cultural life (Art 15 ICESCR), and other substantive rights, if protected and promoted fully, would make a specialist minority provision redundant. See Tomuschat, 'Protection of Minorities under Article 27 of the International Covenant on Civil and Political Rights', in R. Bernhardt et al (eds), *Völkerrecht als Rechtsordnung, Internationale Gerichtsbarkeit, Menschenrechte: Festschrift für Hermann Mosler* (1983) 952; and Rodley, 'Conceptual Problems in the Protection of Minorities: International Legal Developments', 17 *HRQ* (1995) 48 at 54–9.

[120] See I.L. Claude, *National Minorities: An International Problem* (1955) 167.

[121] H. Lauterpacht, *International Law and Human Rights* (1950) 352–3.

[122] 347 US 483 (1954), 74 S Ct 686.     [123] 347 US 483 (1954), 74 S Ct 686 at 493–5.

to learn.[124] It concluded that state-mandated 'separate educational facilities are inherently unequal' and unconstitutional.[125]

The principles enunciated by the US Supreme Court were reaffirmed and extended by the European Court of Human Rights, half a century later, in a case involving indirect discrimination. *D.H. and Others v The Czech Republic* involved the disproportionate enrolment of Roma children in schools for children with special needs including intellectual disabilities.[126] Evidence provided by the applicants shows that despite various legislative and policy changes to integrate Roma children into the ordinary school system in the last two decades, half of Roma children in the Czech Republic attended a special school, where they represented 70 per cent of the enrolments. The applicants argued that this disproportionate representation of Roma children amounted to de facto or indirect discrimination and violated Articles 3 and 14 ECHR and Article 2 of Protocol No 1.

In its judgment, the Grand Chamber noted that the 'vulnerable' plight of the Roma meant that 'special consideration' must be given to their different ways of life and needs in regulatory frameworks and decision-making processes.[127] It added that:

[T]here could be said to be an emerging international consensus among the Contracting States of the Council of Europe recognising the special needs of minorities and an obligation to protect their security, identity and lifestyle, *not only for the purpose of safeguarding the interests of the minorities themselves but to preserve a cultural diversity of value to the whole community.*[128]

The Court noted that although the relevant Czech legislation was neutral on its face, the question arose whether its application disproportionately and adversely impacted upon Roma children, that is, it was indirect discrimination.[129]

The Grand Chamber held that difference in treatment would be discriminatory if 'it has no objective and reasonable justification' and where it is based on race, colour, or ethnic origin 'the notion of objective and reasonable justification must be interpreted as strictly as possible'.[130] It accepted the assessment of independent bodies that the placement of Roma children in these schools was driven by 'real or

---

[124]  347 US 483 (1954), 74 S Ct 686 at 493–5.       [125]  347 US 483 (1954), 74 S Ct 686 at 493–5.
[126]  *D.H. and Others v The Czech Republic*, ECHR (2007) App No 57325/00, judgment of 13 November 2007.
[127]  *D.H. and Others*, para 181. This special vulnerability of the Roma, including in the field of education, has been recognized by other human rights bodies, including the Committee on the Elimination of Racial Discrimination: CERD, *General Recommendation No 27: Discrimination against Roma*, 16 August 2000, paras 17–26. At para 18 it states: 'To prevent and avoid as much as possible the segregation of Roma students, while keeping open the possibility for bilingual or mother-tongue tuition; to this end, to endeavour to raise the quality of education in all schools and the level of achievement in schools by the minority community, to recruit school personnel from among members of the Roma communities and to promote intercultural education.'
[128]  *D.H. and Others*, para 181 (emphasis added).
[129]  *D.H. and Others*, para 189. It found that once the applicant has established a rebuttable presumption that the impact of the practice or policy is discriminatory, the burden of proof shifts to the respondent state to show that it is not discriminatory. It observed that without this shift in the burden of proof, it would be 'extremely difficult in practice' for an applicant to make out indirect discrimination.
[130]  *D.H. and Others*, para 196.

perceived language and cultural differences' between the Roma and the majority.[131] Also, it found that because of the fundamental importance of the prohibition of racial discrimination, even if there had been a waiver through parental consent, it was not permitted because it circumvented 'an important public interest'.[132] The Court found that the placement of Roma children in these special schools further 'isolated' them 'from the wider population', adding:

[T]hey received an education which compounded their difficulties and compromised their subsequent personal development instead of tackling their real problems or helping them to integrate into the ordinary schools and develop the skills that would facilitate life among the majority population.[133]

The Court held that the respondent state had violated Article 14 ECHR and Article 2 of Protocol No 1.

In late 2012, the US Supreme Court in *Fisher v University of Texas at Austin* was asked to consider the constitutionality of remedial measures designed to redress the legacy of racial segregation in public education in Texas.[134] International human rights law, and US domestic law, permit special measures introduced for the 'sole purpose of securing adequate advancement of certain racial or ethnic groups or individuals requiring such protection' as long as it is aimed at protecting their human rights, it does not lead to separate rights for different racial groups, and the measures do not continue after their purpose is fulfilled.[135] A number of arguments were raised in support of special or remedial measures for the effective realization of equality. First, special measures are necessary to ameliorate and reverse disparities in the protection and enjoyment of human rights and fundamental freedoms between particular groups and individuals. While inequality and vulnerability may be the ongoing effect of historic discriminatory practices like racial segregation, this is not required. The focus, as in *Brown*, is on present-day and potential future inequality.[136] Neutral laws, policies, and programmes are inadequate to the task as they are blind to (or worse, freeze) inequalities.[137] The Committee on the Elimination of Racial Discrimination has indicated that '[t]o treat in an equal manner persons or

---

[131] *D.H. and Others*, para 200.     [132] *D.H. and Others*, para 204.
[133] *D.H. and Others*, para 207.     [134] As at April 2013, the Court had not delivered its Opinion.
[135] Articles 1(4) and 2(2) CERD. See CERD, *General Recommendation No 32: The meaning and scope of special measures in the International Convention on the Elimination of All Forms of Racial Discrimination*, 24 September 2009, paras 16–18. This appraisal should be conducted on the basis of accurate data, disaggregated by among other things 'cultural status' (Art 2(2) CERD) and the participation of the group in the social and economic development of the country. Also, the measures must be designed and implemented only with the prior consultation and active participation of the affected group. The US Supreme Court's factors permitting race to be considered in government-funded remedial programmes, include (1) a past history of *de jure* segregation; (2) whether the race-conscious initiative ameliorates the negative impact of the discrimination; (3) whether the harm from the discrimination remains when the policy is operational; and (4) whether the initiative imposes quotes for admission of minorities: Brief of *Amici Curiae* National Association for the Advancement of Colored People (NAACP) et al in support of Respondents in *Fisher v University of Texas at Austin et al*, Docket No 11-345, 13 August 2012, 24.
[136] CERD, *General Recommendation No 32*, para 22.
[137] Data provided by the NAACP showed a significant decrease in the enrolment of African American and Hispanic students following the application of racially neutral admissions policies: NAACP Amicus Brief, 3.

groups whose situations are objectively different will constitute discrimination in effect, as will the unequal treatment of persons whose situations are objectively the same'.[138] The Committee added that the principle of non-discrimination requires that the characteristics of groups be taken into consideration.[139] It has observed that special measures are not an exception to the principle of non-discrimination, but 'integral' to the elimination of inequality.[140] The National Association for the Advancement of Colored People (NAACP), the organization which led the class actions for desegregation of public education, observed:

What the Petition seeks to deny African American and other racial minorities is an admission system that is 'designed to consider each applicant as an individual.'...Under her position, every applicant would be 'holistically' considered except African Americans and other racial minorities, whose personal essays would have to be censored (or self-censored) to remove any mention of experience of race.... [G]ranting the Petitioner's request would deny individuals who had overcome racial adversity the opportunity to demonstrate important accomplishments. Other students, for whom race presented no obstacle, would effectively have an unfair advantage. Many racial minority applicants have pulled themselves up by their bootstraps, and the Court should reject [the] Petitioner's attempt to take away their boots.[141]

Secondly, Article 29(1)(d) of the Convention on the Rights of the Child (CRC) stipulates that education should prepare every child for 'responsible life in a free society, in the spirit of understanding, peace, tolerance, equality of sexes, and friendship among all peoples, ethnic, national and religious groups and persons of indigenous origin'.[142] In *Grutter v Bollinger*, the US Supreme Court found that a university may embrace the educational benefits of diversity (including ethnic and racial diversity) as central to its educational mission for all students and thereby seek to ensure a diverse student population.[143] Finally, in its Amicus Brief in *Fisher*, the Anti-Defamation League observed that '[e]mbracing diversity and promoting a fully integrated society is crucial not only to the struggle to defeat discrimination, but also the continued vitality of our Nation and our society'.[144] The Committee

---

[138] CERD, *General Recommendation No 32*, para 8.

[139] CERD, *General Recommendation No 32*, para 8. Article 1(4) CERD requires that the measures not lead to 'the maintenance of separate rights for different racial groups', which was designed to prevent justifications for state-sanctioned segregation or practices under Apartheid: para 26. See also CERD, *General Recommendation No 14: Definition of discrimination*, 22 March 1993, para 2; and CERD, *General Recommendation No 30*, para 4: that differential treatment will 'constitute discrimination if the criteria for such differentiation, judged in the light of the objectives and purposes of the [CERD], are not applied pursuant to a legitimate aim, and are not proportional to the achievement of this aim.'

[140] CERD, *General Recommendation No 32*, para 20.

[141] NAACP Amicus Brief, 135 at 33–4.

[142] See CRC, *General Comment No 1, Art 29(1): The aims of education*, 17 April 2001, UN Doc CRC/GC/2001/1, para 1: 'The aims [of education] are: the holistic development of the full potential of the child including development of respect for human rights, an enhanced sense of identity and affiliation, and his or her socialization and interaction with others, and with the environment'. See also Benhabib, 'Deliberative Democracy and Multicultural Dilemmas', in S. Benhabib, *The Claims of Culture: Equality and Diversity in the Global Era* (2002) 105 at 123.

[143] 539 US 306 (2003).

[144] Brief of *Amici Curiae* Anti-Defamation League in support of Respondents in *Fisher v University of Texas at Austin et al*, Docket No 11-345, 10 August 2012 at 8. See also Brief of *Amici Curiae* United

on the Rights of the Child, when advocating special measures for the education of indigenous children, stated that it contributes to their individual and collective development and participation in the broader society, in particular, it strengthens children's ability to 'exercise their civil rights in order to influence political policy processes for the improved protection of human rights'.[145] The purpose of non-discrimination is to enable the effective participation of all individuals and realize their role as citizens in a democratic society.

Whilst special measures can attach to a group or an individual, international human rights bodies have indicated that such remedial, non-permanent measures are distinct from specific, permanent human rights recognized by the international community to ensure the existence and identity of groups like minorities and indigenous peoples, and must be treated as such by states parties in their law and practice.[146]

## C. Right to participate in the cultural life of one's own culture

A universal, binding minority protection regime was only realized in 1966 with the adoption of Article 27 ICCPR. It articulates the right of 'members of the minorities to enjoy *their own* culture, practice *their own* religion, and use *their own* language'.[147] The provision revives the interwar minority protection framework in order to afford permanent, specific human rights to certain groups and their individual members. Some liberal theorists have emphasized the significance of *one's own* culture for the enjoyment of all human rights including civil and political rights.[148] It is this interpretation of Article 27 ICCPR and reinterpretation of Article 15 ICESCR which is dominant in the early twenty-first century.

It was only after the large-scale human tragedy and instability caused by civil conflicts in the late twentieth century, that there emerged growing acceptance that dependence on the universal application of individual human rights and non-discrimination alone failed to protect victims targeted because of their membership of an ethnic or religious community. So for example, Article 22, Chapter III (Equality) of the Charter of Fundamental Rights of the European Union stipulates that '[t]he Union shall respect cultural, religious and linguistic diversity'.[149] In addition, new specialist, international instruments which incorporated cultural rights with a collective dimension and promoted cultural diversity were finalized at the international and regional level to protect minorities and indigenous peoples. The most significant of these are the 1992 UN Minorities Declaration,

States in support of Respondents in *Fisher v University of Texas at Austin et al*, Docket No 11-345, 13 August 2012.

[145] CRC, *General Comment No 11: Indigenous children and their rights under the Convention*, UN Doc CRC/C/GC/11, 12 February 2009, paras 57 and 60.

[146] CERD, *General Recommendation No 32*, paras 15 and 26.

[147] GA Res 2200A (XXI), 16 December 1966, in force 23 March 1976 (emphasis added).

[148] See Margalit and Halbertal (1994) 505 and Taylor, 'The Politics of Recognition', in A. Gutmann (ed), *Multiculturalism: Examining the Politics of Recognition* (1994) 25 at 61.

[149] See also second and fourth recitals, Preamble, UNDRIP.

and 2007 Declaration on the Rights of Indigenous Peoples. These instruments go beyond civil and political rights by encompassing recognition of the worth of all cultures.[150] This latter theme is expanded in Part 4 below.

Article 27 ICCPR evolved from the UN General Assembly Resolution on the Fate of Minorities adopted on the same day as the Universal Declaration.[151] Its purpose is 'towards ensuring the survival and continued development of the cultural, religious and social identity of the minorities concerned'.[152] This right is granted over and above other rights contained in the two International Covenants, including non-discrimination.[153] The UN Minorities Declaration similarly augments other international human rights instruments 'by strengthening and clarifying those rights which make it possible for persons belonging to minorities to preserve and develop their group identity'.[154] Since its inclusion in the International Covenant, in spite of its various qualifications, Article 27 has played an important role in defining cultural rights held by minorities and indigenous peoples in international law.

The HRC, which oversees the implementation of Article 27, has underscored its collective aspect. The inclusion of this minority protection within the international human rights framework reinforces the presumption that the right-holder is an individual, rather than the group.[155] Indeed, Article 27 refers to 'persons belonging to such minorities' and not 'minorities' per se. In addition, the ICCPR's complaint mechanism provides standing to states or individuals only.[156] However, the concession to the collective aspect of minority rights comes with the words 'in community with other members of their group' contained in Article 27. The HRC has repeatedly affirmed that the right can only be realized meaningfully when exercised 'in a community', that is as a group.[157] *General Comment No 23* notes that Article 27 protects 'individual rights', but that the obligations owed by states are collective in nature.[158] This interpretation accords with the UN Minorities Declaration,[159] whose commentary stipulates that 'the state cannot

---

[150]  See Taylor (1994) 68.       [151]  GA Res 217C (III), 10 December 1948, UN Doc A/810.

[152]  HRC, *General Comment No 23*, para 9.

[153]  HRC, *General Comment No 23*, paras 4, 5.1, and 9.

[154]  Commentary of the Working Group on Minorities to the United Nations Declaration on the Rights of Persons Belonging to National or Ethnic, Religious and Linguistic Minorities, 4 April 2005, UN Doc E/CN.4/Sub.2/AC.5/2005/2.

[155]  See UN Doc E/CN.4/Sub.2/384/Add.2, paras 125ff; and HRC, *General Comment No 23*, para 1.

[156]  Optional Protocol to the International Covenant on Civil and Political Rights, UNGA Res 2200A (XXI), 16 December 1966, in force 23 March 1976, 999 UNTS 302. Nonetheless, the Committee has noted that 'in principle, [there is] no objection to a group of individuals, who claim to be similarly affected, collectively to submit a communication about the alleged breaches of their rights'. HRC, *Howard v Canada*, Comm No 879/1999, 26 July 2005, UN Doc CCPR/C/84/D/879/1999, para 8.3.

[157]  See *Lubicon Lake Band (Bernard Ominayak) v Canada*, Comm No 167/1984, 26 March 1990, UN Doc A/45/40, Pt 2 (1990) 1, para 32.1; *Länsman v Finland*, 26 October 1994, UN Doc CCPR/52/D/511/1992; and *Länsman v Finland*, 30 October 1996, UN Doc CCPR/C/58/D/671/1995.

[158]  HRC, *General Comment No 23*, para 6.2.

[159]  Articles 1–3, Declaration on the Rights of Persons Belonging to National or Ethnic, Religious and Linguistic Minorities (UN Minorities Declaration), GA Res 47/135, 18 December 1992, UN Doc A/RES/47/135 and UN Doc E/CN.4/Sub.2/AC.5/2005/2, para 14.

fully implement them without ensuring adequate conditions for the existence and identity of the group as a whole'.[160]

The right contained in Article 27 ICCPR is negatively conferred, with the addition of the words 'shall not be denied the right'. However, *General Comment No 23* provides that it also imposes positive obligations on states parties.[161] In the UN Declaration, the cultural rights of the group are accommodated by the restatement of the wording of Article 27, but it does so as a positive rather than negative obligation.[162] The commentary insists that the safeguarding and promotion of the identity of minorities and the effective realization of their cultural rights will often require protective and proactive measures by the state.[163] In addition, according to the Declaration, proactive measures designed to meet these obligations will not prima facie offend the principle of equality contained in the UDHR.[164]

Through its shift in emphasis from national culture to culture as a way of life of individuals and groups, the right to participate in cultural life under Article 15 ICESCR has undergone a metamorphosis which complements the jurisprudence of Article 27 ICCPR. However, importantly Article 15 ICESCR includes and goes beyond the right to participate in one's own culture to encompass the national culture, the cultures of others, and the dialogue between cultures. The 1976 UNESCO Recommendation on the Right to Participate in Cultural Life, which elaborates upon the right, obliges state parties to ensure that minorities have 'full opportunities for gaining access to and participating in the cultural life . . . in order to enrich [the relevant country] with their specific contributions, which safeguards their right to preserve their cultural identity'.[165] However, the Committee for Economic, Social and Cultural Rights (CESCR), in respect of Article 15 ICESCR, has adopted an expansive interpretation of the rightholder and culture, as

[T]he right of everyone—alone, in association with others or as a community—to know and understand his or her own culture and that of others . . . to follow a way of life associated with the use of cultural goods and resources such as land, water, biodiversity, language or specific institutions, and to benefit from the cultural heritage and the creation of other individuals and communities.[166]

Similarly, access to cultural heritage has been defined as 'an important feature of being a member of a community, a citizen and, more widely, a member of society'.[167]

---

[160] UN Doc E/CN.4/Sub.2/AC.5/2005/2, para 14.

[161] HRC, *General Comment No 23*, paras 6.1, 6.2, and 9.

[162] Article 2(1) UN Minorities Declaration.

[163] UN Doc E/CN.4/Sub.2/AC.5/2005/2 at 8, para 33.

[164] Article 8(3) UN Minorities Declaration.

[165] See Art 4(f) 1976 UNESCO Recommendation on the Right to Participate in Cultural Life, adopted on 26 November 1976 by UNESCO General Conference, 19th session.

[166] CESCR, *General Comment No 21*, para15(b) (emphasis added). See also Art 2(a), 1976 UNESCO Recommendation.

[167] UN Doc A/HRC/17/38, para 2. See also HRC Res 6/11 Protection of Cultural Heritage as an important component of the promotion and protection of cultural rights, 28 September 2007, UN Doc A/HRC/RES/6/11.

The CESCR has confirmed that states parties have both negative (non-interference with exercise of cultural practices and access to cultural 'goods and services') and positive (ensuring conditions for participation, facilitation, and promotion of cultural life and access to and preservation of cultural heritage) obligations.[168] The minimum core obligation is defined as '[t]he obligation to create and promote an environment within which a person individually, or in association with others, or within a community or group, *can participate in the culture of their choice*'.[169] This includes the immediate removal of hindrances to accessing one's own culture or other cultures without discrimination and without 'frontiers of any kind'.[170] The Committee requires states parties to report on initiatives to promote awareness of the cultural heritage of indigenous peoples and minorities and establish 'favourable conditions for them to preserve, develop, express and disseminate their identity, history, culture, language, traditions and customs'.[171]

The recalibration of the right to participation in cultural life (Article 15 ICESCR) to harmonize, rather than potentially conflict, with the right to enjoy one's own culture (Article 27 ICCPR) has transformed interpretations of culture and cultural rights in international law through their vernacularization in the claims by indigenous peoples and minorities. The findings of the African Commission of Human and Peoples' Rights in *Centre for Minority Rights Development and Minority Rights Group (on behalf of Endorois Welfare Council) v Kenya*, which brings together self-identification, the right to religious freedom, and the right to culture, illustrates these changes.[172] The Endorois alleged various violations of the African Charter following their removal from ancestral lands by the respondent state to establish a game reserve. The Commission observed that action went to the core of indigenous rights, namely, 'the right to preserve one's identity through identification with ancestral lands, cultural patterns, social institutions and religious systems'.[173]

The respondent state challenged the very categorization of the Endorois as an 'indigenous people' to whom specific, permanent rights attach. The African Commission noted that while the terms 'peoples' and 'indigenous' had eluded definition in international law, the African regional human rights regime specifically encompasses collective rights and recognizes that indigenous peoples are distinguished by the link between people, their land and culture and their self-identification as a distinct community.[174] It acknowledged that self-identification by indigenous

[168] CESCR, *General Comment No 21*, para 6.

[169] CESCR, *General Comment No 21*, para 55 (emphasis added).

[170] CESCR, *General Comment No 21*, para 55(d).

[171] Guidelines on Treaty-Specific Documents to be Submitted by States Parties under Arts 16 and 17 of the International Covenant on Economic, Social and Cultural Rights, 13 January 2009, UN Doc E/C.12/2008/2 at 14, paras 67 and 68.

[172] *Centre for Minority Rights Development and Anor v Kenya*, ACHPR, Comm No 276/03, 4 February 2010.

[173] *Centre for Minority Rights Development and Anor v Kenya*, ACHPR, Comm No 276/03, 4 February 2010, para 157.

[174] *Centre for Minority Rights Development and Anor v Kenya*, ACHPR, Comm No 276/03, 4 February 2010, paras 147–51. See also Report of the African Commission's Working Group of Experts on Indigenous Populations/Communities, adopted at the Twenty-eighth Session (2003).

individuals and acceptance by the community is vital.[175] The African Commission observed that even though they continued to be excluded and discriminated by the dominant culture, indigenous peoples remain determined to preserve, develop, and transmit their ancestral lands and cultural identity to future generations. It added that their continued existence as a 'peoples' was tied to their ability to determine 'their own fate' and live according to 'their own cultural patterns, social institutions and religious systems'.[176] Who could assert communal rights on behalf of the group was to be resolved by the Endorois in accordance with their laws and customs and not by the respondent state.[177] The Commission agreed that the Endorois considered 'themselves to be a distinct people, sharing a common history, culture and religion' and therefore constituted a 'people', and were entitled to the protection of their collective rights under the African Charter.[178]

The African Commission accepted that the Endorois culture, religion, and ways of life are 'intimately intertwined with their ancestral lands' and without access to them, they were unable to fully exercise their cultural and religious rights.[179] In respect of Article 8 (right to freedom of religion), the Commission found that the community's spiritual beliefs and practices constituted a religion under the African Charter and that their continuing inability to access their ancestral lands 'rendered it virtually impossible for the community to maintain religious practices central to their culture and religion'.[180] Also, the restriction of the Endorois' enjoyment of this human right was not justifiable on grounds of economic development or ecological protection.[181]

The complainants also alleged that the removal of the Endorois from their ancestral lands violated the community's cultural rights through the systematic restriction of access to cultural sites and seriously damages their pastoralist way of life.[182] Article 17(2) and (3) ACHPR respectively provide that '[e]very individual may freely take part in the cultural life of his community' and '[t]he promotion and protection of morals and traditional values recognized by the community shall be the duty of the

---

[175] *Centre for Minority Rights Development and Anor v Kenya*, ACHPR, Comm No 276/03, 4 February 2010, para 157. See also Report of the Special Rapporteur R. Stavenhagen on the Situation of Human Rights and Fundamental Freedoms of Indigenous Peoples, 4 February 2002, UN Doc E/CN.4/2002/97, paras 99 and 100.

[176] *Centre for Minority Rights Development and Anor v Kenya*, ACHPR, Comm No 276/03, 4 February 2010, para 157.

[177] *Centre for Minority Rights Development and Anor v Kenya*, ACHPR, Comm No 276/03, 4 February 2010, para 162.

[178] *Centre for Minority Rights Development and Anor v Kenya*, ACHPR, Comm No 276/03, 4 February 2010, para 162.

[179] *Centre for Minority Rights Development and Anor v Kenya*, ACHPR, Comm No 276/03, 4 February 2010, para 156.

[180] *Centre for Minority Rights Development and Anor v Kenya*, ACHPR, Comm No 276/03, 4 February 2010, paras 170 and 173. See Art 26, UNDRIP; CESCR, *General Comment No 21*, para 49(d); Art 13(1) ILO 169; and *Case of the Mayagna (Sumo) Awas Tigni Community v Nicaragua*, I/ACtHR (2001) Series C, No 79, para 149.

[181] *Centre for Minority Rights Development and Anor v Kenya*, ACHPR, Comm No 276/03, 4 February 2010, para 173.

[182] *Centre for Minority Rights Development and Anor v Kenya*, ACHPR, Comm No 276/03, 4 February 2010, para 239.

State'. The Commission confirmed that this right entails negative and positive obligations, that is, 'the protecting of human rights goes beyond the duty not to destroy or deliberately weaken minority groups, but requires respect for, and protection of, their religious and cultural heritage essential to their group identity'.[183] Its interpretation of the twin dimensions of the provision, its individual rightholder and the collective nature of the obligations owed by the state party to the community, accords with those of the UN human rights bodies.[184] Like other international and regional human rights bodies, the African Commission recognized that indigenous peoples embrace a holistic conceptualization of culture which covers land, immovable and movable heritage, tangible and intangible elements.[185] Also, indigenous peoples emphasize the symbiotic relationship between these elements in sustaining and developing their collective identities.[186] UNDRIP recognizes the central importance of land (and resources) to the maintenance and survival of indigenous cultures and identities.[187] Echoing the Permanent Court, the African Commission found that the removal of the Endorois from their ancestral lands meant 'the very essence of the [community's] right to culture [had] been denied, rendering the right, to all intents and purposes, illusory'.[188]

The African Commission found that under Article 17 ACHPR, a state party is under a duty to 'tolerate' diversity and implement positive measures to protect the identity of 'groups different from those of the majority/dominant group' including 'creating spaces for dominant and indigenous cultures to co-exist'.[189] Positive measures were necessary to protect the cultural rights of vulnerable groups like the Endorois against the persistent effects of historic and current policies and practices of exclusion, exploitation, discrimination, forced assimilation, and direct violence and persecution. Also, they are of significance to the broader society as they are designed to promote cultural identity as 'a factor of mutual appreciation among individuals, groups, nations and regions'.[190]

The formulation of the Endorois' claim to encompass the violation of an archetypal liberal right—the right to property (Article 14 ACHPR)—is the site of vernacularization of a human right to accommodate indigenous peoples' worldview and the contestation between the communal right to property and the classical liberal formulation of the right to private property. Drawing on the jurisprudence of the Inter-American and European human rights courts, the Commission

---

[183] *Centre for Minority Rights Development and Anor v Kenya*, ACHPR, Comm No 276/03, 4 February 2010, para 241.
[184] *Centre for Minority Rights Development and Anor v Kenya*, ACHPR, Comm No 276/03, 4 February 2010, para 241.
[185] Articles 11–13, 25, and 31 UNDRIP.
[186] See UN Doc E/CN.4/Sub.2/1995/26, Annex, paras 11–13; UN Doc E/CN.4/Sub.2/2000/26, Annex I, paras 12–14; and UN Doc E/CN.4/Sub.2.AC.4.2006/5, 6–8, paras 1–2.
[187] 10th recital, Preamble, UNDRIP. The CESCR also recognizes this strong communal aspect of indigenous heritage and the integral nature of land and resources in respect of the right to participate in cultural life: *General Comment No 21*, paras 36, 37, and 50(c).
[188] *Centre for Minority Rights Development and Anor v Kenya*, para 251.
[189] *Centre for Minority Rights Development and Anor v Kenya*, para 246.
[190] *Centre for Minority Rights Development and Anor v Kenya*, para 246, citing Guidelines for National Periodic Reports, in Second Annual Activity Report of the African Commission on Human and Peoples' Rights 1988–1989, ACHPR/RPT/2nd, Annex XII.

acknowledged that the rights and interests of indigenous communities in their ancestral lands constituted 'property' under the African Charter.[191] There is a growing awareness in international and regional human rights fora that the relationship between indigenous peoples and their traditional lands goes beyond proprietorship and is primarily defined by its 'spiritual' aspect.[192] Another characteristic of this relationship is that its protection within the relevant community is already governed by their own customs, laws, and practices.[193] While customary law necessarily varies from community to community, it usually recognizes the following inherent characteristics: it affirms that ownership and custodianship of ancestral lands and culture heritage is usually collective or communal in character;[194] that such ownership and custodianship is permanent and inalienable; and it reinforces the intergenerational nature of custodianship and transmission of their cultures.[195] The Inter-American Court of Human Rights, when deciding on similar claims, has noted that human rights law's 'dynamic evolution has had a positive impact on international law in affirming and building up the latter's faculty for regulating relations between States and the human beings within their respective jurisdictions'.[196] The African Commission and the Inter-American Court have recognized that the right to property under their respective human rights instruments must recognize and protect collective aspects of indigenous peoples' relationship with their ancestral lands and its significance for their worldview, religion, and cultural identity.[197] The Inter-American Court has found that to ignore the right of indigenous communities to their ancestral lands affects their right to cultural identity and 'to the very survival of the indigenous community and their members'.[198] In balancing the private right to property of the state or landowners against the communal right to property of indigenous peoples, the African Commission held that the ongoing dispossession of the Endorois from their ancestral lands threatened their cultural survival and therefore tip the proportionality argument in their favour in international law.[199] Similarly, the Inter-American Court has found that restriction of the former may be necessary to realize the 'collective objective of preserving cultural identities in a democratic and pluralist society'.[200]

The HRC has likewise affirmed that protection of rights under Article 27 ICCPR promotes the survival and development of minority cultures for the benefit of these

---

[191] *Centre for Minority Rights Development and Anor v Kenya*, para 187.
[192] Article 26 UNDRIP; CESCR, *General Comment No 21*, para 49(d); Art 13(1) ILO 169; *Mayagna (Sumo) Awas Tigni Community v Nicaragua*, para 149; and *Yakye Axa Indigenous Community v Paraguay*, I/ACtHR (2005) Series C, No 125, para 131.
[193] *Centre for Minority Rights Development and Anor v Kenya*, para 152. See also Art 34 UNDRIP.
[194] *Centre for Minority Rights Development and Anor v Kenya*, para 194. See *Yakye Axa Indigenous Community v Paraguay*, paras 123–31.
[195] *Yakye Axa Indigenous Community v Paraguay*, para 124.
[196] *Centre for Minority Rights Development and Anor v Kenya*, paras 154–; and *Yakye Axa Indigenous Community v Paraguay*, paras 154–156.
[197] *Yakye Axa Indigenous Community v Paraguay*, paras 134–7.
[198] *Yakye Axa Indigenous Community v Paraguay*, para 147.
[199] *Centre for Minority Rights Development and Anor v Kenya*, paras 204 and 235.
[200] *Yakye Axa Indigenous Community v Paraguay*, para 148.

communities and the entire society.[201] This rationale for ensuring the continuation of the diverse cultural, religious, and linguistic identities within and across states and the corresponding rejection of past national assimilation policies has been explicitly reiterated by the United Nations and related bodies.[202] The commentary to the UN Minorities Declaration confirms that 'elimination is illegal' and 'forced assimilation is unacceptable'. However, it notes that a certain degree of integration is required to enable the state to 'respect and ensure human rights to every person within its territory without discrimination'.[203] The purpose of minority protection becomes 'ensur[ing] that integration does not become unwanted assimilation or undermine the group identity of persons living on the territory of States'.[204] It counsels that to achieve this aim, 'minority group identity' acceptance must go beyond 'tolerance' and attract 'a positive attitude towards cultural pluralism', that is not just acceptance but 'respect for the distinctive characteristics and contributions of minorities to the life of the national society as a whole are required' by the state and wider society.[205] The prohibition against forced assimilation encompasses the acts of the state and those of third parties. These concerns are replicated explicitly in multilateral instruments covering indigenous peoples. UNDRIP states that indigenous peoples have a right to 'maintain and strengthen their distinct political, legal, economic, social and cultural institutions, while retaining their right to participate fully, if they so choose, in the political, economic, social and cultural life of the State'.[206] It specifically provides that indigenous peoples and individuals have a right not to be subject to 'forced assimilation or destruction of their culture'. Pursuant to this right, states should provide mechanisms to prevent and enable redress for forced assimilation and acts which deprive them of their cultural identity, dispossess them of their lands or resources, force population transfers, or propaganda which incites racial discrimination.[207]

This negative obligation concerning respect for the worth of all cultures is augmented in the early twenty-first century by specialist multilateral instruments covering cultural diversity designed to protect and promote the flourishing of cultures.

## 4. Diversity

The evolving interpretations of minority protection (Article 27 ICCPR) and the right to participate in cultural life (Article 15 ICESCR) in the final decades of

---

[201] HRC, *General Comment No 23*, para 9.

[202] Article 1(1), UN Minorities Declaration. Article 5(2) Council of Europe FCNM contains a similar prohibition against 'forced' assimilation, while its explanatory report makes clear that 'voluntary' assimilation is not prohibited: Council of Europe, Framework Convention for the Protection of Minorities and Explanatory Report, November 1994, H(94)10, paras 42–6.

[203] UN Doc E/CN.4/Sub.2/AC.5/2005/2, para 21. The CE FCNM also acknowledges the potentially positive role of official integration policies for 'social cohesion' and promotion of 'cultural diversity', which is 'a source and a factor, not of division, but of enrichment of each society': Article 5(2) Council of Europe FCNM.

[204] Article 5(2) Council of Europe FCNM.

[205] UN Doc E/CN.4/Sub.2/AC.5/2005/2, para 28.     [206] Article 5 UNDRIP.

[207] Article 8 UNDRIP.

the twentieth century were accompanied by a reaffirmation of the importance of cultural diversity in various multilateral instruments. The justification for the protection and promotion of diversity goes beyond equality-based arguments to its installation as a common good of humanity. This rationale is contained in instruments adopted in the wake of the Second World War, like the General Assembly Resolution on the Crime of Genocide and the Convention for the Protection of Cultural Property during Armed Conflict, which reference the cultural contribution of all peoples to humanity.[208] It is reiterated in the UNESCO Declaration of Principles of International Cooperation adopted in 1966 which provides that '[i]n their rich variety and diversity, and in their reciprocal influences they exert on one another, all cultures form part of the common heritage of all mankind'.[209] By the beginning of the twenty-first century, several specialist international and regional declarations had been adopted on cultural diversity which replicate this stance.[210] Chief among them, the 2001 UNESCO Universal Declaration on Cultural Diversity provides:

Culture takes diverse forms across time and space. This diversity is embodied in the uniqueness and plurality of the identities of the groups and societies making up humankind. As a source of exchange, innovation and creativity, cultural diversity is as necessary for humankind as biodiversity is for nature. In this sense, it is the common heritage of humanity and should be recognized and affirmed for the benefit of present and future generations.[211]

Cultural diversity has been promoted as a common good for a range of reasons including its importance to peace and stability,[212] progress and prosperity,[213] and

---

[208] First recital, Preamble, Resolution on the Crime of Genocide, GA Res 96 (I), 11 December 1946. It states that genocide 'shocked the conscience of mankind [and] resulted in great losses to humanity in the form of cultural and other contributions represented by these groups'; second recital, Preamble, Convention for the Protection of Cultural Property in the Event of Armed Conflict (1954 Hague Convention), 14 May 1954, entered into force 7 August 1956, 249 UNTS 240, states: '[D]amage to the cultural property belonging to any people whatsoever means damage to the cultural heritage of all mankind, since each people makes its contribution to the culture of the world.'

[209] Article 1(3) UNESCO Declaration of Principles International Cooperation (1966 UNESCO Declaration), resolution adopted by General Conference, 4 November 1966.

[210] Universal Declaration on Cultural Diversity (2001 UNESCO Declaration), adopted by UNESCO General Conference, 2 November 2001; Declaration on Cultural Diversity (CE Declaration), adopted by Council of Europe, Committee of Ministers, 7 December 2000; Charter for African Cultural Renaissance (2006 African Charter), adopted by African Union at Sixth Ordinary Session, 24 January 2006; and Declaration on ASEAN Unity in Cultural Diversity: Towards Strengthening ASEAN Community (ASEAN Declaration), adopted by the Ministers responsible for Culture and Arts of ASEAN Member States, 17 November 2011.

[211] Article 1 2001 UNESCO Declaration. See also third recital, Preamble, UNDRIP; first recital, Preamble, CE Declaration; and fifth recital, Preamble, and Art 5(1) 2006 African Charter. Cf third recital, Preamble, ASEAN Declaration.

[212] Second recital, Preamble, 1966 UNESCO Declaration; second recital, Preamble, 1976 UNESCO Recommendation; second and seventh recitals, Preamble, 2001 UNESCO Declaration; fifth recital, Preamble, 2006 African Charter; fifth recital, Preamble, ASEAN Declaration; sixth and seventh recitals, Preamble, UN Minorities Declaration; and fifth recital, Preamble, CE FCNM.

[213] Fifth recital, Preamble, 1966 UNESCO Declaration; fourth recital, Preamble, 1976 UNESCO Recommendation; sixth recital, Preamble, and Art 3 2001 UNESCO Declaration; CE Declaration generally; fifth recital, Preamble, 2006 African Charter; sixth recital, Preamble, and Part 3, ASEAN Declaration; and sixth and seventh recitals, Preamble, UN Minorities Declaration.

full realization of human rights and fundamental freedoms and a democratic society.[214] These aims in turn impact upon how it is realized on the ground.

This final Part examines how the protection and promotion of diversity is shaping our understandings of rightholders and duty bearers and notions of participation and consensus building in democratic societies. These issues are initially explored in respect of the implementation of cultural diversity through policies of cultural pluralism at the national level; then, the application of cultural pluralism by the international community through voluntary isolation and secession of groups is considered; and finally, diversity within groups themselves through human rights protections is explained with specific reference to women's rights and claims to culture.

## A. Cultural pluralism

Cultural diversity does not mean cultural balkanization, where groups and their cultures are immunized from interaction and evolution, which would lead to potentially greater civil strife and violence.[215] Rather, there is a recognition that cultural diversity and the continuing cultural contributions of communities and individuals is only possible by fostering an environment of inclusion, participation, and open and effective dialogue to facilitate a society of shared, core values. Increasingly, legal and political theorists argue that equality and democracy cannot be effectively realized by focusing on civil and political rights and the public sphere alone. Instead, they maintain that there is a need to acknowledge the cultural sphere, and the varied and dynamic identities and allegiances of groups and individuals, and civil society broadly, the interactions and communications taking place beyond the formal, official state fora. Cultural pluralism is the vehicle by which cultural diversity is implemented and realized on the ground. The UNESCO Cultural Diversity Declaration describes it as 'indissoluble from a democratic framework' because it fosters cultural exchange and 'the creative capacities that sustain public life'.[216]

Africa and Europe, two continents which have been riddled with violent ethnic and religious conflict in recent decades, have adopted multilateral framework conventions focusing on the promotion of cultural diversity and human rights. The Charter for African Cultural Renaissance adopted by the African Union in 2006,[217] and the Council of Europe Framework Convention on the Value of

---

[214] Third recital, Preamble, 1966 UNESCO Declaration; 23rd recital, Preamble, 1976 UNESCO Recommendation; fourth recital, Preamble and Arts 2 and 5 2001 UNESCO Declaration; fourth recital, Preamble, CE Declaration; para 4, ASEAN Declaration; and sixth and seventh recitals, Preamble, CE FCNM. Likewise, human rights instruments and bodies have acknowledged the importance of cultural diversity: Arts 4 and 5, 2001 UNESCO Declaration; Art 5(1) 2006 African Charter; third recital, Preamble, UNDRIP; and CESCR, *General Comment No 21*, para 40.

[215] See Benhabib (2002) 129–30; Taylor (1994) 62; and Raz (1994) 171.

[216] Article 2 2001 UNESCO Declaration.

[217] Replacing the Cultural Charter for Africa, adopted by the Organization of African Unity, 15 July 1976.

Cultural Heritage for Society (Faro Convention) of 2005,[218] shift from emphases on states and national cultures to human rights and cultural diversity.[219] The intent is not to promote unity within a state by bolstering protection of the national cultural identity. Instead, the purpose is a culture within society (regional, national, local) which fosters intercultural and intergenerational dialogue and understanding and respect for human rights.[220] This is augmented by the recognition that this can only be achieved through multilateral cooperation.[221] Two characteristics of these instruments exemplify this human rights focused approach to the international protection of cultural diversity. First, states are no longer the primary holders of rights (and obligations). Instead, they are replaced by communities, groups, and individuals. The Faro Convention recognizes that the right to participate in cultural life entails individual and collective rights and responsibilities, subject to restrictions necessary for a democratic society for the protection of public interest or the rights and freedoms of others.[222] The 2006 African Charter similarly acknowledges the rights and obligations of non-state actors.[223] Secondly, and related to this development, is the promotion of participation, inclusion, dialogue, and consensus not only as between the state and its citizens in the public space, but between communities, groups, and individuals in civil society. The UNESCO Cultural Diversity Declaration's Main Lines of Action provide for 'facilitating, in diversified societies, the inclusion and participation of persons and groups from varied cultural backgrounds'.[224] The African Charter has the stated objective of promoting 'freedom of expression and cultural democracy, which is inseparable from social and political democracy'.[225] The Faro Convention provides that it is the responsibility of public authorities and competent bodies: to encourage critical reflection on the representation of cultures while respecting diverse interpretations; to establish conciliation mechanisms to equitably resolve contradictory values between groups; to develop understandings of cultural heritage which facilitate peaceful coexistence and promote trust and mutual understanding; and to integrate these processes into educational mechanisms.[226]

---

[218] Council of Europe Framework Convention on the Value of Cultural Heritage for Society (Faro Convention), 27 October 2005, ETS 199. See also the Council of Europe, European Cultural Charter, adopted in Paris on 19 December 1954, ETS 18.

[219] Even though both are multilateral instruments intending to promote cooperation on their respective continents. Parts II and III, 1976 African Charter; Art 1, Faro Convention. The 2000 ASEAN Declaration still has a strong state-based approach, eg Arts 1 and 2.

[220] Fifth recital, Preamble, 2006 African Charter; and first and sixth recitals, Preamble, Faro Convention. See also Art 2 UNESCO Diversity Declaration; and 11th recital, Preamble, Art 1, 2000 ASEAN Declaration; and CESCR, *General Comment No 21*, para 50(a).

[221] Eighth recital, Preamble, Faro Convention; sixth recital, Preamble, 2006 African Charter; and 10th recital, Preamble, 2000 ASEAN Declaration.

[222] Articles 1 and 4, Faro Convention. See Arts 3, 8, and 14, 2000 ASEAN Declaration; and UN Doc A/HRC/17/38, paras 61–3.

[223] Articles 4 and 5 and Part III, 2006 African Charter, with references to 'all citizens', 'minorities', 'peoples', 'nations', 'national and regional identities', as well as 'men and women', 'youth', 'elders and traditional leaders', and 'marginalised and underprivileged communities'.

[224] Main Lines of Action Plan for the Implementation, Points 1 to 3, 2001 UNESCO Declaration, Annex.

[225] Article 3(b) 2006 African Charter.     [226] Article 7 Faro Convention.

The Bouchard-Taylor Commission was established in Québec in 2007 in response to escalating public discontent concerning accommodation of minority cultural practices.[227] The events leading up to the Commission were not dissimilar to those discussed earlier in respect of France and Italy concerning religious symbols and practices in public places. In this case, the circumstances were heightened because of the Quebecois' existing anxieties as a minority within predominantly English-speaking Canada. In their recommendations, Bouchard and Taylor deliberately went beyond the narrow legal confines of reasonable accommodation to examine the issues more broadly from a social and economic dimension. Therefore, rather than pursuing harmonization through a legal route, they advocated a citizen path which is informal, reliant on negotiation and compromise, and which leads to adjustment and satisfaction for all parties. For this reason, they observed that the institution of French as the common public language facilitated a framework within society for dialogue but also afforded security for the Quebecois within the Canadian state. More broadly, the norms of 'common public culture' which included integration, intercultural relations, and open secularism needed to be fully and officially defined by the government. They observed that the transplantation of France's strict secularism into Quebec's public schools was incompatible with the province's principle of neutrality on religion. They maintained that integration in a diverse society was not achieved by suppressing identities but 'through the exchange between citizens who thus learn to get to know each other'.[228] Applying these principles in the context of Québec, cultural accommodation would not circumvent core values like gender equality, would not prohibit the wearing of religious symbols or dress in public schools or other public spaces, the display of the crucifix in the parliament or the saying of prayers during parliamentary or council sessions would be prohibited, and while dedicated prayer rooms were not mandatory for state buildings, space could be made available when rooms were temporarily unused.[229] Bouchard and Taylor conclude that any efforts toward 'a common future' between diverse communities would fail if social and economic disparities remain entrenched, if there was a misconception that 'pluriethnicity' was 'so many juxtaposed separate groups perceived as individual islets', and if there was suppression of freedom of religious expression because of anxieties due to past religious oppression.[230]

## B. Voluntary isolation and secession

It is a measure of the importance placed on culture, identity, and the preservation of cultural diversity by contemporary international society that it acknowledges that cultural accommodation may necessitate sanctioning (in very defined and

---

[227] G. Bouchard and C. Taylor, *Building the Future: A Time for Reconciliation. Report of the Commission on Accommodation of Practices Related to Cultural Differences* (2008).

[228] Bouchard and Taylor (2008) 46.

[229] Bouchard and Taylor (2008) 20. See Margalit and Halbertal (1994) 506.

[230] Bouchard and Taylor (2008) 21.

rare circumstances) the voluntary isolation from the dominant culture and society within an existing state or the secession of a group from an existing state to form a new state.

The extreme vulnerability of indigenous peoples in voluntary isolation and initial contact has been recognized by regional and international human rights bodies.[231] These diverse communities share common characteristics, including a highly interdependent relationship with the environment in which they live and develop their cultures; they are 'extremely vulnerable' because of the lack of familiarity with the dominant culture; and are at 'high risk of extinction' because encroachments onto their lands adversely impact their ways of life and ability to preserve their cultures.[232] The case of *Yakye Axa Indigenous Community v Paraguay* involved an indigenous community which had traditionally lived in the Paraguayan Chaco and whose removal from their traditional, communal lands, it was alleged, violated their 'right to life, the right to ethnic identity, the right to culture and to recreate it, the right to survive as an integrated indigenous Community'.[233] The Inter-American Court of Human Rights found that 'possession of their traditional territory is indelibly recorded in their historical memory, and their relationship with the land is such that severing that tie entails the risk of an irreparable ethnic and cultural loss, with the ensuing loss of diversity'.[234] The Court found that the respondent state was under a duty to take positive measures towards realization of a right to a decent life for persons who are 'vulnerable and at risk'.[235] It framed the question it needed to address thus:

[W]hether the State generated conditions that worsened the difficulties of access to a decent life for the members...and whether, in that context, it took appropriate positive measures to fulfil that obligation, taking into account the especially vulnerable situation in which they were placed, given their different manner of life (different worldview systems than those of Western culture, including their close relationship with the land) and their life aspirations, both individual and collective, in the light of the existing international corpus juris regarding the special protection required by the members of indigenous communities....[236]

In their dissenting opinion, Judges Cançado Trindade and Ventura Robles went further, finding that the removal of the community from their ancestral lands

---

[231] People in isolation are defined as indigenous peoples or subgroups who live in remote areas, do not have regular contact with the majority population, and for whom 'isolation is not a voluntary choice but a survival strategy', while indigenous people in initial contact have recent, intermittent contact with the majority population but never become completely aware of its 'patterns and codes of relationships'. Draft Guidelines on the Protection of Indigenous Peoples in Voluntary Isolation and in Initial Contact of the Amazon Basin and El Chaco, Report prepared by the Secretariat, 30 June 2009, UN Doc A/HRC/EMRIP/2009/6, para 7.

[232] UN Doc A/HRC/EMRIP/2009/6, para 13.

[233] *Yakye Axa Indigenous Community v Paraguay*, para 121(h). See more recently in respect of the persistent impact of missionaries on the right to religious freedom of indigenous communities: Report of the Special Rapporteur on freedom of religion or belief, H. Bielefeldt: Mission to Paraguay, 26 January 2012, UN Doc A/HRC/19/60/Add.1, paras 45–53.

[234] *Yakye Axa Indigenous Community v Paraguay*, para 216.

[235] *Yakye Axa Indigenous Community v Paraguay*, para 162.

[236] *Yakye Axa Indigenous Community v Paraguay*, para 163.

and ongoing marginalization caused the deaths of several of its members.[237] They observed that '[c]ultural identity has historical roots, and under the circumstances of the instant case...it [was] tied to ancestral lands. We must emphasize that cultural identity is a component or is attached to the right to life *lato sensu*; thus, if cultural identity suffers, the very right to life of the members of said indigenous community also inevitably suffers'.[238]

In 2009, the UN Office of the High Commissioner for Human Rights (OHCHR), in consultation and collaboration with representative groups, prepared draft Guidelines on the Protection of Indigenous Peoples in Voluntary Isolation and in Initial Contact of the Amazon Basin and El Chaco, which sets out the obligations of states and the international community.[239] States have an obligation to protect the individual and collective rights of indigenous peoples within their territory, especially those that are extremely vulnerable and are at 'high risk of becoming victims of large-scale aggression that ultimately amounts to genocide'.[240] The international community is also required to ensure the adoption and effective implementation of protective measures to guarantee the protection of these peoples' human rights because of their situation of extreme vulnerability and 'fulfil its role and responsibility of guaranteeing that the planet's cultural diversity is protected, as this diversity represents a valuable public good for humanity'.[241] In order to respect the principle of no contact, these communities can only be identified through collaboration with other indigenous peoples that have been contacted and local, regional, or national organizations they may have established, and universities and non-governmental organizations working directly for their protection.[242]

While indigenous peoples in voluntary isolation and initial contact enjoy the full suite of human rights, the OHCHR guidelines identify three overarching and interrelated rights, namely: (1) the right to self-determination—that their decision to live in isolation be respected is described as the 'highest expression of this right' as it guarantees respect for their traditional ways of life; (2) the right to territory—recognizes their dependence on their environment to maintain their ways of life and develop their culture; and (3) the right to culture—that they are able to exercise their cultural rights to guarantee their cultural survival.[243] The rights of indigenous peoples in initial contact, like all indigenous peoples, includes the right to participate or be consulted and the right to free, prior, and informed consent, which has been recognized by international instruments and regional human rights

---

[237] Separate Dissenting Opinion of Judges A.A. Cançado Trindade and M.E. Ventura Robles, in *Yakye Axa Indigenous Community v Paraguay*, paras 6–12.

[238] *Yakye Axa Indigenous Community v Paraguay*, para 18.

[239] Draft Guidelines on the Protection of Indigenous Peoples in Voluntary Isolation and in Initial Contact of the Amazon Basin and El Chaco, UN Doc A/HRC/EMRIP/2009/6. The Spanish version was adopted in May 2012.

[240] UN Doc A/HRC/EMRIP/2009/6, paras 14 and 15.

[241] UN Doc A/HRC/EMRIP/2009/6, paras 16–18.

[242] UN Doc A/HRC/EMRIP/2009/6, para 19.

[243] UN Doc A/HRC/EMRIP/2009/6, paras 20–4.

bodies.[244] Consultation and consensus must accord with the indigenous community's 'own mechanism of consultation, values, customs and customary law'; and it is the community, and not the state, that determines who shall represent them during consultations.[245] Indigenous peoples in voluntary isolation exercise this right by not participating and not providing their consent to encroachments onto their lands.[246] Consent is a mandatory requirement where proposed actions involve the permanent dislocation of communities from their traditional lands, exploitation of natural resources necessary for their subsistence, or the disposal of hazardous materials on their lands. This is an additional safeguard for the rights of indigenous peoples given the direct connection to the right to life and right to cultural identity.[247] It is especially critical for communities in voluntary isolation or initial contact where obtaining consent by force or coercion could amount to 'serious violations of their human rights, including the crime of genocide'.[248] The guidelines encourage the establishment of permanent mechanisms for dialogue among all actors, including all levels of government, indigenous peoples' organizations and non-governmental organizations, involved in the implementation of specific protective measures.[249]

The continuing negotiations concerning the secession of Kosovo from Serbia provide a possible example of the rare circumstances in which the international community will permit recognition of a new state where there has been failure to negotiate between religious or cultural communities. While the international community has persistently denied that the right to external self-determination extends to minorities, the 2005 commentary to the UN Minorities Declaration indicates that they may exercise the right to self-determination as secession 'if participation is denied to a minority and its members'.[250] This view arises from an interpretation of the so-called 'safeguard' clause contained in the 1970 UN Friendly Relations Declaration which reaffirms the applicability of territorial integrity or political unity of states 'conducting themselves in compliance with the principle of equal rights and self-determination of

---

[244] Articles 10, 11, 15, 17, 19, 28, 29, 30, 32, 36, and 38 UNDRIP; Arts 6(1), 6(2), 15(2), 22(3), 27(3), 28 ILO 169 of 1989; *Saramaka People v Suriname (Interpretation of the Judgment on Preliminary Objections)*, I/ACtHR (2008) Series C, No 1, para 16.

[245] *Yakye Axa Indigenous Community v Paraguay*, para 151; and *Sawhoyamaxa Indigenous Community v Paraguay (Judgment)*, I/ACtHR (2006) Series C, No 146, para 135.

[246] UN Doc A/HRC/EMRIP/2009/6, para 68.

[247] Report of the Special Rapporteur on the situation of human rights and fundamental freedoms of indigenous peoples, J. Anaya, 15 July 2009, UN Doc A/HRC/12/34, para 47.

[248] UN Doc A/HRC/EMRIP/2009/6, para 75.

[249] UN Doc A/HRC/EMRIP/2009/6, para 83. As at May 2013, the Rapporteur on the Rights of Indigenous Peoples at the Inter-American Commission on Human Rights is gathering information from states parties concerning their legal and policy practices concerning indigenous peoples in voluntary isolation and initial contact to develop recommendations in accordance with international human rights law.

[250] UN Doc E/CN.4/Sub.2/AC.5/2005/2, paras 15, 19, and 20. See also UN Doc E/CN.4/Sub.2/AC.5/2000/WP.1, paras 18–21, 91. Former Chairperson and Rapporteur of the UN Working Group on Minorities, A. Eide, has noted that if states seek to avail themselves of the principle of state sovereignty and territorial integrity, they must adhere to other elements of United Nations law, including the respect for democracy and human rights inside their states: United Nations Standards on Minorities and Group Accommodation, 23 *Thesaurus Acroasium* (1999) 543 at 545–6.

peoples...and thus possessed of a government representing *the whole people* belonging to the territory without distinction as to race, creed or colour'.[251] In the *Quebec Secession* case, the Canadian Supreme Court also considered that this safeguard clause may justify the exercise of external self-determination or secession 'when a people is blocked from the meaningful exercise of its right to self-determination internally, it is entitled, as a last resort, to exercise it by secession'.[252]

The international recognition of Kosovo's independence proposed by the UN Special Envoy following the failure to reach a negotiated settlement between Serb and Kosovar representatives can be interpreted as a response to a blockage as described by the Canadian Supreme Court.[253] In his separate opinion to the International Court of Justice's *Advisory Opinion on the Unilateral Declaration of Independence in Respect of Kosovo*, Judge Cançado Trindade observed that

States exist for human beings and not vice-versa. Contemporary international law is no longer indifferent to the fate of the population.... The advent of international organizations, transcending the old inter-State dimension, has helped to put an end to... [t]his distortion [which] led States to regard themselves as final repositories of human freedom, and to treat individuals as a means rather than as ends in themselves, with all the disastrous consequences which ensued therefrom.[254]

When making this observation, Judge Cançado Trindade implied that the safeguards applied to the new state of Kosovo, as it did to the state from which it sought to secede. Accordingly, in its declaration of independence, the Kosovo Assembly indicated its acceptance of the obligations proposed by the Special Envoy, particularly those concerning 'the rights of Communities and their members'.[255] In addition to promoting equality, it agreed to refrain from assimilationist policies,[256] and

---

[251] Principle 5, para 7, GA Res 2625 (XXV), 24 October 1970, Annex (emphasis added). This wording, in a slightly modified form, was replicated in the final declaration of the United Nations World Conference on Human Rights, Vienna Declaration and Programme of Action, 25 June 1993, 32 ILM [1993] 1661, at 1665; and expanded by the Secretary-General's High Level Panel Report on Threats, Challenges and Change, A More Secure World: Our Shared Responsibility, 2 December 2004, UN Doc A/59/565, paras 29 and 30.

[252] *Reference re Secession of Quebec* [1998] 2 SCR 217, para 134, and [1998] 115 ILR 536 at 586–7.

[253] See Comprehensive Proposal for the Kosovo Status Settlement, Special Envoy for the future Status Process, M. Ahtisaari, 26 March 2007, UN Doc S/2007/168, paras 1 and 3. On 19 April 2013, Serbia and Kosovo had reached an agreement to normalize relations, including arrangements for Serb-dominated northern Kosovo, following negotiations facilitated by the EU: Statement of EU Council President Van Rompuy, 19 April 2013, reference CL13-032EN. The text of the agreement had not been publicly released as at April 2013.

[254] *Accordance with International Law of the Unilateral Declaration of Independence in Respect of Kosovo*, ICJ Reports (2010) 403, advisory opinion of 22 July 2010, separate opinion of Judge Cançado Trindade, para 239. Despite the submissions of various states in support of this broader interpretation of when the right to self-determination triggers the exercise of secession in international law, the ICJ failed to address this issue.

[255] Kosovo's Declaration of Independence on 17 February 2008, in Introductory Note, Dossier 192, *Accordance with International Law of the Unilateral Declaration of Independence in Respect of Kosovo*; and UN Doc S/2007/168, Annex II. Several states recognizing Kosovo's statehood made specific reference to this undertaking. See United States: Letter President G.W. Bush, 18 February 2008; France: Statement Minister B. Kouchner, 18 February 2010; and United Kingdom: Statement Prime Minister G. Brown, 18 February 2008.

[256] UN Doc S/2007/168, Annex II, Art 2(6).

to implement positive measures conducive for minority communities and their members 'to preserve, protect and develop their identities'.[257] It accepted it had 'a special duty to ensure effective protection of the sites and monuments' of all communities, and promoting their heritages as 'an integral part of the heritage of Kosovo'.[258] The explicit purpose of these guarantees is the promotion of 'a spirit of tolerance, dialogue and [to] support reconciliation between the Communities'.[259]

## C. Human rights, individuals, and the group

Groups and communities, including minorities and indigenous peoples, like states have members with multiple, varying, and dynamic identities, which traverse ethnic and religious affiliations and gender, age, sexual orientation etc.[260] International and regional instruments make clear that neither the state nor groups can invoke culture or religion to derogate from human rights norms, including principles of non-discrimination and equality, which represent core values of the international community. The UN Special Rapporteur on Cultural Rights has stated: 'Cultural diversity is not to be confused with cultural relativism'.[261] The UNESCO Cultural Diversity Declaration explicitly provides that promotion and protection of cultural diversity cannot be used to justify violations of existing human rights norms.[262] Likewise, human rights instruments stipulate that the exercise and enjoyment of cultural rights cannot violate others' human rights.[263] The commentary to the UN Minorities Declaration noted that 'cultural or religious practices which violated human rights law should be outlawed for everyone', so that the qualification is of universal application, to minorities and the majority alike.[264] Article 8(2) of the Declaration provides that agencies of the minority cannot interfere with the human rights of individual members of the group in order to preserve their

---

[257] UN Doc S/2007/168, Annex II, Art 2(1). The implementation of the rights and privileges afforded the Serbian Orthodox Church, its clergy and affiliates, activities and property is overseen by an international monitor: Annex V.

[258] UN Doc S/2007/168, Annex II, Art 2(5).

[259] UN Doc S/2007/168, Annex V, Art 2(1). See *Accordance with International Law of the Unilateral Declaration of Independence in Respect of Kosovo*, Separate Opinion of Judge Cançado Trindade, para 238.

[260] See Harris, 'Race and Essentialism in Feminist Legal Theory', 42 *Stanford Law Review* (1990) 584; and Otto, 'Rethinking the "Universality" of Human Rights Law', 29 *Columbia Human Rights Law Review* (1997) 29.

[261] Report of the Special Rapporteur in the field of cultural rights, F. Shaheed: Enjoyment of Cultural Rights by Women on an Equal Basis with Men, 10 August 2012, UN Doc A/67/287, para 70.

[262] Article 4 2001 UNESCO Declaration. See also sixth recital, Preamble, CE Declaration; and first recital, Preamble, 2006 African Charter. The ASEAN Declaration is silent on this point.

[263] For example, 18th recital, Preamble, 1976 UNESCO Recommendation; Arts 4(2) and 8(2) UN Minorities Declaration; Art 22 CE FCNM; Art 46(2) UNDRIP; and Art 4 Pretoria Declaration on Economic, Social and Cultural Rights in Africa, adopted by the African Commission on Human and Peoples' Rights, meeting at its 36th ordinary session on 17 September 2004, ACHPR/Res 73(XXXVI)04. See CESCR, *General Comment No 21*, para 17, which provides that states are obliged to implement Art 15 ICESCR together with other obligations under the Covenant 'in order to promote and protect the entire range of human rights guaranteed under international law'.

[264] UN Doc E/CN.4/Sub.2/AC.5/2005/2, para 57.

collective identity. The CESCR has indicated in respect of the right to participate in cultural life (Article 15 ICESCR) that 'no one may invoke cultural diversity to infringe upon human rights guaranteed by international law, nor to limit their scope'.[265] The Committee has found that it is mandatory for states parties to ensure equality between men and women in respect of the right to participate in cultural life by eliminating 'institutional and legal obstacles as well as those based on negative practices, including those attributed to customs and traditions'.[266] Yet, as Yvonne Donders meticulously details in this volume, reservation after reservation made by state parties to the Convention on the Elimination of Discrimination against Women (CEDAW) invokes culture and religious practices to circumscribe or deny the human rights of women.

Recent UN reports have been especially alert to the negative effect that claims to culture and religion have on the protection and promotion of women's human rights. The Special Rapporteur on Violence against Women (VAW) noted in 2012 that gender related killings within the family or community, or perpetrated or sanctioned by the state, and justified on cultural grounds was increasing, with the perpetrators rarely being held criminally accountable.[267] For example, in *INTERIGHTS on behalf of Safia Yakubu Husaini and Others v Nigeria*, the African Commission was asked to consider a complaint by Ms Hasaini who was sentenced to death by stoning for adultery following the application of Sharia law by special Sharia Courts in northern Nigeria.[268] Sharia law was only applicable to persons of the Muslim faith and it attached the death penalty to offences which did not attract this form of punishment under the Penal Code of Northern Nigeria, which covers the rest of the population. The complainant alleged that the discriminatory application of these laws and legal process to persons of one faith was a violation of Nigeria's obligations concerning non-discrimination, fair trial, and due process under the African Charter of Human and Peoples' Rights. However, the impact of the discrimination arising because of religious affiliation was compounded because of her gender.[269] Human rights bodies are increasingly cognizant of the need for vigilance in respect of vulnerable groups *within* minorities. The HRC in its General Comments covering Article 27 (Minorities) and Article 3 (Equality between men and women) has stipulated that minority cultural rights do

---

[265] CESCR, *General Comment No 21*, paras 18 and 20.

[266] CESCR, *General Comment No 21*, para 21.

[267] Report of the Special Rapporteur on Violence against Women, its Causes and Consequences, R. Manjoo: Gender-related killing of women, 23 May 2012, UN Doc A/HRC/20.16. See also Report of the Special Rapporteur on Violence against Women, its Causes and Consequences, R. Coomaraswamy: Cultural Practices in the family that are violent toward women, 31 January 2002, UN Doc E/CN.4/2002/83; and Report of Special Rapporteur on Freedom of Religion and Belief, *Étude sur la liberté de religion ou de conviction et la condition de la femme au regard de religion et des traditions*, UN Doc E/CN.4/2002/73/Add.2.

[268] ACHPR, Comm No 269/03, Decision, 27 April 2005.

[269] See UN Doc A/67/287, paras 52 and 53; and Report of the Special Rapporteur on Violence against Women, its Causes and Consequences, Y. Ertürk: Intersection between culture and violence against women, 17 January 2007, UN Doc A/HRC/4/34, para 61.

not authorize the violation of the right to equal enjoyment by women of any rights under the ICCPR, by a state, group, or individual.[270]

The Special Rapporteur on VAW, Yakin Ertürk, has emphasized the need to debunk myths that present cultures as 'static and immutable', 'homogeneous and monolithic', and 'apolitical and detached from the prevailing power relations', and resulting in individuals monopolizing the right to speak on behalf of a cultural or religious community.[271] She has observed that universally agreed values, including the principle that no custom or tradition can be used to justify violence against women, can only be upheld through 'cultural negotiation' where 'positive cultural elements are emphasized, while the oppressive element in cultural-based discourses are demystified'.[272] The UN Special Rapporteur on Cultural Rights, Farida Shaheed, has noted that as 'freedom to participate in cultural life stands at the very core of liberty', such cultural negotiations can only effectively be realized when women enjoy the freedom to participate fully.[273]

Like those of states, the members of a group have human rights and fundamental freedoms recognized in international law. And like states, groups which thwart the full and effective participation of all their members diminish their own legitimacy, and those members who systematically violate human rights in its name are responsible in law.

## 5. Conclusion

The motto of the French Republic took some time to come to a consensus. The first two catch cries of '*liberté*' and '*égalité*' were enunciated immediately and remained consistent. The third in the triumvirate, '*fraternité*'—with its allusions to community rather than the individual—proved less secure. Yet, other republics have embraced similarly communitarian themed mottos. Until 1955, the United States utilized '*E pluribus unum*' ('Out of many, one'). The present-day Republic of South Africa has 'Unity in diversity', as does the European Union ('*In varietate concordia*' or '*Unité dans la diversité*'). All contain within them the kernel of drawing together diverse populaces into a community.

Achieving this community through law remains an incremental process, defined and recalibrated continually since the seventeenth century through the elaboration of civil and political rights in national laws and human rights in international law. Liberty and the promotion of tolerance permitted members of minorities to participate in public life and enjoy related freedoms of beliefs, expression, assembly,

---

[270] HRC, *General Comment No 28: Equality of Rights between Men and Women (Art 3)*, UN Doc A/55/40, annex VI, para 32.

[271] UN Doc A/HRC/4/34, paras 57–63.

[272] UN Doc A/HRC/4/34, para 52; and Report of the Special Rapporteur on Violence against Women, its Causes and Consequences, Y. Ertürk: The Due Diligence Standard as a Tool for the Elimination of Violence Against Women, 20 January 2006, UN Doc E/CN.4/2006/61, paras 85–8.

[273] UN Doc A/67/287, paras 25 and 28, citing M. Sunder, *From Goods to a Good Life: Intellectual Property and Global Justice* (2012) 11.

and association as long they did not interfere with the freedoms of others or offend public morals. The pursuit of equality meant that non-discrimination moved beyond equal enjoyment of civil and political rights by all individuals to cultural (and social and economic) rights and allocation of public resources to ensure that individuals are able to sustain and foster their *own* cultural identity in community with others when it is distinguishable from the national or majoritarian culture. The protection and promotion of cultural diversity by the international community as a common good recognizes the evolving, diverse, and plural identities held by groups and individuals alike. But there is also recognition that diversity can only be sustained in an environment which enables all to participate and engage in dialogue in the formulation and promotion of a society of common, core values (like human rights, racial equality, gender equality) and in which majority and minority cultures can coexist. These processes and the core values which they bring forth are as fundamentally applicable to cultural (and religious) groups and indigenous peoples, as they are to states and the international community.

# PART II

# 3

# Protecting Minority Groups through Human Rights Courts

## The Interpretive Role of European and Inter-American Jurisprudence[*]

*Gaetano Pentassuglia*

## 1. Introduction

As the principal organs of the Organization of American States' (OAS) human rights system, both the Inter-American Court of Human Rights (hereinafter: 'the Inter-American Court' or 'the Court') and Inter-American Commission of Human Rights (hereinafter: 'the Inter-American Commission') have rendered decisions on cases involving the cultural and physical integrity of indigenous groups living within the boundaries of OAS member states. Partly initiated in the course of the 1980s and 1990s in connection with the Inter-American Commission's reporting and occasionally quasi-judicial work,[1] the core of the jurisprudence on indigenous issues squarely lies in the recent contribution of the Inter-American Court to reconceptualizing the role of the 1969 American Convention on Human Rights (ACHR) in this fast evolving area of international human rights law.

For its part, the European Court of Human Rights (hereinafter: 'the European Court' or 'the Court') has delivered judgments in a variety of matters involving minority groups under the 1950 European Convention on Human Rights (ECHR). In a 1973 report, a Council of Europe Committee of Experts on Human Rights explained that while there was no need for an additional protocol on the subject, 'there was no overriding obstacle of a legal character' against this either.[2] Nearly 40 years on, a protocol on minorities remains unavailable. However, major

---

[*] Much of the case law used in this chapter is updated as much as possible as of September 2011. Comments on further developments are occasionally provided in footnotes.

[1] See eg *Yanomami v Brazil*, Resolution No 12/85, Case No 7615, 5 March 1985.

[2] Rights of National Minorities, Report of the Committee of Experts on Human Rights to the Committee of Ministers, DH/Exp (1973) 47, para 12.

developments such as the post-1989 eastward expansion of the ECHR system and the adoption of new texts of relevance to minority groups by Council of Europe and other European and global institutions over the past 20 years, appear to have been conducive to a more sensitive approach of the European Court to issues of pluralism, identity, and non-discrimination regarding minority groups.

As is known, both the ECHR and the ACHR followed in the footsteps of the global human rights movement created with the establishment of the United Nations in 1945. Like the United Nations Charter and the Universal Declaration of Human Rights, both of them embrace the universalistic thrust of human rights protection and do not make specific provision for minority groups defined by ethnicity, language, and/or religion. As in the context of the Universal Declaration of Human Rights, proposals for introducing minority clauses in the ECHR—in the late 1940s and early 1960s, respectively—proved unsuccessful. The right to non-discrimination in Article 14 mentions 'association with a national minority' as part of an egalitarian effort to secure Convention rights for all.

Given these general systemic similarities, the judicial nature of decisions, as well as the largely parallel developments concerning ethno-cultural groups, the present chapter seeks to juxtapose the two regimes in order to expose—directly or indirectly—convergences and divergences in addressing minority group issues under general human rights treaties. It does not aim to provide a comprehensive overview or strictly analytical discussion of the case law. Rather, it reflects on a set of four questions, including the substantive and procedural elements underpinning the Inter-American and European Courts' respective jurisprudence (section 2), the role of positive obligations and proportionality reviews (section 3), the relation of the ACHR and ECHR to 'external' instruments as part of the interpretive process (section 4), as well as the real or potential implications of the case law for the very understanding of minority groups for purposes of human rights protection (section 5). I will consider each question from the perspective of the regime in question, and then offer some additional comparative thoughts. Based on these four lines of inquiry, I will discuss the broad themes which are reflected in Inter-American and European human rights judicial proceedings (and other global and regional jurisprudence as well, as appropriate), the sort of reading of the ACHR and ECHR that that litigation generates, as well as the impact of the Inter-American and European Courts on the wider system of minority group protection in international law.

## 2. Unearthing Human Rights Rationales: Substantive and Procedural Elements

### A. European Court

Beginning in the late 1990s, the European Court started to receive applications, initially from Turkey and Greece and subsequently from countries from the former Soviet bloc, affecting the assertion and manifestation of minority groups' identity in the public sphere. They variably involved the refusal by state authorities to register associations claiming to represent a national minority group or to be pursuing a pro-minority agenda, the dissolution of political parties having similar objectives, or bans on public meetings.

In the vast majority of these cases, the Court rejected the state's argument that the measures in question served to prevent disorder and/or protect the rights of others. Instead, it found a breach of the right to freedom of association in Article 11 by making three interrelated general arguments. First, it confirmed that the 'existence of minorities and different cultures in a country [is] a historical fact that a "democratic society" [has] to tolerate and even protect and support according to the principles of international law'.[3] Secondly, it explained that the dissolution of pro-minority political parties or associations does not meet the requirement of proportionality implicit in the relevant limitations clause if campaigning is conducted through non-violent and democratic means. Thirdly and more significantly, it broadly endorsed cultural pluralism as a value protected by the ECHR. As the Grand Chamber put it in *Gorzelik v Poland*, 'pluralism is...built on the genuine recognition of, and respect for, diversity and the dynamics of cultural traditions, ethnic and cultural identities'.[4] This is even more so when it comes to allowing relevant meetings to be held or refraining from physically attacking party or association structures and members.

The Court has hardly addressed the question of whether the communities concerned were minority groups in the sense of international law. It has even conceded that self-identification as a national minority may be limited by general state interests where it is linked to additional benefits under domestic law.[5] Crucially, though, it has upheld freedom of association (and expression) to articulate the theme of a post-Cold War open society in which national and subnational identities can be freely asserted and debated, and for which protection can be sought. It establishes a fundamental connection between 'seeking an ethnic identity or asserting a minority consciousness' and the quality of the democratic process. The Court sets out a minimum standard which enables claims to minority protection, including language rights or autonomy (or even secession), to be appropriately located within a human rights-driven pluralistic agenda rather than a narrowly defined security context. Moreover, the standard of pluralism inevitably pervades a range of other culture-related restrictions considered by the Court, including the denial of registration and legal capacity of minority churches in multireligious societies or the denial of recognition of the group's internal organization and religious leadership. While religion as a broader theme may not involve minority groups per se, this jurisprudence unquestionably affords significant protection to religious minorities.[6]

---

[3] *Sidiropoulos and Others v Greece*, ECHR (1998) Reports 1998-IV, judgment of 10 July 1998, para 41; see also *Tourkiki Enosi Xanthis and Others v Greece*, ECHR (2008) App No 26698/05, judgment of 27 March 2008, para 51.

[4] *Gorzelik and Others v Poland*, ECHR (2004) App No 44158/98, judgment of 17 February 2004, para 92.

[5] *Gorzelik and Others v Poland*, paras 97–103.

[6] See eg *Metropolitan Church of Bessarabia and Others v Moldova*, ECHR (2001) App No 45701/99, judgment of 13 December 2001; *Canea Catholic Church v Greece*, ECHR (1997) Reports 1997-VIII,

More specific identity considerations under Article 8 represent another area where recently progress has been made by the Court. The then European Commission on Human Rights first paved the way for accepting claims relating to the way of life of a minority group as being pertinent to the right to private and family life under that provision. In *G and E v Norway* from the early 1980s, the impact of a hydroelectric dam within traditional Sami areas was deemed to be proportionate to the aim pursued by the government.[7] However, in language which was somehow reminiscent of Article 27 of the International Covenant on Civil and Political Rights (ICCPR), the point was made that Article 8 was in principle applicable to this sort of interference—a proposition which seems to be borne out by more recent acknowledgments of the Sami way of life.[8] Whatever the weight of minority issues behind the 1983 finding, it was effectively not until *Chapman v United Kingdom* in 2001 that the Court not only confirmed the link between private and family life and minority identity but also found an 'emerging international consensus recognising the special needs of minorities and an obligation to protect their security, identity and lifestyle'.[9] As part of a wider set of similar cases, *Chapman* brought to the fore the particular position of Roma members being unable to find accommodation compatible with their lifestyle because of a denial of planning permissions by local authorities, the insufficiency of public caravan sites, or the practical unavailability of private sites. In *Connors v United Kingdom*, the Roma applicant, unlike Sandra Chapman, had been lawfully residing in a local authority site at the time of his eviction, although the point made by the Court signalled a more general pattern: '[i]t would rather appear that the situation in England as it has developed, for which the authorities must take some responsibility, places considerable obstacles in the way of gypsies pursuing an actively nomadic lifestyle while at the same time excluding from procedural protection those who decide to take up a more settled lifestyle'.[10]

In *Chapman*, the Court conceded that, while there is no immunity from general laws, the way in which such laws are implemented may have an impact on the way of life of the Roma community. It went as far as to argue that given the position of the group as a vulnerable minority, 'some special consideration should be given to their needs and their different lifestyle both in the relevant regulatory planning framework and in reaching decisions in particular cases', and that to that extent a positive obligation 'to facilitate the Gypsy way of life' derived from Article 8. The applicant lost the case because of a wide margin of appreciation in planning matters which the state was said to enjoy. However, a similar line of reasoning was

---

judgment of 16 December 1997; *Hasan and Chaush v Bulgaria*, ECHR (2000) App No 30985/96, judgment of 26 October 2000; *Serif v Greece*, ECHR (1999) App No 38178/97, judgment of 14 December 1999; *Holy Synod of the Bulgarian Orthodox Church (Metropolitan Inokentiy) and Others v Bulgaria*, ECHR (2009) App Nos 412/03 and 35677/04, judgment of 22 January 2009.

[7] Application Nos 9278/81 and 9415/81, DR 35, 35.

[8] For a recent analysis, see Koivurova, 'Jurisprudence of the European Court of Human Rights Regarding Indigenous Peoples: Retrospect and Prospects', 18 *Int'l Journal on Minority and Group Rights* (2011) 1 at 25–6.

[9] ECHR (2001) App No 27238/95, judgment of 18 January 2001, para 93.

[10] ECHR (2001) App No 66746/01, judgment of 27 May 2004, para 94.

confirmed in *Muñoz Díaz v Spain*, involving the impact of marriages according to Roma rites and traditions on the implementation of marriage laws.[11] Here the Court found in favour of a member of the traditional Roma minority in Spain, though in the context of non-discrimination. Moreover, in *Noack v Germany*, involving a contested relocation of a Sorbian village in the *Land* of Brandenburg, the rationale for declaring the application inadmissible was that extensive consultations with the group had taken place before the decision to relocate the village had been made, and that the group would continue to enjoy adequate protection in accordance with the Constitution of that *Land*.[12] This jurisprudence suggests that state discretion under Article 8 is not unlimited. Ethnic identity falls within the scope of the article,[13] and the impact of state measures on minority groups' traditional practices, particularly their level of participation in the decision-making process, must be reviewed on a case-by-case basis.

The broader discourse of equality under Article 14 has provided additional substance to the Strasbourg Court's evolving engagement with minority issues. In retrospect, the famous *Belgian Linguistics* decision—the first ECHR case on non-discrimination ever—effectively set the tone for a wider approach to non-discrimination more than three decades later, conceptually and practically. The Court confirmed that differential treatment is permissible if it rests on a reasonable and objective justification (ie one which pursues a legitimate aim and is proportionate to that aim). In fact, as it was noted, 'Article 14 does not prohibit distinctions which are founded on an objective assessment of essentially different factual circumstances';[14] those distinctions may be 'called for' to correct factual inequalities. At the same time, the Court noted that non-discrimination can be found in relation to the 'aim and effects of the measure under consideration'.[15] *Thlimmenos v Greece*[16] and *D.H. and Others v The Czech Republic*[17]—from 2000 and 2007, respectively—both expand on *Belgian Linguistics* in that they both endorse—implicitly and explicitly—the notion of indirect discrimination deriving from seemingly neutral measures regarding access to a specific profession and access to education. In the 1968 case, the language legislation in Belgium affected the French-speaking children of (Dutch-speaking) Flanders but the formal admission criterion to the schools in the relevant communes on the periphery of Brussels was residency, not language. Discrimination on this particular count was found in this early case despite the fact that the territorial unilingualism embedded in that legislation was deemed to have been justified by the aim of accommodating the dominant language communities in the Dutch- and French-speaking regions. In the aftermath of *Thlimmenos*, the notion was explicitly consolidated that 'a general

---

[11] ECHR (2007) App No 49151/07, judgment of 8 December 2009.

[12] ECHR (2000) App No 46346/99, admissibility decision of 25 May 2000.

[13] See eg *Ciubotaru v Moldova*, ECHR (2010) App No 27138/04, judgment of 27 April 2010.

[14] *Case Relating to Certain Aspects of the Laws on the Use of Languages in Education in Belgium*, ECHR (1968) Series A, No 6, 44.

[15] ECHR (1968) Series A, No 6, 34.

[16] ECHR (1997) App No 34369/97, judgment of 6 April 2000.

[17] ECHR (2007) App No 57325/00, judgment of 13 November 2007.

policy or measure that has disproportionately prejudicial effects on a *particular group* may be considered discriminatory notwithstanding that it is not specifically aimed at that group'.[18] The recent case law on Roma-only schools or classes in the Czech Republic, Greece, and Croatia[19] has made it clear that not only may discrimination occur indirectly as a result of general policies on, for instance, learning disabilities or language deficiencies, but also proof of discriminatory intent is not required if a rebuttable prima facie case of indirect discrimination has been made out.

Generally speaking, the proactive reading of Article 14 stems from the interplay of substantive and procedural obligations. 'Special vigilance' is required of states parties in the context of racial violence and racial discrimination more broadly, compared with cases with no racist connotations. Protection against such discrimination cannot be waived. Discrimination can be hidden behind legislation or official policy and thus fighting it requires enhanced modalities of intervention. Conceptually, the thrust of this line ties up with the pluralism jurisprudence, on the one hand—centred as it is on respect for diversity—and the principle of 'special protection' upheld in the more specific area of Article 8, on the other. Operationally, the Court has used the parameter of special vigilance under Article 14 to find a positive duty upon states to investigate possible racist motives behind physical attacks on individuals and property by state or non-state actors, in conjunction with Article 2 (right to life) or Article 3 (prohibition of degrading treatment). Moreover, the admissibility of cases of suspected institutional racism has become inextricably linked to new thinking about evidential issues. In *Nachova and Others v Bulgaria*,[20] involving the killing of two Roma conscripts by Bulgarian army officers, the Court held that shifting the burden of proof on to the state in cases of alleged discrimination may be difficult to transpose to cases where it is being argued that an act of violence by particular individuals has been racially motivated. However, the Grand Chamber did recognize that that technique does facilitate proof of (indirect) discrimination in cases concerning employment or provision of services. It is precisely in relation to provision of services such as school education that new ground has been broken by both allowing the reversal of the burden of proof in circumstances where prima facie evidence is available and expanding that evidence to include previously inadmissible statistical data. In short, the Court has responded to criticism of its standard of proof 'beyond reasonable doubt' voiced in previous cases by accepting 'less strict evidential rules' in certain cases of alleged indirect discrimination.[21] Central to this line is a view

---

[18] *Kelly v United Kingdom*, ECHR (2001) App No 30054/96, judgment of 4 May 2001, para 154 (emphasis added).

[19] *D.H. and Others v The Czech Republic*, ECHR (2007) App No 57325/00, judgment of 13 November 2007; *Sampanis and Others v Greece*, ECHR (2008) App No 32526/05, judgment of 5 June 2008 (in French); *Oršuš and Others v Croatia*, ECHR (2010) App No 15766/03, judgment of 16 March 2010.

[20] ECHR (2005) App Nos 43577/98 and 43579/98, judgment of 6 July 2005.

[21] *D.H. and Others v The Czech Republic*, ECHR (2007) App No 57325/00, judgment of 13 November 2007, para 186.

of the case at issue that boldly enables the Court to give greater consideration to the impact of the measures in question on the minority group concerned, not merely the individual applicants taken out of their community context.[22] While the impact can be measured even without statistical evidence,[23] it is clear that the use of such evidence from international and national sources has strongly contributed to exposing the plight of individuals as part of an entire community being affected. Finally, the focus on non-violent acts or measures signalled by *Nachova* has not ruled out a shift of the burden of proof to the state when strong inferences exist suggesting that the alleged racial violence occurred in a *context* which was generally not racially neutral, over and above the position of specific individuals directly responsible for acts of brutality.[24]

## B. Inter-American Court

The complex body of judgments of the Inter-American Court relies on a range of general clauses contained in the ACHR. It reveals a fundamentally holistic approach to the field. This is hardly surprising, given the lack of specific ACHR provisions on indigenous rights and the almost inherent multidimensionality of indigenous issues. The central theme from which most of the ramifications of the Court's jurisprudence derive is access to traditional lands and natural resources which are found on or beneath them. In 2001, the decision in the *Mayagna (Sumo) Awas Tingni Community v Nicaragua* case famously recognized 'the right to property in a sense which includes, among others, the rights of members of the indigenous communities within the framework of communal property'.[25] This unprecedented ruling was based on both the realization of a distinctive material and spiritual connection between indigenous peoples and their traditional land tenure systems—one which could not be characterized as merely 'a matter of possession and production'—and the fact that the terms of the ACHR (and indeed, international human rights treaties generally) were to be given a meaning separate from the one possibly given to them in domestic law. As explained in the case of *Indigenous Community Xákmok Kásek v Paraguay* nearly ten years on, the concept of indigenous property differs from the classic concept of property but deserves to be equally protected on the basis that the Article 21 right to 'property' is capable of accommodating different ways of using and arranging goods 'that come from the culture, uses, customs, and beliefs of different peoples'.[26]

---

[22] For some critical reactions to these innovative dimensions of the Court's review, see *D.H. and Others*, Dissenting Opinion of Judge Borrego Borrego; *Oršuš and Others v Croatia*, ECHR (2010) App No 15766/03, judgment of 16 March 2010, Joint Partly Dissenting Opinion of Judges Jungwiert, Vajić, Kovler, Gyulumyan, Jaeger, Myjer, Berro-Lefèvre, and Vučinić, para 15. Still, some level of analysis of the inter-group dimension appears inevitable: see also *Sejdić and Finci v Bosnia and Herzegovina*, ECHR (2009) App Nos 27996/06 and 34836/06, judgment of 22 December 2009.

[23] *Oršuš and Others v Croatia*, ECHR (2010) App Nos 15766/03, judgment of 16 March 2010, para 153.

[24] *Stoica v Romania*, ECHR (2008) App No 42722/02, judgment of 4 March 2008, paras 127–32.

[25] IACtHR (2001) Series C, No 79, judgment of 31 August 2001, para 148.

[26] IACtHR (2010) Series C, No 214, judgment of 24 August 2010, para 87.

In this sense, the Court's most significant contribution lies in the decoupling of the right to property in the ACHR from property title as regulated by national law. Indeed, the Court has, on the one hand, allowed traditional indigenous possession to override lack of registration at the domestic level. Arguments based on failure by the community to meet internal legal requirements have been dismissed. As a result, factual elements rooted in traditional practices (and established through indigenous customs and laws as well as expert testimonies) are legally equated to full property title granted by the state. On the other hand, dispossession of traditional indigenous lands or severe encroachments on the community's ability to sustain a material and spiritual connection with those lands due to state or non-state action have been said not to affect the community's right to recover them or to obtain other lands of equal quality and size to the extent that the relationship with such lands has been maintained. A continuing relationship with land is in turn based on a contextual analysis of local circumstances affecting the group and, as implied by the construction, may include time periods in which access to land was precluded for reasons beyond the group's will or control. In *Yakye Axa Indigenous Community v Paraguay*,[27] the Court crucially indicated that it is for the state, in full consultation with the community concerned, to consider expropriating privately own land in conformity with Article 21(2), in the event of a conflict between indigenous property and private property resulting from transfers to 'innocent' third parties.

Another turning point in the Court's jurisprudence has been the recognition of natural (subsoil) resources as integral to the notion of indigenous property falling within the scope of Article 21. In *The Saramaka People v Suriname*,[28] the Court confirmed the autonomous role of international human rights law upheld in *Awas Tingni* by discussing indigenous rights under the ACHR as separate from rights over lands and resources under domestic law. The case essentially turned on whether the state had failed both to recognize the right to property of the members of the Saramaka people over the territory that they had traditionally used and occupied, and to allow effective judicial protection of such right under the ACHR. Suriname's Constitution did not recognize a right to communal property for members of indigenous or tribal communities, and, together with statutory legislation, vested all ownership rights over natural resources with the state. Working within the framework of earlier jurisprudence, the Court not only explicitly acknowledged that 'the right to use and enjoy their territory would be meaningless in the context of indigenous and tribal communities if said right were not connected to the natural resources that lie on and within the land',[29] but also established special requirements to be met in the event of state measures aiming at limiting the enjoyment of indigenous rights over such natural resources under Article 21. It was noted that the general requirements for permissible limitations on property rights set out in Article 21(2) do not exhaust the range of conditions that must be satisfied in order

---

[27] IACtHR (2005) Series C, No 125, judgment of 17 June 2005, paras 146, 217.
[28] IACtHR (2007) Series C, No 172, judgment of 28 November 2007.
[29] IACtHR (2007) Series C, No 172, judgment of 28 November 2007, para 122.

to ensure the survival of indigenous and tribal communities in relation to their traditional lands and resources. Indeed, any restrictions may be justified only to the extent that, in addition to those requirements, they have specifically guaranteed (a) effective participation, ie the ability of the group to be involved meaningfully in the decision-making process regarding the 'development, investment, exploration or extraction plan' in question; (b) benefit-sharing, ie the capacity of the group to share in the benefits expected to derive from the project affecting their land and its natural resources; and (c) environmental and social impact assessment, ie the provision of independent surveys providing benchmarks to the parties concerned as to the likely individual and cumulative effects of the proposed development activity. Suriname was found to be in breach of those requirements in relation to logging concessions and small-scale goldmining concessions. The Court crucially explained, though, that in the event of large-scale development or investment projects which are bound to have a major impact on the community's way of life and subsistence economy, the requirement of effective participation must take place in the form of free, prior, and informed consent to the relevant measures, 'mere' consultation being inadequate to secure proper involvement of the community. While the pre-*Saramaka* jurisprudence establishes the process for regaining the land, *Saramaka* sets out general conditions in the event that rights and land use are already there. In that sense, *Saramaka* builds on previous cases, particularly *Yakye Axa*, to expand the justificatory test for permissible restrictions.

In essence, the Court's case law on land rights—and the similar jurisprudence of the Commission[30]—is built around five broad elements: (1) property, in the autonomous sense of the Inter-American system, allowing for both traditional land tenure systems and multiple points of connection with land, including links surviving denial of access to it; (2) historic claims, which must be rooted in continuing effects of dispossession and require, as in the case of recent taking of land by state or non-state actors, restitution (*restitutio in integrum*) or alternative lands (or, absent those, financial compensation) when restitution is not possible; (3) natural resources to the extent necessary to sustain the group's way of life, in connection with special requirements to justify limitations on the group's ability to benefit from those resources as part of indigenous property; (4) effective indigenous participation as a general requirement involving all major aspects of indigenous land disputes, including possible title extinguishment; and (5) access to judicial protection based on distinctive legal capacities to seek enforcement of land rights in court and to obtain reparation of damage suffered by the group as part of a wider concept of access to justice.[31]

---

[30] For a recent comprehensive survey, see Indigenous and Tribal Peoples' Rights over Their Ancestral Lands and Natural Resources, OEA/Ser.L/V/II., Doc 56/09 (2010), available at <http:www.cidh.org> (accessed 17 June 2013).

[31] Since the present chapter was completed, the Inter-American Court delivered judgment in the case of *The Kichwa Indigenous People of Sarayaku v Ecuador*, IACtHR (2012) Series C, No 245, judgment of 27 June 2012. Turning on a lack of consultation by Ecuador with the Sarayaku people prior to beginning or authorizing oil extractive activity within their traditional territory, the decision reinforces the scope of this case law's effective participation component. Indeed, the consultation process and its objectives are further set out and made an even stronger test for respondent states to pass. Importantly,

While reconceptualizing property under Article 21, the Court has come to recognize the impact of physical and cultural access to traditional lands on the enjoyment of the right to life under Article 4. In *Yakye Axa*, it understood this right both in the traditional sense (ie as a protection against arbitrary taking of life by the state) and as an entitlement to a 'dignified existence', that is, to live under conditions that are—as further explained in *Sawhoyamaxa Indigenous Community v Paraguay*[32]—'minimally compatible with the dignity of the human person' and the cultural identity associated with it. In essence, the notion that land tenure systems define the physical, cultural, and economic space within which indigenous identities manifest themselves, has led the Court to emphasize the detrimental consequences arising from lack of access to land for the very wellbeing of indigenous communities. This inextricable connection between physical integrity and land-based identity does not simply derive from failure to protect indigenous property, but rests on autonomous findings concerning the treatment suffered by the community over a significant period of time while living in different areas. In line with earlier case law, *Xákmok Kásek* broadly elaborated on 'dignified existence' in connection with rights to water, food, health, and education as set out mainly in the UN International Covenant on Economic, Social and Cultural Rights, in order to articulate the ramifications of that concept under Article 4. Moreover, it has been gradually accepted that violations of the right to life may go as far as to include the deaths of members of the community to the extent that a persuasive causal relationship between those deaths and their condition of vulnerability due to state-generated land deprivation has been established.

As I mentioned, the Court's (and Commission's) reading of indigenous issues rests on a rather hybrid, holistic human rights approach. A further illustration of this is the case of *Yatama v Nicaragua*[33] which involved refusal by the authorities to allow indigenous candidates to run for political office at the local level. The Court offered a nuanced understanding of the right to political participation in Article 23 ACHR. For one thing, it found the requirements for candidate registration set out by an electoral law of 2000 to be unduly restrictive on indigenous groups. On the other hand, it held that the very requirement of presenting indigenous candidates only through political parties infringed on uniquely indigenous conceptions and

---

the ramifications of the duty to consult are said to be part of general international law. One could argue that the very strengthening of indigenous participation in decision-making, coupled with the typical inadequacies of consultation as a background to much contemporary indigenous rights litigation, would ordinarily suffice for the Court to find a breach of the ACHR, independently of specific matters of free, prior, and informed consent for large-scale development plans as explained in *Saramaka*. For access to justice elements, see *The Saramaka People v Suriname*, IACtHR Series C, No 127, judgment of 28 November 2007, paras 172, 188–9; for an account of various access to justice approaches, see more generally Pentassuglia, *Minority Groups and Judicial Discourse in International Law: A Comparative Perspective* (2009) 20–1, Ch 5. For specific applications of the concept of access to justice to indigenous women, see eg *Fernández Ortega et al v Mexico*, IACtHR (2010) Series C, No 215, judgment of 30 August 2010, para 200.

[32] *Sawhoyamaxa Indigenous Community v Paraguay*, IACtHR 2006 Series C, No 126, judgment of 29 March 2006. See also *The Kichwa Indigenous People of Sarayaku v Ecuador*, IACtHR (2012) Series C, No 245, judgment of 27 June 2012, paras 248, 249.

[33] IACtHR (2005) Series C, No 127, judgment of 23 June 2005.

methods of association and organization, and was therefore in breach of Article 23 together with the principle of equality set out in Article 24.

## C. Comparative reflections

It is clear from the above *tour d'horizon* of cases that both Courts have engaged with issues regarding minority groups by revisiting the scope of relevant provisions in the ECHR and ACHR. Both of them have construed them in functional and pragmatic ways in order to match their own distinctive language and logic. The outcome of this process inevitably varies, not least because of the nature and scope of the issues raised. The European Court's jurisprudence deals with issues of pluralism, identity, and non-discrimination mainly in the context of transition to more open systems or special cases, whereas the Inter-American Court's reflects the peculiar social and historical background of indigenous peoples in the Americas.

Although the degree of protection somewhat mirrors the sociological and legal exchanges on human rights matters within the respective systems, both Courts have importantly acknowledged—explicitly or implicitly—the group or collective dimension of rights of relevance to minority identities. Examples of this tendency include the group-related impact of freedom of association and freedom of religion, the interplay of individual and collective way of life in matters of private and family life, and group-based non-discrimination and associated evidential issues under the ECHR, as well as the collective dimension of property and related rights under the ACHR.[34] The group-oriented view of indirect discrimination under the ECHR, and the reassessment of ACHR access to justice guarantees as group-based access to juridical personality, participation in proceedings and reparation, are largely the effects rather than the cause of evolving deeper understandings of the significance of the treaties in question to minority communities. In point of fact, this increasingly expansive view echoes and reinforces parallel jurisprudential developments which have occurred both under Article 27 ICCPR (minority rights) and the African Charter on Human and Peoples' Rights.

Especially in the *Ogoni* case and, more recently, the *Endorois* case decided by the African Commission on Human and Peoples' Rights,[35] the protection of indigenous communities appears to have been spread along a scale of 'general' individual and collective guarantees, ranging from basic cultural and land-related rights, to property rights *stricto sensu*, to rights to natural resources. 'Peoples' rights' are

---

[34] In *Moiwana Village v Suriname*, the Inter-American Court also found that the fact that the Moiwana community members could neither bury their loved ones in accordance with fundamental norms of N'djuka culture, nor enjoy their own traditional way of life as being inextricably linked to their land, was in breach of the right to physical and moral integrity in Art 5(1) ACHR. For an explicit endorsement of the collective approach, see *The Kichwa Indigenous People of Sarayaku v Ecuador*, IACtHR (2012) Series C, No 245, judgment of 27 June 2012, para 231.

[35] *The Social and Economic Rights Action Center for Economic and Social Rights v Nigeria*, Comm No 155/96 (2001); *Centre for Minority Rights Development (Kenya) and Minority Rights Group International on behalf of Endorois Welfare Council v Kenya*, Comm No 276/2003 (2009).

being made available at the subnational level.[36] The (collective) right to natural resources (Article 21 African Charter on Human and Peoples' Rights—hereinafter 'ACHPR') works largely (though by no means exclusively) within the constraints of the (individual) right to property in Article 14 ACHPR. At the same time, individual cultural rights in Article 17 ACHPR have been read as affording protection to ethno-cultural minority groups and entailing a duty to take 'positive steps' to achieve this objective.[37] Irrespective of the obvious distinctive features of each human rights treaty, it seems fair to argue that jurisprudential analyses across human rights systems are de facto transcending longstanding rigid dichotomies between the individual and the (ethno-cultural) group within human rights law. The Inter-American Court's case law demonstrates that reading group-oriented guarantees into traditional individual human rights clauses is both possible and indeed desirable.

Having said that, the Inter-American Court's line, unlike the European Court's, has been supported by relatively more coherent legal circumstances, such as national legislation, ratification of the 1989 International Labour Organization Convention Concerning Indigenous and Tribal Peoples in Independent Countries (ILO Convention 169), a more favourable group-oriented approach to 'indigenous peoples' in international law compared to 'minorities', but also and more crucially—as I discuss below—a more assertive evolutionary method of interpretation generally. While the European Court protects associative freedoms and their functional possibilities for minority groups as necessary in a democratic society so as to make state interference normally unacceptable, the Inter-American Court goes as far as to conceive of restrictions on existing 'rights of others' in order to secure a democratic society which is genuinely pluralistic and thus respectful of cultural diversity,[38] including one represented by minority groups. Whereas the European Court has recognized identity rights but is still unclear about its ramifications, the Inter-American Court has gone as far as to develop a complex body of jurisprudence on the implications of reading indigenous rights into the ACHR—from conceptual to operational aspects. Whereas the Strasbourg Court has importantly expanded its understanding of non-discrimination under Article 14 ECHR to include group dimensions and the general notion of indirect discrimination, the Inter-American Court has effectively mainstreamed the principle of equality throughout the cases by making it one of the cornerstones of its interpretation.[39]

---

[36] For an overview, see Pentassuglia, 'Towards a Jurisprudential Articulation of Indigenous Land Rights', 22 *EJIL* (2011) 165 at 184–90.

[37] *Centre for Minority Rights Development (Kenya) and Minority Rights Group International on behalf of Endorois Welfare Council v Kenya*, Comm No 276/2003 (2009), para 248.

[38] *Yakye Axa Indigenous Community v Paraguay*, IACtHR (2005) Series C, No 125, judgment of 17 June 2005, para 148. See also *The Kichwa Indigenous People of Sarayaku v Ecuador*, IACtHR (2012) Series C, No 245, judgment of 27 June 2012, para 217.

[39] *The Kichwa Indigenous People of Sarayaku v Ecuador*, para 51.

## 3. Constraining the State: Positive Obligations, Proportionality Reviews, or Both?

### A. European Court

Despite the lack of specific ECHR provisions on minority groups, the censuring or consideration of interferences with pluralism (Article 11), identity (Article 8), or non-discrimination rights (Article 14) over the past ten to 15 years, including a set of modalities derived from the principle of 'special vigilance' in matters of racial discrimination, is arguably at the core of a wider legal reasoning which is rendering the ECHR an increasingly functional instrument in the field of minority protection. The extent to which the European Court is prepared to read positive obligations into relevant Convention rights as a way of limiting state discretion is difficult to measure. I think it would be fair to suggest that, in response to mounting pressure to encompass minority issues within the scope of the ECHR, the Strasbourg case law has reflected varying degrees of judicial intervention. Proportionality reviews of state action appear to capture the general basis for such intervention irrespective of substantive positive obligations based on autonomous (ie non-domestic law reliant) readings of the ECHR.[40]

The pluralism jurisprudence—primarily revolving around (the lifting of) restrictions on pro-minority entities or events—largely reinforces negative obligations, while still upholding diversity as a positive value, as 'a source of enrichment'.[41] In fact, the Court has found positive obligations in relation to several classic ECHR rights, including the right to life, freedom of association, freedom of religion and family and private life. As in the context of Article 27 ICCPR, positive measures may be required to support the assertion or manifestation of minority diversity (think of protection of minority organizations, churches, or individuals against attacks from private parties).[42] Nevertheless, what lies at the core of this jurisprudence is the broad notion that pluralism (political, religious, and ultimately 'cultural') must be allowed to flourish without undue interference. Far from restating the obvious, it lays down the foundations for constructive forms of personal autonomy through private law organizations, including political parties, foundations or religious denominations, in line with the requirements of United Nations as well as European instruments and practice.[43] As partly suggested by the ECHR jurisprudence itself,[44] OSCE and Council of Europe standards are of critical importance to

---

[40] For an account of the doctrine of autonomous concepts, see Letsas, 'The Truth in Autonomous Concepts: How to Interpret the ECHR', 15 *EJIL* (2004) 279.

[41] *Timishev v Russia*, ECHR (2005) App Nos 55762/00 and 55974/00, judgment of 13 December 2005, para 55.

[42] See eg *mutatis mutandis*, *X and Y v The Netherlands*, ECHR Series A, No 91, judgment of 26 March 1985, para 23.

[43] Suksi, 'Personal Autonomy as Institutional Form—Focus on Europe Against the Background to Article 27 of the ICCPR', 15 *Int'l Journal on Minority and Group Rights* (2008) 157.

[44] *Sidiropoulos and Others v Greece*, ECHR (1998) Reports 1998–IV, judgment of 10 July 1998, para 44.

reinforce this line of thinking under the ECHR in ways that consolidate and expand on a traditional yet dynamic component of minority protection.

The boundaries of this line are tellingly reflected in recent cases on political participation of minorities or political parties supporting minority representations. The Court has been clear in rejecting internal arrangements formally excluding members of minority groups from electoral processes, even when those arrangements had been based on an international treaty like the 1995 Dayton Peace Agreement ending the conflict in the former Yugoslavia.[45] While limitations on Article 3 of Protocol 1 have sometimes been broadly accepted,[46] denial of access of members of minority groups to active and passive electoral rights has been deemed to be incompatible with that provision, as have unnecessary restrictions on minority candidates' opportunities to run for political office. However, the censuring of political exclusion in cases such as *Sejdić and Finci v Bosnia and Herzegovina* and *Aziz v Cyprus*[47] has not provided the background to distinctive positive obligations aimed to ensure certain modalities of political pluralism. For example, in *Grosaru v Romania*,[48] involving political representation of the Italian minority in Parliament, the Court commented on the generosity of the special arrangements that had been made to secure special representation for minorities but did not comment on positive duties on states parties to do so. Even more significantly, in *Yumak and Sadak v Turkey*, the Grand Chamber expressed concern about the 10 per cent threshold electoral rule for political parties to gain representation in Parliament but still recognized its legality in that particular context. The decision came in contrast to claims from interveners and dissenting judges that the rule in question effectively constituted a failure to secure representation of regional or minority parties (particularly Kurdish organizations) in the Turkish Grand National Assembly.[49]

As I mentioned earlier, *Chapman* recognizes a specific positive obligation 'to facilitate the Gypsy way of life' under Article 8. However, the Court was quick to dismiss extensive readings of this obligation requiring states to provide Roma communities with an adequate number of suitably equipped caravan sites to support their specific way of life. A strong dissent criticized this position pointing to an obligation to take positive steps in line with European developments in the field. While 'special protection' for Roma groups has been repeatedly recognized in later cases on racial violence and segregation, the contours of the positive obligation found in *Chapman* remain undefined. The main problem seems to lie in the decoupling of Article 8 from the right to non-discrimination. The notion that a positive obligation exists for states parties to facilitate a minority group's way of life under that provision, appears difficult to reconcile—both conceptually and practically—with the notion that such obligation would not in itself justify differential treatment.[50] If 'private and family

---

[45] *Sejdić and Finci v Bosnia and Herzegovina*, ECHR (2009) App Nos 27996/06 and 34836/06, judgment of 22 December 2009.

[46] See eg *Ždanoka v Latvia*, ECHR (2006) App No 58278/00, judgment of 16 March 2006.

[47] *Aziz v Cyprus*, ECHR (2004) App No 69949/01, judgment of 22 June 2004.

[48] ECHR (2010) App No 78039/01, judgment of 2 March 2010.

[49] ECHR (2008) App No 10226/03, judgment of 8 July 2008.

[50] ECHR (2001) App No 27238/95, judgment of 18 January 2001, para 95; contrast with the view of the joint dissent, para 8.

life' is to be given broader scope in order to proactively include elements of minority group identity in the *public* sphere, then the dissent in *Chapman* and other cases such as *Noack* seem in principle to provide a more appropriate basis for that. Minority participation in relevant decision-making processes may well emerge as part of a wider principle requiring positive protection under Article 8, but it is unclear whether the Court would see it more like a major indicator of compliance in proportionality reviews under Article 8(2) than a strict positive obligation. In *Connors*, it confirmed the *Chapman* case law but did narrow the state's margin of appreciation by holding that the lack of judicial review of the eviction at issue was reflective of more general and significant obstacles being faced by the Roma group in the United Kingdom in pursuing either a nomadic or more settled lifestyle. It agreed that the eviction of the applicant and his family constituted a serious interference with Article 8 rights— deemed to be of 'central importance to the individual's identity'—for which 'weighty reasons of public interest by way of justification' had not been provided.[51]

Equally significant is the jurisprudence on Sami rights. Several applications have been lodged over the years by Sami from Norway (as in the well-known *G and E* case, mentioned earlier), Finland, and Sweden. Most of these applications were declared inadmissible by the then European Commission on Human Rights. However, important progress has been made in terms of acknowledging the Sami way of life as falling within the protective reach of the ECHR. The early, rather limited, 1980s jurisprudence on Article 8 appears to have been reinforced—at least in conceptual terms—by later cases which have recognized the validity of the claim that the culture and way of life of the Sami be respected or that protracted legal proceedings over Sami land claims are in breach of Article 6(1) ECHR.[52] In fact, Sami villages and associations have consistently argued that the Sami have rights over their traditional lands as a matter of property to be protected under Article 1 of Protocol 1. The property claim has been made on several occasions, both in relation to traditional Sami land tenure practices[53] and as part of specific

---

[51] ECHR (2004) App No 66746/01, judgment of 27 May 2004, paras 82, 86. Since the present chapter was completed, the European Court delivered judgment in the case of *Yordanova and Others v Bulgaria*, ECHR (2012) App No 25446/06, judgment of 24 April 2012. It held that enforcing an eviction order issued by the municipal authorities in Sofia to dismantle an unlawful Roma settlement of several hundred persons which had been de facto tolerated by those authorities since the 1960s, would be in breach of the applicants' rights to home and private and family life under Art 8 ECHR. The Court found that no adequate proportionality assessment had been undertaken by the domestic authorities which accounted for the applicants as members of an especially vulnerable group. Breaking new ground in a way which is bound to impact future Roma eviction cases, the Court read Art 8 in light of Art 14 and found deficiencies in decision-making relating to the timing and modalities of removal, and possible arrangements for alternative shelter. While positive action is clearly implied— and indeed justified—by the Court's reasoning, the central line of the judgment seems to confirm the suggestion that the primary focus tends to be more on an enhanced proportionality test based on robust compliance indicators and less on specific or strictly worded positive obligations.

[52] See eg *Halvar From v Sweden*, ECmHR (1998) App No 34776/97, admissibility decision of 4 March 1998; *Könkämä and 38 Other Saami Villages v Sweden*, ECmHR (1996) App No 27033/95, admissibility decision of 25 November 1996; *Handölsdalen Sami Village and Others v Sweden*, ECHR (2010) App No 39013/04, judgment of 30 March 2010.

[53] For a recent reaffirmation of such a claim, see *Handölsdalen Sami Village and Others v Sweden*, ECHR (2009) App No 39013/04, admissibility decision of 17 February 2009.

disputes—including *Hinqitaq 53 and Others v Denmark*[54] and *The Chagos Islanders v United Kingdom*[55]—involving past relocations of indigenous communities. At this stage, some positive developments which may be traced in the line of Sami cases from the last 25 years or so are being counterbalanced by the lack of autonomous positive obligations relating to the recognition of Sami—and by implication, indigenous—property rights. While the Court has not ruled out the possibility that Sami traditional rights may constitute 'possessions' in the sense of Article 1 of Protocol 1, it has done so by refraining to derive a positive duty upon the parties to secure those rights directly from the ECHR. Instead, it has deferred judgment over land claims to domestic authorities absent any manifest errors of fact or law, even though the Court's doctrine and practice of autonomous concepts (as well as comparative human rights jurisprudence) arguably do not require it to do so.[56]

Article 8 is the main, but not only Convention provision which may have an impact on minority groups' identity. Article 2 of Protocol 1 has been occasionally invoked in an attempt to mainstream minority education within the scope of the ECHR. Here again, the tendency by the Court has been to guard the perimeters of state action rather than articulating a specific positive obligation. As famously established in the *Belgian Linguistics* case, the ECHR does not include a right to receive education in a particular language or in a particular way. More recently, though, in *Cyprus v Turkey*, the Court was keen to emphasize that it would find a violation of the right to education if a properly functioning system of mother tongue education for a minority group were to be subsequently withdrawn.[57] It held that failure to provide continuing Greek-speaking secondary education for Greek-Cypriots living in northern Cyprus infringed the latter's right to education. The line seems in principle to offer an important, if indirect, legal defence of the *status quo ante* in the event that—as has been the case in some Central and Eastern European states—the previous regime has been abruptly abolished due to changing political circumstances. At the same time, it allows the drawing of parallels with the impact of certain policies on minority education from the broader perspective of equality. In 1935, the Permanent Court of International Justice ruled that the closing down of private minority schools together with other private schools in Albania, coupled with the provision of a uniform system of public education in Albanian, was incompatible with that country's international obligations to ensure 'equality in fact' for minority groups.[58] Both cases were considered against the backdrop of preexisting international undertakings, and both of them reflected the logic and language of the regime under which judicial pronouncements were

---

[54] ECHR (2006) App No 18584/04, admissibility decision of 12 January 2006.

[55] ECHR (2012) App No 35622/04 (filed on 20 September 2004, but declared inadmissible on 11 December 2012 by the Fourth Section of the Court). See also the 2009 submissions by Human Rights Watch and Minority Rights Group International as interveners at <http://www.hrw.org/en/news/2009/10/02/chagos-islanders-v-united-kingdom> (accessed 29 June 2013).

[56] See generally, Pentassuglia (2011) 177–82. See also *Doğan and Others v Turkey*, ECHR (2004) App Nos 8803–8811/02, 8813/02 and 8815–8819/02, judgment of 29 June 2004, paras 137–9.

[57] ECHR (2001) App No 25781/94, Judgment of 10 May 2001, paras 277–8.

[58] *Minority Schools in Albania*, 1935 PCIJ Series A/B, No 64.

made. Both of them, though, support a general principle according to which the abolishment of private minority schools or minority education within the public educational system that is bound to prove detrimental to the minority group is not allowed. These cases illustrate the importance of conducting careful judicial enquiries into the permissibility (proportionality) of measures affecting minority groups.

Greater emphasis on non-discrimination under Article 14 can generate stricter forms of control over state action. As I indicated earlier, the Court's supervision may be supported by positive obligations, such as the duty to investigate prima facie cases of racially motivated violence or other forms of 'special protection'. The test of indirect discrimination crucially polices the edges of state intervention. It may go as far as to challenge their impact on entire communities[59] or implicitly point to 'reasonable accommodation' in individual circumstances.[60] It does constrain state discretion through enhanced proportionality tests, including issues of burden of proof and evidence. It may thus, over time, constructively permeate aspects most directly related to minority groups' identity, as the early *Belgian Linguistics* case and the seminal principle of special consideration of 'vulnerable minorities' in the Article 8 case law would seem to allow. Yet, the rationale for this jurisprudence as it currently stands appears to be primarily 'negative' in nature. It generally focuses on stringent *ex post facto* assessments rather than the enforcement of *ex ante* positive duties to guarantee differential treatment.

This scenario helps appreciate how the Court has dealt with the notion of proactive measures which do provide for complex forms of group-differentiated rights. The equality jurisprudence does not appear to yield a specific obligation to address structural (majority/minority) imbalances within society. Nevertheless, it does provide grounds for justifying proportionate autonomy regimes or other group measures on political representation, language/education, or religion. Whether it's a proportional representation system allowing a minority group to be represented in the legislature, an educational and language system based on territorial criteria, or even forms of cultural autonomy defined by religious affiliations, the Strasbourg jurisprudence has reflected essentially proportionality reviews aimed to mark out the boundaries of permissible action under the ECHR, not to set out a priori substantive obligations. In this sense, broad permission of pro-group policies—such as a special voting system in Northern Ireland or special minority representation in Romania—does provide them with the necessary legitimacy in human rights terms. Conversely, criticism of those policies or aspects of them—such as 'illiberal'

---

[59] *D.H. and Others v The Czech Republic*, ECHR (2007) App No 57325/00, judgment of 13 November 2007. See also *Yordanova and Others v Bulgaria*, App No 25446/06, judgment of 24 April 2012.

[60] *Thlimmenos v Greece*, ECHR (2000) App No 34369/97, judgment of 6 April 2000. For the concept of 'reasonable accommodation' in Canadian legislation and case law, see Woehrling, 'L'obligation d'accommodement raisonnable et l'adaptation de la société à la diversité religieuse', 43 *McGill Law Journal* (1998) 325; the concept of (denial of) reasonable accommodation (as discrimination) can be found in Art 2 of the UN Convention on the Rights of Persons with Disabilities, UNTS 2515, 3 13 December 2006.

or state control-free religious personal laws or potentially abusive electoral legislation—point to adjustments which are required to make them compatible with the ECHR in future.[61] I think it is instructive to note that recent (and still evolving) data seem to indicate that European *domestic* courts have primarily engaged in proportionality reviews when using the Council of Europe's Framework Convention for the Protection of National Minorities in cases challenging the constitutionality of special legislative measures on minority political participation, language and/ or education. They seem to be concentrating on the necessity and proportionality of the legislation concerned under Article 4(2) of the Framework Convention (full and effective equality) irrespective of whether that particular measure can be claimed under the treaty.[62] Indeed, both global and European standards on political participation or language/education generally recognize a considerable degree of discretion on the part of states in relation to advanced modalities of minority group involvement including public law forms of functional autonomy.[63] Also, private minority associations may not automatically claim public law status in connection with special legislation on minority groups.[64] International minimum standards must be upheld, but the ways and means of securing effective protection (and, a fortiori, measures that withdraw guarantees previously enjoyed by the group) are generally subject to a sort of sliding-scale approach to the intensity of proportionality reviews. From this perspective, the Strasbourg judges have a greater legitimacy-enhancing role to play irrespective of any specific positive obligations which they are (or may be) prepared to derive dynamically or incrementally from the ECHR in certain circumstances with a view to further limiting states' margin of appreciation.

## B. Inter-American Court

The Inter-American Court's jurisprudence is construed around a web of positive obligations which are derived from ACHR rights. The jurisprudence on land rights and the right to life lies at the core of this proactive approach. In *Saramaka*, the point was confirmed—and more forcefully made—that delimiting, demarcating, and titling the land are essential components of a positive obligation designed to protect traditional indigenous lands against state and non-state incursions which encroach on the group's effective ability to sustain the relationship with its subsistence and cultural base.[65] Titling in law is thus a necessary implication of enjoying

---

[61] For discussion from a comparative perspective, see Pentassuglia (2011) 125–33.

[62] For an overview of constitutional court cases, see Palermo, 'Domestic Enforcement and Direct Effect of the Framework Convention for the Protection of National Minorities: On the Judicial Implementation of the (Soft?) Law of Integration', in Verstichel et al (eds), *The Framework Convention for the Protection of National Minorities: A Useful Pan-European Instrument?* (2008) 187 at 206–9.

[63] Suksi, 'Functional Autonomy: The Case of Finland with Some Notes on the Basis of International Human Rights Law and Comparisons with Other Cases', 15 *Int'l Journal on Minority and Group Rights* (2008) 195 at 210–23.

[64] *Gorzelik and Others v Poland*, ECHR (2004) App No 44158/98, judgment of 17 February 2004.

[65] IACtHR (2007) Series C, No 172, judgment of 28 November 2007, para 115.

protection under Article 21. It is meant to provide legal certainty to the community and its members in ways that guarantee the permanent use and enjoyment of the land. In this sense, the obligation to recognize indigenous property rights is not exhausted by generic domestic enactments. It does involve an elaborate process of physical identification and legal protection of the land to the immediate benefit of the community concerned. Unsurprisingly, the positive duty of land delimitation, demarcation, and titling has been found both in relation to a principled elaboration on Article 21 and in the context of reparations awarded to indigenous victims. In fact, impermissible occupation of land triggers off *restitutio in integrum* as the principal remedy to be sought under Article 63(1). Only when restitution is not possible can alternative remedies be provided. On this reading, positive obligations are directed not only at regaining the land, as in the *Yakye Axa* and similar scenarios, but also protecting the community while still in possession of it. Against the backdrop of a general (negative) duty to refrain from granting concessions while land is being disputed, demarcated, or returned, a more general positive obligation has been linked to the prevention of, and investigation into, illegal extractive activities such as illegal mining, logging, or fishing in traditional lands of indigenous groups.[66]

The language of positive obligations ultimately permeates a wider range of ramifications of indigenous land rights protection, including specific procedural requirements for development activities affecting indigenous natural resources, access to judicial review of relevant governmental decisions through recognition of legal personality which allows for practical protection of land rights in a communal manner, as well as effective participation of community representatives in all aspects of land rights disputes. The discourse about the right to life in Article 4 has been construed around positive obligations too. As explained in *Sawhoyamaxa* and confirmed in *Xákmok Kásek*, states are required to take all appropriate steps to protect and promote the right to life. The Court has made it clear, though, that no 'impossible or disproportionate burden' can be imposed on the state, due to resource or other operational constraints.[67] In fact, for responsibility to arise, the state must have known, and failed to respond to a situation of immediate and certain risk to the life of individuals or a group of individuals in a way that could have been reasonably expected. This obligation of due diligence has been applied to indigenous communities in relation to particular individuals affected by land deprivation such as children, pregnant women, or the elderly, as well as a more general failure to protect the right to a dignified existence through adequate socioeconomic services. It is in this context that responsibility for the deaths of community members has also been found, in connection with a lack of necessary positive measures within the realm of the state's capabilities. One might argue that

---

[66] See eg Indigenous and Tribal Peoples' Rights over Their Ancestral Lands and Natural Resources, OEA/Ser.L/V/II., Doc 56/09 (2010), available at <http://www.cidh.org> (accessed 29 June 2013), paras 268–70.

[67] *Sawhoyamaxa Indigenous Community v Paraguay*, IACtHR (2006) Series C, No 146, judgment of 29 March 2006, para 155.

the proactive approach to Article 4 in *Sawhoyamaxa* and *Xákmok Kásek* mirrors the land rights jurisprudence in that the positive obligations generated by the former are clearly intended to serve as the most obvious preconditions for enjoying the positive protection arising out of Article 21.

Positive obligations are clearly at the centre of the Court's line of reasoning. They constitute the principal means of limiting state autonomy under the ACHR in matters of indigenous rights, generating strict reviews of state performance. For example, the due diligence-based duty construed in connection with the right to life in Article 4 has involved intense control over state measures relating to health risks such as preventable diseases stemming from lack of access to land or encroachments on it.[68] But the Court has also been keen to tighten proportionality tests when it comes to justifying restrictions on existing rights. Assuming the legal validity of both private and indigenous property claims, the Court has firmly qualified state discretion over the way to address such competing claims or to consider limiting indigenous property rights over natural resources. In *Yakye Axa* and later cases, the Court has come to refine its jurisprudence relating to the adequacy of measures favouring private over indigenous property or making concessions to third parties to carry out development activities within traditional indigenous areas. The Court has recognized that limitations on the property rights of 'innocent' third parties in the form of expropriation under Article 21(2) may be necessary 'to attain the collective objective of preserving cultural identities in a democratic and pluralist society',[69] provided that fair compensation is paid to those affected. Central to this line is the notion that, while it is for the state to make decisions on a case-by-case basis, a number of arguments traditionally made by the state to justify continuing protection of individual private property will be deemed unacceptable, thereby making any measures to that effect disproportionate. Aside from more obvious cases where the 'innocence' of third parties cannot be established[70] or the state simply appeals to the group's lack of title or status, such arguments ordinarily include the fact that the land has long been in private hands, that it is being used productively, or that it is being covered by bilateral investment treaties (BITs). In the latter case, the Court has offered justifications for prioritizing human rights obligations over commercial undertakings, at least from the perspective of the ACHR. Apart from indicating the possibility of limiting or nationalizing capital investments in the name of 'public purpose or interest' under the relevant BIT, the Court has interpreted the role of BITs in a way that is generally compatible with the state's obligations under human rights treaties. As I will argue below, although this line is unlikely to prove compelling as regards an assumed hierarchy of norms

---

[68] *Indigenous Community Xákmok Kásek v Paraguay*, IACtHR (2006) Series C, No 214, judgment of 24 August 2010; *Yakye Axa Indigenous Community v Paraguay*, IACtHR (2005) Series C, No 125, judgment of 17 June 2005; *Sawhoyamaxa Indigenous Community v Paraguay*, IACtHR (2006) Series C, No 136, judgment of 29 March 2006.

[69] *Yakye Axa Indigenous Community v Paraguay*, IACtHR (2005) Series C, No 125, judgment of 17 June 2005.

[70] Indigenous and Tribal Peoples' Rights over Their Ancestral Lands and Natural Resources, OEA/Ser.L/V/II., Doc 56/09 (2010), available at <http://www.cidh.org> (accessed 29 June 2013), para 118.

in international law, it most certainly provides a persuasive view that constrains state discretion from within the scope of the ACHR. The same can be said of the *Saramaka* test of effective participation, benefit-sharing and environmental and social impact assessment—this time in the context of restrictions on existing indigenous property rights. By setting out special criteria complementing the ones set forth in Article 21(2), the Court has essentially redefined the test of proportionality relating to property rights restrictions to account for special considerations regarding indigenous communities. Indeed, both positive obligations and strict proportionality tests in mutually supporting areas such as life, land, and political participation are ultimately the end result of a broad reading of the ACHR requiring states parties to take the specific characteristics of indigenous communities into account when assessing the scope and content of the treaty.[71]

## C. Comparative reflections

The above jurisprudence seems to indicate a relatively cautious move by the Strasbourg Court towards positive obligations relating to certain aspects of minority group protection. For example, positive elements such as horizontal protection or participation in the decision-making process may be read into rights to freedom of association and respect for private and family life in Articles 10 and 8, respectively. However, the general line is tentative, and seemingly incremental. Positive obligations in the area of non-discrimination may create a space for a more ambitious approach and broadly define the kind of 'special protection' for minority groups (particularly Roma groups) required of states parties. In fact, procedural obligations (eg under Articles 8 and 14) are more likely to be at the forefront of the Court's increasingly expansive view of minority issues. Although findings of positive obligations are largely piecemeal and ad hoc, proportionality reviews appear to provide a general basis for judicial intervention, particularly in relation to severe interferences with existing rights, withdrawal of guarantees previously enjoyed, or the adoption of structural measures for complex forms of group accommodation.

By contrast, the San José Court's body of cases, while similarly acknowledging the special features of the communities concerned, is directly grounded in positive obligations derived from an essentially holistic evolutionary reading of such rights as those to life, property, participation, and access to a judicial remedy. However, in the Inter-American Court's jurisprudence, positive obligations still combine (and unsurprisingly so) with a demanding proportionality test to measure state performance (eg in relation to due diligence-based obligations relating to Article 4) and/or to justify restrictions on existing rights (eg in regard to limitations on indigenous property rights to be found under Article 21). Both Courts thus engage in proportionality reviews that generate different levels of intensity in regard to the extent to which state measures come under judicial scrutiny. Whereas

---

[71] *Yakye Axa Indigenous Community v Paraguay*, IACtHR (2005) Series C, No 125, judgment of 17 June 2005, para 51.

the Inter-American Court's line rests on revisiting the very substance of the ACHR and then understanding 'proportionality' against that reading, the European Court appears to have been so far more comfortable with qualifying and guarding the boundaries of state action under explicit or implicit limitations clauses or advanced views of non-discrimination rather than through direct or systemic (re)appraisals of Convention rights as they relate to minority groups.

But, aside from substantive reconceptualizations of life, property, or political participation under the ACHR, most obligations are procedural in nature—from land demarcation to effective involvement in decision-making, to access to justice. This is significant in terms of constraining state discretion as much as the fact that, even assuming new substantive readings of rights, complex issues regarding minority groups (and indeed, complex human rights issues generally) can hardly be addressed effectively under human rights treaties unless they are linked to solid benchmarks relating to process (including reparation). In this sense, while ambitious reconsiderations of concepts or terms (eg indigenous property) appear to be less forthcoming in the European Court, emerging ECHR procedural obligations relating to prevention/protection, participation, investigation and remedy, as well as specific procedural issues of evidence and burden of proof, should arguably be seen as part of a general 'proceduralist' trend in international human rights jurisprudence.[72]

Having said that, the Inter-American Court has been clearly more inclined to engage in a comprehensive reassessment of the ACHR in ways that cannot be said of the European Court's reading of the ECHR. This is partly reflective of evolving modalities of human rights treaty interpretation and the effectively distinctive impact of the Inter-American Court on the understanding of indigenous rights. I will now turn to these aspects of the two Courts' case law in relation to what appears to be the key driving factor in the interpretive process, namely external human rights instruments.

## 4. Mainstreaming Accommodation through 'Systemic' Readings: From Restraint to Cross-fertilization

### A. European Court

In this context, the impact of 'external' international human rights instruments on the Court's jurisprudence appears to be evolving. In *Sidiropoulos v Greece*,[73] the Court referred to the CSCE Copenhagen Document on the Human Dimension and the Charter of Paris for a New Europe to uphold the right to freedom of

---

[72] The African Commission on Human and Peoples' Rights has combined autonomous positive duties (due diligence-based horizontal protection, access to information, participation in decision-making, remedies) with firm proportionality tests (*Ogoni, Endorois*). These variations reflect regional circumstances and the structure of the relevant human rights regime. At the same time they should be seen as part of a dynamic, potentially open-ended interpretive process across systems.
[73] ECHR (1998) Reports 1998-IV, judgment of 10 July 1998, para 44.

association of minority members in Article 11. By appealing to a 'strictly super-visory role', the majority in *Chapman* effectively refrained from using the Framework Convention for the Protection of National Minorities as a specific interpretive tool. However, as I mentioned earlier, the Court did rely on an 'emerg-ing international consensus recognising the special needs of minorities and an obli-gation to protect their security, identity and lifestyle'[74] to accept the argument that a minority group's way of life may attract the guarantees of Article 8, and to limit state discretion in the decision-making process.

More constructively than in *Chapman*, the Grand Chamber in *Gorzelik v Poland*[75] quoted from the Framework Convention to further articulate the sub-stance of Article 11, and by implication, the more general procedural significance of freedom of association within a democratic society. In the 2007 judgment in *D.H. and Others*, the Court explicitly drew on findings relating to the Framework Convention's monitoring process, and upheld indirect discrimination and its procedural ramifications in the wake of leading domestic, international and European jurisprudence and legislation on the subject (including the Framework Convention, EU anti-discrimination legislation and case law, and domestic juris-prudence). In *Muñoz Díaz*, the Court took the view that 'the collective beliefs of a community that is well-defined culturally cannot be ignored'.[76] In particular, it noted that 'under the Framework Convention for the Protection of National Minorities...the States Parties to the Convention are required to take due account of the specific conditions of persons belonging to national minorities'.[77] While the finding of a breach of Article 14 in conjunction with Article 1 of Protocol 1 was based on a contextual assessment of the case, it did implicitly support the dissent in the Spanish Constitutional Court arguing for a positive reading of the Constitution in light of the Framework Convention.

The implications of this emerging connection between the Strasbourg jurispru-dence and the international (at least European) law system of minority protection are fluid and potentially open-ended. In one sense, the Court has broadly recog-nized the systemic unity of international law by emphasizing that the ECHR does not stand in a vacuum and thus needs to be interpreted in light of the general legal framework of which that treaty is a component. The rationale for this approach mainly lies in striking a balance between the values protected by the ECHR and more traditional state values rooted in classical areas of general international law such as state immunity.[78] But, in another more familiar sense, one can argue that the widely accepted concept of the ECHR as a 'living instrument' equally works

---

[74] ECHR (2001) App No 27238/95, judgment of 18 January 2001, para 93.

[75] ECHR (2004) App No 44158/98, judgment of 17 February 2004, para 93.

[76] ECHR (2009) App No 49151/07, judgment of 8 December 2009, para 59.

[77] ECHR (2009) App No 49151/07, judgment of 8 December 2009, para 64.

[78] Voyiakis, 'Access to Court v State Immunity', 52 *ICLQ* (2003) 297. For a vivid illustration of the tension in this area, see the International Court of Justice's decision in *Jurisdictional Immunities of the State (Germany v Italy: Greece Intervening)*, ICJ Reports (2012), judgment of 3 February 2012 (on the key issue of reparation for gross human rights abuses, see the dissenting opinions of Judges Yusuf, Cançado Trindade, and Gaja).

for a more integrated view of the system to the extent that it requires consideration of international (and domestic) practice as a way of informing—wholly or partially—the Court's dynamic or evolutionary readings of Convention rights. As I will argue below, the Vienna Convention on the Law of Treaties (Article 31) and jurisprudential practice, including recent regional litigation, would appear to buttress, or even actively promote this general view of human rights treaty interpretation.[79]

The jurisprudence mentioned above should be seen as part of a gradual implicit acknowledgment of the inevitable intrusion of international standards on minority groups into the Court's interpretive function. The anxiety reflected in *Chapman* about Strasbourg's 'strictly supervisory role' and the vagueness of the Framework Convention, has not prevented the Court and/or individual judges from openly engaging with relevant external instruments in later case law (and indeed, in that same case and the earlier *Sidiropoulos* as well). This line may also prove useful to reinforce parallel moves at the domestic level regarding the use of the Framework Convention by constitutional courts as an aid to interpretation and source of internal obligation.[80] From the perspective of international law, the Court will increasingly be drawn into discussions about minority groups in their various dimensions. Against the background of clashes between human rights and state concerns in other areas of ECHR jurisprudence, the notion that the Convention cannot be interpreted in an international legal vacuum does not seem to rule out, *mutatis mutandis*, the downplaying of minority group considerations, particularly where reinforced by a generous understanding of the state's margin of appreciation in areas traditionally perceived as falling within the scope of domestic jurisdiction. On the other hand, the dynamic reading of the ECHR as the most genuine hallmark of that jurisprudence calls for a more consistent interaction with relevant standards and practices as pertinent group issues arise. The reach of this systemic approach is difficult to foresee, being largely a function of how the Court views its interpretive role and the relationship with its state constituencies. As in earlier cases unrelated to minority issues, it might in principle draw on a considerable range of sources including treaties which have not been widely ratified, such as the European Charter for Regional and Minority Languages, Protocol 12 (aside from cases directly construed around this text) or general recommendations, to support proactive interpretations of the ECHR. While there is evidence to suggest that progressive interpretations of human rights treaties informed by external instruments may be based on minimum standards clauses linked to state consent (one of which can be found in Article 53 ECHR), systemic readings (including the ones supported by the Court itself) generally rest on wider views of human rights developments irrespective of narrowly construed state consent.[81] Recent cases involving indigenous groups may well point in the same direction as they expose regional and global developments in the field, including Inter-American

---

[79] For a discussion of non-European human rights case law, see Pentassuglia (2011).
[80] See note 62.    [81] Pentassuglia (2011) 180–2. See also Letsas (2004).

jurisprudence and UN practice.[82] As noted, the Court seems in the main to prefer proportionality reviews to findings based on specific (or clearly worded) positive obligations, which in turn suggests an incrementally constructive yet cautious use of external human rights instruments and practice. In *Grosaru*, for example, the 1999 Lund Recommendations on the Effective Participation of National Minorities in Public Life—adopted by independent experts under the auspices of the OSCE—and the work of the European Commission for Democracy Through Law (otherwise known as the Venice Commission) were included among the areas of practice relevant to the case, but the judgment did not elaborate on such practice while noting the importance of special electoral rules for national minorities in Romania. On the other hand, elements of that same practice are reinforced by the Court's findings on freedom of association as a way of upholding evolving understandings of personal autonomy. Also, the participatory elements which are reflected in cases like *Noack* and the Article 8 case law on Roma groups echo increasingly strong participatory standards arising out of the jurisprudence of the UN Human Rights Committee under Article 27 ICCPR.[83] The interpretation of the ECHR ultimately depends on evolving conceptions of the state's margin of appreciation and inevitably variable degrees of involvement with the general corpus of hard and soft international (human rights) law under particular circumstances.

## B. Inter-American Court

The Inter-American body of case law has relied on a range of specialized human rights standards to inform the interpretation of the Inter-American instruments. Of special relevance to this 'external' approach is Article 29(b) ACHR which provides that no provision thereof may be interpreted as 'restricting the enjoyment or exercise of any right or freedom recognized by virtue of the laws of any State Party or by virtue of another convention to which one of the said states is a party'. The Court has consistently interpreted this clause as enabling it to read the ACHR in light of standards upheld by the party outside the framework of the treaty, whether in the form of domestic law or international conventions binding on it. On this reading, the San José judges have emphasized the respondent state's consent to the relevant norms, be they the Constitution of Nicaragua in *Awas Tigni*, ILO Convention 169 and its respective domestic legislation in *Yakye Axa* and *Sarayaku*, or the UN Covenants in *Saramaka*.[84]

---

[82] *The Chagos Islanders v United Kingdom*, ECHR (2012) App No 35622/04, admissibility decision of 11 December 2012. The interveners had previously argued that indigenous rights should inform the Court's approach to the case; *Handölsdalen Sami Village and Others v Sweden*, ECHR (2010) App No 39013/04, judgment of 30 March 2010, partially dissenting opinion of Judge Ziemele.

[83] For the strongest statement on participatory rights so far, see HRC, *Angela Poma Poma v Peru*, UN Doc CCPR/C/95/D/1457/2006, 27 March 2009.

[84] *Mayagna (Sumo) Awas Tingni Community v Nicaragua*, IACtHR (2001) Series C, No 79, judgment of 31 August 2001, paras 152–3; *Yakye Axa Indigenous Community v Paraguay*, IACtHR (2005) Series C, No 125, judgment of 17 June 2005, para 138; *The Saramaka People v Suriname*, IACtHR (2007) Series C, No 172, judgment of 28 November 2007, paras 92, 131; *The Kichwa Indigenous People of Sarayaku v Ecuador*, IACtHR (2012), Series C, No 245, judgment of 27 June 2012. For a similar approach by the IACmHR, see *Mary and Carrie Dann v United States*, Report No 75/02,

One might argue that this type of clause only deals with the 'negative' side of the equation, namely that of disallowing the use of the treaty as a pretext for cutting down higher levels of protection being provided outside of that treaty.[85] Also, while domestic property law is not a bar to the protection of indigenous property under the Inter-American system, divergent interpretations of the same provision could potentially result from different combinations of external instruments that apply to the state against which a complaint has been brought.

However, irrespective of Article 29(b) ACHR, the Inter-American Court and Commission have generally employed a dynamic, evolutionary method of interpretation on the basis of a variety of international law texts and, where available, domestic law as well. Indeed, it is a comprehensive (re)assessment of the Inter-American instruments that has proved essential to valuing indigenous issues within their own purview. By regarding the ACHR as having an 'autonomous meaning' (compared to domestic law) and being a 'living instrument' (ie in accordance with present-day conditions and the wider legal system), the Court in *Awas Tigni* essentially reaffirmed (and adjusted) the teleological line generally endorsed by the European Court when interpreting the ECHR.[86] Also, in its Advisory Opinion on *The Right to Information on Consular Assistance within the Framework of the Guarantees of Due Process*, it elaborated upon the International Court of Justice's jurisprudence in *South West Africa (Second Phase)* by holding that 'the interpretation of a treaty must take into account not only the agreements and instruments related to the treaty...but also the system of which it is part'.[87] The *Yakye Axa* decision confirmed the understanding of the interpretive context embraced by the Court in that advisory opinion by valuing the '*corpus iuris* of international human rights law' as the relevant framework for interpretation.[88]

The Inter-American Commission has embraced this line to justify reliance on international instruments as indicators of emerging or existing consensus rather than narrowly defined state consent. In *Mary and Carrie Dann v United States*,[89] the respondent argued that the ACHR, the Draft American Declaration on the Rights of Indigenous Peoples, and ILO Convention 169, were all irrelevant to the case because the United States was not a party to the first and third instruments, and the second one was merely 'soft law'. A similar point was made by Ecuador in *The Kichwa Peoples of the Sarayaku Community and its Members v Ecuador*,[90] in relation

---

Case 11.1140, 27 December 2002, paras 124, 131; *Maya Indigenous Communities of the Toledo District v Belize*, Report No 96/03, Case 12.053, 24 October 2003, paras 85, 111–19.

[85] For discussion in a different setting, see Liisberg, 'Does the EU Charter of Fundamental Rights Threaten the Supremacy of Community Law? Article 53 of the Charter: a fountain of law or just an inkblot?' Harvard Jean Monnet Working Papers 4/01 (2001).

[86] *Loizidou v Turkey (Preliminary Objections)*, ECHR (1995) 20 EHRR (1995) 99, 71. See generally Mowbray, 'The Creativity of the European Court of Human Rights' 5 *Human Rts L Rev* (2005) 57.

[87] OC-16/99, IACtHR (1999) Series A, No 16, para 113. See also *Legal Consequences for States of the Continued Presence of South Africa in Namibia (South West Africa) notwithstanding Security Council Resolution 276 (1970)*, ICJ Reports (1971), 16 at 31.

[88] IACtHR (2005) Series C, No 125, judgment of 17 June 2005, paras 126–8.

[89] Report No 75/02, Case 11.1140, 27 December 2002.

[90] Report No 64/04, Petition 167/03, Admissibility, 13 October 2004.

to ILO Convention 169. In both cases, the Commission dismissed the claim by linking the American Declaration on the Rights and Duties of Man (ADRDM) to the wider (treaty and customary law based) canon of international indigenous rights in general, and indigenous land rights in particular. The Court's approach to 'external' standards has been slightly more cautious in that the integration of indigenous instruments or general human rights such as the civil and political as well as socioeconomic rights set out in the UN Covenants has been largely premised on the consent of the state to be bound by the relevant treaty, as I illustrated earlier, or that state's adherence to the soft law instrument in question (as was the case in *Saramaka* with regards to the 2007 Declaration on the Rights of Indigenous Peoples—hereinafter 'DRIP'). In a broadly similar vein, the implicit integration of human rights considerations into the interpretation of BITs through the element of 'public purpose' in the context of possible expropriations of foreign investment-related property has been considered against the state's existing obligations under international human rights law, particularly the ACHR.[91] However, this seemingly more prudent line has not always been applied to all aspects of the case. In *Saramaka*, notions of economic self-determination and identity, natural resources as part of (indigenous) property and the additional requirements of consultation or consent, benefit-sharing and environmental and social impact assessment for lawful restrictions on the (indigenous) right to property, are crucially borrowed from multiple jurisdictions or otherwise authoritative sources, thereby making the treaty a proxy for cross-fertilization processes.[92] Moreover, the Court has not established consent to the relevant 'external' instrument in other types of cases.[93]

In sum, the broad reading of indigenous issues within the Inter-American system rests on a cross-fertilization interpretive process, whereby the scope of relevant clauses are being expanded on the basis of the wider framework of international hard and soft law regarding indigenous rights.[94] In this sense, the substantive and procedural aspects of Article 21 and Article 4 ACHR, as I described them earlier, have come to embrace elements that elaborate and expand on the jurisprudence of other bodies.

This line comes very close to the one reflected in Article 31(3)(c) of the Vienna Convention on the Law of Treaties (VCLT),[95] in the sense of allowing the

---

[91] *Sawhoyamaxa Indigenous Community v Paraguay*, IACtHR (2006) Series C, No 146, judgment of 29 March 2006, para 140.

[92] IACtHR (2007) Series C, No 172, judgment of 28 November 2007, paras 92–6, 103, 118–23, 128–40. On benefit-sharing, further input is likely to derive from the (not yet in force) Nagoya Protocol on Access to Genetic Resources and the Fair and Equitable Sharing of Benefits Arising from their Utilization to the Convention on Biological Diversity, adopted in October 2010 (implementing inter alia Art 8(j) of the Convention), available at <http://www.cbd.int/abs/> (accessed 29 June 2013).

[93] See eg Lixinski, 'Treaty Interpretation by the Inter-American Court of Human Rights: Expansionism at the Service of the Unity of International Law', 21 *EJIL* (2010) 585.

[94] As for the IACmHR, see *Mary and Carrie Dann v United States*, Report No 75/02, Case 11.1140, 27 December 2002, paras 124, 131; *Maya Indigenous Communities of the Toledo District v Belize*, Report No 96/03, Case 12.053, 24 October 2003, paras 85, 111–19; *Garifuna Community of Cayos Cochinos and its Members v Honduras*, Report No 39/07, Petition 1118-03, Admissibility, 24 July 2007, para 49.

[95] Article 31(3)(c) VCLT refers to 'any relevant rules of international law applicable in the relations between the parties'. For discussion, see Simma, 'Universality of International Law from the

integration of 'external' standards by way of interpretation which may or may not be strictly tied up with the individual consent of the state party as opposed to more general references to international law as it has evolved in the spirit of the evolutionary approach pioneered in the field of human rights by the Strasbourg Court. If evolutionary interpretation by definition accords with wider legal developments rather than the judges' own preferences and values or specific national practices, then the positive reading of Article 29(b) ACHR upheld by the Court, whatever the uncertainties that may surround it, might be said to reinforce this systemic approach and thus its 'neutrality', for more specific, essentially evidential purposes linked to the case at hand. Given the strong political sensitivities associated with indigenous issues, especially in matters of land and natural resources, the Court's insistence on relevant 'higher' standards upheld by the respondent state in a separate setting further supports the interpretation in question so as to make it acceptable as much as possible from within that state's legal practice.

The ever greater use of international standards as a way of reinforcing the Court's expansive approach to the ACHR has at least three elements to it which are worth noting. On the one hand, reliance on Article 29(b) and (directly or indirectly) the VCLT to make the case for a dynamic reading of the ACHR as part of a wider set of relevant international instruments connects the treaty to the body—or *corpus iuris*, in the Court's words—of general international law. In other words, it shows the intention of the Court not to challenge the fundamental unity of international law, but rather to acknowledge it in ways that can only enrich the scope of the human rights regime in question.[96] This, in turn, aims to functionally adjust the treaty as a 'living instrument' by locating it within a wider set of developments—or 'subsequent practice' ex Article 31(3)(b) VCLT—in the relevant field. At the same time, two important variations on this theme stand out—one internal to the area of indigenous rights, the other of a more structural nature. The first variation turns on the expansive reading of the ACHR. A closer look at the pertinent framework of international human rights law suggests that this reading has consisted not just of integrating the content of 'external' standards 'lock, stock, and barrel', as it were, but has involved a considerable degree of creative judicial elaboration which has deepened or clarified points of substance or procedure still fraught with uncertainty or ambiguity at the level of international instruments, especially in the context of indigenous land rights. Indeed, crucial issues including demarcation, restitution of ancestral lands, natural resources, or benefit-sharing have arguably benefited from the Court's dynamic interpretation of the ACHR in such a way as to establish, as a matter of principle, the sort of solid legal benchmarks that specialized standards seem unable to provide aside from basic (not infrequently vague) starting points. As I have sought to demonstrate elsewhere,[97]

---

Perspective of a Practitioner', 20 *EJIL* (2009) 265 at 276–7; Christoffersen, 'Impact on General Principles of Treaty Interpretation', in M.T. Kamminga and M. Scheinin (eds), *The Impact of Human Rights Law on General International Law* (2009) 37 at 47–50. For a clearer (re)statement of the Inter-American Court's position, see recently *The Kichwa Indigenous People of Sarayaku v Ecuador*, IACtHR (2012) Series C, No 245, judgment of 27 June 2012, paras 161, 216, 231.

[96]  See eg Lixinski (2010).        [97]  Pentassuglia (2011).

while all of the above cases use or refer to ILO and UN instruments, all of them some-what transcend them in ways that deepen the role of international human rights law relative to indigenous communities. From a practical standpoint, specialized instruments on indigenous land rights are not necessarily at the forefront of the international norm advancement process.[98]

The other important variation concerns the way in which the Court sees the very relationship between the ACHR and human rights law more generally, and international law as a whole. As hinted at earlier, the Court has explained that the implementation of obligations deriving from commercial treaties such as BITs may not provide a justification for a failure to comply with the ACHR (and human rights obligations generally). In *Sawhoyamaxa*, it held that Peru could not invoke a BIT with Germany in order to free itself from obligations relating to the affected community. As well as suggesting ways of reconciling undertakings under foreign investment treaties and human rights obligations from within the language of the BIT in question, the Court more fundamentally argued that a multilateral treaty on human rights 'stands in a class of its own', generating rights for 'individual human beings' and the functioning of which is not dependent on state reciprocity.[99] While this view does not project human rights law as a self-contained regime (at least in the sense of it being disconnected from general international law), it does advance the view that human rights law should be seen as *lex specialis* compared to international law with no human rights dimensions. Unsurprisingly, the specific hierarchical argument—that is, that human rights treaties are hierarchically superior to other treaties such as commercial agreements—has proved controversial, not least because, in the event of a 'pure' conflict of treaty obligations, the systemic interpretation of international law could equally be said to limit, not to expand, the reach of human rights duties, and, conversely, the body of international human rights clearly does not qualify *en bloc* as *ius cogens*.[100] In

---

[98] Current non-adjudicatory practice illustrates this further. In Observations on the situation of the Charco la Pava community and other communities affected by the Chan 75 hydroelectric project in Panama, the UN Special Rapporteur on the situation of human rights and fundamental freedoms of indigenous people considered specialized instruments on indigenous land rights applicable to Panama, including ILO Convention 107 (the only ILO convention that has been ratified by Panama) and the DRIP (UN Doc A/HRC/12/34/Add.5, 7 September 2009). While they provided significant background to the discussion, central aspects of recommended protection in accordance with international law, were all drawn from the Inter-American jurisprudence in its own right. Unsurprisingly, the case of the Ngöbe communities in Panama has been put to the Inter-American bodies: see eg *Four Ngöbe Indigenous Communities and their Members*, Order of the Inter-American Court of Human Rights, 28 May 2010; and note 127 below.

[99] *Sawhoyamaxa Indigenous Community v Paraguay*, IACtHR (2006) Series C, No 146, judgment of 29 March 2006, para 140. This proposition was endorsed by the African Commission in *Centre for Minority Rights Development (Kenya) and Minority Rights Group International on behalf of Endorois Welfare Council v Kenya*, Comm No 276/2003 (2009), para 235, fn 130.

[100] For discussion, see eg Nikken, 'Balancing of Human Rights and Investment Law in the Inter-American System of Human Rights', in Dupuy, Francioni, and Petersmann (eds), *Human Rights in International Investment Law and Arbitration* (2009) 246 at 265–70. In some cases, the very recognition of a human rights dimension to a BIT-related dispute may prove problematic: see eg *Chevron Corpn & Texaco Petroleum Co v Republic of Ecuador*, Permanent Court of Arbitration, Case No 2009-23, at <http://www.pca-cpa.org/showpage.asp?pag_id=1408> (accessed 29 June 2013).

fact, the search for an overarching rationale for addressing potentially competing treaty obligations tends to shift from the legal to the policy or ethical dimension of conflict, interpretive techniques aiming to read human rights standards into BITs *ex post facto* (as was implicitly argued in *Sawhoyamaxa*), or even preemptive strategies which can facilitate their explicit coordination at the time of drafting the investment treaty.[101] But, leaving that particular argument aside, it can hardly be implausible of the Court—as the body empowered to interpret and apply the ACHR—to expect states which are party to it to comply with their treaty obligations irrespective of obligations they may have undertaken in other areas. The prioritization of human rights obligations, including those affecting indigenous communities, arguably appears to be a reasonable justification for limiting state discretion under the human rights treaty in question and thus informing the judicial body's own judgment of proportionality.

## C. Comparative reflections

This analysis shows that both Courts recognize or assume the unity of the international legal order in that both of them seek to relate the specifics of cases to wider developments in the field and/or show awareness of relevant principles of international law more generally. However, the impact of 'external' instruments on the way in which they frame issues regarding minority groups does vary. While the Strasbourg Court has been traditionally assertive in terms of how to read the ECHR over time,[102] it was not until recently that it began to engage with those issues and, even more so, with specialized instruments adopted within the Council of Europe or other international organizations. The degree to which the European Court will be prepared to both use other international instruments to inform the reading of the ECHR and have that reading prevail over 'statist' views normally built around the notion of margin of appreciation and/or classic 'sovereignty-based' rules of international law, remains to be seen.

By contrast, the Inter-American Court's understanding of the ACHR has expanded on the Strasbourg general model of human rights interpretation by adapting the instrument to changing social and cultural circumstances and grounding its own readings of rights in the wider context of hard and soft law instruments pertaining to indigenous communities, ie the *corpus* of international human rights law. It was in 2001, at a time when the European Court delivered its first more progressive

---

[101] Simma, 'Foreign Investment Arbitration: A Place for Human Rights?', 60 *ICLQ* (2011) 573. For a partial acknowledgment of this line in the context of a foreign investment dispute involving indigenous issues, see the NAFTA Award in *Grand River Enterprises Six Nations Ltd et al v United States of America*, 12 January 2011, at <http://www.state.gov/documents/organization/156820.pdf> (accessed 29 June 2013), sections IV, VIII. At the same time, it has been convincingly argued that the impact of commercial agreements on human rights obligations raises important issues regarding the responsibility of the *home* state's corporate nationals and their subsidiaries acting extraterritorially: McCorquodale and Simons, 'Responsibility Beyond Borders: State Responsibility for Extraterritorial Violations by Corporations of International Human Rights Law', 70 *Modern Law Review* (2007) 598 at 621–3.
[102] See eg Letsas (2004).

yet cautious decision on minorities in *Chapman*, that the Inter-American Court delivered its groundbreaking judgment in *Awas Tigni*. The multidimensional line of the Inter-American Court is reflected in the Inter-American Commission's juris-prudence and was recently echoed in the jurisprudence of the African Commission on Human and Peoples' Rights in the *Endorois* case. More than that, the 'systemic approach' based on a presumption of coherence with existing international law ex Article 31(3)(c) VCLT has gained ground in discourses of treaty interpretation, as shown in the 2003 *Oil Platforms* case before the International Court of Justice and the efforts to integrate human rights standards and practice into foreign invest-ment treaties.[103] The reach of 'external' standards and practice may prove more or less problematic depending on the case, but the Inter-American Court's broad reading of indigenous issues based on both domestic and international undertak-ings under Article 29(b) ACHR appears largely to adapt the logic of the VCLT in a narrow sense. In this respect, the European Court appears to be lagging behind in terms of consolidating a systemic view of the ECHR that rests on a firm legal methodology geared towards mainstreaming minority group issues into the treaty.

Functional readings based on the *effet utile* and similar doctrines support effect-ive minority group-friendly interpretation of (regional) human rights treaties while at the same time creating a space for judicial cross-fertilization on treaty interpreta-tion. Indeed, mainstreaming elements of minority group protection into human rights jurisprudence can be supported by interjudicial dialogue (eg on the extent of evolutionary treaty interpretations in the field) and broad appreciation of jurispru-dential developments across global, regional, and domestic lines. The asymmetry in domestic laws and practices on ethno-cultural minorities in Europe is as real as the fact that most European states are bound by or have adhered to key global and regional instruments, just as most states of the Inter-American system are bound by ILO Convention 169 and have adhered to the DRIP—both of which have a prominent place in the Inter-American Court's 'systemic' jurisprudence on indigenous rights. Moreover, seen retrospectively, the most progressive traits of the European Court's case law have hardly had any obvious connection with specific or uniform domestic practices across Europe, although implicit or explicit consensus amongst European states is most likely to impact on the Court's interpretation of ECHR rights.

Having said that, a word of caution is in order. Judicial practice shows that 'external' standards on minority groups are not necessarily, or not always, at the heart of the interpretive process. For one thing, the indigenous rights jurispru-dence shows that it may well be domestic legislation (including legislation incor-porating ratified international conventions) or otherwise state consent that opens up interpretive possibilities which are only subsequently reinforced by a systemic assessment of international human rights instruments as such. More crucially, those instruments, particularly specialized ones, generally turn out to be more of

---

[103] Simma and Kill, 'Harmonizing Investment Protection and International Human Rights: First Steps Towards a Methodology', in C. Binder et al, International Investment Law for the 21st Century: Essays in Honour of Christoph Schreuer (Oxford University Press, 2009) 678; Simma (2011). *Oil Platforms (Islamic Republic of Iran v United States of America)*, ICJ Reports (2003) 161.

an authoritative source of inspiration than a source of predefined rules. To put it differently: the systemic approach still requires *judicial elaboration* as both the Inter-American and European Courts deal with the complexities of minority protection and the uncertainties left by specialized instruments themselves. It is the resulting jurisprudence rather than the wider legal context that is most likely to generate responses to particular legal issues.

## 5. The Understanding of Minority Groups: Treaty Implications and Beyond

### A. European Court

The Court will be reluctant to recognize self-identification as the only criterion for supporting the international or domestic legal existence of a minority group. In *Ciubotaru v Moldova*,[104] it upheld the argument that a claimed ethnicity cannot be based on purely subjective grounds. In *Gorzelik*, it controversially accepted the government's position that—at least in the circumstances of the case involving potential electoral benefits for the applicant association—the Silesians were not entitled to self-define themselves as a national minority independently of decisions by Polish authorities. This point is in effect linked to a more general thinking about the role of the Court in matters of group recognition.

*Gorzelik* indicated that there is no obligation under international law to adopt a particular concept of 'national minority' or 'a procedure for the official recognition of minority groups'.[105] The Polish government was thus not at fault in failing to adopt either of them. This is arguably correct to the extent that international law does not preclude variations on the legal understanding of the concept or on the modalities of, or approach to group recognition within domestic systems. On one reading, *Gorzelik* might be seen as ultimately surrendering the task of minority group recognition to domestic practices, with no role left for international law as such. It would be for states to determine the very criteria for minority group status, not just to determine if those criteria (as supplied by international law) are met. The Court—and indeed any other international human rights adjudicatory body—would then be a somewhat silent spectator of state policies and preferences, especially when it comes to allocating benefits resulting from positive measures.

On a different reading, *Gorzelik* does not warrant such a view, as the case recognizes neither self-identification nor domestic practices as the *exclusive* sources to determine minority group status for international legal purposes. The lack of an obligation to adopt internal definitions and mechanisms does not in itself affect the more general question of the impact of human rights standards on group status issues. The lack of an internal procedure to seek legal recognition can still be considered on the basis that international law need not be based on domestic

---

[104] ECHR (2010) App No 27138/04, judgment of 27 April 2010.
[105] ECHR (2004) App No 44158/98, judgment of 17 February 2004, para 68.

mechanisms, and the lack of a particular concept of 'national minority' (in the *Gorzelik* scenario) does not tell us whether or not the position of the state is generally compatible with international law.[106] Indeed, the common theme reflected in human rights jurisprudence has always been that the existence of the group cannot be determined by the state alone other than in the sense of confirming—or possibly augmenting—the scope of protection already upheld at the international level on factual grounds.[107] The Court did shy away from definitional matters in light of the approach of several specialized human rights instruments. But it still reserved for itself a degree of control over the state's margin of appreciation under the ECHR, acknowledged a 'commonly shared European view' that minority protection is essential for a democratic society, and found that the power conferred on Polish courts to determine national minority status in the context of the 1993 Elections Act did not amount to 'an unlimited and arbitrary power of appreciation'.[108] I have argued elsewhere that the way in which the Court addressed the case, particularly in relation to the adequacy and reliability of domestic assumptions and court findings against minimal international law parameters on ethno-cultural minorities and the Court's own jurisprudence, was questionable.[109] But this is not to suggest that the Court cannot perform a robust supervisory role. For one thing, this case law—however unconvincing in its practical output—implicitly retains the element of protection against abuse as a matter of principle. In future cases, the Court would do well to link this element to more assertive proportionality reviews of the kind it has undertaken in other cases in connection with the extent of state discretion and the implications of state measures on the principle of equality under Article 14.[110] This is likely to require greater attention to the autonomous import of international law in matters of recognition. On the other hand, the Strasbourg jurisprudence as it exists or is being developed has afforded protection of minority groups or allowed consideration of relevant group matters regardless of definitional controversies.

---

[106] For example, a formally stated broad concept would ordinarily not run counter to international law since there is no obligation to adopt a narrower definition for domestic purposes; conversely, a highly restrictive or selective one which is implicitly assumed in public policy would be in breach of international law to the extent that it fails to cover traditional groups which would ordinarily be regarded as stable communities qualifying for minority protection. The gist of the latter line has been endorsed by the Advisory Committee operating under the Framework Convention for the Protection of National Minorities, although what constitutes an 'arbitrary distinction' varies depending on the approach to minority groups generally. For a discussion in the context of indigenous communities, see Macklem, 'Indigenous Recognition in International Law: Theoretical Observations', 30 *Michigan Journal of International Law* (2008–09) 177.

[107] See eg HRC, *General Comment 23: The rights of minorities (Article 27)*, UN Doc CCPR/C/21/Rev.1/Add.5, 8 April 1994, para 5.2. The special prominence of self-identification in relation to indigenous communities (Art 1(2) ILO Convention 169; Art 33 DRIP) further reinforces this notion. See generally Pentassuglia, *Minorities in International Law: An Introductory Study* (2002) 72–4; and further comments in section B.

[108] ECHR (2004) App No 44158/98, judgment of 17 February 2004, paras 67, 68, 70.

[109] Pentassuglia (2009) 220–1.

[110] It has been generally accepted that measures going beyond the requirements of the ECHR are still subject to the Court's review under Art 14 as long as the relevant subject-matter falls within the scope of the Convention.

The Court has recognized 'ethnic' identity as falling within the scope of the ECHR, requiring states to enable applicants to prove their claimed ethnicity; it has accepted Roma claims to a particular way of life and non-discrimination rights from an individual and collective point of view; it has engaged with Sami rights; it has indirectly supported traditional minorities such as Turkish Kurds or German Sorbians; it has shown awareness of European historical factors involving national minorities, and even reviewed issues of inter-group equality or accommodation; it has considered the extent to which cultural differences or other circumstances typically associated with migrants' condition or certain religious groups in Europe merit protection (in addition to issues of physical integrity such as expulsion of or refusal to entry to asylum seekers).[111]

## B. Inter-American Court

In *Moiwana Village v Suriname* and *Saramaka*, the Inter-American Court noted an 'all-encompassing relationship' between the Maroon groups in question and their land. Both groups are amongst the descendents of African slaves who were forcibly taken to Suriname during the colonization period in the seventeenth century. In *Saramaka*, the state disputed whether the Maroon group concerned could be regarded as a tribal community under international human rights law. Rejecting this assertion, the Court found that the Saramaka people had a distinctive identity associated with their ancestral land tenure system and its attendant social, cultural, and economic characteristics. It concluded that, despite the fact that it was not indigenous to the region, the group fell within the purview of the Court's jurisprudence regarding indigenous peoples' rights to property because of the obvious commonalities of the Saramakas and indigenous communities in the narrow sense of 'first inhabitants'. In practice, the Court relied upon expert evidence to articulate the legal existence of the Saramaka people as a group entitled to protection within the context of Article 21 ACHR and related provisions. The point was further reinforced by the notion that the existence of individual members of the Saramaka people who lived outside the traditional territory and did not follow Saramaka traditions and laws could not in itself affect the distinctiveness of the Saramakas as a group for the purposes of the ACHR.

As in other cases such as *Sawhoyamaxa*, land serves as the principal marker of the group's factual existence and legal significance. It combines with a broad and contextual assessment of multiple manifestations of identity. However, what distinguishes these cases from others is that the Court entertains—and upholds—the claim that the communities should be regarded as 'tribal' peoples, although it offers no specific elaboration on either Article 1 ILO Convention 169[112] or other

---

[111] See eg *Leyla Sahin v Turkey*, ECHR (2005) App No 44774/98, judgment of 10 November 2005; Cumper, 'Europe, Islam and Democracy—Balancing Religious and Secular Values under the European Convention on Human Rights', 3 *European Yearbook of Minority Issues* (2003–04) 163; *Thlimmenos v Greece*, ECHR (2000) App No 34369/97, judgment of 6 April 2000; *Turan Cakir v Belgium*, ECHR (2009) App No 44256/06, judgment of 10 March 2009 (in French).

[112] The Convention provides a general understanding of 'tribal' groups in Art 1.1(a).

texts to support a genuinely distinctive international law category. In fact, the proposed understanding in such cases is based on factual evidence and then transposed into the area of indigenous rights. I would submit that the fundamental rationale for this line is effectively to expand the very concept of 'indigeneity', at least from the perspective of the Inter-American system. *Moiwana* and *Saramaka* have broadly interpreted that concept to include non-native and land-dependent traditional communities including Afro-descendants who are linked to patterns of abuse and exploitation dating back to European colonization.

Decided in 2005 and 2007 respectively, both cases seem to echo an emerging understanding of indigenous communities in Africa which had been first signalled by the African Commission on Human and Peoples' Rights' Working Group on Indigenous Populations/Communities (AWGIPC) in a landmark report from 2003. In this report, the AWGIPC linked some 'peoples' rights' under the 1981 African Charter on Human and Peoples' Rights—particularly the right to existence and self-determination (Article 20), the right to natural resources (Article 21), and the right to development (Article 22)—to an expansive conception of African indigenousness which is not linked to 'prior occupancy' of traditional communal lands and resources.[113] By relying on the criteria of self-identification, territorial connection, cultural distinctiveness, and exclusion (broadly understood), in line with some definitional attempts at the international level, the African Commission has generally endorsed the post-colonial reading of the AWGIPC. Indeed, it specifically built upon it in its 2007 Advisory Opinion on *The United Nations Declaration on the Rights of Indigenous Peoples*[114] and the recent landmark decision in the *Endorois* case against Kenya. In this case, they recognized the pastoralist community in question as an indigenous community for the purposes of the African Charter, based on a connection with traditional lands and associated long-standing cultural practices, 'beyond the "narrow/aboriginal/pre-Colombian" understanding of indigenous peoples'.[115]

This jurisprudence impacts on the recognition of indigenous groups in ways that deepen the role of international human rights law in matters of group status. For one thing, the lack of specific definitions in the ACHR and ADRDM (and African Charter as well) facilitates rather than constrains dynamic and functional readings (in the above-mentioned sense) of general human rights provisions. At the same time they sow the seeds of a wider reconsideration of the role of international law in recognizing the groups which are entitled to protection. On one level, strict definitions are widely regarded as unnecessary, yet a flexible international legal

[113] Report of the African Commission's Working Group of Experts on Indigenous Populations/ Communities, submitted in accordance with the Resolution on the Rights of Indigenous Populations/ Communities in Africa, IWAGIA (Copenhagen) and ACHPR (Banjul) (2005), Section 4.2. More broadly, this report articulates in the context of indigenous rights a general reassessment of 'peoples' rights' under the African Charter to include entitlements for sub-national groups, Report etc (2005), Ch III; see also *Kevin Mgwanga Gunme et al. Cameroon*, Comm No 266/2003 (2009).

[114] Resolution on the United Nations Declaration on the Rights of Indigenous Peoples, ACHPR/ Res 121 (XXXXII) 07, 28 November 2007, paras 9–13.

[115] *Centre for Minority Rights Development (Kenya) and Minority Rights Group International on behalf of Endorois Welfare Council v Kenya*, Comm No 276/2003 (2009), para 159.

concept of 'indigenous peoples' is fast gaining ground.[116] However, rooted as it is in international law as such, this concept does not surrender the task of identifying the groups to state legislation or purely (not infrequently unfavourable) domestic practices, and neither does it surrender it to the group through a notion of self-identification that does away with socio-historical evidence appropriate to the case.[117] Rather, the flexible view reflected in the Inter-American and African case law arguably repositions—and effectively reaffirms—international human rights law in the field in ways that allow for more context sensitive and practical responses which still account for distinctive protective rationales for the groups concerned.

In another sense, the reconceptualization of indigeneity driven by an implicitly revisited understanding of the connection between specific historical and territorial circumstances and structural patterns of group non-dominance, could possibly lead to a more general recalibration of the conceptual and legal relationship between 'indigenous peoples' and 'national minorities' (in the sense of traditional groups) as international law categories.[118] As the African Commission shies away from rigid distinctions between 'indigenous peoples' and ethno-cultural 'minorities' under the African Charter, traditional *non*-autochthonous communities are being brought within the indigenous fold by the Inter-American Court and Commission despite the initial exclusive focus on 'New World' indigenous communities in general international law. One can assume that the Inter-American approach to Afro-descendants reflects *au fond* functional protections associated with land, participation and/or culture rather than dogmatic classifications of the type still envisaged by international human rights instruments.

The UN Human Rights Committee (HRC) may well be pointing in the same direction when articulating the substance of Article 27 ICCPR. In *Ángela Poma Poma v Peru*, involving members of the Aymara community in Peru, the HRC noted that, where state measures 'substantially compromise or interfere with the culturally significant economic activities of a minority or indigenous community', group participation must be seen as a central element of the decision-making process—it requires not 'mere' consultation, but 'the free, prior and informed consent of the members of the community'.[119] Aside from the details of the case, the HRC's broad reference to a 'minority or indigenous community' seems to suggest that certain degrees of group participation may well apply to *all* Article 27 traditional

---

[116] One of the first authors arguing for a flexible concept was Kingsbury, ' "Indigenous Peoples" in International Law: A Constructivist Approach to the Controversy', 92 *American Journal of Int'l Law* (1998) 414; for a critique of this conceptual expansion within the African context, see F.M. Ndahinda, *Indigenousness in Africa: A Contested Legal Framework for Empowerment of 'Marginalized' Communities* (2011).

[117] For concerns relating to an unbounded approach to 'indigenous peoples' as a legal concept, see Macklem (2008–09); domestic policy and legislation in Africa frequently involve issues of group recognition and land security against the backdrop of restrictive internal requirements: see eg ILO/ ACHPR, Overview Report of the Research Project by the International Labour Organization and the African Commission on Human and Peoples' Rights on the Constitutional and Legislative Protection of the Rights of Indigenous Peoples in 24 African Countries (2009), paras 117–21.

[118] See eg Kymlicka, *Multicultural Odysseeys: Navigating the New International Politics of Diversity* (2007), 273–91.

[119] UN Doc CCPR/C/95/D/1457/2006, 27 March 2009, para 7.6.

minorities, not just 'indigenous peoples' in the original sense of first inhabitants of a particular land.

In short, the emerging decoupling of territory from narrowly construed priority in time (ie the initially unique requirement for indigenous status) raises the question of whether there is scope for an overarching view of minority protection that (re)considers the multiple ways in which history and territory—including the legacy of colonialism and later changes in territorial sovereignty, distribution, or configuration—affect the identity and claims of traditional ethno-cultural communities in general.

## C. Comparative reflections

When looking at such a burgeoning case law comprehensively, one might argue that the broader question is not so much the role of the European and Inter-American Courts in theoretically defining minority groups, as the role of these Courts in generating practical protection for minority groups generally. Indeed, with both the Strasbourg and San José judges shying away from rigid definitional constraints and/or the vagaries of domestic recognition, the answer lies less in conceptual nuances on group status and more in understanding what is at stake when it comes to interpreting group issues under the ECHR and ACHR. General human rights treaties apply to all the individuals (and groups) subject to states parties' jurisdiction. They create comprehensive frameworks which allow for flexibility and dynamic judging across systems. Roma rights are being considered under the ECHR independently of the specific status of Roma communities in international law. The same applies to non-citizen ethnic Russians in the Baltic States or the de facto minority of Greek-Cypriots living in Turkish-occupied Northern Cyprus. The approach to racial discrimination under Article 14, too, in principle transcends specific issues of group status while still creating a framework for meaningful protection. The contextual understanding of indigeneity embraced by the Inter-American Court under the ACHR resonates with similar thinking under the African regime.

The opening up of the ECHR and ACHR to an increasing variety of group considerations induced by the very nature of the treaty raises the issue of the degree to which such considerations can and should affect the interpretation and development of international law in the field. A major question is whether this case law, in spite of its real or potential dynamic interpretation, is rendering minority group-related human rights more or less 'generic' because of its inherently general jurisdictional scope. In reality, while international jurisprudence creates openings for multilayered judicial governance, it also requires a proper understanding of the sort of issues or 'projects' that may benefit from judicial interventions.[120] I argue that the contribution of the Inter-American and European Courts in this area, especially the Strasbourg Court's, depends on these Courts' ability to distinguish

---

[120] See eg Letsas (2004) 535.

between cases and/or levels of protection and to recognize or expose broad similarities where appropriate.

International human rights jurisprudence can reflect different degrees of intervention over issues of ethno-cultural justice. It can uphold state neutrality (eg on religious matters) while rejecting a monocultural concept of nation-building and supporting multiple forms of private law autonomy for minority groups.[121] It can endorse cultural diversity and rights based on a survivalist conception of cultural preservation[122] or a universalist idea of cultural identity as inherent in all individuals, including minorities. But a purely universalist account does not easily square with what are normally assessments predicated on contingent features of minority groups. More often than not, the jurisprudential analyses that underpin the recent and past history of minority protection in international law have considered the position of minority groups as a special case rather than the manifestation of generic circumstances of cultural difference.[123] They have typically assumed or elaborated upon territorial and historical patterns as well as views of structural non-dominance involving (directly or indirectly) communities as such. For constitutional purposes, major national courts have distinguished between individual human rights protection and special (targeted) forms of group protection such as language or education rights.[124] The latter are now widely accepted as part of the international human rights framework. Yet one may argue that distributive justice or other pluralist equality-based remedial strategies can provide alternative or concurrent conceptual bases for the protection of those rights in international human rights law (in conjunction with specific minority rights instruments). They do not prejudge the particular outcome of cases but in principle direct the interpreter to normative questions which help her read those cases against distinctive socio-political settings.[125]

In short, general concerns for non-discrimination and cultural identity stand alongside or combine with specific assumptions about history, territory, inequality and/or other structural elements associated with group identity. The fact that the European and Inter-American Courts have engaged in different ways with

---

[121]   This is the line which largely underpins the European Court's case law on freedom of religion and political pluralism, as I described it earlier.

[122]   For a critique of this rationale against the principle of freedom of choice, see Patten, 'Beyond the Dichotomy of Universalism and Difference: Four Responses to Cultural Diversity', in Choudhry (ed), *Constitutional Design for Divided Societies: Integration or Accommodation?* (2008) 91 at 101–5.

[123]   See eg the 1935 *Minority Schools in Albania* case, or the Belgian, Roma, and Sami cases under the ECHR mentioned above. For a broader perspective, including Art 27 ICCPR as well as regional jurisprudence in the Americas and Africa, see Pentassuglia (2011); Pentassuglia (2009) Ch 4.

[124]   Woehrling, '"Droits", "liberté" et "accommodements" linguistiques dans la jurisprudence de la Cour suprême du Canada', in *Humanisme et Droit: Ouvrage en Hommage au Professeur Jean Dhommeaux* (2013) 447. For a general discussion, Woehrling, 'Les trois dimensions de la protection des minorités en droit constitutionnel comparé', 34 *Revue de droit de l'Université de Sherbrooke* (2003–04) 93.

[125]   See eg Macklem, 'Minority Rights in International Law', 6 *Int'l Journal of Constitutional Law* (2008) 531. Recent scholarship has gone so far as to provide a defence of collective moral rights and a set of contextual but principled considerations for their realization: eg D. Newman, *Community and Collective Rights: A Theoretical Framework for Rights Held by Groups* (2011).

minority groups arguably adds to the creation of hybrid and sophisticated sites of legal analysis and discussion but does not—or should not—obscure the reasons why certain groups generally merit protection in the way they do.

From this perspective, a distinction should be drawn between generic claims to accommodation based on cultural or religious diversity and the impact of the ECHR and ACHR jurisprudence on ethno-cultural justice in the above-mentioned sense. Whereas *Thlimmenos*, the Muslim veiling controversies or the cases on religious symbols in schools under the ECHR, speak to the particular question of negotiating fair terms of integration through varying degrees of tolerance or religious-cultural accommodation within society, many of the cases from Central, Eastern, and Western Europe raising issues of pluralism (including political participation), identity and/or equality, together with a whole host of decisions regarding indigenous groups' physical and cultural integrity on the Inter-American continent, can be traced back to more permanent features of the minority group phenomenon in ways that enable the ECHR and the ACHR to play a greater or lesser instrumental role depending on the context of the case and the issues raised.[126] Common themes of discourse such as (racial) discrimination—including indirect discrimination—as well as the right to identity and a distinctive way of life, property (and related) rights, the right to education or voting rights, have allowed both Courts to make their respective treaty work for the benefit of a variety of minority communities irrespective of internal or external definitional hurdles such as citizenship, territorial settlement, priority in time (aboriginality), or state recognition.[127] It is fair to assume that the more 'generic' the case at issue (eg on non-discrimination), the wider its scope of application is likely to be, regardless of the type of group affected. However, the background position of the group against the rationales for its protection in international human rights law should provide, where appropriate, the basis for a nuanced and targeted approach to interpretation. In this sense, much of the above-mentioned jurisprudence (eg on associative pluralism, Roma and Sami members, land rights, and so on) arguably signals a more ambitious reading of the ECHR and ACHR when it comes to incrementally expanding the substantive and procedural reach of specific treaty rights or the impact of the instrument as a whole for mainly traditional groups. The Inter-American Court's reconsideration of rights in relation to indigenous communities, lumping native and non-native groups together, is an obvious case in point. Alternatively, the European Court tends to address complex issues of ethno-cultural justice such as corrections to the political or education system primarily (though by no means exclusively) from a procedural rather than substantive angle, with a major emphasis on Article 14.

Approaching this area requires a modicum of methodology: we need to understand why certain groups merit protection, what kind of protection can be reasonably claimed or expected because of that understanding, and whether existing

---

[126] The dimensions of this contribution can relate to either process or substance, as indicated in previous sections. For detailed discussion from a comparative point of view, see Pentassuglia (2009).

[127] On the controversial citizenship requirement for minority status, see the Venice Commission's Report on Non-Citizens and Minority Rights, Study no 294/2004, CDL-AD(2007)001.

jurisprudence—wittingly or unwittingly—points to normative instabilities in international law which need to be resolved over the longer term. Longstanding or more recent controversies over definitional matters across the whole spectrum of 'minorities' and 'indigenous peoples' in international law generate tensions which can be usefully assuaged by courts or court-like bodies whose jurisdiction *ratione personae* is unencumbered by particular textual requirements. The practical impact of ECHR jurisprudence on Roma and the ethnic Russians in the Baltic states, or the ACHR jurisprudence on Afro-descendants, illustrate the point, at least in terms of bringing particular claims within those Courts' jurisdiction. Judicial interventions are far from exhausting the range of international responses to issues involving minority groups. But they do provide vitally important guidance to the legal process. International jurisprudence ultimately shapes, and is shaped by this process dynamically. It holds the promise of consciously reflecting existing rationales for protection as relevant issues affecting a diverse range of groups arise within the interpretive practice.

## 6. Conclusions: Towards a New Interpretive Ethos

Ill-equipped to deal with issues relative to minority groups on their face, the ECHR and ACHR as interpreted by the European and Inter-American Courts have nevertheless started to generate meaningful protection for such groups in connection with issues of ethnicity, language, religion or, more specifically, indigeneity. Construed around the broad areas of pluralism, identity, and non-discrimination, on the one hand, as well as traditional access to land and resources, on the other, the contemporary jurisprudence of the Strasbourg and San José judges reflects a view of the ECHR and ACHR which is arguably more complex than the one projected onto the European and Inter-American legal landscapes at the time of their adoption.

Universalist in style and content, as they should be, the ECHR and ACHR are nevertheless part of a dynamic international human rights system in which varying degrees of interaction and dialogue are both necessary and desirable. In this regard, the impressive work of regional and global institutions in the broad field of minority group protection, coupled with major changes in territorial sovereignty which occurred in the late 1980s and early 1990s in Europe and elsewhere, could hardly have left the judicial interpretation of those treaties unaffected. In reality, the evolving readings of Articles 11, 8, and 14 ECHR (among others), and, even more so, several ACHR provisions revolving around protection of traditional land tenure systems of indigenous communities, epitomize a new stage of these treaties as 'living instruments' within such a multilayered legal framework. Setting benchmarks for asserting, debating, or reconsidering national and subnational identities in the public sphere, upholding respect for cultural diversity, and increasingly acknowledging the *collective*, not merely individual, dimension of protecting minority groups—from physical and culture-related integrity to inter-group equality—are significant achievements. They de facto reinforce, and are reinforced by international minimum standards. Indeed, one may argue that the acknowledgment of the collective dimension of general rights pertaining to ethno-cultural 'minorities' in Europe and 'indigenous peoples' in the Americas, as varied and distinctive as it certainly is, brings to the fore stages of a fundamentally similar legal process, namely the progressive internalization of the interpretive impact of international human rights adjudication on minority protection (and indeed, human rights law more generally). In this sense, judicial practice looks very much like 'subsequent practice' in the application of the treaty within the meaning of Article 31(3)(b) VCLT.

It is unclear whether the European Court will be prepared to fully embrace the language of positive obligations as a way of limiting states' margin of appreciation in the above-mentioned areas of pluralism, identity, and non-discrimination, or fully endorse the implications of a systemic interpretation of the ECHR through external instruments and practice. For its part, the experience of the Inter-American Court suggests that the evolutionary method of treaty interpretation long used by the Strasbourg Court can be based on a constructive interplay of 'autonomous' meanings compared to domestic practices and provisions, and positive obligations read into the instrument in light of the general body of international human rights law.[128]

The complexities and diversity of European history and individual country contexts, as distinct from the relatively more homogeneous setting for indigenous rights protection in the Americas, may have the European Court lean towards enhanced, 'externally informed' proportionality tests under relevant limitations clauses or general principles rather than clearly worded positive duties. In other words, the level of 'systemic integration' (in the above-mentioned sense of the Vienna Convention or general international law) of the wider corpus of international standards (eg the Framework Convention and global instruments) is likely to remain fluid and relatively lower in Strasbourg than in San José. However, positive obligations have been found by the European Court on a number of occasions and proportionality tests can prove as important as positive obligations in reducing state autonomy, reinforcing democratic debate in Europe, or providing baselines for measuring the impact of state action. In fact, 'proportionality' appears to be a key principle running through the whole body of both the European and Inter-American jurisprudence, covering obvious instances of state interference together with more complex cases of competing claims. Conceptually, it frames the discussion about minority groups in terms of a balancing act within society which is respectful of and compatible with human rights rather than a legal battle

---

[128] Pentassuglia (2011). Interestingly, in the recent *Sarayaku* judgment, the Inter-American Court references other human rights jurisprudence, including case law from the European Court, in order to further entrench a connection between rights to land and rights to culture under Art 21 ACHR, thereby acknowledging the comparative spirit of contemporary human rights treaty interpretation as advocated in this chapter, especially in the context of dynamic exchanges between the European and Inter-American systems. *The Kichwa Indigenous People of Sarayaku v Ecuador*, IACtHR (2012) Series C, No 245, judgment of 27 June 2012, para 216.

for one-sided views. At the same time, the more progressive reading of the ACHR by the Inter-American Court has often (though by no means always) been used to support a measure of domestic consent and has led to a high level of judicial elaboration beyond the normative detail of specialized instruments to encompass substantive obligations and complex procedural elements as diverse as varying degrees of effective participation and collective forms of reparation grounded in *restitutio in integrum* and its attendant access to justice (adjudicatory) processes.[129]

In both jurisdictions, progressive interpretation appears to have been triggered by the perceived scale of the problem or level of 'gravity' of the case at issue. Illustrations of this varied intensity of judicial articulation include a sustained and increasingly multifaceted view of indigenous rights arising from deep-seated patterns of abuse regarding access to land and natural resources,[130] prioritization of socioeconomic dimensions of protection and remedial action linked to humanitarian emergencies (and echoed by leading case law such as *Ogoni* under the African system), a firmly proactive approach to non-discrimination against Roma and other vulnerable groups, particularly in the context of violent incidents, and a primarily indirect approach to advanced domestic arrangements or complex forms of group-differentiated rights as components of the 'day-to-day' political process. Here it is interesting to note that the right to life has started to feature significantly in the jurisprudence of both Courts. However, while the European Court's general approach to that right (including, for example, positive obligations to prevent predictable risks or to investigate)[131] has so far revolved around situations such as environmental disasters or acts of brutality, the Inter-American Court's 'adaptation' of the European Court's line has encompassed specific group identity issues in connection with a wider concept of 'dignified existence' that connects individual physical wellbeing and collective dimensions of cultural protection.[132]

Indeed, comparatively speaking, the more assertive line of the Inter-American Court (and Commission) could be explained by reference to a consistent embrace of multicultural policies in most Latin American countries' constitutions and statutory legislations, against a traditional European legal and political thinking informed by notions of domestic jurisdiction, nation-state and/or strictly

---

[129] Unlike the European Court's jurisprudence, this has included, for example, consistent recourse to the doctrine of 'continuing effects' of rights violations: see Pentassuglia (2009) 163–7.

[130] Partly echoing the recent *Endorois* case before the African Commission on Human and Peoples' Rights, two cases are currently pending before the Inter-American Commission on Human Rights in which local indigenous communities challenge nature conservation measures involving their traditional land: *Garifuna Community of Cayos Cochinos and its Members v Honduras*, Report No 39/07, Petition 1118-03, Admissibility, 24 July 2007; *The Kaliña and Lokono Peoples v Suriname*, Report No 76/07, Petition 198-07, Admissibility, 15 October 2007. See also *Ngöbe Indigenous Community and their members in the Changuinola River Valley v Panama*, Report No 75/09, Petition 286-08, Admissibility, 5 August 2009.

[131] For example *Öneryildiz v Turkey*, ECHR (2004) App No 48389/99, judgment of 30 November 2004.

[132] See Section 2 above. In this respect, an increasing recognition of group issues by the European Court in the context of racial violence or racial segregation might generate more imaginative views of Art 2 ECHR as well.

individual civil and political rights.[133] But this view would be a simplistic one, since the constitutional turn to multiculturalism in Latin America is a relatively recent phenomenon compared to earlier conceptions of state sovereignty and human rights in the region, whereas European states do have a longstanding tradition of accommodating ethnic and cultural diversity through a wide variety of legal domestic and international mechanisms. More importantly, the jurisprudential expansion of regional human rights treaties discussed in this chapter is generally independent of domestic practices as it seeks to provide *new* ways of responding to challenges posed by minority groups under those treaties. There is no reason why the European Court's approach to minority groups cannot build upon its jurisprudential mantras of pluralism, identity, and non-discrimination to provide an incrementally imaginative and more systemically integrated view of minority issues under the ECHR against the backdrop of concerns voiced by minority groups, regulatory moves within the European space, or even the extra-territorial effects of states parties' measures.[134]

It goes without saying that the implementation of both European and Inter-American judgments is a major test of this increasingly transformative interpretive jurisprudence. Here a significant difference between the two systems is given by the 'devolved' (ECHR) or 'centralized' (ACHR) mechanism of monitoring. Whereas the ECHR tasks the Committee of Ministers with supervising the execution of judgments (Article 46(2)), a traditionally (more) assertive approach to remedies under the ACHR (Article 63(1)) has been coupled with direct and continuing monitoring by the Inter-American Court of respondent states' compliance with its judgments.[135] The recently embraced concept of pilot or quasi-pilot judgments in the European Court's jurisprudence could possibly lead to a parallel expansion of remedial powers,[136] including 'class actions' of sorts for systemic

---

[133] This individualistic understanding of rights has been a basis for a critique of an otherwise progressive ECHR case law in certain areas: see eg Francioni, 'International Human Rights in an Environmental Horizon', 21 *EJIL* (2010) 41.

[134] In terms of post-Lisbon EU law, see eg Case T-18/10, *Inuit Tapiritt Kanatami and Others v Parliament and Council*, order of 6 September 2011 (not yet published), which was declared inadmissible by the CJEU; Ahmed, *The Impact of EU Law on Minority Rights* (2011). For a review of issues relating to indigenous (intellectual) property and the scope of Art 1 Protocol 1 to the ECHR, see eg Vezzani, 'Il Primo Protocollo alla Convenzione europea dei diritti umani e la tutela della proprietà intellettuale di popoli indigeni e comunità locali', 1 *Diritti umani e diritto internazionale* (2007) 305; for the extra-territorial dimension of state responsiblity, see also note 101.

[135] For example, the leading case of *Awas Tigni* was declared closed by the Court in April 2009 following a whole range of measures progressively undertaken by Nicaragua under San José's supervision, in accordance with the 2001 judgment: *Mayagna (Sumo) Awas Tingni Community v Nicaragua*, Monitoring Compliance with Judgment, Order of 3 April 2009. Other leading cases such as *Sawhoyamaxa* or *Saramaka* remain under the Court's active periodic review. On the other hand, the political pressure exerted by the Committee of Ministers over respondent states against which breaches of the ECHR have been found by the European Court has contributed towards the implementation of judgments notwithstanding a cautious approach of this Court to affording specific remedies for those breaches.

[136] For ECHR developments relating to remedies more generally, see Wildhaber, 'The Execution of Judgments of the ECtHR: Recent Developments', in Dupuy et al (eds), *Common Values in International Law: Essays in Honour of Christian Tomuschat* (2006) 671.

issues affecting minority groups. However, the substantive reach of this technique remains to be seen.[137]

The paradox of international jurisprudence under general human rights treaties is that the more it embraces progressive readings of provisions relevant to minority groups, the more conscious it becomes of the interpretive value of external specialized instruments pertinent to the case at issue, and the more assertive it proves to be vis-à-vis domestic laws, the more it produces creative judging which propels it as an indispensable point of reference to vest minority protection with greater 'constitutional' legal significance.[138] Regional variations are inevitable, induced as they are by the distinctive language and scope of treaty regimes, changing perceptions of states parties' sensitivities as well as different socio-political and/or domestic legal circumstances. Yet judicial cross-fertilization is inevitable too, being as it is a function of a rapidly expanding dialogue across jurisdictions, both internationally and domestically.[139] In fact, as human rights adjudicatory bodies generally seek to develop broadly comparable understandings of human rights treaties, domestic courts increasingly rely on such bodies' findings to construe their interpretation of internal provisions and effectively contribute to the development and/or implementation of international standards.[140] Judges cannot and should not substitute for the political process addressing minority group concerns. But they can and should inform that process with dynamic understandings of international human rights law. Indeed, the human rights jurisprudence on minority groups reflects emerging degrees of international legality which qualify political consensus or help compensate for the relative lack of it. Whatever lies ahead in the jurisprudence of both the European and Inter-American Courts, it will open up further possibilities for a range of groups irrespective of definitional hurdles. Claimants' expectations should be reasonable and proportionate to the scope of the treaty in question. Judicial persuasiveness will hinge on a modicum of methodology—a new interpretive ethos, as it were—as to how to handle relevant claims, and what is at stake when it comes to considering them.

---

[137] For recent commentary, see Sitaropoulos, 'Implementation of the European Court of Human Rights' judgments concerning national minorities or why declaratory adjudication does not help', European Society of International Law, Conference Paper No 4/2011, 1 ESIL Conference Paper Series (2011) 1. On the other hand, Protocol 14 ECHR further refines the interaction between the European Court and the Committee of Ministers by enabling the latter to refer the case back to the former for interpretation or for failure by the state to comply with a judgment rendered against it.

[138] Whether and to what extent elements of the jurisprudence discussed in this chapter underpin specific—emerging or existing—norms of customary international law was beyond the purpose of the inquiry.

[139] That this process can hardly leave even traditional adjudicatory bodies unaffected is confirmed by the recent judgment of the International Court of Justice in *Ahmadou Sadio Diallo (Republic of Guinea v Democratic Republic of the Congo)*, ICJ Reports (2010) 639.

[140] See eg Higgins, 'A Babel of Judicial Voices? Ruminations from the Bench', 55 *ICLQ* (2006) 791 at 798. For examples of interactions in the field of indigenous rights, see Pentassuglia (2011); Courtis, 'Notes on the Implementation by Latin American Courts of the ILO Convention 169 on Indigenous Peoples', 18 *Int'l Journal on Minority and Group Rights* (2011) 433.

# 4

# Culture and the Rights of Indigenous Peoples

*Siegfried Wiessner**

Centuries have gone by since Columbus first landed in Hispaniola. The process of colonization subjugated the original inhabitants of many continents, often resulting in the denial of the very humanity of peoples outside the mostly European imperial ambit. The lust for power and economic gain as well as unquestioned feelings of cultural superiority fueled the project of Conquest, which, in many ways, has shaped the contours of the world today. Indigenous peoples were driven aside, forced to assimilate and, in many cases, had to give up their time-honoured ways of life. A more subtle, but, in the long run, more formidable threat was posed by the lures of modern science and technology, the siren song of progress. So, as one by one their members integrated themselves into modern society, their culture died. Or so it seemed.

It turned out, however, that indigenous peoples' beliefs and traditions never completely vanished from the Earth. Even though they had to adapt to modernity, go underground, many of them survived—a sufficient number to start a renascence of indigenous values and communities around the globe. Beginning in the 1970s, the First Nations reappeared in strength, and they demanded their place at the table of those who made decisions over their fate—within states and at the international level. They asked for respect for their mistreated cultures, their right to self-determination, and their right to live on their land according to their ancient traditions.

Cultural difference, at times a radical one, provides the key context within which the indigenous peoples' claims to self-government arose. Unlike the claims of other groups, indigenous peoples' claims are often couched in the verbiage of 'sovereignty'.[1] Vine Deloria, Jr, revered leader of the American Indian resurgence, spoke in terms of 'indigenous sovereignty'.[2] Even today, US courts use 'tribal sovereignty' as a term of art when they analyse cases involving American Indian tribes

* The author draws freely, though with significant changes and updates, upon his articles entitled 'The Cultural Rights of Indigenous Peoples: Achievements and Continuing Challenges', 22 *EJIL* (2011) 121, and 'Re-Enchanting the World: Indigenous Peoples' Rights as Essential Parts of a Holistic Human Rights Regime', 15 *UCLA J Int'l L & Foreign Affairs* (2010) 239.

[1] Wiessner, 'Indigenous Sovereignty: A Reassessment in Light of the UN Declaration on the Rights of Indigenous Peoples', 41 *Vanderbilt J Transnat'l L* (2008) 1141.

[2] Deloria, 'Self-Determination and the Concept of Sovereignty', in J.R. Wunder (ed), *Native American Sovereignty* (1996) 118, 121, 123.

or, as they prefer to be called, 'nations'.[3] Other states also face indigenous peoples' demands for sovereignty.[4] While these terms are in usual parlance understood in a political sense, ie as claims for power, in the case of indigenous peoples they are motivated by the existential desire to keep alive their ways of life, their traditions, and their culture. As the late Vine Deloria clarified, indigenous sovereignty 'consist[s] more of a continued cultural integrity than of political powers and to the degree that a nation loses its sense of cultural identity, to that degree it suffers a loss of sovereignty'.[5] 'Sovereignty', explains another great Native American leader, Kirke Kickingbird, 'cannot be separated from people or their culture'.[6]

The safeguarding and flourishing of their cultures is thus the preeminent basis of indigenous peoples' claims; the goal of preservation of cultural diversity on the planet, in turn, arguably propelled the overwhelming consensus of states to recognize these aspirations, as expressed in the 2007 United Nations Declaration on the Rights of Indigenous Peoples (UNDRIP).[7] The present state of the law has been expressed in the International Law Association's (ILA) Resolution No 5/2012 on the Rights of Indigenous Peoples of 30 August 2012,[8] an authoritative statement on the reach of customary international law in the field.

[3] For a recent case law summary, see D.H. Getches, C.F. Wilkinson, and R.A. Williams, Jr (eds), *Cases and Materials on Federal Indian Law* (5th edn, 2005) 377–413. As to the original Marshall trilogy of cases, see 104–27. Felix S. Cohen, in his seminal handbook of federal Indian law, referred to powers of Indian tribes as 'inherent powers of a limited sovereignty which has never been extinguished'. F.S. Cohen, *Handbook of Federal Indian Law* (1942) 122, quoted in *United States v Wheeler*, 435 US 313 (1978) at 322. North American indigenous peoples often style themselves as a 'nation'. See eg The Navajo Nation, <http://www.navajo-nsn.gov> (accessed 21 July 2013); The Oneida Indian Nation, <http://www.oneidaindiannation.com> (accessed 29 June 2013); The Shasta Indian Nation, <http://www.shastaindiannation.org/index.html> (accessed 29 June 2013); The Catawba Indian Nation, <http://catawbaindiannation.com> (accessed 29 June 2013).
[4] See Carlson, 'Premature Predictions of Multiculturalism?', 100 *Michigan L Rev* (2002) 1470 at 1475–6 (referring to Latin American states' recognition of indigenous sovereignty claims); see also Otto, 'A Question of Law or Politics? Indigenous Claims to Sovereignty in Australia', 21 *Syracuse J Int'l L & Commerce* (1995) 65 at 79–80; cf Kahn, 'The Legal Framework Surrounding Maori Claims to Water Resources in New Zealand: In Contrast to the American Indian Experience', 35 *Stanford J Int'l L* (1999) 49 at 81 (referring to the 'importance of a confined resource base to the retention of indigenous sovereignty'); Christie, 'Indigeneity and Sovereignty in Canada's Far North: The Arctic and Inuit Sovereignty', 110 *South Atlantic Q* (2011) 329. See generally Corntassel and Hopkins Primeau, 'Indigenous "Sovereignty" and International Law: Revised Strategies for Pursuing "Self-Determination"', 17 *Human Rts Q* (1995) 343; S. Curry, *Indigenous Sovereignty and the Democratic Project* (2004).
[5] Deloria (1996).
[6] K. Kickingbird et al, *Indian Sovereignty* (1977) 2.
[7] United Nations Declaration on the Rights of Indigenous Peoples (UNDRIP), GA Res 61/295, 13 September 2007. For an expert commentary on this Declaration and indigenous peoples' rights in general, see ILA Committee on the Rights of Indigenous Peoples, Interim Report to the 74th ILA Conference in The Hague, 15–20 August 2010 (hereinafter 2010 ILA Interim Report), and Final Report to the 75th ILA Conference in Sofia, 27–31 August 2012 (hereinafter 2012 ILA Final Report), both available at <http://www.ila-hq.org/en/committees/index.cfm/cid/1024> (accessed 29 June 2013). See also Anaya and Wiessner, 'The UN Declaration on the Rights of Indigenous Peoples: Towards Re-empowerment', *JURIST Forum*, 3 October 2007, available at <http://jurist.law.pitt.edu/forumy/2007/10/un-declaration-on-rights-of-indigenous.php> (accessed 29 June 2013).
[8] Rights of Indigenous Peoples, Resolution No 5/2012, 75th Biennial Meeting of the International Law Association, Sofia, adopted 30 August 2012, available at <http://www.ila-hq.org/en/committees/index.cfm/cid/1024> (accessed 17 June 2013).

This chapter starts with the discussion of culture as a collective phenomenon and the attendant need to safeguard it through individual and collective rights (1). It then traces the development of indigenous peoples' claims and aspirations (2), in response to which international legal protections have been developed prior to UNDRIP (3). It moves on to present the comprehensive treatment of those claims in UNDRIP (4); and it ends with the discussion of its legal effect and the extent to which it reflects customary international law as laid out in the International Law Association's Final Report and historic Resolution No 5/2012 (5).

## 1. Culture as Collective Phenomenon and the Need to Protect It through Individual and Collective Rights

As law, in essence, ought to serve human beings, any effort to design a better law should be conceived as a response to human needs and aspirations.[9] These needs and aspirations vary from culture to culture and they change over time. From the need to make sense of one's individual and cultural experiences arise inner worlds, or each person's inner reality. The international human rights system is, in this context,

concerned with protecting, for those who wish to maintain them, the integrity of the unique visions of these inner worlds, from appraisal and policing in terms of the cultural values of others. This must be, for these inner world cosmovisions, or introcosms, are the central, vital part of the individuality of each of us. This is, to borrow Holmes' wonderful phrase, 'where we live.' Respect for the other requires, above all, respect for the other's inner world.[10]

---

[9] Law as a process of authoritative and controlling decision is most felicitously used as a vehicle to establish and promote a public order of human dignity. It ought to be designed to provide maximum access by all to all things humans value in life. The essence of this theory about law, variously called the New Haven School, Policy-Oriented Jurisprudence, or Law, Science, and Policy, has been laid out in H.D. Lasswell and M.S. McDougal, *Jurisprudence for a Free Society: Studies in Law, Science and Policy* (1992). See also Reisman, 'International Lawmaking: A Process of Communication', 75 *Proc Am Soc'y Int'l L* (1981) 101; Reisman, 'The View from the New Haven School of International Law', 86 *Proc Am Soc'y Int'l L* (1992) 118; Wiessner, 'International Law in the 21st Century: Decisionmaking in Institutionalized and Non-Institutionalized Settings', 26 *Thesaurus Acroasium* (1997) 129; Wiessner and Willard, 'Policy-Oriented Jurisprudence and Human Rights Abuses in Internal Conflict: Toward a World Public Order of Human Dignity', 93 *AJIL* (1999) 316; Reisman, Wiessner, and Willard, 'The New Haven School: A Brief Introduction', 32 *Yale J Int'l L* (2007) 575; Wiessner, 'Law as a Means to a Public Order of Human Dignity: The Jurisprudence of Michael Reisman', 34 *Yale J Int'l L* (2009) 525; Wiessner, 'The New Haven School of Jurisprudence: A Universal Toolkit for Understanding and Shaping the Law', 18 *Asia Pacific L Rev* (2010) 45.

[10] As to the concept of 'inner worlds', see p 25:

Surely one of the most distinctive features of our species is the need to create and ascribe meaning and value to the immutable experiences of human existence: the trauma of birth, the discovery of the self as separate from others, the formation of gender or sexual identity, procreation, the death of loved ones, one's own death, indeed, the mystery of it all. Each culture, in its unique context, records these experiences in ways that provide meaning, guidance and codes of rectitude that serve as compasses for the individual as he or she navigates the vicissitudes of life. These are the inner worlds, the inner reality each person inhabits.

It is readily agreed upon that individual members of particular cultural or religious communities enjoy the freedoms of speech, assembly, association, and the freedom to hold a religious belief and practice its tenets. This provides indigenous persons the legally enforceable opportunity to defend themselves against abridgments of this general right to develop and express their inner worlds. In fact, there is scant argument that, as stated in the Preamble to UNDRIP, 'indigenous individuals are entitled without discrimination to all human rights recognized in international law'. While the realization of this right is far from being achieved in many parts of the globe, the legal entitlement as such is unquestioned. What has been objected to more often is the second part of this quote from the Preamble: '[I]ndigenous peoples possess collective rights which are indispensable for their existence, well-being and integral development as peoples.' Yet it is exactly these rights held communally that are central to indigenous peoples' survival as such.

The very term 'collective human rights' has engendered, at times, fierce opposition. This may have had different reasons. For one, the first human rights declarations could only conceive of the dichotomy between the individual and the state; *tertia non datur*. One such example is the 1789 *Déclaration des droits de l'homme et du citoyen*;[11] the other one is the American Bill of Rights of 1791. Based on thoughts of the Enlightenment and the natural rights philosophy of John Locke, Jean-Jacques Rousseau, and Immanuel Kant, the individual rights to liberty and property were seen as central to the happiness of the individual; to protect them was seen as the first task of the state. In John Locke's mind, if these rights were violated by the government of the state, the citizen had a right to revolution. A second consideration was that the modern territorial state, having thrown off the personal rulers of feudal origin, was jealously guarding its preeminence, the all-encompassing power of sovereignty. It was afraid that intermediate groups vested with rights might mitigate, even weaken and check its own projections of control over the land and its people. In the twentieth century, especially after the Second World War, the Cold War generated another source of suspicion regarding collective rights: they were seen as closely tied conceptually to the collectivization of individually held lands and industrial properties in various totalitarian revolutions and takeovers of the time.

The latter at least does not hold true for the rights claims of indigenous peoples: they are typically based on their existential need to survive and flourish as a culture, not as a political or economic unit. Indigenous peoples also are not competing for economic or political power with the state, the cultural groundedness and cultural boundedness[12] of their claims to autonomy and lands insulate them

---

[11] Cf N. Torbisco Casals, *Group Rights as Human Rights: A Liberal Approach to Multiculturalism* (2006), 106, 108 ('Undoubtedly, the drafters of the *Déclaration des droits de l'homme et du citoyen* must have known that "the people" from which they derived political legitimacy comprised not only the French, but also the Alsatians, Basques, Bretons, Catalans and Occitants.... In sum, despite existing diversity, all states have tried to promote the identification of its [sic] citizens with a single official language and culture, often through extremely coercive means'.)

[12] Wiessner, 'The Cultural Rights of Indigenous Peoples: Achievements and Continuing Challenges', 22 *EJIL* (2011) 121 at 129.

from any such charge. Most importantly, however, their rights termed 'collective' are the ones that are necessary to their happiness and full self-realization as individuals. If the law should serve human beings and allow them to realize their dreams, it must recognize that an empirical assessment of human beings yields the result that individuals cannot flourish alone; they are social animals, as Aristotle recognized in his characterization of a human being as a *zoon politicon*.[13] Interaction with and reliance upon others are *conditiones sine qua non* for human existence.[14]

Thus a reduction of the legal systems' response to human needs and wants to solely individual freedoms and entitlements is at least incomplete. It is also counterproductive to the human rights project, as it runs against the inherent goal of fostering the full development of a human being's potential. The interaction between the individual and the group into which he or she was born or has chosen to affiliate with, is an empirical reality which cannot be denied and which the law ignores at its peril. After all, 'no man is an iland, intire of itselfe; every man is a peece of the Continent, a part of the maine'.[15]

As far as the philosophical moorings of human rights are concerned,[16] it has been pointed out that Immanuel Kant's ethical system revolving around the axiom of inviolate human dignity[17] does not limit itself to rigidly individualist conceptions of a good order. As Neil MacCormick stated, '[t]he Kantian ideal of respect for persons implies...an obligation in each of us to respect that which in others constitutes any part of their sense of their own identity'.[18] That identity is formed by participation in what he calls 'cultural communities', which need appropriate institutional protection.[19] Similarly, Will Kymlicka has pointed out that whereas groups provide the cultural structures which constitute the context of choice for individual action,[20] they need to have rights in order to foster individuals' well-being.[21] Others have argued that these groups have distinctive collective interests whose moral value is on a par with the interests of individuals.[22]

---

[13] Kullmann, 'Der Mensch als politisches Lebewesen bei Aristoteles', 108 *Hermes* (1980) 419.

[14] Wiessner, 'Re-Enchanting the World: Indigenous Peoples' Rights as Essential Parts of a Holistic Human Rights Regime', 15 *UCLA J Int'l L & Foreign Affairs* (2010) 239 at 260, with further references.

[15] J. Donne, *Meditations* 17 (1624). Individual liberalism has thus been criticized for cutting the citizen off from the person and constructing a 'cripple of a man, lacking moral or political nature, without roots'. Bay, 'From Contract to Community: Thoughts on Liberalism and Postindustrial Society', in F.R. Dallmayr (ed), *From Contract to Community* (1978) 29 at 30.

[16] For a good overview of this problématique, see Underkuffler, 'Human Genetics Studies: The Case for Group Rights', 35 *J L Med & Ethics* (2007) 383 at 384–5.

[17] Cf eg I. Kant, *Grounding for the Metaphysics of Morals* (J.W. Ellington trans, 3rd edn, 1993) (1785).

[18] N. MacCormick, *Legal Rights and Social Democracy: Essays in Legal and Political Philosophy* (1982) 261.

[19] MacCormick (1982) 261.

[20] W. Kymlicka, *Liberalism, Community, and Culture* (1989) 167.

[21] W. Kymlicka, *Multicultural Citizenship: A Liberal Theory of Minority* Rights (1995) 13.

[22] See Addis, 'Individualism, Communitarianism, and the Rights of Ethnic Minorities', 67 *Notre Dame L Rev* (1992) 615; Addis, 'On Human Diversity and the Limits of Toleration', in I. Shapiro and W. Kymlicka (eds), *Ethnicity and Group Rights* (1997) 112; McDonald, 'Should Communities Have Rights? Reflections on Liberal Individualism', 4 *Can J L & Juris* (1991) 217 at 237 ('Individuals are regarded as valuable because they are choosers and have interests. But so also do communities make choices and have values. Why not then treat communities as fundamental units of value?'). See also

This philosophical consideration is buttressed by the empirical fact of the individual influencing the group and the group influencing the individual—a reciprocal dynamic. George Herbert Mead has presented the critical insight that in the constant interplay between the individual and society's constituent groups, not only is the individual self shaped and changed, but general patterns of group behaviour are reconstructed and modified as well.[23] In that sense, groups of meaning to individuals are essential extensions of self, necessary parts of a person's identity. Culture, in particular, is a group phenomenon; it cannot be developed by the solipsistic effort of an individual human being. The concept of an 'individual culture' has been rejected, with good grounds, particularly in the context of indigenous peoples.[24]

In order to respond holistically to human needs and aspirations, one needs to aim at protecting both individuals and the groups relevant to them. Vulnerability of individuals created the need for individual human rights; the vulnerability of groups—particularly of cultural communities—creates the need for their protection. The critical question of relevance to the human rights project is: what deprivations of values targeting individuals as members of groups have taken place in recent history, and in order to achieve a world public order of human dignity, how might these deprivations be remedied? To answer this question, we need to understand exactly what the claims are that arise in the essential interaction between individuals and the groups relevant to them.

To that end, I would like to introduce a helpful empirical distinction, the distinction between an 'organic' and a 'non-organic group'.[25] The first category encompasses collectivities of human beings, commonly designated as a 'nation' or

Réaume, 'Individuals, Groups, and Rights to Public Goods', 38 *U Toronto LJ* (1988) 1 at 13–17, 24; Garet, 'Communality and Existence: The Rights of Groups', 56 *S Cal L Rev* (1982–83) 1001.

[23]  See eg C.W. Morris (ed), *George Herbert Mead, Mind, Self and Society: From the Standpoint of a Social Behavioralist* (1934); A. Strauss (ed), *George Herbert Mead, On Social Psychology: Selected Papers* (1964).

[24]  Torres, 'Indigenous Education and "Living Well": An Alternative in the Midst of Crisis', in L. Meyer and B.M. Alvarado (eds), *New World of Indigenous Resistance* (2010) 213 at 217 ('The notion of individual culture is unacceptable for indigenous peoples who claim the collective production, throughout history, of all systemic expressions of their particular cultures'). See also Estevez, 'Beyond Education', in Meyer and Alvarado (2010) 115 at 121 ('Among all indigenous peoples, the condition of the strong "we" is expressed existentially and in the language itself, for this is the subject of *comunalidad*, the first layer of existence, formed by the interlocking of the networks of real relationships that make up each person'). On the other hand, Kay Warren and Jean Jackson state that rather than focusing on 'uniformly shared cultures rooted in a particular place…anthropologists favor studies that engage multiple interacting identities, globalized flows of culture and peoples, and conflicting views and subject positions in contemporary society.' Warren and Jackson, 'Introduction: Studying Indigenous Activism in Latin America', in K.B. Warren and J.E. Jackson (eds), *Indigenous Movements, Self-Representation and the State in Latin America* (2003) 1 at 8.

[25]  For details, see Wiessner, 'Faces of Vulnerability: Protecting Individuals in Organic and Non-Organic Groups', in G. Alfredsson and P. Macalister-Smith (eds), *The Living Law of Nations: Essays on Refugees, Minorities, Indigenous Peoples and the Human Rights of Other Vulnerable Groups in Memory of Atle Grahl-Madsen* (1996) 217. This distinction, focusing on the classification of the pertinent group itself, differs from Emile Durkheim's dichotomy between mechanical and organic solidarity. 'Mechanical solidarity', in his view, referred to the social cohesion based on kinship ties in traditional, small-scale societies, while 'organic solidarity' applied to modern industrial societies signifying the feeling of interdependence between society members generated by their specialized roles and the ensuing need to coordinate. Cf E. Durkheim, *The Division of Labour in Society* (1933).

a 'people', who have made and maintain a conscious decision—in Ernest Renan's words, the *plébiscite de tous les jours*—which manifests their will to live together as a community.[26] 'Non-organic groups', such as women, children, even many religious communities, do not have the same interest in sharing all aspects of life. They are primarily concerned with not being discriminated against by the ruling elites. The focus of members of such groups is thus not 'the protection of group identity, but differential treatment by both arbitrary and authoritative power.... In contrast, the ultimate expression of solidarity within an organic group, the quest for cultural, political, and other forms of autonomy, constitutes a demand to be treated differentially *ab initio*.'[27] The vulnerability of an organic group can be measured by the 'intensity of threat to the group's identity, defined by its distinctive cultural, linguistic, ethnic, religious or other bonds'.[28] Denials of their claims to be separate, to determine their own fate, to govern themselves, constitute deprivations of essential values of the members of the organic group as well as of the groups themselves.

Indigenous peoples typically are, by definition, organic groups, ie collectivities that are characterized by the desire and practice of sharing virtually all aspects of life together.[29] This classification as an organic group facilitates inclusion in the legal regime of autonomy of not only indigenous communities with distinct territories, but also of those indigenous peoples who have lost most of their land base, thus constituting largely personal associations.

While the philosophical and empirical arguments against the recognition of rights of groups are less than convincing, even the historic arguments of positivist legal tradition hold little weight, as these legal formulations are somewhat specious, and have faded in the recent past. The exclusion of group rights from the American Bill of Rights and the French *Déclaration* can be explained by the fact that both 'democratic revolutions' saw the loyalties of individuals to organizations other than the ones represented by the ruling elite of the state as fundamentally threatening.[30] These fears were augmented if the interests of these intermediate

---

[26] Cf S. Wiessner, *Die Funktion der Staatsangehörigkeit* (1989), 102–5. Martínez Luna describes this comprehensive interdependence as follows: 'The community is like a virtual gigantic family. Its organization stems initially and always from respect. Everything is done together, a practice obviously reinforced by the policy of the Spanish colonizers of concentrating populations. Still, it is a natural reaction, naturally linked up with the use of a common language.' Martínez Luna, 'The Fourth Principle', in Meyer and Alvarado (2010) 85 at 94.

[27] Wiessner (1996) 222.

[28] Wiessner (1996) 221.

[29] Wiessner (1996) 221.

[30] There are no group rights enumerated in the American Bill of Rights, as even the Second Amendment right of 'the people' to keep and bear arms is interpreted as an individual right. *District of Columbia v Heller*, 554 US 570 (2008). As to France, see A. Knapp and V. Wright, *The Government and Politics of France* (5th edn, 2006) 312:

> The political culture of Jacobinism, as inherited from the French Revolution, has even less use for interest groups than for parties. Jacobins opposed the narrow, 'particular' (and inevitably selfish) interests represented by the groups to the 'general interest' which only the state could incarnate. The Le Chapelier Law of 1791, whose effective ban on such organisations as trade unions was confirmed in 1810 by Napoleon's penal code, was the legislative expression of the Jacobin view (Napoleon's code also helpfully banned gatherings of over twenty people).

groups were perceived to be in some way antithetical to the desires of the ruling elites.[31] Similar worries explain the absence of group rights in early United Nations instruments.[32] This taboo of group entitlements has, however, long been overcome in positive law, both domestically and internationally, as extant treaty protections of the right to self-determination (Article 1 of both UN human rights covenants of 1966); culture, cultural diversity, and cultural heritage (UNESCO conventions referred to below);[33] minorities (Council of Europe Framework Convention on the Protection of National Minorities[34]); and indigenous and tribal communities (as in ILO Convention No 169[35]) amply demonstrate.

Collective entitlements in the field of human rights are thus here to stay.[36] They are essential for the protection of cultural diversity and indispensable to the protection of indigenous peoples and their ways of life. They complete the needed holistic response of the law to the human condition and their vulnerabilities.

As stated above, indigenous peoples constitute the prototype of an organic group: ideally, they aspire to spend their lives together—in virtually all aspects, not just a few. Their essential characteristics are not only those of heteronomously defined collectivities of human beings, discriminated against over time, but also now autonomously, self-defined as communities with specific ways of life and a view of the world characterized by their strong, often spiritual relationship with the land of which the outside world regards them as the original inhabitants.[37]

---

[31] Wiessner (1996) 219.

[32] Goldman, 'The Need for an Independent International Mechanism to Protect Group Rights: A Case Study of the Kurds', 2 *Tulsa J Comp & Int'l L* (1994) 45 at 51; Robinson, 'International Protection of Minorities: A Global View', 1 *Israeli YB Human Rts* (1971) 61 at 77.

[33] See notes 96–106 below.

[34] Framework Convention for the Protection of National Minorities, CETS 157, 2 January 1995, available at <http://www.legislationline.org/documents/action/popup/id/8152> (accessed 29 June 2013).

[35] See ILO Convention No 169 Concerning Indigenous and Tribal Peoples in Independent Countries, adopted 27 June 1989, 28 ILM 1382.

[36] Cf Vrdoljak, 'Self-Determination and Cultural Rights', in F. Francioni and M. Scheinin (eds), *Cultural Human Rights* (2008) 41 at 59, with reference to Professors Tomuschat and Rodley who share the opinion that a variety of individual guarantees make minority rights redundant. Tomuschat, 'Protection of Minorities under Article 27 of the International Covenant on Civil and Political Rights', in R. Bernhardt et al (eds), *Völkerrecht als Rechtsordnung—Internationale Gerichtsbarkeit—Menschenrechte. Festschrift für Hermann Mosler* (1983) 952; and Rodley, 'Conceptual Problems in the Protection of Minorities: International Legal Developments', 17 *Human Rts Q* (1995) 48 at 54–9.

[37] See the understanding of the term as advanced in the UN Permanent Forum on Indigenous Issues (Fifth Session, Fact Sheet 1: Indigenous Peoples and Identity, at <http://social.un.org/index/IndigenousPeoples/UNPFIISessions/PreviousSessions/Fifth.aspx> (accessed 21 July 2013)) and the discussion on the issue of definition in the 2010 ILA Interim Report, 6–9, and 2012 Final Report, 2–3. This understanding also reflects the criteria advanced in the literature by Wiessner, 'Rights and Status of Indigenous Peoples: A Global Comparative and International Legal Analysis', 12 *Harvard Human Rts J* (1999) 57 at 115, and Scheinin, 'The Rights of an Individual and a People: Towards a Nordic Sámi Convention', in M. Åhrén, M. Scheinin, and J.B. Henriksen (eds), *The Nordic Sami Convention: International Human Rights, Self-Determination and Other Central Provisions* (2007) 40 at 43ff, as well as Scheinin, 'The Right of a People to Enjoy Its Culture: Towards a Nordic Saami Rights Convention', in F. Francioni and M. Scheinin (eds), *Cultural Human Rights* (2008) 151 at 154–8.

This *differentia specifica* of indigenous peoples,[38] the collective spiritual relationship to their land, thus appears to be what separates them also from other groups generally, and diffusely, denominated 'minorities', and what has created the need for a special legal regime transcending the general human rights law on the universal and regional planes.[39] There have been eclectic interpretations of human rights conventions that protect certain minority traditions, as in the jurisprudence of the European Court of Human Rights regarding the Roma,[40] and there have been specific treaties, albeit not widely ratified, that protect indigenous peoples, such as ILO Convention No 169. The most comprehensive effort to safeguard indigenous peoples' cultures has, however, been made with the United Nations Declaration on the Rights of Indigenous Peoples of 13 September 2007, passed in the General Assembly by an overwhelming vote, and now enjoying virtually universal support.

The threat to the survival of indigenous peoples' culture and their identity is what has motivated the claims listed above. It underlies the peoples' demands to live on their traditional lands, to continue their inherited ways of life, to self-government. Their cultural preservation and ability to flourish is thus at the root of the claims as recognized by the states; this goal, not primarily political or economic objectives, inspires the positive law guarantees. In this sense, all the rights of indigenous peoples are, broadly speaking, cultural rights, and any interpretation of these rights, whether in UNDRIP or other instruments and prescriptions recognizing rights of indigenous peoples, ought to keep this *telos* in mind.

## 2. Indigenous Peoples' Claims and Aspirations

In order to achieve an order of human dignity, ie the utmost opportunity for human beings to realize their dreams and aspirations, it is essential to inquire into indigenous peoples' views of the world fueling their claims. Pursuant to this inquiry, Reisman concluded that political and economic self-determination are important for indigenous peoples, 'but it is the integrity of the inner worlds of peoples—their rectitude systems or their sense of spirituality—that is their distinctive

---

[38] As to the importance of cultural difference for the international indigenous movement, see Erueti, 'The International Labour Organization and the Internationalization of the Concept of Indigenous Peoples', in S. Allen and A. Xanthaki (eds), *Reflections on the UN Declaration on the Rights of Indigenous Peoples* (2011) 93 at 115ff.

[39] Will Kymlicka warns against the pursuit of exclusive special rights for indigenous peoples as, among other reasons, possibly undermining support for their cause. Kymlicka, 'Beyond the Indigenous/Minority Dichotomy?', in Allen and Xanthaki (2011) 83 at 207 ('We need to recognize that indigenous peoples aren't the only group in need of targeted rights—this is also true, in different ways, of national minorities, the Roma, Dalits, immigrants, and others'). I would suggest, though, that the success of the indigenous peoples' movement should be taken as encouragement for other groups with special needs to pursue a similar path of international legal empowerment, rather than a possibly negative outcome to be lamented.

[40] European Court of Human Rights, Factsheet—Roma and Travellers (May 2013), available at <http://www.echr.coe.int/Documents/FS_Roma_ENG.pdf> (accessed 21 July 2013).

humanity. Without an opportunity to determine, sustain, and develop that integrity, their humanity—and ours—is denied.'[41]

Empirically and historically speaking, virtually all indigenous peoples share a common set of problems resulting from the tortured relationship between the conqueror and the conquered. First, the conqueror took away the land that indigenous peoples, in line with their cosmovision, had freely shared. Secondly, the conqueror's way of life was imposed. Thirdly, political autonomy was drastically curtailed. Fourthly, indigenous peoples have often been relegated to a status of extreme poverty, disease, and despair.[42]

Five basic claims of indigenous peoples arose from this condition: (1) traditional lands should be respected or restored, as a means to their physical, cultural, and spiritual survival; (2) indigenous peoples should have the right to practice their traditions and celebrate their culture and spirituality with all their implications; (3) they should have access to welfare, health, educational, and social services; (4) conquering nations should respect and honour their treaty promises; and (5) indigenous nations should have the right to self-determination.[43]

From the very first statements of the indigenous peoples' movement at the international level,[44] self-determination was the top and unrenounceable demand. It was vital to maintaining the indigenous peoples' culture and spirituality, which, in turn, was inextricably tied to their land. The image of a triangle of self-determination, culture, and land encapsulates these three claims' essential interrelatedness,[45] with culture critically informing and defining both.

The safeguarding of their land is crucial to the effective protection of indigenous peoples' cultures. Being 'indigenous' means to live within one's roots.[46] Indigenous peoples, in a popular definition, have thus 'always been in the place where they are'.[47] While this definition may not reflect empirical truth as, historically, a great many migrations of human communities have taken place, the collective consciousness of indigenous peoples, often expressed in creation stories or similar

---

[41] Reisman (1996) 33.

[42] Cf K.S. Coates, *A Global History of Indigenous Peoples: Struggle and Survival* (2004); Hitchcock, 'The Plight of Indigenous Peoples', 49 *Soc. Educ.* (1985) 457; R.D. Edmunds, F.E. Hoxie, and N. Salisbury, *The People: A History of Native America* (2006); V. Deloria, Jr, *Custer Died For Your Sins: An Indian Manifesto* (1969); R. Jaulin, *La Paix Blanche: Introduction à l'ethnocide* (1970); F. Jennings, *The Invasion of America: Indians, Colonialism, and the Cant of Conquest* (1975); M.A. Jaimes (ed), *The State of Native America: Genocide, Colonization, and Resistance* (1992); T.R. Berger, *A Long and Terrible Shadow: White Values, Native Rights in the Americas 1492–1992* (1991).

[43] Wiessner (1999) 98–9.

[44] See eg Declaration of Principles Adopted by the Fourth General Assembly of the World Council of Indigenous Peoples in Panama, September 1984, Principle 1, reprinted in C. Charters and R. Stavenhagen (eds), *Making the Declaration Work: The United Nations Declaration on the Rights of Indigenous Peoples* (2009) 48, 49.

[45] Cf P. Aikio and M. Scheinin (eds), *Operationalizing the Right of Indigenous Peoples to Self-Determination* (2000).

[46] Etymologically, the Latin word '*indigena*' is composed of two words, '*indi*', meaning 'within' and '*gen*' or '*genere*' meaning 'root', *Longman Dictionary of Contemporary English* (3rd edn, 1995) 724.

[47] *The Longman Dictionary of Contemporary English Online*, Definition of 'indigenous', available at <http://www.ldoceonline.com/dictionary/indigenous> (accessed 11 May 2009).

sacred tales of their origin,[48] places them unequivocally and since time immemorial at the location of their physical existence. More importantly, their beliefs make remaining at that place a compelling dictate of faith.

This claim of a special, deeply spiritual bond with the land has at times been seen as overly romantic, essentialized, thus reductionist, strategically so. Such an opinion, however, would miss the point in various ways. It is in itself reductionist of the empirical reality of human beings, caricaturing individuals as purely economic actors interested solely in power and wealth. Human life and human flourishing extend far beyond the econocentric view of cost/benefit analysis and wealth maximization. Man (and woman) does not live by bread alone. A comprehensive view of human nature would see that beyond power and wealth, human beings are motivated by a range of other goals: respect, well-being, affection, skills, enlightenment, and rectitude.[49] Individual human beings differ in their setting of priorities of aspiration, and the empirical description of such aspirations does not portend any hierarchy between them. There might be, indeed, there often are, mixed human motives or aspirations. The law is ever increasingly called upon to allow access by all persons to the processes of shaping and sharing all of these aspirations, ie things human beings value. This is what any public order of human dignity[50] demands.

Indigenous peoples may be, and often are, at the bottom of the social and economic ladder in virtually all societies they live in.[51] That is why one of their strong claims is the quest for social and economic rights such as food, health care, and shelter.[52] This is, however, not their only, or most characteristic, claim. Their other, more embracing claims have historically asked for preservation of their endangered culture, their language, their lands.[53] This enters a realm not easily assessed or included by materialist *matrices*.

---

[48] P.V. Beck, A.L. Walters, and N. Francisco, *The Sacred: Ways of Knowledge, Sources of Life* (1977) 102 (Medicine men or shamans interpret the creation stories and determine how people 'must live in order to keep the balance of relationships that order the world').

[49] Cf H.D. Lasswell and A. Kaplan, *Power and Society: A Framework for Political Inquiry* (1950); Lasswell and McDougal (1992) 336ff.

[50] Professor Francioni has spoken of human dignity as the 'central notion' of the Universal Declaration of Human Rights. Francioni, 'Culture, Heritage and Human Rights: An Introduction', in Francioni and Scheinin (2008) 1 at 8. See also D. Kretzmer and E. Klein (eds), *The Concept of Human Dignity in Human Rights Discourse* (2002).

[51] For example, '[a]boriginal people [in Canada] are on the bottom of every list where it's a bad place to be, such as regarding life span, income and so forth, and on the top of the list, where that is the worst place to be, such as concerning unemployment, suicide, diabetes and the like'. Morse, 'A View from the North: Aboriginal and Treaty Issues in Canada', 7 *St Thomas L Rev* (1995) 671 at 674. For other country situations, see Wiessner (1999) 60–93.

[52] Due to their frequent relegation to a status of extreme poverty, disease, and despair, they often claim 'access to welfare, health, educational and social services'. Wiessner (1999) 98–9.

[53] Due to the conquerors' taking of their ancestral lands, the drastic curtailment of their ways of life and autonomy, the indigenous peoples mainly claim that 'traditional lands should be respected or restored, as a means to their physical, cultural, and spiritual survival;...indigenous peoples should have the right to practice their traditions and celebrate their culture and spirituality with all its implications;...conquering nations should respect and honor their treaty promises; and...indigenous nations should have the right to self-determination.' Wiessner (1999) 98–9.

It is the realm of spirituality. It is the reality of their inner worlds, their cosmo-visions.[54] It is a world often foreclosed to the modern mind and its overweening idea of progress.[55] It may be characterized as made-up, unprovable, irreal. Still, it is a powerful force that motivates people across the globe in many places at least as powerfully as greed or the desire to remove vast material inequality.

The Coordinator of the Indian Nations Union in the Amazon has articulated the link between culture and land in timeless prose, making this statement of claim:

When the government took our land…they wanted to give us another place…But the State, the government, will never understand that we do not have another place to go. The only possible place for [indigenous] people to live and to re-establish our existence, to speak to our Gods, to speak to our nature, to weave our lives, is where our God created us.…We are not idiots to believe that there is possibility of life for us outside of where the origin of our life is. *Respect our place of living, do not degrade our living conditions, respect this life.… The only thing we have is the right to cry for our dignity and the need to live in our land.*[56]

It is difficult to justify calling such professions of indigenous spirituality pre-textual or strategic, or emanating from a false consciousness. There may be some indigenous persons who do live inauthentic lives, but so do members of other groups. The mystery of faith is a powerful reality common to many human beings around the globe.[57] Religion is not, as it has been called, the 'opiate of the people'. In a multicultural global community, indigenous peoples' value systems and world views, which are deeply spiritual, are at the centre of their demands. Jaime Martínez Luna, a Zapotec anthropologist, makes this important point:

The need to survive causes us to view everything from a materialistic perspective.…But here is where the difference from indigenous thinking springs forth. *Comunalidad* is a way of understanding life as being permeated with spirituality, symbolism, and a greater integration with nature. It is one way of understanding that human beings are not the center, but simply a part of the great natural world. It is here that we can distinguish the enormous difference between Western and indigenous thought.[58]

As Michael Reisman concluded, it is the integrity of the inner worlds of peoples—their rectitude systems or their sense of spirituality—that is their distinctive humanity,[59] and represents their cultural identity in need of being safeguarded by the law.

---

[54] Reisman (1996) 25.

[55] Wiessner (2008) 1143; F. Wilmer, *The Indigenous Voice in World Politics: Since Time Immemorial* (1993); and R. Koselleck, *The Practice of Conceptual History: Timing History, Spacing Concepts* (2002).

[56] Ailton Krenak, World Commission on Environment and Development (WCED), Public Hearing in Sao Paulo, Brazil (28–29 October 1985), in Report of the WCED: Our Common Future, UN Doc A/42/427/Annex (1987), para 69 (emphasis added).

[57] For details, see eg M. Eliade, *The Sacred and the Profane* (1959). See also Beck, Walters, and Francisco (1977).

[58] Martínez Luna (2010) 93–4.

[59] Reisman (1996) 33.

## 3. International Legal Protections of Indigenous Culture Prior to UNDRIP

Despite the rise of other international actors, the state is still the most important and effective generator and enforcer of the law.[60] Both within the state and beyond, in the sphere of international law, indigenous peoples' claims have found increasing resonance and acceptance, with the states shifting from a policy of assimilation and termination to one of indigenous self-determination and cultural survival. This somewhat surprising indigenous resurgence, starting in the 1960s and 1970s, is to a great extent owed to influential crossborder movements facilitated by modern communications technology. The present high point of reempowerment was the 2007 United Nations Declaration on the Rights of Indigenous Peoples (UNDRIP).[61] Still, the law developed in this direction long before the UN General Assembly adopted UNDRIP overwhelmingly.[62]

Before UNDRIP was adopted, a number of the claims raised by indigenous peoples had been addressed in the context of individual human rights regimes. This applies to the right to physical survival; to social and economic rights, to the extent they are accepted; and to the general freedom of religion. None of these individual rights and rules, however, dealt comprehensively with the indigenous condition, even though their interpretation has made enormous strides towards effective safeguarding of key indigenous demands, particular in the area of culture.

### A. ICCPR

The International Covenant on Civil and Political Rights (ICCPR),[63] for example, guarantees the right to life, to privacy, and to family.[64] While these safeguards are important to indigenous persons, the key protection for them as members of cultural minority groups is to be found in Article 27. It reads:

In those States in which ethnic, religious or linguistic minorities exist, persons belonging to such minorities shall not be denied the right, in community with the other members of their group, to enjoy their own culture, to profess and practice their own religion, or to use their own language.

The ICCPR's monitoring body, the Human Rights Committee (HRC), broadly interprets this norm safeguarding cultural integrity;[65] for indigenous peoples,

---

[60] While other communities gain ever more importance, states remain the primary organizations and value providers. Reisman, 'Designing and Managing the Future of the State', 8 *EJIL* (1997) 409 at 416.

[61] UN Declaration on the Rights of Indigenous Peoples, GA Res 61/295, 13 September 2007.

[62] This overview of the legal responses draws freely on my Introductory Note to the UN Declaration on the Rights of Indigenous Peoples, GA Res 61/295, Annex, UN Doc A/RES/61/295, 13 September 2007, available at <http://untreaty.un.org/cod/avl/historicarchives.html> (accessed 17 June 2013).

[63] International Covenant on Civil and Political Rights (ICCPR), GA Res 2200A (XXI), UN Doc A/6316, opened for signature 16 December 1966, entered into force 23 March 1976, available at <http://www.ohchr.org/EN/ProfessionalInterest/Pages/CCPR.aspx> (accessed 21 July 2013).

[64] ICCPR, Arts 6, 17, 23.     [65] ICCPR, Art 27.

it includes essential rights to lands and resources.[66] The same is true regarding self-government, under the right to self-determination of Article 1,[67] reviewed under the state reporting procedure.

This formulation may well reflect the desire of important nation-states to protect culture through (individual) rights of members of the group rather than (collective) rights of the groups themselves.[68] The jurisprudence of the respective treaty monitoring body has, however, moved ever more strongly in the direction of 'collectivizing'[69] these rights. The HRC's *General Comment No 23* on Article 27 ICCPR states that this provision protects 'individual rights', but that the obligations owed by states are collective in nature.[70] In its jurisprudence, it has consistently stated that the right to enjoyment of culture, practice of religion, or use of language can only be meaningfully exercised 'in a community', ie as a group.[71] In the *Kitok* case, the Committee held that reindeer husbandry is a protected activity under Article 27 as the traditional livelihood of the Sami people.[72] In *Ominayak*, it concluded that the exploitation of timber, oil, and gas in the Lubicon Lake Band's lands destroyed the indigenous people's traditional hunting and fishing grounds and thus violated Article 27.[73] The two *Länsman* cases[74] as well as the *Apriana Mahuika* case[75] also state that Article 27 includes a dimension that safeguards indigenous peoples' collective culture.[76] The right to self-determination under Article 1 applies to indigenous peoples as such, as clarified in the HRC's *General Comment No 23*.[77] The HRC monitors this right, however, only under the state reporting procedure, not the individual complaint procedure under the Optional Protocol to the ICCPR.[78]

[66] UN Human Rights Committee (HRC), *General Comment No 23: The Rights of Minorities (Art 27)*, UN Doc CCPR/C/21/Rev.1/Add.5, 8 April 1994, para 7.

[67] HRC, *General Comment No 12: The Right to Self-Determination of Peoples (Art 1)*, UN Doc 13/03/84, 13 March 1984, para 5, available at <http://www.unhchr.ch/tbs/doc.nsf/0/f3c99406d 528f37fc12563ed004960b4?Opendocument> (accessed 29 June 2013). See also Scheinin, 'The Right to Self-Determination under the Covenant on Civil and Political Rights', in Aikio and Scheinin (2000) 179 at 198 (referring to the 'economic or resource dimension of the right to self-determination').

[68] Cf Vrdoljak, 'Genocide and Restitution: Ensuring Each Group's Contribution to Humanity', 22 *EJIL* (2011) 17 at 31.

[69] Åhren, 'Protecting Peoples' Cultural Rights: A Question of Properly Understanding the Notion of States and Nations?', in Francioni and Scheinin (2008) 91 at 107.

[70] HRC, *General Comment No 23: The Rights of Minorities (Art 27)*, UN Doc CCPR/C/21/Rev.1/ Add.5, 8 April 1994, para 6.2.

[71] Vrdoljak (2008) 61, with further references.

[72] *Kitok v Sweden*, No 197/1985, UN Doc A/43/40 (1988), at 221ff.

[73] *Lubicon Lake Band (Bernard Ominayak) v Canada*, No 167/1984, UN Doc A/45/40 (1990), Pt 2 at 1.

[74] *Ilmari Länsman v Finland*, UN Doc CCPR/52/D/511/1992 and *Jouni E. Länsman v Finland*, UN Doc CCPR/C/58/D/671/1995.

[75] *Apriana Mahuika et al v New Zealand*, UN Doc A/56/40 (2000), at 11ff.

[76] Åhren (2008) 107–8.

[77] HRC, *General Comment No 23: The Rights of Minorities (Art 27)*, UN Doc CCPR/C/21/ Rev.1/Add.5, 8 April 1994, para 3(2) (self-determination is a 'right belonging to peoples'). Vrdoljak (2008) 61.

[78] An example of such scrutiny is contained in the Concluding Observations on the Second and Third Reports of the United States of America: 'The State party should take further steps to secure the rights of all indigenous peoples, under articles 1 and 27 of the Covenant, so as to give them greater influence in decision-making affecting their natural environment and their means of subsistence as

One of the other legal issues has been whether Article 27 requires positive measures to be taken to protect a culture. In its *General Comment No 23*, the HRC observed that

culture manifests itself in many forms, including a particular way of life associated with the use of land resources, especially in the case of indigenous peoples. That right may include such traditional activities as fishing or hunting and the right to live in reserves protected by law. The enjoyment of those rights may require positive legal measures of protection and measures to ensure the effective participation of members of minority communities in decisions which affect them.[79]

The logic is this: 'Although the rights protected under article 27 are individual rights, they depend in turn on the ability of the minority group to maintain its culture, language or religion'.[80] It follows that 'positive measures by States may...be necessary to protect the identity of a minority and the rights of its members to enjoy and develop their culture and language and to practise their religion, in community with the other members of the group'.[81]

It has also been argued that the establishment and development of indigenous cultural institutions and systems (that is, indigenous cultural autonomy) is properly located within the concept of collective cultural rights addressed by provisions such as Article 27, and not within the sphere of self-determination addressed by Article 1 of the ICCPR, for example—a concept referred to as essentially belonging to the political, or power, domain.[82] The better argument is, probably, a fusion of both: an understanding of indigenous sovereignty, like that offered by Native American leader and scholar Vine Deloria Jr, as it is based on an essentially cultural foundation.[83]

## B. ICESCR

Similar to Article 27 ICCPR, according to Article 15(1)(a) of the International Covenant on Economic and Social Rights (ICESCR),[84] 'the States Parties to the present Covenant recognize the right of everyone to take part in cultural life'.[85] The UN Committee for Economic, Social and Cultural Rights has stated that minorities and indigenous peoples are guaranteed the freedom to practice and promote

---

well as their own culture.' Concluding Observations of the Human Rights Committee, United States of America, UN Doc CCPR/C/USA/CO/3/Rev.1 (18 December 2006) 12, para 37. For further examples, see Åhren (2008) 108, n 100.

[79] HRC, *General Comment No 23* (1994), para 7.
[80] HRC, *General Comment No 23* (1994), para 6.2.
[81] HRC, *General Comment No 23* (1994), para 6.2.
[82] A. Xanthaki, *Indigenous Rights and United Nations Standards: Self-Determination, Culture and Land* (2007) 215.
[83] See note 2 above.     [84] 993 UNTS 3.
[85] This right to participate in cultural life has been incorporated in a number of other human rights instruments, as listed by Vrdoljak, 'Human Rights and Illicit Trade in Cultural Objects', in S. Borelli and F. Lenzerini (eds), *Cultural Heritage, Cultural Rights, Cultural Diversity: New Developments in International Law* (2012) 107 at 133.

awareness of their culture,[86] defined in both individual and collective dimensions and as reflecting 'the community's way of life and thought'.[87] More recently, the Committee affirmed that the 'strong communal dimension of indigenous peoples' cultural life is indispensable to their existence, well-being and full development, and includes the right to the lands, territories and resources which they have traditionally owned, occupied or otherwise used or acquired'.[88] It has formulated general comments on the rights to adequate housing, food, water, and health as they pertain to indigenous peoples.[89] Regarding the right to health under Article 12, it stated that health services specifically designed for certain communities (especially indigenous peoples) 'should be culturally appropriate, taking into account traditional preventive care, healing practices and medicines'.[90]

## C. Other human rights treaties

The Committee on the Elimination of All Forms of Racial Discrimination has promulgated a general recommendation that expounds upon the states' duty of non-discrimination against indigenous peoples regarding the protection of their culture, their economic and social development, their effective participation and their rights over lands, territories, and resources.[91] State reports are reviewed under these standards and individual situations are monitored under the Committee's early warning/urgent action procedure relating to indigenous communities and peoples.[92]

The Convention on the Rights of the Child[93] includes express protections of the rights of indigenous children to their own cultures, religions, and languages. Article 30 reflects virtually verbatim the right granted under Article 27 ICCPR,

---

[86] General Discussion on the Right to Take Part in Cultural Life as recognized in Art 15 of the International Covenant on Economic, Social and Cultural Rights, UN Doc E/1993/23, Ch VII, para 205, as cited by Vrdoljak (2008) 58.

[87] UN Doc E/1993/23, Ch VII, paras 204, 209, 210, and 213.

[88] *General Comment No 21: The right of everyone to take part in cultural life (Art 15, para 1 (a), of the International Covenant on Economic, Social and Cultural Rights)*, UN Doc E/C.12/GC/21, 21 December 2009, para 36.

[89] *General Comment No 7, The right to adequate housing—forced evictions (Art 11(1) of the International Covenant on Economic, Social and Cultural Rights)*, UN Doc E/1998/22, annex IV, 20 May 1997, para 10; *General Comment No 12: The right to adequate food (Art 11 of the International Covenant on Economic, Social and Cultural Rights)*, UN Doc E/C.12/1999/5, 12 May 1999, para 13; *General Comment No 15: The right to water (Arts 11 and 12 of the International Covenant on Economic, Social and Cultural Rights)*, UN Doc E/C.12/2002/11, 20 January 2003, para 16(d).

[90] *General Comment No 14 (2000): The right to the highest attainable standard of health (Art 12 of the International Covenant on Economic, Social and Cultural Rights)*, UN Doc E/C.12/2000/4, 11 August 2000, para 27.

[91] UN Committee on the Elimination of Racial Discrimination (CERD), *General Recommendation No 23: Indigenous Peoples*, UN Doc A/52/18, Annex V, 18 August 1997. It is now including UNDRIP in its set of normative standards. Thornberry, 'Integrating the UN Declaration on the Rights of Indigenous Peoples into CERD Practice', in Allen and Xanthaki (2011) 61.

[92] Cf CERD, Decision 1 (68): Early Warning and Urgent Action Procedure, UN Doc CERD/C/USA/DEC/1, 11 April 2006.

[93] Convention on the Rights of the Child, GA Res 44/25, Annex, 44, UN GAOR Supp (No 49) 167, UN Doc A/44/49, 20 November 1989.

whereas Article 29(d) mandates the directing of a child's education, inter alia, to the development of 'his or her own cultural identity, language and values'.[94]

Reviews of state reports under the Convention against Torture, the Convention on the Elimination of All Forms of Discrimination against Women and the Convention on the Protection of the Rights of All Migrant Workers and Members of Their Families have paid special attention to indigenous persons.[95]

## D. UNESCO instruments

The key contribution of indigenous peoples to the cultural diversity of this planet has been recognized in various United Nations Educational, Scientific and Cultural Organization (UNESCO) instruments, spearheaded by the 2001 Declaration on Cultural Diversity.[96]

UNESCO is a place particularly dedicated to the protection of the cultural property of indigenous peoples. Tangible immovable items of indigenous cultural property may be inscribed in the World Heritage List under the 1972 UNESCO World Heritage Convention,[97] albeit in the United States—and, according to the UN Expert Mechanism on the Rights of Indigenous Peoples and the African Commission on Human and Peoples' Rights, globally—not without the free, prior, and informed consent of the indigenous peoples.[98]

Similar involvement of indigenous peoples in the designation and management of intangible cultural resources is mandated in the 2003 UNESCO Convention for the Safeguarding of the Intangible Cultural Heritage (CSICH).[99] Still, it is only states that can ultimately determine what will be added to the List of Representative Intangible Heritage of Mankind.[100]

---

[94] Convention on the Rights of the Child, Art 30 (reflecting Art 27 ICCPR), and Art 29(c) (mandating the directing of a child's education towards, inter alia, the 'development of respect for the child's parents, his or her own cultural identity, language and values').

[95] Wiessner, Introductory Note to the UN Declaration on the Rights of Indigenous Peoples, GA Res 61/295, Annex, UN Doc A/RES/61/295, 13 September 2007, available at <http://untreaty.un.org/cod/avl/historicarchives.html> (accessed 17 June 2013).

[96] UNESCO Universal Declaration on Cultural Diversity, UNESCO Doc 31C/Res 25, Annex I, 2 November 2001, available at <http://portal.unesco.org/en/ev.php-URL_ID=13179&URL_DO=DO_TOPIC&URL_SECTION=201.html> (accessed 21 July 2013).

[97] UNESCO Convention concerning the Protection of the World Cultural and Natural Heritage, 1972.

[98] For details, see Lenzerini, 'Cultural Rights and Cultural Heritage', in 2012 ILA Final Report, 23.

[99] 2012 ILA Final Report, 24–5. UNESCO Convention for the Safeguarding of the Intangible Cultural Heritage, UNESCO Doc MISC/2003/CLT/CH/14, 17 October 2003. See also Lenzerini, 'Intangible Cultural Heritage: The Living Culture of Peoples', 22 *EJIL* (2011) 101.

[100] 'The Convention…leaves to the states, and not the communities, the faculty of determining which manifestations of heritage should be inventoried and protected, both at the national and, most importantly, at the international level, through the List of Representative Intangible Heritage of Mankind.…As states are the only ones which can nominate manifestations of heritage for the list, it is very easy to see that states will prefer those manifestations of heritage that are not politically controversial.' Lixinski, 'Selecting Heritage: The Interplay of Art, Politics and Identity', 22 *EJIL* (2011) 81 at 82. An indigenous people's heritage can, however, not be listed without its free, prior, and informed consent. Lenzerini, 2012 ILA Final Report, 25.

'Intangible cultural heritage' is defined by Article 2 CSICH as:

the practices, representations, expressions, knowledge, skills—as well as the instruments, objects, artefacts and cultural spaces associated therewith—that communities, groups and, in some cases, individuals recognize as part of their cultural heritage. This intangible cultural heritage, transmitted from generation to generation, is constantly recreated by communities and groups in response to their environment, their interaction with nature and their history, and provides them with a sense of identity and continuity, thus promoting respect for cultural diversity and human creativity.

This definition denotes a key philosophical difference between the approach taken by the World Heritage Convention and the Intangible Heritage Convention: while tangible heritage is seen to deserve international protection in light of its 'outstanding *universal* value', ie is *objectively* determined, intangible cultural heritage adds to the definition the self-recognition of its manifestations as part of the cultural heritage by the communities concerned, or, as Federico Lenzerini put it, the *'subjective* perspective of its creators and bearers, who recognize the heritage concerned as an essential part of their idiosyncratic cultural inheritance, even though it may appear absolutely worthless to external observers'.[101] This convention provides potentially broad protection for indigenous cultural heritage, but has attracted criticism for its weak implementation scheme, leading to a call for effective intangible cultural heritage safeguarding by international human rights bodies.[102]

Of interest for indigenous peoples is also the 2005 Convention for the Protection of the Diversity of Cultural Expression.[103] Its guiding principles include the 'protection and promotion of the diversity of cultural expression' and the 'recognition of equal dignity of and respect for all cultures, including the cultures of persons belonging to minorities and indigenous peoples'.[104] Its objectives include: 'to encourage dialogue among cultures with a view to ensuring wider and balanced cultural exchanges in the world in favour of intercultural respect and a culture of peace'; and 'to foster interculturality in order to develop cultural interaction in the spirit of building bridges among peoples'.[105] 'Interculturality' is defined as 'the existence and equitable interaction of diverse cultures and the possibility of generating shared cultural expressions through dialogue and mutual respect'.[106]

## E. Related conventions and statutes

In addition, indigenous peoples are specifically protected if their cultural heritage is stolen or illegally exported. According to Article 5(3)(d) of the 1995 UNIDROIT

---

[101] Lenzerini (2011) 108.

[102] Lenzerini (2011) 115.

[103] UNESCO Convention on the Protection and Promotion of the Diversity of Cultural Expressions, UNESCO Doc CLT-2005/CONVENTION DIVERSITE-CULT REV, 20 October 2005. For a critical assessment, see Graber, 'The New UNESCO Convention on Cultural Diversity: A Counterbalance to the WTO?', 9 *J Int'l Economic L* (2006) 553.

[104] UNESCO Convention on the Protection and Promotion of the Diversity of Cultural Expressions, Art 2 (hereinafter UNESCO Diversity Convention).

[105] UNESCO Diversity Convention, Arts 1(c) and (d).

[106] UNESCO Diversity Convention, Art 4(8).

Convention on Stolen or Illegally Exported Cultural Objects,[107] a court or other competent authority of a state party must order the return of an illegally exported cultural object if the requesting state establishes that the removal of the object from its territory significantly impairs 'the traditional or ritual use of the object by a tribal or Indigenous community'. Also, where the object was created by indigenous communities for their traditional use, it shall be returned to that community.[108]

Of particular interest to indigenous peoples is the return of remains of their loved ones. The US Native American Graves Protection and Repatriation Act (NAGPRA)[109] has led the way. A similar practice exists in Australia.[110] And a recent campaign by the Museum of New Zealand effectuated the return from museums or private collections abroad to New Zealand of 300 to 500 mummified Māori heads (*Mokomokai*) to be returned for burial according to Māori traditions to the relatives of the person to whom the head belonged in life—when they may be identified—or to be kept in the museum.[111]

Article 8(j) of the Convention on Biological Diversity[112] affirmed indigenous peoples' rights to their traditional knowledge and has led to continued protective efforts in this forum. The World Intellectual Property Organization also discusses the protection of traditional knowledge and cultural expressions.[113]

## F. The UN Draft Principles and Guidelines on the Protection of the Heritage of Indigenous People

In 2000, the United Nations Sub-Commission on the Promotion and Protection of Human Rights approved the revised United Nations Draft Principles and Guidelines on the Protection of the Heritage of Indigenous People,[114] suggesting a comprehensive *sui generis* regime of protection of indigenous heritage.[115] The

---

[107] 34 ILM 1322.

[108] 34 ILM 1322, Art 7(2). See also Vrdoljak (2012) 122.

[109] Public Law 101-601 of 16 November 1990.

[110] Lenzerini, 2010 ILA Final Report, 21–2, with reference to European Network for Indigenous Australian Rights, 'Repatriation of Aboriginal Human Remains', available at <http://archive.eniar.org/repatriation.html> (accessed 21 July 2013).

[111] Lenzerini, 'The Tension between Communities' Cultural Rights and Global Interests: The Case of the Māori *Mokomokai*', in Borelli and Lenzerini (2012) 157.

[112] United Nations Convention on Biological Diversity, Art 8(j), UN Doc ST/DIP/1307, 5 June 1992, available at <http://www.cbd.int/convention/text/> (accessed 29 June 2013).

[113] Cf World Intellectual Property Organization (WIPO), Traditional Knowledge, <http://www.wipo.int/tk/en/tk> (accessed 29 June 2013).

[114] UN Economic and Social Council (ECOSOC), Commission on Human Rights, Human Rights of Indigenous Peoples: Report of the Seminar on the Draft Principles and Guidelines for the Protection of the Heritage of Indigenous People, UN Doc E/CN.4/Sub.2/2000/26, 19 June 2000, available at <http://www.unhchr.ch/Huridocda/Huridoca.nsf/0/42263fd3915c047ec1256929004f1f fc?Opendocument> (accessed 29 June 2013) (hereinafter Indigenous Heritage Report). This 2000 UN seminar reviewed and revised the original draft principles and guidelines contained in an elaborate research report and study by Mrs Erica-Irene A. Daes, 'Protection of the Heritage of Indigenous People', UN Sales No E 97. XIV.3 (1997).

[115] Wiessner and Battiste, 'The 2000 Revision of the United Nations Draft Principles and Guidelines on the Protection of the Heritage of Indigenous People', 13 *St Thomas L Rev* (2000) 383 at 384. The authors served as facilitators for the 2000 UN seminar.

concept of 'heritage', as the object of protection, was chosen because the alternatives 'cultural property' and 'intellectual property' were considered inappropriate
in the context of indigenous peoples. First, 'property' with its inevitable connotation of individual exclusive right could not adequately reflect indigenous peoples'
view of connectedness with their land and attendant community and individual
responsibilities.[116] Secondly, the distinction between 'cultural' and 'intellectual'
property was seen, from the indigenous perspective, as 'not very useful' as it
reflected an 'artificial' separation of heart and mind.[117] The term 'heritage', in contrast, is 'everything that belongs to the distinct identity of a people'[118] and 'includes
all expressions of the relationship between the people, their land, and the other
living beings and spirits which share the land'.[119]

Importantly, the concept of indigenous peoples' heritage was delimited very
broadly. In accordance with the earlier draft, it includes all artifacts, cultural
expressions such as works of art, music, dance, and ceremonies; traditional knowledge, including scientific, agricultural, medicinal, and other use of flora and
fauna; human remains; burial grounds; and sacred sites.[120] This comprehensive
approach reflects the indigenous holistic worldview of interconnectedness of all
beings and things, material and immaterial. It also provides the backdrop for a
coherent policy with respect to the diverse items or elements of indigenous heritage. To achieve consistency, consensus was reached on the suggestion to replace
the earlier draft's terms 'culture, arts and sciences' with the term 'heritage' throughout the document.[121] With respect to sacred sites, the original draft provided for
protection of such sites only against unauthorized entry or use. The new version
of the guidelines also provides for protection against destruction and deterioration.[122] As to traditional knowledge, other international organizations and treaty
regimes have addressed the phenomenon of dispossession and the need for protection.[123] Since they, however, come at the issue from different angles and with
potentially different objectives, such as the protection of biodiversity and the sharing of biodiversity-related knowledge, or the limited purposes of intellectual property regimes, they 'run, in indigenous eyes, the danger of losing the forest for the
trees'.[124] The holistic approach of the draft principles and guidelines therefore is,
to them, of special appeal.

In 2005, an expanded working paper by Yozo Yokota and the Saami Council on
the Draft Principles and Guidelines retained the broad definition of the heritage of

---

[116] Daes (1997) 3, para 26.      [117] Daes (1997) 3, para 21.
[118] Daes (1997) 3, para 24.      [119] Daes (1997) 21, para 164.
[120] Draft Guideline 13, Indigenous Heritage Report, 13.
[121] Wiessner and Battiste (2000) 386.
[122] Draft Guideline 25, Indigenous Heritage Report, 15.
[123] See Wiessner, 'Indigenous Peoples: General Report', 10 *YB Int'l Envtl L* (2000) 193, with
reference to pertinent activities by, inter alia, the Commission on Sustainable Development, the
Intergovernmental Forum on Forests, the Conference of the Parties to the Biodiversity Convention,
the World Intellectual Property Organization (WIPO), UNESCO, the United Nations Environmental
Programme (UNEP), and the United Nations Development Programme (UNDP).
[124] Wiessner and Battiste (2000) 388.

indigenous peoples.[125] It reiterated that indigenous peoples' heritage must not be exploited without their free, prior, and informed consent.[126]

## G. The World Bank

The World Bank Operational Policy and Bank Policy on Indigenous Peoples (OP/BP 4.10) of 2005[127] continued an early involvement of indigenous peoples in their projects as demonstrated in Operational Directive 4.20 of 17 September 1991.[128] It demanded, wherever possible, the active participation of indigenous peoples in the development process itself.

## H. The Inter-American Human Rights Convention

On the regional level, the Inter-American Commission and Court of Human Rights have interpreted the American Declaration of the Rights and Duties of Man and the American Convention on Human Rights in ways tailored to the specific needs of indigenous peoples. These include the right to life, including a dignified communal existence, the right to collective property over lands, territories, and natural resources, the right to consultation and consent, and the right to political participation in accordance with their traditional ways of life.[129] The cultural grounding was manifest in these decisions, particularly in the landmark *Awas Tingni* judgment of the Inter-American Court of Human Rights (IACtHR) of 31 August 2001,[130] affirming the existence of an indigenous people's collective right to its land. It stated:

Through an evolutionary interpretation of international instruments for the protection of human rights, taking into account applicable norms of interpretation and pursuant to article 29(b) of the Convention—which precludes a restrictive interpretation of rights—, it is the opinion of this Court that article 21 of the Convention protects the right to property

---

[125] Expanded Working paper submitted by Yozo Yokota and the Saami Council on the substantive proposals on the draft principles and guidelines for the protection of the heritage of indigenous peoples, UN Doc E/CN.4/Sub.2/AC.4/2005/3, para III.A.1.

[126] Review of the draft principles and guidelines on the heritage of indigenous peoples, prepared by Yozo Yokota and the Saami Council, UN Doc E/CN.4/Sub.2/AC.4/2004/5.

[127] Cf Operational Directive 4.10 on Indigenous Peoples, *World Bank Operational Manual* (July 2005, rev April 2013), available at <http://web.worldbank.org/WBSITE/EXTERNAL/PROJECTS/EXTPOLICIES/EXTOPMANUAL/0,,contentMDK:20553653~menuPK:4564185~pagePK:64709096~piPK:64709108~theSitePK:502184,00.html> (accessed 29 June 2013).

[128] Operational Directive 4.2 on Indigenous Peoples, *World Bank Operational Manual* (17 September 1991).

[129] See eg *Mayagna (Sumo) Awas Tingni Community v Nicaragua*, IACtHR (2001) Series C, No 79, 31 August 2001; *Moiwana Village v Suriname*, IACtHR (2005) Series C, No 124, 15 June 2005; *Yakye Axa Indigenous Community v Paraguay*, IACtHR (2005) Series C, No 125, 17 June 2005; *Sawhoyamaxa Indigenous Community v Paraguay*, IACtHR (2006) Series C, No 146, 29 March 2006; *Saramaka People v Suriname*, IACtHR (2007) Series C, No 172, 28 November 2007.

[130] *Awas Tingni*, see note 129 above. For details of this case, see Anaya and Grossman, 'The Case of Awas Tingni v. Nicaragua: A New Step in the International Law of Indigenous Peoples', 19 *Arizona J Int'l & Comp L* (2002) 1.

in a sense which includes, among others, the rights of members of the indigenous communities within the framework of communal property, which is also recognized by the Constitution of Nicaragua.

Given the characteristics of the instant case, some specifications are required on the concept of property in indigenous communities. Among indigenous peoples there is a communitarian tradition regarding a communal form of collective property of the land, in the sense that ownership of the land is not centered on an individual but rather on the group and its community. Indigenous groups, by the fact of their very existence, have the right to live freely in their own territory; the close ties of indigenous people with the land must be recognized and understood as the fundamental basis of their cultures, their spiritual life, their integrity, and their economic survival. For indigenous communities, relations to the land are not merely a matter of possession and production but a material and spiritual element which they must fully enjoy, even to preserve their cultural legacy and transmit it to future generations.[131]

Other decisions in the same vein followed.[132] In *Moiwana Village v Suriname*, this cultural motivation was vividly present when the Court saw the right of members of the indigenous community to their physical, mental, and moral integrity (Article 5(1)) violated by the state denying them the right to bury their dead in line with their traditions. The Court reasoned:

If the various death rituals are not performed according to N'djuka tradition, it is considered a profound moral transgression, which will not only anger the spirit of the individual who died, but also may offend other ancestors of the community.... This leads to a number of 'spiritually-caused illnesses' that become manifest as actual physical maladies and can potentially affect the entire natural lineage... [O]ne of the greatest sources of suffering for the Moiwana community members is that they do not know what has happened to the remains of their loved ones, and, as a result, they cannot honor and bury them in accordance with fundamental norms of N'djuka culture.[133]

Judge Cançado Trindade, in his separate opinion, stated that only by properly honouring the dead can their collective memory of the deceased be saved from oblivion. Deciding this way was an essential prerequisite of 'safeguarding their right to life *lato sensu*, encompassing the right to cultural identity, which finds expression in their acknowledged links of solidarity with their dead'.[134] In a later interpretation of this decision, the same key judge declared that the law applied by the IACtHR in such a case found its material source in the universal juridical conscience which 'has evolved towards a clear recognition of the relevance of cultural diversity for the universality of human rights, and vice-versa'.[135]

---

[131] *Awas Tingni*, see note 129 above, paras 148–9.    [132] See note 129 above.
[133] See note 129 above, paras 98ff.
[134] See Separate Opinion of Judge Cançado Trindade, para 92. See also Lenzerini (2011) 116.
[135] *Moiwana Village v Suriname*, IACtHR (2006) Series C, No 145, Interpretation of the Judgment of Merits, Reparations and Costs, judgment of 8 February 2006, Separate Opinion of Judge Cançado Trindade, para 24; Lenzerini, (2011) 116.

## I. The African Charter on Human and Peoples' Rights

In 2000, the African Commission on Human and Peoples' Rights established a working group of experts on indigenous populations/communities, which submitted its first report in 2005.[136] It identified a number of indigenous peoples, detailing mainly different groups of hunter-gatherers and pastoralists,[137] and reporting a great number of violations of their rights, including their rights to land and other resources[138] as well as their cultural and language rights.[139]

These were important measures of progress. Arguably missing in the broad-based universal human rights instruments, however, was a specific protection of the distinctive cultural and group identity of indigenous peoples as well as the spatial and political dimension of that identity, namely, their ways of life. The clearest example of the 'general human rights gap' in the global instruments, not the Inter-American instruments, may be the lack of a legal guarantee to indigenous peoples, as communities, to maintain control over the traditional lands with which they have deep, often spiritual, ties. Other such distinctive claims are those for the return of sacred remains, artifacts, and sites, and their demand of governments to honour treaty obligations.

## J. ILO Convention No 169

Focusing on many of these communal needs and aspirations, in 1989, the International Labour Organization (ILO) promulgated the Convention Concerning Indigenous and Tribal Peoples in Independent Countries (ILO Convention No 169).[140] Deliberately created to supersede the more assimilationist Convention No 107 of 1957,[141] this treaty has played an important role in identifying and codifying the rights of indigenous peoples. It has now been ratified by virtually all of the Latin American countries with significant indigenous populations.[142] It ensures indigenous peoples' control over their legal status, internal structures, and environment,[143] and it guarantees indigenous peoples' rights to ownership and possession of the total environment they occupy or use.[144]

---

[136] Commission on Human Rights, Sub-Commission on the Promotion and Protection of Human Rights, Working Group on Minorities, Report of the African Commission's Working Group of Experts on Indigenous Populations/Communities, UN Doc E/CN.4/Sub.2/AC.5/2005/WP.3, 22 April 2005 (hereinafter African Commission Expert Working Group Report).

[137] African Commission Expert Working Group Report, 15ff.

[138] African Commission Expert Working Group Report, 21ff.

[139] African Commission Expert Working Group Report, 40ff.

[140] Convention No 169 Concerning Indigenous and Tribal Peoples in Independent Countries, adopted 27 June 1989, 28 ILM 1382.

[141] Convention No 107 Concerning Indigenous and Tribal Peoples in Independent Countries, entered into force 2 June 1959, UNTS 328, 247.

[142] As of 15 April 2012, Convention No 169 has been ratified by 22 countries. For details, see NORMLEX Database of International Labour Standards at <http://www.ilo.org/dyn/normlex/en/f?p=1000:1:0::NO:::> (accessed 29 June 2013).

[143] Cf Firestone, Lilley and Torres de Noronha, 'Cultural Diversity, Human Rights, and the Emergence of Indigenous Peoples in International and Comparative Environmental Law', 20 *American University Int'l L Rev* (2005) 219.

[144] Convention No 169, Arts 1–19.

Still, a global, comprehensive, inclusive, and integrated prescriptive effort was needed to listen to and address all of the concerns of indigenous peoples. The forum for these efforts was the United Nations, and the ultimate result is the 2007 UNDRIP.

## 4. The United Nations Declaration on the Rights of Indigenous Peoples

In 1971, as the plight of indigenous peoples had become ever more visible, the United Nations Economic and Social Council appointed a Special Rapporteur, Mr José Martínez Cobo of Ecuador, to study patterns of discrimination against indigenous peoples around the globe.[145] In 1982, upon receipt of his reports documenting a wide range of human rights issues, the United Nations Sub-Commission on Prevention of Discrimination and Protection of Minorities (the 'Sub-Commission') appointed a Working Group on Indigenous Populations with the twofold mandate: (1) to review national developments pertaining to the promotion and protection of the human rights and fundamental freedoms of indigenous peoples; and (2) to develop international standards concerning the rights of indigenous peoples.[146]

In 1985, under the determined leadership of Chairperson-Rapporteur Mrs Erica-Irene A. Daes,[147] this working group of independent experts began drafting a declaration on the rights of indigenous peoples, taking into account the comments and suggestions of participants in its sessions, particularly representatives of indigenous peoples and governments.[148] At its 11th session, in July 1993, the Working Group agreed on a final text for the draft declaration and submitted it to the Sub-Commission.[149] In August 1994, the Sub-Commission adopted the draft declaration and submitted it to the Commission on Human Rights for consideration.[150]

---

[145] Cf ECOSOC Res 1589 (L), UN Doc E/5044, 21 May 1971, 16; ECOSOC, Commission on Human Rights, Sub-Commission on Prevention of Discrimination and Protection of Minorities, Report on the Work of its Twenty-Fourth Session, UN Doc E/CN.4/Sub.2/323, 1 August 1971. For an account of the inception of the United Nations' involvement with indigenous peoples' issues, see the recollections by an official spearheading the effort, Augusto Willemsen-Díaz, 'How Indigenous Peoples' Rights Reached the UN', in Charters and Stavenhagen (2009) 16.

[146] ECOSOC Res 1982/34, Supp No 1, UN Doc E/1982/59, 7 May 1982, 26 (Study of the problem of discrimination against indigenous populations).

[147] For a summary of her efforts, in her own voice, see E.-I. Daes, *Indigenous Peoples: Keepers of Our Past, Custodians of Our Future* (2008).

[148] Daes, 'The Contribution of the Working Group on Indigenous Populations to the Genesis and Evolution of the UN Declaration on the Rights of Indigenous Peoples', in Charters and Stavenhagen (2009) 48.

[149] ECOSOC, Sub-Commission on Prevention of Discrimination and Protection of Minorities, Report of the Working Group on Indigenous Populations on its 11th Session, UN Doc E/CN.4/SUB.2/1993/29, Annex 1, 23 August 1993.

[150] ECOSOC, Sub-Commission on Prevention of Discrimination and Protection of Minorities, Report on its 46th Session, UN Doc E/CN.4/Sub.2/1994/5, 28 October 1994.

In 1995, the Commission on Human Rights appointed a new Working Group, with predominantly government participation, charged with achieving a consensus on the draft declaration.[151] As the Commission on Human Rights was transformed into the Human Rights Council (the 'Council'), the second act of the Council was to approve the draft of UNDRIP by adopting Resolution 1/2 of 29 June 2006 by a vote of 30 in favour to two against, with 12 abstentions.[152] In doing so, the Council adopted without change a joint draft resolution submitted by Peru based on the final compromise text proposed by the Chairman of the Working Group, Mr Luis-Enrique Chávez of Peru.[153] On 28 November 2006, the Third Committee of the General Assembly, by a vote of 82 in favour to 67 against, with 25 abstentions, decided to defer consideration pending further consultations, with a view to taking action on UNDRIP before the end of the 61st session of the General Assembly, ie early September 2007.[154] The last changes were made over the course of 2007, primarily to accommodate some of the demands of the African states which had resulted in the deferral.[155]

The final version of UNDRIP was adopted on 13 September 2007 by an affirmative vote of 143 states in the General Assembly. Four countries—the United States, Canada, Australia, and New Zealand—voted against it, while 11—Azerbaijan, Bangladesh, Bhutan, Burundi, Colombia, Georgia, Kenya, Nigeria, Russia, Samoa, and Ukraine—abstained.[156] The US no vote at the time focused on UNDRIP's right to self-determination in Article 3, which, in its view, despite limiting language in Articles 4 and 46, did not exclude the option of secession with sufficient clarity. Also, the idea of collective rights was seen as possibly colliding with the principle 'that one group cannot have human rights that are denied to other groups within the same nation-state' and possibly violating the rights of individuals within the group. Similarly, a veto power of one group regarding issues that

---

[151] ECOSOC, Sub-Commission on Prevention of Discrimination and Protection of Minorities, Report on its 51st Session, UN Doc E/1995/23, 1 January 1995; ECOSOC Res 1995/32, 52nd plen mtg, Supp No 4, UN Doc E/CN.4/1995/32, 25 July 1995, 110.

[152] Human Rights Council, Working Group of the Commission on Human Rights to Elaborate a Draft Declaration in Accordance with Paragraph 5 of the General Assembly Resolution 49/214 of 23 December 1994, UN Doc A/HRC/RES/1/2 (13 November 2006). For a detailed account of the diplomatic engineering of this surprising feat, see De Alba, 'The Human Rights Council's Adoption of the United Nations Declaration on the Rights of Indigenous Peoples', in Charters and Stavenhagen (2009) 108.

[153] ECOSOC, Commission on Human Rights, Report of the Working Group Established in Accordance with Commission on Human Rights Resolution 1995/32 of 3 March 1995 on its 10th Session, UN Doc E/CN.4/2005/89/Add.2, 1 April 2005; ECOSOC, Commission on Human Rights, Report of the Working Group Established in Accordance with Commission on Human Rights Resolution 1995/32 of 3 March 1995 on its 11th Session, UN Doc E/CN.4/2006/79, 22 March 2006. For background, see Chávez, 'The Declaration on the Rights of Indigenous Peoples Breaking the Impasse: The Middle Ground', in Charters and Stavenhagen (2009) 96.

[154] Human Rights Council, Report of the Third Committee to the General Assembly, UN Doc A/61/448, 6 December 2006; GA Res 61/178, UN Doc A/RES/61/178, 6 March 2007.

[155] For an excellent exposé and discussion of African positions regarding UNDRIP, see Van Genugten, 'Protection of Indigenous Peoples on the African Continent: Concepts, Position Seeking, and the Interaction of Legal Systems', 104 *AJIL* (2010) 29 at 34.

[156] United Nations Declaration on the Rights of Indigenous Peoples, GA Res 61/295, 13 September 2007.

may affect them would run against principles of democratic decision-making. In addition, UNDRIP's land, resource, and redress rights were seen as 'overly broad', 'unworkable', and 'inconsistent'.[157] Canada, Australia, and New Zealand issued similar statements.[158]

Subsequently, Australia had a change of government and change of heart: it endorsed UNDRIP in April 2009.[159] Similarly, on 19 April 2010, the government of New Zealand declared its support for the Declaration.[160] On 12 November 2010, Canada formally endorsed UNDRIP.[161] Colombia and Samoa, originally abstaining countries, have now expressed their support for UNDRIP.[162] Most importantly, on 16 December 2010, President Barack Obama endorsed the Declaration on behalf of the United States of America.[163] We have thus arrived at a global consensus on UNDRIP.

UNDRIP formulates the rights of indigenous peoples to the extent, as well as in the structure and format, that the international community of states has recognized them. In UN practice, as a 'declaration', it is a 'solemn instrument resorted to only in very rare cases relating to matters of major and lasting import-ance where maximum compliance is expected'.[164] The state practice and *opinio juris* backing up the claim of customary international law predating key parts of the Declaration, and involving the triangle of culture, self-determination and land, will be dealt with later.[165]

The safeguarding of indigenous cultures plays a dominant role in UNDRIP: at least 17 of the 46 articles are about cultural rights; it has been stated that 'in fact, one can find the cultural rights angle in each article of the Declaration'.[166]

---

[157] Press Release, Robert Hagen, US Advisor, US Mission to the UN (USUN), Observations of the US with Respect to the Declaration on the Rights of Indigenous Peoples, Annex (13 September 2007), available at <http://www.shunpiking.com/ol0406/0406-IP-positionofUS.htm> (accessed 29 June 2013).

[158] Cf Press Release, General Assembly Adopts Declaration on Rights of Indigenous Peoples; 'Major Step Forward' Towards Human Rights For All, Says President, UN Doc GA/10612, 13 September 2007, available at <http://www.un.org/News/Press/docs/2007/ga10612.doc.htm> (accessed 29 June 2013).

[159] Press Release, Michael Dodson, Forum Rapporteur, UN Permanent Forum on Indigenous Issues, Australian Government Announcement on the United Nations Declaration on the Rights of Indigenous Peoples. 3 April 2009, available at <http://www.un.org/esa/socdev/unpfii/documents/Australia_official_statement_endorsement_UNDRIP.pdf> (accessed 29 June 2013).

[160] Press Release, John Key, Prime Minister, New Zealand Government, 'National Govt to Support UN Rights Declaration', 20 April 2010, available at <http://www.beehive.govt.nz/release/national+govt+support+un+rights+declaration> (accessed 29 June 2013).

[161] See Press Release, Indian and Northern Affairs Canada, 'Canada's Statement of Support on the United Nations Declaration on the Rights of Indigenous Peoples', 12 November 2010, available at <http://www.ainc-inac.gc.ca/ap/ia/dcl/stmt-eng.asp> (accessed 29 June 2013).

[162] 2010 ILA Interim Report, 5.

[163] 'Remarks by the President at the White House Tribal Nations Conference', 16 December 2010, available at <http://www.whitehouse.gov/the-press-office/2010/12/16/remarks-president-white-house-tribal-nations-conference> (accessed 29 June 2013).

[164] ECOSOC, 19 March–14 April 1962, Report of the Commission on Human Rights, UN Doc E/3616/Rev, para 105.

[165] Cf text at notes 185ff below.

[166] Stamatopoulou, 'Taking Cultural Rights Seriously: The Vision of the UN Declaration on the Rights of Indigenous Peoples', in Allen and Xanthaki (2011) 392.

The preamble affirms that indigenous peoples are 'equal to all other peoples', and that 'all peoples contribute to the diversity and richness of civilization and cultures, which constitute the common heritage of mankind'. Even though their situation 'varies from region to region and from country to country',[167] indigenous peoples and persons enjoy all human rights (Articles 1, 17(1)), and they are free and equal to all others (Article 2). The essential novelty of this instrument is its recognition of 'indispensable' collective rights,[168] which include: self-determination, the preservation and flourishing of their cultures, and the protection of indigenous peoples' rights to their lands. The rights of indigenous peoples to their heritage include their exclusive control over it, as stated in Article 31(1) UNDRIP:

Indigenous peoples have the right to maintain, control, protect and develop their cultural heritage, traditional knowledge and traditional cultural expressions, as well as the manifestations of their sciences, technologies and cultures, including human and genetic resources, seeds, medicines, knowledge of the properties of fauna and flora, oral traditions, literatures, designs, sports and traditional games and visual and performing arts. They also have the right to maintain, control, protect and develop their intellectual property over such cultural heritage, traditional knowledge, and traditional cultural expressions.[169]

Article 3 of UNDRIP recognizes indigenous peoples' claims to self-determination broadly as the right to 'freely determine their political status and freely pursue their economic, social and cultural development',[170] while Article 4 guarantees their 'right to autonomy or self-government in matters relating to their internal and local affairs, as well as ways and means for financing their autonomous functions'.[171] Also, in reaction to various states' articulated fears of the spectre of secession, Article 46(1) excludes any interpretation that would 'authorize or encourage any action which would dismember or impair, totally or in part, the territorial integrity or political unity of sovereign and independent States'.[172]

The claim to indigenous sovereignty is primarily founded upon indigenous peoples' aspirations to preserve the indigenous peoples' inherited ways of life, change those traditions as they see necessary, and, in sum, allow indigenous cultures to flourish. The effective protection of indigenous culture is thus key to its understanding. This fundamental policy goal undergirds, in particular, the novel prohibition of forced assimilation, sometimes referred to as 'ethnocide', against indigenous peoples (Article 8(1)—going beyond the prohibition of genocide against them, as enunciated in Article 7(2)),[173] the prohibition of their forced removal and relocation (Article 10).

Key cultural rights in a narrow sense are contained in Articles 11 through 13. Article 11 guarantees the right to practise and revitalize indigenous peoples' cultural

---

[167] UNDRIP, preamble.    [168] UNDRIP, preamble.
[169] Xanthaki, 'Cultural Rights and Identity', in 2010 ILA Interim Report, 21 at 25, noting the 'comprehensiveness' of this concept of cultural heritage.
[170] UNDRIP, Art 3.    [171] UNDRIP, Art 4.    [172] UNDRIP, Art 46(1).
[173] Even though Art 8(1) UNDRIP does not use the word 'ethnocide', it captures its essence: 'Indigenous peoples and individuals have the right not to be subjected to forced assimilation or destruction of their culture.'

traditions and customs, including 'the right to maintain, protect and develop the past, present and future manifestations of their cultures, such as archaeological and historical sites, artefacts, designs, ceremonies, technologies and visual and performing arts and literature' and customs. Article 12 enshrines the rights of indigenous peoples 'to manifest, practise, develop and teach their spiritual and religious traditions, customs and ceremonies'; 'to maintain, protect, and have access in privacy to their religious and cultural sites'; 'to the use and control of their ceremonial objects'; as well as 'to the repatriation of their human remains'. Article 13 addresses indigenous intangible heritage, emphasizing that '[i]ndigenous peoples have the right to revitalize, use, develop and transmit to future generations their histories, languages, oral traditions, philosophies, writing systems and literatures, and to designate and retain their own names for communities, places and persons', requiring states to 'take effective measures to ensure that this right is protected' and 'to ensure that indigenous peoples can understand and be understood in political, legal and administrative proceedings, where necessary through the provision of interpretation or by other appropriate means'. An indigenous people's language is central to its culture—an ever more important issue in view of the accelerating threat that those languages will vanish and the need for this alarming downward spiral to be brought to a halt.[174]

Article 14 articulates 'individual and collective rights to education', including the right of indigenous peoples to 'develop and control educational systems that are consistent with their linguistic and cultural methods of teaching and learning' as well as the right of 'indigenous pupils' to be placed on an 'equal footing with non-indigenous pupils' regarding 'access to all levels and forms of education within the State'.[175] Article 15 guarantees indigenous peoples the right to have 'their cultures, traditions, histories and aspirations...appropriately reflected in education and public information'. This includes the state's duty to combat prejudice and discrimination and to develop tools that 'promote tolerance, understanding and good relations among indigenous peoples and all other segments of society'. Article 16 grants indigenous peoples the right to 'establish their own media in their own languages', an important aspect of self-determination, and to have non-discriminatory access to non-indigenous media; also states have a 'duty to ensure that indigenous cultural diversity is duly reflected in non-indigenous media'.[176] These articles are aimed at 'redressing wrongs (such as in the form of forced assimilation or discrimination in education, media, and public life), as well as repairing, restoring, and strengthening indigenous communities and cultures'.[177]

The protection of indigenous peoples' communal rights to their land is inextricably intertwined with their right to their culture. Thus, Article 25 emphasizes

---

[174] For a recent discussion of these issues, see Dussias, 'Indigenous Languages under Siege: The Native American Experience', 3 *Intercultural Human Rights L Rev* (2008) 5; Kibbee, 'Minority Language Rights: Historical and Comparative Perspectives', 3 *Intercultural Human Rights L Rev* (2008) 79. See also Mancini and De Witte, 'Language Rights as Cultural Rights: A European Perspective', in Francioni and Scheinin (2008) 247.

[175] Graham, 'Education and the Media', 2010 ILA Interim Report, 25.

[176] Graham (2010) 26.          [177] Graham (2010) 27.

indigenous peoples' 'distinctive spiritual relationship' with their lands,[178] and Article 26 affirms their 'right to the lands, territories, and resources which they have traditionally owned, occupied or otherwise used or acquired' (Section 1) and their 'right to own, use, develop, and control the lands, territories, and resources that they possess by reason of traditional ownership or other traditional occupation or use, as well as those which they have otherwise acquired' (Section 2).[179] It also mandates that 'States shall give legal recognition and protection to these lands, territories, and resources. Such recognition shall be conducted with due respect to the customs, traditions and land tenure systems of the indigenous peoples concerned' (Section 3; see also Article 32).[180]

Related key guarantees include indigenous peoples' rights to participate in decision-making on matters which would affect their rights (Article 18), and the obligations of states to 'consult and cooperate in good faith with the indigenous peoples concerned' to obtain their 'free, prior, and informed consent' to legislative and administrative decisions that 'may affect them' (Articles 19, 32(2)).[181] There are also rights to the improvement of their social and economic conditions (Articles 17, 21, 22, and 24), rights to development (Article 23) and international cooperation (Articles 36, 39, 41, and 42), treaty rights (Article 37), and certain rights to redress and reparations (eg Articles 8(2), 28).

Substantive limits to indigenous peoples' autonomy, where stated, are formulated in terms of universal standards of human rights (Articles 34, 46(2)). According to Article 46(3), the provisions of UNDRIP shall be interpreted in accordance with 'principles of justice, democracy, respect for human rights, equality, non-discrimination, good governance, and good faith'. These principles are intended to serve as an interpretative framework of UNDRIP and not as a substantive limit to its rights.[182] In particular, these rather sweeping interpretive provisions listed in Article 46(3) cannot be allowed to undermine the fundamental purpose and policies of the document.[183] Overall, UNDRIP sees itself as a minimum 'standard of achievement to be pursued' (Preamble, Article 43),[184] but it does not preclude the development of additional rights in the future (Article 45).

## 5. The Legal Effect of UNDRIP, Customary International Law and ILA Resolution No 5/2012

### A. UNDRIP and customary international law

As stated above, though not legally binding per se, a declaration may become binding to the extent that its various provisions are reflected in conforming state

---

[178] UNDRIP, Art 25.    [179] UNDRIP, Art 26(1) and (2).    [180] UNDRIP, Arts 26(3), 32.
[181] UNDRIP, Arts 19, 32(2).    [182] Wiessner (2011) 138.
[183] Wiessner, 'The United Nations Declaration on the Rights of Indigenous Peoples: Selected Issues', in A. Constantinides and N. Zaikos (eds), *The Diversity of International Law: Essays in Honour of Professor Kalliopi K. Koufa* (2009) 343 at 354.
[184] UNDRIP, preamble.

practice and *opinio juris*. This distinct body of customary international law concerning indigenous peoples, not necessarily coextensive with the full reach of the current UNDRIP, may have formed long before this vote occurred, and may emerge thereafter.[185] UNDRIP organizes all the claims of indigenous peoples to the extent the international community of states has chosen to approve them and according to the structure articulated. Some of these claims acknowledged as 'rights' form part of customary international law, while others may become the *fons et origo* of later-emerging customary international law.[186] As Richard Lillich classically stated 25 years ago:

> Whether a transmutation from mere resolution into binding international law has occurred is determined, broadly, by the degree of acceptance by the international legal community of the norms contained in the resolution. The process is one of juridical osmosis, there being no identifiable instant at which a resolution suddenly bursts forth as a binding legal norm. As the process is necessarily a gradual one, disagreement will often occur over whether, at any given time, the magic point has been attained.[187]

The starting point for such evaluation is the clarification of the meaning of customary international law as listed in the 1969 ICJ decision in the *North Sea Continental Shelf Case*.[188] A useful amplification is offered by the ILA Report on the Formation of Customary International Law.[189]

Regarding UNDRIP's legal effect, another new development has to be taken into account: there may be standards of evaluation of state conduct, applied by intergovernmental bodies that cannot be counted among the traditional 'sources' of international law enumerated in Article 38(1) of the ICJ Statute. The vanguard in this development is the process of 'universal periodic review' instituted by the Council. The standard of evaluation in this review, the Council announced, aside from treaties the various countries are parties to, would be the Universal Declaration of Human Rights (UDHR).[190] Similarly, in August 2008, Professor S. James Anaya, the United Nations Special Rapporteur on the rights of indigenous peoples, announced that he would measure state conduct vis-à-vis

---

[185]　Anaya and Wiessner (2007).

[186]　Anaya and Wiessner (2007). *Accord* Van Genugten (2010) 51 ('Whether that label [ie customary international law] fits cannot be said about the Declaration as a whole but should be elaborated upon on an article-by-article basis', referring to the pertinent work of the ILA Committee on the Rights of Indigenous Peoples). As to the latter's interim assessment, see Lenzerini, 'Rights of Indigenous Peoples under Customary International Law', in 2010 ILA Interim Report, 43–52.

[187]　R.B. Lillich, *The Human Rights of Aliens in Contemporary International Law* (1984), 44. As to the UDHR, Lillich concluded that 'there is fairly persuasive authority which maintains that that point has been reached, at least with respect to many of the rights guaranteed by the Declaration'.

[188]　*North Sea Continental Shelf*, ICJ Reports (1969), 3, paras 73–4 (requiring a very widespread practice of states, including states specially affected, in conformity with the purported new rule of customary international law, a practice motivated by a sense of legal obligation (*opinio juris*)).

[189]　International Law Association, London Conference Report, Statement of Principles Applicable to the Formation of General Customary International Law (2000), available at <http://www.ila-hq.org/download.cfm/docid/A709CDEB-92D6-4CFA-A61C4CA30217F376> (accessed 29 June 2013).

[190]　United Nations Human Rights Council, Institution Building, Resolution 5/1, Annex, UN Doc A/HRC/RES/5/1, 18 June 2007, para 1, available at <http://ap.ohchr.org/documents/E/HRC/resolutions/A_HRC_RES_5_1.doc> (accessed 29 June 2013).

indigenous peoples by the yardstick of UNDRIP.[191] The duty of UNDRIP implementation by states, laid down in Article 38, has been seen as the next challenge, including, but not limited to, systems of monitoring.[192] At the Durban Review Conference in April 2009, 182 states adopted by consensus an outcome document in which they *welcome[d]* the adoption of the UN Declaration on the rights of indigenous peoples which has a positive impact on the protection of victims and, in this context, *urge[d]* States to take all necessary measures to implement the rights of indigenous peoples in accordance with international human rights instruments without discrimination'.[193] In conformity with Articles 41 and 42 of UNDRIP and as a matter of policy direction, the standards of UNDRIP have also been urged to be mainstreamed into the UN's, the ILO's, and UNESCO's policies and programmes.[194] In addition, the concept of soft law has been offered to characterize the legal significance of UNDRIP[195] and its extraordinary legitimacy, generated through the inclusive *processes* from which it has sprung, the justice inherent in its *content*, and the extent to which international actors, be they individuals, civil society, trans-national corporations, states, indigenous peoples, and

---

[191] According to UN Special Rapporteur S. James Anaya, UNDRIP represents 'an authoritative common understanding, at the global level, of the minimum content of the rights of indigenous peoples, upon a foundation of various sources of international human rights law.... The principles and rights affirmed in the Declaration constitute or add to the normative frameworks for the activities of United Nations human rights institutions, mechanisms and specialized agencies as they relate to indigenous peoples.' UN Human Rights Council, Report of the Special Rapporteur on the Situation of Human Rights and Fundamental Freedoms of Indigenous People, UN Doc A/HRC/9/9, 11 August 2008, paras 85, 88, available at <http://www2.ohchr.org/english/bodies/hrcouncil/docs/9session/A-HRC-9-9AEV.doc> (accessed 29 June 2013). He also states that 'the Declaration relates to already existing human rights obligations of States, as demonstrated by the work of United Nations treaty bodies and other human rights mechanisms, and hence can be seen as embodying to some extent general principles of international law. In addition, insofar as they connect with a pattern of consistent international and State practice, some aspects of the provisions of the Declaration can also be considered as a reflection of norms of customary international law' (referring to Anaya and Wiessner (2007)). UN Doc A/HRC/9/9, 11 August 2008, para 41.

[192] Rodríguez-Piñero Royo, '"Where Appropriate": Monitoring/Implementing of Indigenous Peoples' Rights under the Declaration', in Charters and Stavenhagen (2009) 14. See also Dorough, 'The Significance of the Declaration on the Rights of Indigenous Peoples and Its Future Implementation', in Charters and Stavenhagen (2009) 264; Burger, 'Making the Declaration Work for Human Rights in the UN System', in Charters and Stavenhagen (2009) 304; Stavenhagen, 'Making the Declaration Work', in Charters and Stavenhagen (2009) 352.

[193] UN Office of the High Commissioner for Human Rights, Outcome document of the Durban Review Conference, 24 April 2009, para 73.

[194] Mr Koïchiro Matsuura, UNESCO Director-General, highlighted his organization's participation in the 'U.N. Task Team to elaborate the United Nations Development Group (UNDG) Guidelines on Indigenous People Issues, which will orient U.N. country teams in their efforts to mainstream the principles of the U.N. Declaration on the Rights of Indigenous Peoples in development programmes.' He added, '[w]e believe that it is only through intercultural dialogue between generations, cultures and civilizations, as well as between indigenous peoples, societies and States at large that indigenous cultures can fully flourish'. Koïchiro Matsuura, Director-General of UNESCO, Message on the Occasion of the International Day of the World's Indigenous People, 9 August 2008, available at <http://unesdoc.unesco.org/images/0016/001619/161906e.pdf> (accessed 29 June 2013).

[195] Barelli, 'The Role of Soft Law in the International Legal System: The Case of the United Nations Declaration on the Rights of Indigenous Peoples', 58 *Int'l & Comp LQ* (2009) 957.

so on, *engage* with it', has been stressed as enhancing the prospect of compliance by states.[196]

Under customary international law, states at least have the obligation not to prohibit or impair indigenous peoples' teaching of their own language or transmitting through the generations their traditional knowledge and cultural heritage.[197] This negative right is not yet coupled with a positive obligation of states to take all possible measures in order to allow indigenous peoples to preserve and revitalize their languages and transmit them to future generations—although best practices are being developed around the world. This negative right may, however, turn positive if the state mandates education in public schools rather than indigenous schools: in this case, the state would be obligated to provide instruction in the indigenous language; otherwise, the national policy of compulsory education would place an unacceptably huge burden in the path of indigenous children to learn their own language.

In addition, global comparative research on state practice and *opinio juris* over a period of five years in the late 1990s reached certain conclusions about the content of newly formed customary international law regarding the rights and status of indigenous peoples. The worldwide indigenous renascence had led to significant changes in constitutions, statutes, regulations, case law, and other authoritative and controlling statements and practices of states that had substantial indigenous populations. These changes included the recognition of indigenous peoples' rights to preserve their distinct identity and dignity and to govern their own affairs—be they 'tribal sovereigns' in the United States, the Sami in Lappland, the *resguardos* in Colombia, or Canada's Nunavut.[198] This move towards recognition of indigenous self-government was accompanied by an affirmation of native communities' title to the territories they traditionally used or occupied.

In many countries, domestic law now mandates a practice that would have been unthinkable only a few years ago: the demarcation and registration of First Nations' title to the lands of their ancestors. Indigenous people achieved this dramatic victory through several means: a peace treaty in Guatemala, constitutional and statutory changes in countries such as Brazil,[199] and modifications of the common law in Australia and other states. Indigenous culture, language, and tradition, to the extent they have survived, are increasingly inculcated and celebrated.[200] Treaties of the distant past are being honoured, and agreements are fast becoming the preferred

---

[196] Charters, 'The Legitimacy of the UN Declaration on the Rights of Indigenous Peoples', in Charters and Stavenhagen (2009) 280.

[197] 2010 ILA Interim Report, 51.        [198] Wiessner (2008) 1156.

[199] For a recent reaffirmation of the Constitution's guarantee to indigenous peoples of their right to their traditional lands, see the 19 March 2009 decision of the Brazilian Supreme Court in the case of *Raposa Serra do Sol*, a vast indigenous area located in the Amazonian state of Roraima defended against the claims of invading rice farmers and senators of the state; 'Supreme Court upholds Indians' rights in historic ruling' (20 March 2009), <http://www.survivalinternational.org/news/4354> (accessed 29 June 2013).

[200] As to the developments in Africa, see Van Genugten (2010) 30–62. See also the most recent decision of the African Commission on Human and Peoples' Rights recognizing collective rights to land of the Endorois people in Kenya, *Centre for Minority Rights Development (Kenya) and Minority*

mode of interaction between indigenous communities and the descendants of the former conquering elites. A close analysis of state practice and *opinio juris* of the specially affected states at the end of the last century could only conclude that customary international law was not only emerging, but had arisen and included indigenous peoples' rights to cultural integrity, autonomy, and their traditional lands.[201] Other scholars reviewed this evidence and largely concurred in the result.[202]

The Inter-American Commission on Human Rights made the key step from the global research effort to a practical application of those conclusions to the international legal status of indigenous peoples. Referring to this study and the opinions of other international legal scholars to argue for a new principle of customary international law,[203] the Inter-American Commission submitted the case of an indigenous group in the rainforest of Nicaragua to the Inter-American Court of Human Rights. The tribunal, in its celebrated *Awas Tingni* judgment of 31 August 2001,[204] affirmed the existence of an indigenous people's collective right to its land. Other decisions in the same vein followed, as detailed above.[205] The decisions of the Inter-American Court of Human Rights broke new ground as they radically reinterpreted Article 21 of the American Convention, the right to property—a

---

*Rights Group International on behalf of Endorois Welfare Council v Kenya*, 276/03, paras 187 and 205, following the earlier decision to the same effect in *The Social and Economic Rights Action Center for Economic and Social Rights v Nigeria*, 155/96, para 63; and the South African Constitutional Court's restoration of indigenous lands in *Alexkor Ltd v The Richtersveld Community and Others*, 2003 (19) SA 48-51 (CC).

[201] Wiessner (1999) 127, concluding, as to the content of customary international law:

First, indigenous peoples are entitled to maintain and develop their distinct cultural identity, their spirituality, their language, and their traditional ways of life. Second, they hold the right to political, economic and social self-determination, including a wide range of autonomy and the maintenance and strengthening of their own system of justice. Third, indigenous peoples have a right to demarcation, ownership, development, control and use of the lands they have traditionally owned or otherwise occupied and used. Fourth, governments are to honor and faithfully observe their treaty commitments to indigenous nations.

[202] S.J. Anaya, *Indigenous Peoples in International Law* (2nd edn, 2004), 49–72; Anaya and Williams, 'The Protection of Indigenous Peoples' Rights over Lands and Natural Resources under the Inter-American Human Rights System', 14 *Harvard Human Rights J* (2001) 33; Oguamanam, 'Indigenous Peoples and International Law: The Making of a Regime', 30 *Queen's LJ* (2004) 348. For a concurring analysis of indigenous land rights under customary international law and UNDRIP, see Stevenson, 'Indigenous Land Rights and the Declaration on the Rights of Indigenous Peoples: Implications for Maori Land Claims in New Zealand', 32 *Fordham Int'l LJ* (2008) 298. A recent monograph on the protection of groups in international law also concluded that 'there is sufficient proof of State practice and *opinio juris* among States to suggest the existence of a right to autonomy for indigenous peoples in international law'. N. Wenzel, *Das Spannungsverhältnis zwischen Gruppenschutz und Individualschutz im Völkerrecht* (2008), 508. *Accord* Weller, 'Settling Self-Determination Conflicts: Recent Developments', 20 *EJIL* (2009) 111 at 116. But see also Xanthaki, 'Indigenous Rights in International Law Over the Last 10 Years and Future Developments', 10 *Melbourne J Int'l L* (2009) 27.

[203] 'Final Written Arguments of the Inter-American Commission on Human Rights before the Inter-American Court of Human Rights in the Case of *Mayagna (Sumo) Indigenous Community of Awas Tingni Against the Republic of Nicaragua*', 19 *Arizona J Int'l & Comp L* (2002) 327 at 349.

[204] See note 129 above.      [205] See note 129 above.

provision, like all the other guarantees of the document, originally focused on the rights of individuals.

Such a radical reinterpretation of the treaty can only be based on a significant shift in the normative expectations of the states. It is most conceivable that the evidence for such a shift is found in the same material that has been adduced to prove customary international law: pertinent state practice and *opinio juris.* Upon such analysis, on 18 October 2007, Chief Justice A.O. Conteh of the Belize Supreme Court concluded: 'Treaty obligations aside, it is my considered view that both customary international law and general international law would require that Belize respect the rights of its indigenous people to their lands and resources'.[206]

The right to autonomy, part of the right to self-determination, is guaranteed in Article 4 UNDRIP as power over local and internal affairs. In this sense, backed up by very widespread state practice and *opinio juris,* it also forms part of customary international law.[207] Indigenous peoples generally do not claim a right to external self-determination, ie secession.[208] Therefore, the issue as to whether a claim to secession can be based on Article 3 UNDRIP, appears to be moot. In any event, while Article 46(1) UNDRIP does not expressly banish the spectre of secession by indigenous peoples—it could be argued that such remedy could be justified, in the words of the Canadian Supreme Court, if an indigenous people, like any other definable group, is 'denied meaningful access to government'[209]—it severely restricts the argument that a right to secession or external self-determination is guaranteed by Article 3's broadly formulated right to self-determination.

The claim to indigenous peoples' self-determination is essentially founded upon the aspiration to preserve their inherited ways of life, change those traditions as *they* see necessary, and allow their cultures to flourish.[210] That goal drives the claim for independent decision-making as to the structures and functions of decision-making within the indigenous community. Internal autonomy thus asks of modern nation-states to recognize formally 'democratic' as well as formally 'non-democratic' forms of indigenous government—as long as they are essential to their traditional ways of life. This would include the recognition of law-making and law-applying powers by traditional leaders in their various spheres of authority—peace chiefs, war chiefs, shamans, elders, etc. An obligation to have indigenous peoples accede to modern formal processes of periodic election and change

---

[206] *Aurelio Cal v Attorney General of Belize,* Supreme Court of Belize, Judgment, 18 October 2007, para 127, available at <http://www.elaw.org/node/1620> (accessed 29 June 2013).

[207] Wheatley, 'Autonomy or Self-Government', 2010 ILA Interim Report, 15–16. See also note 202 above.

[208] Van Dyke, 'Self-Determination', 2010 ILA Interim Report, 9.

[209] The Canadian Supreme Court, in its *Québec* Opinion, concluded that:

> [T]he international law right to self-determination only generates, at best, a right to external self-determination in situations of former colonies; where a people is oppressed, as for example under foreign military occupation; or where a definable group is denied meaningful access to government to pursue their political, economic, social and cultural development.

*Reference Re: Secession of Québec* [1998] 2 SCR 217 (Can), reprinted in 37 ILM [1998] 1340 at 1373, para 138.

[210] Wiessner (2010) 275.

of leaders may run against the spirit of preservation of the innermost core of their culture, ie decisions about how their decisions are made. It might complete, as previous policies of extermination and assimilation did, the circle of conquest. On the other hand, indigenous peoples themselves might want to change the way decisions have been made. But that decision, according to UNDRIP, should be theirs, and theirs alone, not forced upon them by the outside world.

## B. The International Law Association and ILA Resolution No 5/2012

As the rights and status of indigenous peoples was a novel field to investigate, and in order to clarify authoritatively, through updated and indepth research, the content of international law in this field, the International Law Association (ILA)[211] at its 72nd Biennial Meeting in Toronto established a Committee on the Rights of Indigenous Peoples. The Committee on the Rights of Indigenous Peoples was given the task of writing an authoritative commentary on indigenous peoples' rights, including, as stated later, the meaning of the 2007 UN Declaration. In its final composition, the Committee featured no less than 30 expert members from all inhabited continents.[212]

The ILA Committee on the Rights of Indigenous Peoples' 2010 Interim Report updated the search for state practice and *opinio juris* and independently reached, with ever more examples of domestic and international practice, many of the results arrived at earlier, including the finding of customary international law including the right to the recognition and preservation of cultural identity; the right to traditional lands and natural resources; and the right to reparation and redress for the wrongs suffered.[213] That research was completed and brought up to date in the Final Report of the ILA as submitted to the 75th ILA Biennial Meeting in Sofia.[214]

---

[211] The International Law Association, now headquartered in London, was founded in Brussels in 1873. Its objectives are 'the study, clarification and development of international law, both public and private, and the furtherance of international understanding and respect for international law'. The ILA has consultative status, as an international non-governmental organization, with various United Nations specialized agencies. Its membership, presently about 3,500, 'ranges from lawyers in private practice, academia, government and the judiciary, to non-lawyer experts from commercial, industrial and financial spheres, and representatives of bodies such as shipping and arbitration organisations and chambers of commerce' <http://www.ila-hq.org/en/about_us/index.cfm> (accessed 29 June 2013).

[212] For a list of all members, see <http://www.ila-hq.org/en/committees/index.cfm/cid/1024/member/1> (accessed 29 June 2013). The original Chair of the Committee was Professor S. James Anaya. In 2008, Professor Anaya was appointed UN Special Rapporteur on the Rights of Indigenous Peoples. In this position, he could no longer lead the Committee, and he resigned. At the 73rd ILA Biennial Meeting in Rio de Janeiro the same year, the author of this paper was appointed Chair of this Committee. The Committee then established ten subcommittees dealing with distinct themes such as the legal nature of the Declaration and its rights, the definition *vel non* of indigenous peoples, the right to self-determination and autonomy, the rights to cultural identity, education, and the media, the rights to traditional lands, including free, prior, and informed consent, treaty rights, and the right to development.

[213] For detailed research, see the chapter by the Committee's Rapporteur, University of Siena Professor Federico Lenzerini, 'The Rights of Indigenous Peoples under Customary International Law', 2010 ILA Interim Report, 43–52, and 2012 ILA Final Report, 28–9.

[214] The Rapporteur integrated work done at an intersessional workshop at the European University Institute in Florence, Italy, and combined subcommittee reports in a 52-page interim report for the

The package of both interim and final report plus the resolution were adopted at the Open Session of the Committee on 28 August 2012, with all ILA members present in the room voting in favour of it, save one abstention.[215] Resolution No 5/2012 was formally adopted at the final session of the Sofia Conference two days later.[216]

This resolution is historic. Not only does it recognize collective human rights[217] it also specifies a number of rights, essentially culture-based, that have become part and parcel of customary international law. These include:

(1) The right to self-determination to the extent it is recognized under international law.[218] Using the template of the distinction between external and internal self-determination, the interim report, as integrated into the final report and resolution, made clear that indigenous peoples would have a right to secede only if such a right, under any

---

ILA's 74th Biennial Meeting in The Hague. After another intersessional meeting conducted at the University of Anchorage in Alaska in August 2011, at the invitation of Inuit Committee member Dalee Sambo Dorough, the final report of the committee and a resolution for the ILA's 75th Biennial Meeting in Sofia was prepared. The final report supplemented the interim report of 2010.

[215] The session was chaired by Ralph Wilde (University College London) and was well attended. Following presentation of the report and resolution by the Chair and Rapporteur, interventions from the floor from amongst the Committee members present, and comments and questions from non-Committee members of the ILA, all supportive and informative, the Chairman of the Session put the Committee's proposal to a vote. All ILA members voting in that room raised their hands in favour—save one abstention. After this adoption of the resolution, the ILA Steering Committee put its finishing touches on the resolution, without changing the substance of the Committee's proposal. A question was asked as to why the resolution did not include a definition of the term 'indigenous peoples'. The Chair of the Indigenous Peoples' Rights Committee responded that the Committee as a whole, in particular its indigenous members, was unwilling to present a formal definition as this was seen, inter alia, as another attempt at colonization. Still, in the final report, a section had been included to clarify the understanding of the term. Two essential elements of that multifactorial description of indigenous peoples were self-identification as such, and indigenous peoples' special, often spiritual relationship with their ancestral lands (see 2012 ILA Final Report, note 7 above, at 2–3). The Steering Committee accepted this explanation.

[216] At the closing plenary session of 30 August 2012 in the aula of the University of Sofia, the Chairman of the ILA Executive Council, Lord Mance, Justice of the United Kingdom Supreme Court, and Open Session Chairman Wilde introduced Resolution No. 5/2012. Dr Wilde stated:

This resolution represents the culmination of six years of very hard work on this important and cutting-edge topic. Its conclusions and recommendations are based on a wide-ranging and rigorous study of state practice in this area, as reflected in the Committee's two lengthy reports. The resolution and those reports are clearly destined to play a major role in influencing the understanding and development of international law in this field.

Then he commended the adoption of the Resolution—to the rousing applause of the audience. As with the other resolutions, Lord Mance, after waiting for objections which did not come, declared the resolution properly offered, seconded, and passed.

[217] ILA Resolution No 5/2012, Conclusion No 1: 'Indigenous peoples are holders of collective human rights aimed at ensuring the preservation and transmission to future generations of their cultural identity and distinctiveness...'.

[218] ILA Resolution No 5/2012, Conclusion No 4: 'States must comply with the obligation—consistently with customary and applicable conventional international law—to recognize, respect, protect, fulfil and promote the right of indigenous peoples to self-determination, conceived as the right to decide their political status and to determine what their future will be, in compliance with relevant rules of international law and the principles of equality and non-discrimination.'

condition, were to be recognized by the international community with respect to any other people as well.[219] Indigenous peoples would have the same rights as other peoples in this respect, no less.[220]

(2) More content-filled is the right to autonomy, the right to internal and local self-government as laid down in Article 4 of the Declaration.[221] It includes, inter alia, the right of an indigenous people to continue its structures of leadership and traditions, commonly designated as their customary law.[222] In its generality and global reach, this specific right of indigenous peoples under international law is unprecedented.[223] This autonomy can take many forms; as every provision in the Declaration and the general law of indigenous peoples it has to be interpreted from its *telos*, ie the safeguarding and flourishing of indigenous peoples' cultures and traditions.[224] As against the rights of individual members, limits to this self-rule of the group are the customary international law of individual human rights as well as rights under treaties the state, on whose territory the indigenous peoples reside, has accepted.[225]

(3) Indigenous peoples' rights to their cultural identity have to be recognized, respected, protected, and fulfilled by the state.[226] The customary

---

[219] In the extra-colonial context, legal affirmations of such a right have been few and far between. Cf *Re: Secession of Quebec* [1998] 2 SCR 217 (Can), reprinted in 37 ILM [1998] 1340 at 1373, para 138.

[220] Van Dyke, 'Self-Determination', 2010 ILA Interim Report, 10 ('In this and other self-determination-related respects, indigenous peoples must be exactly considered as all other peoples').

[221] ILA Resolution No 5/2012, Conclusion No 5: 'States must also comply—according to customary and applicable conventional international law—with the obligation to recognize and promote the right of indigenous peoples to autonomy or self-government, which translates into a number of prerogatives necessary in order to secure the preservation and transmission to future generations of their cultural identity and distinctiveness. These prerogatives include, *inter alia*, the right to participate in national decision-making with respect to decisions that may affect them, the right to be consulted with respect to any project that may affect them and the related right that projects significantly impacting their rights and ways of life are not carried out without their prior, free and informed consent, as well as the right to regulate autonomously their internal affairs according to their own customary laws and to establish, maintain and develop their own legal and political institutions.'

[222] It helps here to understand law, in line with policy-oriented jurisprudence, as a process of authoritative and controlling decision within any community, be it territorial or personal. Reisman, Wiessner, and Willard, 'The New Haven School: A Brief Introduction', 32 *Yale J Int'l L* (2007) 575, 587–8, 591–2; Wiessner, 'The New Haven School of Jurisprudence: A Universal Toolkit for Understanding and Shaping the Law', 18 *Asia Pacific L Rev* (2010) 45, 47–9.

[223] There have been a number of minority rights arrangements under specific treaty regimes, especially after the First World War, but no such general legal right of a group under international law has been recognized before. Domestic law, on the other hand, knows of many such arrangements, which created, inter alia, the basis for the customary international law conclusion. For details, see Klein, 'Minderheitenschutz im Völkerrecht', 123 *Schriftenreihe Kirche und Gesellschaft* (1994); Klein, 'Minderheiten', 'Minderheitenrechte', 'Minderheitenschutz', in M. Honecker et al (eds), *Evangelisches Soziallexikon* (2001), paras 1083–8.

[224] Wiessner (2011) 129.      [225] 2012 ILA Final Report, 3.

[226] ILA Resolution No 5/2012, Conclusion No 6: 'States are bound to recognize, respect, protect and fulfil indigenous peoples' cultural identity (in all its elements, including cultural heritage) and to cooperate with them in good faith—through all possible means—in order to ensure its preservation and transmission to future generations.'

international law obligation here does not translate into a general positive right.[227] Rather, it is to be seen as a right not to be denied the right to speak and teach their own language, the ever more threatened anchor of their culture.[228] They also have the right to establish schools and media of their own.[229]

(4) The key culture-based right of indigenous peoples under customary international law translates into a state obligation to 'recognize, respect, safeguard, promote and fulfil the rights of indigenous peoples to their traditional lands, territories and resources',[230] which includes, in the first place, the demarcation, titling, and equivalent forms of legal recognition of these resources. This right recognizes the conceptually indispensable link of the peoples to the areas with which they have a special, often spiritual connection. It also recognizes the special role indigenous peoples have played in the preservation of these lands, making them their trusted guardians. Their use typically was oriented not at the exploitation of the resource to the point of exhaustion, but at the preservation of those lands for future generations, making them a model for modern environmental law's quest for sustainability. Maybe this right is the most consequential one as it may collide with the interests of other actors in the use of these very lands, sometimes with the national interest.[231]

(5) The right to free, prior, and informed consent to governmental measures affecting indigenous peoples leads usually only to the right of the affected communities to be consulted. This consultation, however, must include the active participation of indigenous peoples in the planning of such projects. If a project significantly endangers the very essence of an indigenous people's culture, then consent is required, under customary international law.[232] It, however, ought not to be arbitrarily denied.

---

[227] 2012 ILA Final Report, 15: 'At the moment, . . . the legal evolution occurred in this respect has probably not yet reached the point of leading to the existence of a rule of customary international law dictating a *positive* State obligation to take all possible measures in order to allow indigenous peoples to preserve their languages and transmit them to future generations. At the same time, it is reasonably indubitable that such an obligation actually exists in *negative* terms, in the sense that States are bound not to create any obstacles to the efforts and activities carried out by indigenous peoples in order to preserve their own languages as an element of their cultural identity.'

[228] Dussias (2008); as to the importance of language, see Klein, 'Menschenwürde und Sprache', in K. Grözinger (ed), *Sprache und Identität im Judentum* (1998) 59.

[229] ILA Resolution No 5/2012, Conclusion No 8: 'States must recognize the right of indigenous peoples to establish their own educational institutions and media, as well as to provide education to indigenous children in their traditional languages and according to their own traditions. States have the obligation not to interfere with the exercise of these rights.' For details, see 2012 ILA Final Report, 15.

[230] ILA Resolution No 5/2012, Conclusion No 7.

[231] For a good analysis, see Vadi, 'When Cultures Collide: Foreign Direct Investment, Natural Resources, and Indigenous Heritage in International Investment Law', 42 *Columbia Human Rights L Rev* (2011) 797.

[232] 'When the essence of their cultural integrity is at significant risk, obtaining the free, prior and informed consent of the indigenous peoples concerned becomes mandatory.' 2012 ILA Final Report, 10.

(6) Reparations and redress for wrongs are also addressed, with due regard for their proper format, adequacy, and effectiveness.[233]

## 6. Conclusion

UN Special Rapporteur James Anaya, in his enthusiastic endorsement of the ILA report and resolution, wrote that the resolution is 'highly authoritative' and may, as intended, assist him and other decision-makers in their work of interpreting, applying, and implementing indigenous peoples' rights.[234] Earlier, in 2011, the ICSID Arbitral Tribunal in the *Grand River Case* had referred to the work of the Committee and its interim report in finding that there 'may well be...a principle of customary international law requiring governmental authorities to consult indigenous peoples on governmental policies or actions significantly affecting them'.[235]

Generally, resolutions of the International Law Association, just as those of the International Law Commission, have been recognized as evidence of international law. The *Third Restatement of Foreign Relations Law of the United States* affirms this characterization,[236] as does the most recent leading textbook of international law in Germany. As Graf Vitzthum stated there, global resolutions of a body as qualified and diverse as the International Law Association are stating a rare consensus

---

[233] ILA Resolution No 5/2012, Conclusion No 10: 'States must comply with their obligations—under customary and applicable conventional international law—to recognize and fulfil the rights of indigenous peoples to reparation and redress for wrongs they have suffered, including rights relating to lands taken or damaged without their free, prior and informed consent. Effective mechanisms for redress—established in conjunction with the peoples concerned—must be available and accessible in favour of indigenous peoples. Reparation must be adequate and effective, and, according to the perspective of the indigenous communities concerned, actually capable of repairing the wrongs they have suffered.' For different ways to effectuate reparations, see F. Lenzerini (ed), *Reparations for Indigenous Peoples: International and Comparative Perspectives* (2008).

[234] S. James Anaya, Statement of Endorsement of Committee Final Report and Resolution, at ILA Final Report 2012, 31–2:

The committee's work before you reflects the highest standards of our profession.... Given the thorough research undertaken by the committee, the conclusions as formulated in its final report and resolution are highly authoritative. I am confident that, as intended, this expert commentary will reduce confusion and contention over the content and normative status of the provisions of the UN Declaration and of indigenous peoples' rights in general. It will help me in my work as Special Rapporteur as I endeavor to guide states toward ever close compliance with the new regime of indigenous peoples' human rights.

The commentary will be available to practitioners and advocates, governments, courts and tribunals, academics and indigenous organizations, to draw on and refer to in dealing with the important issues that concern indigenous peoples. Accordingly, it will be a hallmark of the work of the International Law Association in the new environment of the values-based international law of the 21st century.

[235] *Grand River Enterprises Six Nations, Ltd, et al v United States of America*, 12 January 2011, para 210, available at <http://www.state.gov/documents/organization/156820.pdf> (accessed 25 October 2012).

[236] American Law Institute, *Third Restatement of the Foreign Relations Law of the United States* (1987), § 103 Reporters' Notes No 1.

amongst, at times, radically different cultures and value traditions, and thus should be especially appreciated and valued.[237] This is particularly true when, as in this case, they pass not only uncontested, but with emphatic support.

On such firm ground, Resolution No 5/2012 transcends the writings of individual scholars. It reflects general international law on the rights and status of indigenous peoples. Its substance has come to help complete the circle of protection for the most vulnerable peoples on the face of the Earth. In assisting these threatened cultures in their struggle for survival and flourishing, law may approximate its noblest end: to make peace through justice, ever aiming for a public order in which dignity for all is assured.

---

[237] Vitzthum, 'Begriff, Geschichte und Quellen des Völkerrechts', in W. Graf Vitzthum (ed), *Völkerrecht* (3rd edn, 2004) 72, para 147.

# PART III

# 5

# The European Union and Cultural Rights

*Evangelia Psychogiopoulou*

## 1. Introduction

More than half a century of conceptual elaboration and policy evolution in support of human rights protection and promotion shows that the attention afforded to civil, political, social, and economic rights has not been paralleled by a comparable level of attention given to cultural rights. Although the division of human rights in different categories implies no hierarchy among them, cultural rights have not developed at an equal pace.[1] Largely accounting for this has been the vagueness of the concept of 'culture',[2] which has substantially complicated the formulation, scope, and understanding of cultural rights. In major human rights instruments and treaties, there has so far been no precise definition of cultural rights as such. Rather specific lists of rights have been marked as 'cultural', while more familiar categories of civil and political rights have been acknowledged, mainly by means of judicial practice, as having a cultural dimension.

The purpose of this chapter is to examine how the European Union (EU) has been confronted with the issue of cultural rights, and investigate whether it has developed policies that are directly or indirectly concerned with their protection and promotion. Is the EU bound to respect cultural rights and, if yes, what do these 'cultural rights' actually stand for? Furthermore, is the EU under a duty to promote the realization of cultural rights and, if yes, what are the mechanisms and instruments that it possesses for that purpose?

The rhetoric of rights has accompanied and played an important role in the development of the EU legal system. Initially conceived as a means to strengthen the process of European integration, the language of rights has been used to facilitate attainment of the EU's core objectives and reinforce acceptance of the EU polity by its member states. Respect for fundamental rights has thus been recognized

---

[1] Symonides, 'Cultural Rights', in J. Symonides (ed), *Human Rights: Concepts and Standards* (2000) 175 at 175–6; Donders, 'A Right to Cultural Identity in UNESCO', in F. Francioni and M. Scheinin (eds), *Cultural Human Rights* (2008) 317 at 318.

[2] Stavenhagen, 'Cultural Rights: A Social Science Perspective', in A. Eide, C. Krause, and A. Rosas (eds), *Economic, Social and Cultural Rights: A Textbook* (2001) 85 at 87–91.

early as an EU obligation subject to judicial scrutiny. Presently, with the Charter of Fundamental Rights of the European Union having acquired legal force, the EU appears to enjoy all the necessary components for the development of an ambitious fundamental rights policy.[3] What is the place that cultural rights occupy in such a policy, and are cultural rights to be fulfilled only by means of an EU fundamental rights policy proper?

In order to shed some light on the EU's approach to, and engagement with, cultural rights, this chapter is structured as follows. Sections 2 and 3 discuss the place of cultural rights in the EU legal system. Whereas section 2 focuses on the EU constitutional framework, section 3 identifies the EU's normative commitment to the protection of cultural rights, as reflected in the UNESCO Convention on the Protection and Promotion of the Diversity of Cultural Expressions, to which the EU is party. Sections 4 and 5 examine the contribution of the EU to the fulfilment of cultural rights by means of its fundamental rights and cultural policies. Section 6 concludes with some final remarks concerning the ways in which cultural rights have been integrated in the EU legal order and its policy practice and how such integration could be reinforced.

## 2. Cultural Rights and EU Constitutional Law

The founding Treaties of the European Communities in the 1950s did not contain a commitment to the protection and promotion of human rights. Although human rights protection formed the basis of intensive discussion in the pursuit of European political integration, the failure of the European Defence Treaty and the downfall of the European Political Community significantly diluted ambitions.[4] As a result, similarly to the European Coal and Steel Community Treaty, the 1957 Treaties on the European Economic Community (EEC) and the European Atomic Energy Community made no mention of human rights. The tasks and duties of these two Communities were strictly defined in line with the common market mandate of the Messina conference, the issue of human rights being relinquished to the constitutional orders of the member states to cope with.

Minds, however, progressively evolved due to the endorsement by the then European Court of Justice (now the Court of Justice of the European Union, hereinafter the CJEU or the Court) of a human rights discourse—a response to national allegations that constitutionally protected human rights at member state level should act as limitation on the powers of the Communities.[5] A preliminary mention of fundamental rights was made in the preamble of the 1986

---

[3] Communication from the Commission: Strategy for the effective implementation of the Charter of Fundamental Rights by the European Union, COM(2010) 573, 19 October 2010, 2.

[4] De Búrca, 'The Evolution of EU Human Rights Law', in P. Craig and G. de Búrca (eds), *The Evolution of EU Law* (2nd edn, 2011), 465 at 467–75.

[5] See in particular Case 29/69, *Erich Stauder v City of Ulm—Sozialamt* [1969] ECR 419; Case 11/70, *Internationale Handelsgesellschaft mbH v Einfuhr- und Vorratsstelle für Getreide und Futtermittel* [1970] ECR 1125; Case 4/73, *Nold v Commission* [1974] ECR 491.

Single European Act,[6] but it was the 1992 Maastricht Treaty on European Union (TEU) which formally recognized human rights as part of EU law, reflecting the CJEU's jurisprudence on the issue. Article F(2) of the Treaty of Maastricht provided that fundamental rights, as guaranteed by the European Convention for the Protection of Human Rights and Fundamental Freedoms (hereinafter ECHR or the Convention), and as resulting from the constitutional traditions common to the member states, amounted to *general principles of EU law*. The 1997 Treaty of Amsterdam went one step further. Article 6(1) TEU proclaimed that '[t]he Union is founded on the principles of liberty, democracy, respect for human rights and fundamental freedoms, and the rule of law, principles which are common to the Member States', while Article 49 TEU granted treaty status to the 'Copenhagen criteria', including respect for human rights and fundamental freedoms, for EU accession.[7] Also, the Treaty of Amsterdam extended the powers of the CJEU to cover a fundamental rights observance test as regards the actions of the European institutions (Article 46 TEU), and established a sanctioning mechanism against serious and persistent breaches of fundamental rights by the member states, which was reinforced by the 2000 Treaty of Nice to incorporate situations of a clear risk of a serious breach of fundamental rights (Article 7 TEU). Shortly after the entry into force of the Treaty of Amsterdam, the Charter of Fundamental Rights of the European Union (hereinafter CFR or the Charter) was drafted and then proclaimed in 2000. Following the non-ratification of the Treaty establishing a Constitution for Europe, the CFR was given binding legal status by the Lisbon Treaty in 2009. Hence, presently, besides affirming that fundamental rights, as guaranteed by the ECHR and as resulting from the constitutional traditions common to the member states, constitute general principles of EU law (Article 6(3) TEU), Article 6 TEU stipulates that the EU recognizes the rights, freedoms, and principles set out in the CFR, which has the same legal value as the Treaty on European Union and the Treaty on the Functioning of the European Union (TFEU) (Article 6(1) TEU). Article 6 TEU also requires the EU to accede to the ECHR (Article 6(2) TEU). Moreover, in accordance with Article 21 TEU, '[t]he Union's action on the international scene shall be guided by the principles which have inspired its own creation, development and enlargement, and which it seeks to advance in the wider world: democracy, the rule of law, the universality and indivisibility of human rights and fundamental freedoms, respect for human dignity, the principles of equality and solidarity, and respect for the principles of the United Nations Charter and international law.'

The above mentioned provisions, reflective of the progressive constitutional attention afforded to fundamental rights and freedoms within the EU legal framework, do not make explicit reference to cultural rights. This is also the case

---

[6] The preamble to the Single European Act mentioned that member states are '[d]etermined to work together to promote democracy on the basis of fundamental rights recognised in the constitutions and laws of the Member States, in the Convention for the Protection of Human Rights and Fundamental Freedoms, and the European Social Charter, notably freedom, equality and social justice'.

[7] Article 49 TEU proclaimed that 'any European State which respects the principles set out in Art 6(1) may apply to become a member of the Union'.

concerning Article 2 TEU which proudly pronounces that '[t]he Union is founded on the values of respect for human dignity, freedom, democracy, equality, the rule of law and respect for human rights', including 'the rights of persons belonging to minorities'.[8] Admittedly, 'respect for human rights', including 'the rights of persons belonging to minorities', covers all different categories of human rights, thus cultural rights as well. In addition, the ECHR, whose norms amount to general principles of EU law, contains several provisions that enjoy a cultural dimension,[9] despite the fact that it is focused on political and civil rights for the most part. Article 8 ECHR on respect for private and family life, Article 9 ECHR on freedom of thought, conscience and religion, Article 10 ECHR on freedom of expression, Article 11 ECHR on freedom of assembly and association, Article 14 ECHR prohibiting discrimination on the grounds of sex, race, colour, language, religion, political or other opinion, national or social origin, association with a national minority, property, birth or other status, and Article 2 of the first protocol to the ECHR on the right to education can all be construed as covering cultural rights in the broad sense.

Largely driven by the fundamental rights account of the CJEU, the constitutional proclamation of the provisions of the ECHR as general principles of EU law—besides the concurrent affirmation of member states' common constitutional traditions as general principles of EU law—had important consequences for the human rights foundations of the EU polity, particularly in a pre-CFR context but also in the post-Charter era. Declared as an autonomous source of EU fundamental rights principles—insubordinate to national constitutionally protected human rights—the ECHR functions as a limitation on EU action. The CJEU is entrusted with the task of ensuring respect for its provisions by the European institutions, while national rules falling with the scope of EU law are also required to be compatible with the ECHR.[10]

Notably, the CJEU has ruled that international treaties on which the member states have collaborated or of which they are signatories can supply guidelines for the protection of fundamental rights and freedoms as general principles of EU law.[11] On this basis, it can be argued that Article 27 of the Universal Declaration of Human Rights (UDHR) on the right to freely participate in the cultural life of a community and to enjoy the arts may inform fundamental rights protection as a general principle of EU law. The same could be said fairly regarding Article 27 of the International Covenant on Civil and Political Rights (ICCPR) concerning the right of ethnic, religious, and linguistic minorities to enjoy their own culture,

---

[8] Article 2 TEU goes on to say that '[t]hese values are common to the member states in a society in which pluralism, non-discrimination, tolerance, justice, solidarity and equality between women and men prevail'.

[9] On this, see Donders, 'The Protection of Cultural Rights in Europe: None of the EU's Business?', 10 *Maastricht Journal of European and Comparative Law* (2003) 117 at 127–35.

[10] See indicatively Joined Cases C-60 and C-61/84, *Cinéthèque v Fédération Nationale des Cinémas Français* [1985] ECR 2605, Rec 25 of judgment; Case C-12/86, *Demirel v Stadt Schwaebisch Gmund* [1987] ECR, Rec 28.

[11] See Case 4/73, *Nold v Commission* [1974] ECR 491, Rec 13.

to profess and practice their own religion, and to use their own language, in community with the other members of their group, and Articles 13 and 15 of the International Covenant on Economic, Social and Cultural Rights (ICESCR) concerning, respectively, the right to education, and the right to take part in cultural life, the right to benefit from the protection of the moral and material interests resulting from any literary or artistic production of which the beneficiary is the author, and the freedom indispensable for creative activity.

Nevertheless, it should be noted that the CJEU and the European institutions more broadly, have so far shown little interest in integrating the cultural provisions of the UDHR, the ICCPR, and the ICESCR in their reasoning. At the time of writing, for instance, there has been no CJEU judgment specifically referring to Article 27 UDHR, Article 27 ICCPR, or Articles 13 and 15 ICESCR in the context of culture-related cases brought to the Court's attention. Moreover, the Court has taken the position that the member states cannot rely on the provisions of the ICESCR (and arguably, on the provisions of the UDHR and the ICCPR as well) in order to justify restrictive domestic measures that are not compatible with other provisions of primary EU law, such as Articles 18 and 21 TFEU on the prohibition of discrimination on grounds of nationality, and the right of every EU citizen to move and reside freely within the territory of the member states.[12]

That being so, the TFEU provisions on free movement and the principle of equal treatment merit attention, as they generate rights for individuals that can be exercised in the cultural domain. To illustrate, Articles 34 and 35 TFEU, which prohibit quantitative restrictions and all measures having equivalent effect for intra-EU trade, apply to trade in cultural goods,[13] and can be interpreted as ensuring individuals' freedom to unconstrained imports and exports of cultural goods. The free movement of workers, the freedom of establishment and the freedom to provide services, enshrined in Articles 45, 49, and 56 TFEU, apply to cultural workers, self-employed cultural practitioners, and operators providing cultural services.[14] Moreover, Article 18 TFEU prohibits any discrimination on grounds of nationality, while Article 19 TFEU provides the European institutions with the power to take measures to combat discrimination based, among others, on racial or ethic origin, religion or belief, which are important features of one's cultural identity.

Article 36 TFEU establishes that discriminatory barriers to trade in goods can be justified, inter alia, on grounds of 'the protection of national treasures possessing artistic, historic or archaeological value' and 'the protection of industrial and commercial property', provided that they do not constitute a means of arbitrary discrimination or a disguised restriction of trade. Although the justification concerning the protection of national treasures has seldom been advanced before the

---

[12] Case C-73/08, *Bressol and Others* [2010] ECR I-2735.
[13] Case 7/68, *Commission v Italy* [1968] ECR 423.
[14] Case C-290/94, *Commission v Greece* [1996] ECR I-3285; Case 155/73, *Sacchi* [1974] ECR 409; Case 197/84, *P. Steinhauser v City of Biarritz* [1985] ECR 1819.

CJEU,[15] in the early 1990s the EEC introduced uniform controls for the export of member states' cultural goods outside the EEC customs territory, and also enacted rules to secure their return when these are unlawfully removed from the member states.[16] Relevant norms sought to ensure the proper functioning of the internal market,[17] but at the same time reflected steps taken to reconcile the principle of free movement of goods with domestic cultural policy concerns pertaining to heritage protection.

Protection of literary and artistic property by copyright was found, in turn, to be covered by 'the protection of industrial and commercial property', set out in Article 36 TFEU as one of the grounds justifying national restrictions to free movement.[18] Alerted by the jurisprudence of the CJEU, the European legislator adopted various harmonizing measures in the area of copyright and related rights—an attempt to mitigate or altogether eliminate differences between national copyright regimes that could distort the internal market while seeking to ensure a high level of protection for cultural operators.[19] Concurrently, the CJEU has ruled in a number of cases that obstacles to free movement arising from generally applicable national rules that do not distinguish on grounds of origin can be justified by imperative reasons relating to the public interest.[20] The notion of public interest has been broadly interpreted to encompass national cultural policy goals that may be viewed from a cultural rights perspective, such as protecting national historical and artistic heritage; facilitating the widest possible dissemination of knowledge of a country's patrimony;

---

[15] On this see Case C-531/07, *Fachverband der Buch- und Medienwirtschaft v LIBRO Handelsgesellschaft mbH* [2009] ECR I-3717, where the CJEU held that the protection of books as cultural objects and thus, 'the protection of cultural diversity in general cannot be considered to come within the "protection of national treasures possessing artistic, historic or archaeological value"' within the meaning of Art 36 TFEU (para 32).

[16] Council Regulation 3911/92/EEC of 9 December 1992 on the export of cultural goods, OJ 1992 L 395/1; Council Directive 93/7/EEC of 15 March 1993 on the return of cultural objects unlawfully removed from the territory of a member state, OJ 1993 L 74/74.

[17] Regulation 3911/92/EEC was adopted on the basis of what was then Art 113 EEC (now Art 207 TFEU on common commercial policy) whereas Directive 93/7/EEC was based on Art 100a EEC (now Art 114 TFEU concerning the adoption of measures for the approximation of the provisions laid down by law, regulation, or administrative action in member states which have as their object the establishment and functioning of the internal market). The two instruments thus dealt with the external and internal facets of the internal market.

[18] See, indicatively, Joined Cases 55/80 and 57/80, *Musik-Vertrieb Membran GmbH v GEMA* [1981] ECR 147.

[19] See, for instance, Council Directive 92/100/EEC of 19 November 1992 on rental right and lending right and on certain rights related to copyright in the field of intellectual property, OJ 1992 L 346/61 (repealed by Directive 2006/115/EC, OJ 2006 L 376/28); Council Directive 93/83/EC of 27 September 1993 on the coordination of certain rules concerning copyright and rights related to copyright applicable to satellite broadcasting and cable retransmission, OJ 1993 L 248/15; Council Directive 93/98/EC of 29 October 1993 harmonizing the term of protection of copyright and certain related rights, OJ 1993 L 290/9 (repealed by Directive 2006/116/EC, OJ 2006 L 372/18 and amended by Directive 2011/77/EU, OJ 2011 L 265/1); Directive 2001/29/EC of the European Parliament and of the Council of 22 May 2001 on the harmonization of certain aspects of copyright and related rights in the information society, OJ 2001 L 167/10; Directive 2001/84 of the European Parliament and of the Council of 27 September 2001 on the resale right for the benefit of the author of an original work of art, OJ 2001 L 272/32.

[20] Case 120/78, *Rewe/Bundesmonopolverwaltung für Branntwein* [1979] ECR 649.

and safeguarding freedom of expression of the various social, cultural, religious, and philosophical components of a member state.[21] In other instances, ensuring member states' compliance with free movement requirements has served to facilitate access to local cultural activity, and thus participation in the cultural life of a member state other than the state of origin or residence, for the nationals of the member states who exercise their free movement rights.[22] Moreover, in cases concerning free movement, the principle of non-discrimination and also EU citizenship (Article 20 TFEU), the Court's jurisprudence has provided support for the preservation of the cultural identity of member states' nationals who move freely within the EU.[23] In a set of more recent cases drawing mainly on EU citizenship and the right of EU citizens to free movement and residence, the Court has dealt extensively with discrepancies in the attribution, composition, and spelling of a person's name, acknowledging that names are a constituent element of one's identity.[24]

Signalling the EU's resolve to render fundamental rights protection more visible to the EU citizens, the enactment of the CFR and the subsequent recognition of its legally binding nature have substantially diversified the human rights sources of the EU's constitutional legal order. As evidenced by the drafting mandate of the Cologne European Council, the CFR was not intended to develop any new rights.[25] Rather it should contain and codify the fundamental rights and freedoms, together with basic procedural rights, safeguarded by the ECHR and derived from the constitutional traditions common to the member states; include the EU citizenship rights; and incorporate the economic and social rights laid down in the European Social Charter and the Community Charter of the Fundamental Social Rights of Workers. In the preamble to the CFR, it is indeed explained that the Charter 'reaffirms … the rights, as they result, in particular, from the constitutional traditions and international obligations common to the Member States, the Treaty on European Union, the Community Treaties, the European Convention for the Protection of Human Rights and Fundamental Freedoms, the Social Charters adopted by the Community and by the Council of Europe and the case-law of the Court of Justice of the European Communities and of the European Court of Human Rights'. Accordingly, the CFR essentially contains civil and political rights, EU citizenship rights, and social and economic rights. However, as is the case with the ECHR, many of its provisions enjoy a cultural dimension in the broad sense. The CFR includes, for example, the right to respect for private and

---

[21] Case C-180/90, *Commission v Italy* [1991] ECR 709; Case C-154/89, *Commission v France* [1991] ECR I-659; Case C-353/89, *Commission v The Netherlands* [1991] ECR 4069.

[22] Case 197/84, *P. Steinhauser v City of Biarritz* [1985] ECR 1819; Case 45/93 *Commission v Spain* [1994] ECR I-911; Case C-234/01, *Arnoud Gerritse v Finanzamt Neukölln-Nord* [2003] ECR I-5933.

[23] Case 137/84, *Criminal proceedings against Rober Heinrich Maria Mutsch* [1985] ECR 2681; Case C-168/91, *Christos Konstantinidis v Stadt Altensteig—Standesamt and Landratsamt Calw—Ordnungsamt* [1993] ECR 1191; Case C-148/02, *Garcia Avello* [2003] ECR I-11613.

[24] Case C-353/06, *Grunkin and Paul* [2008] ECR I-7639; Case C-208/09, *Sayn-Wittgenstein* [2010] ECR I-13693; Case C-391/09, *Runević-Vardyn and Wardyn* [2011] ECR I-3787.

[25] Cologne European Council, 3–4 June 1999, Conclusions of the Presidency, Annex IV, European Council Decision on the drawing up of a Charter of Fundamental Rights of the European Union, <http://www.europarl.europa.eu/summits/kol2_en.htm#an4> (accessed 28 May 2012).

family life (Article 7), freedom of thought, conscience, and religion (Article 10), freedom of expression and information (Article 11), freedom of assembly and of association (Article 12), and the right to education (Article 14), which correspond to Articles 8, 9, 10, 11 ECHR and Article 2 of the first protocol to the ECHR, respectively. According to Article 52(2) CFR, the meaning and scope of these fundamental rights and freedoms must be the same as those laid down in the ECHR, whereas in accordance with Article 53 CFR, the CFR provisions must not be interpreted as restricting or adversely affecting the rights and freedoms recognized by the ECHR. Consequently, limitations on the rights enshrined in Articles 7, 10, 11, 12, and 14 CFR may not exceed those considered legitimate by virtue of the corresponding ECHR articles.[26] However, as made clear by Article 52(3) CFR, the EU may provide more extensive protection than that afforded by the ECHR.

In addition to the above-mentioned articles, the CFR includes several other provisions that are of relevance to cultural rights protection, such as Article 13 CFR on freedom of the arts, Article 25 CFR which refers to the rights of the elderly, including the right to participate in cultural life, and Article 17 CFR on the right to property, which covers protection of intellectual property, extending to literary and artistic property. Article 21 CFR deals with non-discrimination. Drawing mainly on Article 19 TFEU[27] and Article 14 ECHR,[28] it states in paragraph 1 that 'any discrimination based on any grounds such as sex, race, colour, ethnic or social origin, genetic features, language, religion or belief, political or any other opinion, membership of a national minority, property, birth, disability, age or sexual orientation shall be prohibited'. Going beyond Article 19 TFEU, Article 21 CFR incorporates a reference to 'language' and 'membership of a national minority', which are closely related to one's cultural identity.

The Charter also makes explicit mention of cultural diversity. In the preamble, it is stated that the EU contributes to the preservation and to the development of common values, such as human dignity, freedom, equality and solidarity, democracy and the rule of law, 'while respecting the diversity of the cultures and traditions of the peoples in Europe as well as the national identities of the Member States'. A similar provision can be found in Article 3(3) TEU, which expressly provides that the Union 'shall respect its rich cultural and linguistic diversity, and shall ensure that Europe's cultural heritage is safeguarded and enhanced', while Article 4(2) TEU provides that '[t]he Union shall respect the equality of Member States before the Treaties as well as their national identities, inherent in their fundamental structures, political and constitutional'. Consequently, both the CFR and the TEU

---

[26] See also, in this respect, Explanations relating to the Charter of Fundamental Rights, OJ 2007 C 303/17.

[27] Article 19(1) TFEU reads: 'Without prejudice to the other provisions of the Treaties and within the limits of the powers conferred by them upon the Union, the Council, acting unanimously in accordance with a special legislative procedure and after obtaining the consent of the European Parliament, may take appropriate action to combat discrimination based on sex, racial or ethnic origin, religion or belief, disability, age or sexual orientation.'

[28] See Explanations relating to the Charter of Fundamental Rights, OJ 2007 C 303/17 at 24. Article 21 CFR also builds on Art 11 of the Convention on Human Rights and Biomedicine.

acknowledge the EU's duty to respect the national identities of the member states and cultural diversity, though the CFR reference to the diversity of the cultures and traditions of *the peoples in Europe*—in addition to the national identities of the member states—arguably shows that the EU not only values diversity *between* the national cultural identities of the member states but also diversity of cultural identities *within* the member states.

Article 22 CFR is not explicit on this point, as it generally affirms that '[t]he Union shall respect cultural, religious and linguistic diversity'. Bearing in mind that the drafting of Article 22 CFR was mainly based on Article 6 TEU and Article 167(1) and (4) TFEU concerning the cultural powers of the EU,[29] guidance for its interpretation may be sought from Article 167 TFEU. Article 167(1) TFEU provides that '[t]he Union shall contribute to the flowering of the cultures of the Member States, while respecting their national and regional diversity....' Mention of both national and regional diversity entails that both diversity *between* and *within* the member states must be respected. On this basis, it may be derived that reference to cultural diversity in Article 22 CFR refers to both diversity *between* and *within* the member states.

In accordance with Article 51(1) CFR, the provisions of the CFR, and thus its culture-related rights, freedoms, and principles, 'are addressed to the institutions, bodies, offices and agencies of the Union with due regard for the principle of subsidiarity and to the Member States only when they are implementing Union law'. Accordingly, although the EU courts have the power to review the compatibility with the CFR of measures adopted by the European institutions (understood broadly as covering all the authorities set up by EU primary and secondary law), they still lack the power to review compliance with EU fundamental rights of national rules when the member states act within national competence. This was established in the pre-Lisbon case law of the CJEU.[30]

Article 51(2) stipulates that the Charter neither establishes any new powers or tasks for the EU, nor modifies the EU powers and tasks as these are defined by the Treaties. In a similar vein, Article 6(1) TEU provides that 'the provisions of the Charter shall not extend in any way the competences of the Union as defined in the Treaties'. According to the Explanations relating to the Charter of Fundamental Rights, which, as provided by Article 6(1) TEU, must be given due regard when interpreting the rights, freedoms and principles of the Charter,[31] 'the reference to the Charter in Article 6 of the Treaty on European Union cannot be understood as extending by itself the range of Member State action considered to be "implementation of Union law"'.[32]

---

[29] Explanations relating to the Charter of Fundamental Rights, OJ 2007 C 303/17 at 25.

[30] See indicatively, Case 36/75, *Roland Rutili v Minister for the Interior* [1975] ECR 1219; Case 5/88, *Wachauf* [1989] ECR 2609; Case C-260/89, *Elliniki Radiophonia Tileorassi* [1993] ECR I-2925.

[31] In accordance with the general provisions contained in Title VII of the Charter, governing its interpretation and application.

[32] See Explanations relating to the Charter of Fundamental Rights, OJ 2007 C 303/17 at 32, Title VII—General provisions governing the interpretation and application of the Charter, Explanation on Article 51—Field of application.

The question when national measures come within the scope of EU law, or to paraphrase Article 51(1) CFR, when they 'implement EU law', is contentious and has received significant attention by legal scholars.[33] Broadly speaking, in line with the jurisprudence of the CJEU, EU fundamental rights bind the member states when they 'implement' and 'apply' EU law, that is, when they adopt legal and administrative acts in order to implement EU rules and when they interpret or apply domestic provisions whose subject-matter is governed by EU primary and/or secondary law. EU fundamental rights also bind national authorities when they seek to justify national measures derogating from EU law[34] either on the basis of an express derogation clause contained in the Treaties or by relying on the broader range of public interest justifications developed by the CJEU for non-discriminatory national measures.[35] From this perspective, the Charter could be criticized for apparently narrowing the pre-Lisbon scope of judicial review of national measures on fundamental rights grounds, precisely on account that Article 51(1) CFR appears to suggest that national authorities must respect the Charter's provisions *only* when they implement EU law. True, at the time of the drafting of the CFR, there were strong political calls in support of limiting its relevance for the member states and stressing as far as possible its importance for the European institutions.[36] However, a cursory look at the clarifications provided in the CFR Explanations—and the CJEU case law mentioned therein—shows that in all likelihood, the circumscription of the scope of judicial scrutiny on fundamental rights grounds was not the intention of the CFR drafters.[37] According to the CFR Explanations, 'it follows unambiguously from the case-law of the Court of Justice that the requirement to respect fundamental rights defined in the context of the Union is only binding on the Member States when they act in the scope of Union law'.[38] Thus, mention in Article 51(1) CFR of member states' duty to respect the CFR provisions *only* when they implement EU law might very well be a drafting deficiency of the CFR. The final decision has rested of course with the CJEU and, indeed, the Court has confirmed that the fundamental rights guaranteed by the Charter must be complied with 'where national legislation falls within the scope of European Union law'.[39] In consequence, what needs to be stressed here is that a 'link' with EU law is necessary for the provisions of the CFR, including those of a cultural nature, to be invoked before the EU judiciary. Such a link to EU law is similarly required for the provisions of the CFR to be invoked before national courts. National courts are bound to review national measures in the light

---

[33] See P. Craig and G. de Búrca, *EU Law: Text, Cases and Materials* (4th edn, 2008), 395–402; A. Rosas and L. Armati, *EU Constitutional Law: An Introduction* (2010), 148.

[34] See Case C-260/89, *Elliniki Radiophonia Tileorassi* [1993] ECR I-2925; Case C-368/95, *Familiapress* [1997] ECR I-3689.

[35] Case 120/78, *Rewe/Bundesmonopolverwaltung für Branntwein* [1979] ECR 649.

[36] See Craig and De Búrca (2008) 402.

[37] The explanations refer for instance to the seminal *Elliniki Radiophonia Tileorassi* judgment, which clarified the Court's stance in relation to fundamental rights protection in the case of member states' derogations from EU law.

[38] Explanations relating to the Charter of Fundamental Rights, OJ 2007 C 303/17 at 32.

[39] On this see Case 617/10, *Åkerberg Fransson*, judgment of 26 February 2013, *nyr*, para 21.

of the CFR when these are connected with the EU legal order, so as to fall within its scope.

Notably, the emphasis placed by Article 22 CFR on *respecting* cultural diversity rather than *promoting* cultural diversity implies that Article 22 CFR imposes a negative obligation of non-interference on the EU to avoid jeopardizing cultural diversity. The Charter attributes no proactive role to the European institutions to promote cultural diversity by conferring positive rights on individuals or groups.[40] It then becomes essential to probe into the cultural powers bestowed on the EU by means of the TFEU, in order to verify whether their delineation assigns the European institutions with duties to *both* respect and promote cultural diversity.

The cultural powers of the EU, laid down in Article 167 TFEU, enjoy an explicit and implicit facet.[41] The EU explicit cultural powers depict a carefully demarcated cultural mandate, as responsibility for cultural affairs primarily rests with the member states. According to Article 167(1) TFEU, the role of the EU is strictly limited to contributing to the flowering of the cultures of the member states, with due *respect* to their national and regional diversity, while 'bringing the common cultural heritage to the fore'. Paragraph 2 of Article 167 TFEU determines that action by the EU shall be aimed at encouraging cooperation between the member states and, if necessary, at supporting and supplementing their action in specifically defined areas: improving the knowledge and dissemination of the culture and history of the European peoples; safeguarding the cultural heritage of European significance; promoting non-commercial cultural exchanges; and facilitating artistic and literary creation, including in the audiovisual sector. The EU and its member states are also to foster cooperation with third countries and competent organizations in the sphere of culture, particularly the Council of Europe, as established by Article 167(3) TFEU.[42] In terms of instruments, pursuant to Article 167(5) TFEU, the EU may only make use of incentive measures, excluding any harmonization of the laws and regulations of the member states, and recommendations. Incentive measures are to be adopted under the ordinary legislative procedure, in which both the European Parliament and the Council are involved, after consulting the Committee of the Regions. Recommendations are to be adopted by the Council on a proposal from the European Commission (hereinafter the 'Commission').

The implicit cultural powers of the EU are set out in Article 167(4) TFEU, according to which '[t]he Union shall take cultural aspects into account in its

---

[40] The same pattern of 'negative obligation' is also discernible in Art 13 CFR on freedom of the arts and Art 25 CFR concerning the right of the elderly to participate in cultural life.

[41] On the cultural powers of the EU, see generally De Witte, 'The cultural dimension of Community law', IV-1 *Collected Courses of the Academy of European Law* (1993) 229; E. Psychogiopoulou, *The Integration of Cultural Considerations in EU Law and Policies* (2008), 25–38 and 54–61; Craufurd Smith, 'The Evolution of Cultural Policy in the European Union', in P. Craig and G. de Búrca (eds), *The Evolution of EU Law* (2nd edn, 2011) 869.

[42] Note also that pursuant to Art 207(4) TFEU, the Council shall act unanimously for the negotiation and conclusion of agreements with one or more third countries or international organizations 'in the field of trade in cultural and audiovisual services, where these agreements risk prejudicing the Union's cultural and linguistic diversity'.

action under other provisions of the Treaties, in particular in order to *respect* and
to *promote* the diversity of its cultures' (emphasis added). By requiring the accommodation of cultural considerations in EU action taken via use of legal bases other
than Article 167(5) TFEU, Article 167(4) TFEU reveals that EU measures with a
cultural component may be adopted in the context of EU policies other than the
EU cultural policy proper. Cultural policy objectives can thus be integrated in,
and pursued by, EU measures that are primarily designed to attain other legitimate
EU policy goals. These 'policy-linking' efforts of the European institutions, also
known as 'cultural mainstreaming',[43] must specifically target both *respect* and *promotion* of the EU's cultural diversity. Respect and promotion of cultural diversity
thus amounts to a transversal policy concern that needs to be reflected in overall
EU practice.

   The preceding analysis shows that although the cultural powers of the European
institutions do not make explicit reference to cultural rights per se, they allow for
the development of policies that can indirectly contribute to their protection and
promotion. True, the role of the EU is particularly constrained when it comes to
the exercise of its explicit cultural powers, yet respect for member states' national
and regional cultural diversity constitutes the overarching policy consideration
that must determine EU cultural action. Also, the four areas of Article 167(2)
TFEU in which the European institutions may take action are closely connected
to the very essence of cultural rights, that is, improving access to and facilitating
participation in cultural life: they are concerned with stimulating engagement in
cultural activity, promoting enjoyment of cultural assets, and facilitating the diffusion of cultural information and knowledge. Quite importantly, by means of the
implicit cultural powers of the EU, respect and promotion of cultural diversity is
recognized as a cross-cutting policy concern to be integrated in EU action on the
whole. This means that the EU is not solely required to abstain from compromis-
ing cultural plurality when developing activities in the various areas of competence
that it enjoys; it is also under a duty to take adequate measures to support and
encourage it.

### 3.  Cultural Rights in the UNESCO Convention on the Protection and Promotion of the Diversity of Cultural Expressions

Besides the constitutional provisions mentioned above, the EU's commitment
to cultural diversity also finds expression in international conventions and agreements to which the EU is a party. Among these, the UNESCO Convention on
the Protection and Promotion of the Diversity of Cultural Expressions (hereinafter CDC or the 'Cultural Diversity Convention') figures prominently. The CDC

---

[43] Psychogiopoulou, 'The Cultural Mainstreaming Clause of Article 151(4) EC: Protection and
Promotion of Cultural Diversity or Hidden Cultural Agenda?', 12 *European Law Journal* (2006) 575.

entered into force on 18 March 2007, three months after the date of deposit of the instruments of ratification of 12 EU member states[44] and the instrument of accession of the then European Community, now succeeded by the EU as a result of the Treaty of Lisbon. The EU and its member states thus contributed to the critical number of ratifications required by Article 29 CDC, for the Cultural Diversity Convention to enter into force. Affirming that the 'UNESCO Convention constitutes a relevant and effective pillar for promoting cultural diversity and cultural exchanges, to which both the Community [now the Union], as reflected in Article 151(4) of the EC Treaty [now Article 167(4) TFEU], and its Member States, attach the greatest importance', the Council approved the CDC on 18 May 2006.[45] In line with Article 216(2) TFEU which states that 'agreements concluded by the Union are binding upon the institutions of the Union and on its Member States', the Cultural Diversity Convention is binding on the EU and forms part of EU law. This means that the EU must conform to, and implement, its provisions when exercising the competences assigned to it by the Treaties and falling within the areas covered by the CDC.

A central actor behind its drafting and negotiation, the interest of the EU in the Cultural Diversity Convention can be traced back in the early 2000s when discussions on the desirability of an international legal instrument on cultural diversity intensified. Responsive to the Universal Declaration on Cultural Diversity and its Action Plan, which called on the UNESCO member states to initiate reflection on an international legal instrument on cultural diversity,[46] the Commission issued a Communication 'Towards an international instrument on cultural diversity',[47] which viewed positively the adoption of a legally binding instrument. According to the Commission, this new instrument should consolidate certain cultural rights, besides committing parties to international cooperation, creating a forum for debate on cultural policies and establishing global monitoring on the state of cultural diversity worldwide. For the Commission, cultural rights in this context should be understood within the meaning of the UDHR and Article 5 of the UNESCO Declaration on Cultural Diversity (without prejudice to intellectual property rights and their exploitation), which reads as follows:

Cultural rights are an integral part of human rights, which are universal, indivisible and interdependent. The flourishing of creative diversity requires the full implementation of cultural rights as defined in Article 27 of the Universal Declaration of Human Rights and in Articles 13 and 15 of the International Covenant on Economic, Social and Cultural Rights. All persons should therefore be able to express themselves and to create and disseminate

---

[44] Finland, Austria, France, Spain, Sweden, Denmark, Slovenia, Estonia, Slovakia, Luxembourg, Lithuania, and Malta ratified the Convention on 18 December 2006.

[45] Council Decision 2006/515/EC of 18 May 2006 on the conclusion of the Convention on the Protection and Promotion of the Diversity of Cultural Expressions, OJ 2006 L 201/15.

[46] Article 1 Universal Declaration on Cultural Diversity, 2 November 2001, <http://portal.unesco.org/en/ev.php-URL_ID=13179&URL_DO=DO_TOPIC&URL_SECTION=201.html> (accessed 28 May 2012).

[47] See Communication from the Commission to the Council and the European Parliament: Towards an international instrument on cultural diversity, COM(2003) 520, 27 August 2003.

their work in the language of their choice, and particularly in their mother tongue; all persons should be entitled to quality education and training that fully respect their cultural identity; and all persons should be able to participate in the cultural life of their choice and conduct their own cultural practices, subject to respect for human rights and fundamental freedoms.

Also, for the new international instrument to garner full EU support, the Commission noted, it should be based on, and fully respect, human rights. Thus, beyond the recognition of cultural rights, notably the right to participate freely in the cultural life of one's choice, the new instrument should also pay attention to the UDHR. The UDHR, the Commission explained, established an approach to culture based on the concepts of human dignity, equality, and freedom, further developed in the UNESCO Universal Declaration on Cultural Diversity. The latter provided in Article 4 that no one could invoke cultural diversity to infringe upon human rights or limit their scope.[48]

Welcoming the decision of the UNESCO General Conference on 17 October 2003 to commence negotiations on the drawing-up of a convention, the European Parliament underlined that 'cultural diversity cannot be preserved unless every individual has access to, and can participate in, his or her own culture'.[49] The European Parliament agreed with the Commission that the new legal binding instrument on cultural diversity should, inter alia, consolidate cultural rights, and called on the General Conference of UNESCO 'to guarantee . . . the right to freedom of information, freedom of opinion, intellectual property, the protection of fundamental rights and cultural human rights'.[50] For the European Parliament, however, 'the Convention's main aims ought to lie in recognizing the special nature of cultural products and services, enshrining in international law the legitimate right of any State or group of States to determine their cultural policies freely, a right taking the form, in particular, of legislative, regulatory or financial measures, and strengthening international cooperation policies and solidarity in the sphere of culture'.[51] In a resolution produced a few months following the preparation of a preliminary draft convention,[52] the European Parliament insisted on the convention being based upon the principles of individual human rights as laid down in international instruments, including the right to freedom of information and opinion, and the right to intellectual property.[53] It also noted that access to a diversified supply of cultural content, both national and from all regions of the world,

[48] UNESCO Universal Declaration on Cultural Diversity, 2 November 2001, <http://portal. unesco.org/en/ev.php-URL_ID=13179&URL_DO=DO_TOPIC&URL_SECTION=201.html> (accessed 28 May 2012).

[49] EP Resolution of 14 January 2004 on preserving and promoting cultural diversity: The role of the European regions and international organisations such as UNESCO and the Council of Europe, OJ 2004 C 92E/322, point C.

[50] OJ 2004 C 92E/322, paras 30 and 39.          [51] OJ 2004 C 92E/322, para 31.

[52] UNESCO, Preliminary draft of a Convention on the Protection of the Diversity of Cultural Contents and Artistic Expressions, UNESCO Doc CLT/CPD/2004/CONF-201/2 (July 2004), <http://www.incd.net/docs/UNESCOdraft04.pdf> (accessed 28 May 2012).

[53] EP Resolution of 14 April 2005 on working towards a Convention on the protection of the diversity of cultural content and artistic expression, OJ 2006 C 33E/591, para 14.

should be understood as a fundamental right, and stressed that the convention should clearly underline the right of parties to develop, maintain, and implement policies and laws designed to protect and promote cultural diversity.[54]

The final text of the CDC reveals that the Convention is not a cultural rights instrument. Rather its purpose, as stipulated in Article 1 CDC, is 'to protect and promote the diversity of cultural expressions'; 'to create the conditions for cultures to flourish and to freely interact in a mutually beneficial manner'; 'to reaffirm the sovereign rights of States to maintain, adopt and implement policies and measures that they deem appropriate for the protection and promotion of the diversity of cultural expressions on their territory'; and to 'strengthen international cooperation and solidarity in a spirit of partnership', among others. Hence, far from conferring cultural rights on individuals and communities, the CDC focuses on the rights and obligations of its parties with the aim of protecting and enhancing the diversity of cultural expressions at the national level and throughout the world. However, the CDC also includes several references to human rights. For instance, the preamble acknowledges the importance of cultural diversity for the full realization of human rights and fundamental freedoms, and underlines that 'freedom of thought, expression and information…enable cultural expressions to flourish within societies'. The guiding principles of the CDC, set out in Article 2 CDC, include the 'principle of respect for human rights and fundamental freedoms', according to which cultural diversity can only be protected and promoted 'if human rights and fundamental freedoms, such as freedom of expression, information and communication, as well as the ability of individuals to choose cultural expressions are guaranteed'. The provisions of the CDC, Article 2 adds, cannot be invoked to infringe human rights and fundamental freedoms or limit their scope.

Evidently, the Cultural Diversity Convention refrains from addressing cultural rights per se. However, many of its provisions refer to measures that are closely related to the implementation of cultural rights. Telling is Article 6(2) CDC, which identifies a series of measures that the parties to the CDC, including the EU, may adopt in order to preserve and enhance cultural diversity domestically. These cover measures that provide opportunities for the creation, production, dissemination, distribution, and enjoyment of cultural activities, goods, and services, including in relation to the language used; measures aimed at providing public financial assistance; measures designed to establish and support public institutions; and measures to nurture and sustain artists as well as others involved in the creation of cultural expressions. Additionally, in accordance with Article 7(1) CDC, the parties to the CDC commit to 'endeavour' to create in their territory an environment encouraging individuals and social groups 'to create, produce, disseminate, distribute and have access to their own cultural expressions, paying due attention to the special circumstances and needs of…persons belonging to minorities and indigenous peoples'.[55]

---

[54] OJ 2006 C 33E/591, paras 8 and 5.

[55] Mention of minorities and indigenous peoples is also made in other provisions. The preamble stresses, for instance, the significance of indigenous peoples' traditional knowledge systems and the need for their adequate protection and promotion. It also points to the importance of the vitality of cultures, 'including for persons belonging to minorities and indigenous peoples, as manifested in their

## 4. Cultural Rights and EU Human Rights Policy

The new fundamental rights dimension of the EU polity, ensuing from the legally binding CFR, has signalled a new era in the development and further consolidation of a genuine fundamental rights culture underpinning the work of the European institutions and the member states, when these act within the scope of EU law. In its Strategy for the effective implementation of the Charter of Fundamental Rights by the European Union, the Commission has laid down a detailed process for respecting fundamental rights in EU legislative acts, that is, from the initial drafting of Commission proposals, to the amendments brought by the Council and the European Parliament as co-legislators, and the implementation of relevant acts by the member states.[56] The Commission has reinforced, in particular, the evaluation of the impact of its proposals on fundamental rights by establishing a 'checklist' to ensure systematic compliance with the Charter.[57] Moreover, it has identified a series of measures devised to strengthen compliance with the CFR, including preparatory consultations, impact assessments, training and operational guidance, and targeted recitals in proposals that have a specific link with fundamental rights. Further, it has called for transparent interinstitutional dialogue when issues of compatibility arise, based on the understanding that each European institution— the Commission, the European Parliament and the Council—are responsible for assessing the impact of their own proposals and amendments on fundamental rights and freedoms. Turning to the member states, the Commission has stressed that 'the upholding of fundamental rights by Member States when they implement Union law is in the common interest of all the Member States because it is essential

---

freedom to create, disseminate and distribute their traditional cultural expressions and to have access thereto'. Moreover, the principle of 'equal dignity of and respect for all cultures', recognized in Art 3 CDC, makes explicit reference to the cultures of persons belonging to minorities and indigenous peoples.

[56] See Communication from the Commission: Strategy for the effective implementation of the Charter of Fundamental Rights by the European Union, COM(2010) 573, 19 October 2010.

[57] The 'fundamental rights check list' contains the following questions:

1. What fundamental rights are affected?
2. Are the rights in question absolute rights (which may not be subject to limitations, examples being human dignity and the ban on torture)?
3. What is the impact of the various policy options under consideration on fundamental rights? Is the impact beneficial (promotion of fundamental rights) or negative (limitation of fundamental rights)?
4. Do the options have both a beneficial and a negative impact, depending on the fundamental rights concerned (eg a negative impact on freedom of expression and beneficial one on intellectual property)?
5. Would any limitation of fundamental rights be formulated in a clear and predictable manner?
6. Would any limitation of fundamental rights:
   – be necessary to achieve an objective of general interest or to protect the rights and freedoms of others (which)?
   – be proportionate to the desired aim?
   – preserve the essence of the fundamental rights concerned?

to the mutual confidence necessary for the operation of the Union'.[58] On this basis, it announced its intention to guarantee respect for the Charter and enforce fundamental rights by making use of all available means: preventive measures designed to raise domestic authorities' awareness during the implementation process; and initiation of infringement proceedings for non-compliance with the CFR.[59]

While the efforts deployed to systematically streamline human rights into the EU legislative process might facilitate the implementation of the culture-related provisions of the CFR, the system is limited to highlighting problematic aspects in the drafting of Commission proposals and the subsequent legislative and implementation phases. Most of the measures laid down focus on identifying the fundamental rights liable to be affected by specific legislative initiatives. The strategy falls short of directing efforts towards identifying policy areas where legislative action might be required to ensure protection of fundamental rights, and thus towards 'mainstreaming' fundamental rights into EU policies in a proactive manner. At the same time, it is plain to see that the European institutions are for the most part to act in an autonomous manner;[60] no arrangements have been made to ensure the establishment of structures conducive to thorough and systematic interinstitutional coordination that would have enabled the European institutions to share the findings acquired through the conduct of independent compatibility checks.

In its strategy, the Commission has also announced the publication of an annual report on the application of the Charter with a view to taking stock of progress in a continuous and consistent manner, while allowing for the exchange of views with the European Parliament and the Council on a sustainable basis. The 2010, 2011 and 2012 reports disclose limited attention paid to the implementation of the provisions of the Charter that are concerned with culture and cultural diversity, save those regarding the principle of non-discrimination and respect for equality.[61] Clearly, the EU enjoys a broad set of instruments to promote equality and fight discrimination, many of which were adopted prior to the CFR acquiring binding legal effect. The Race Equality Directive, for instance, addresses discrimination based on racial or ethnic origin, both in the workplace and other areas of life

---

[58] Communication from the Commission: Strategy for the effective implementation of the Charter of Fundamental Rights by the European Union, COM(2010) 573, 19 October 2010, 9.

[59] The Commission has also stressed the importance of member states' own systems of fundamental rights protection for those cases in which it has no power to intervene as the guardian of the Treaties, namely when breaches of fundamental rights at the national level have no connection to EU law.

[60] See, in particular, Commission Staff Working Paper: Operational Guidance on taking account of Fundamental Rights in Commission Impact Assessments, SEC(2011) 567 final, 6 May 2011; Art 36 of the Rules of Procedure of the European Parliament, <http://www.europarl.europa.eu/sides/getLastRules.do?language=EN&reference=TOC> (accessed 28 May 2012); General Secretariat of the Council, Guidelines on methodological steps to be taken to check fundamental rights compatibility at the Council's preparatory bodies, 10140/11, 18 May 2011, <http://register.consilium.europa.eu/pdf/en/11/st10/st10140.en11.pdf> (accessed 28 May 2012).

[61] European Commission, 2010 Report on the application of the EU Charter of Fundamental Rights, <http://ec.europa.eu/justice/policies/rights/docs/report_EU_charter_FR_2010_en.pdf> (accessed 28 May 2012); 2011 Report on the application of the EU Charter of Fundamental Rights, <http://ec.europa.eu/justice/fundamental-rights/files/charter-brochure-report_en.pdf> (accessed 28 May 2012); 2012 Report on the application of the EU Charter of Fundamental Rights, <http://ec.europa.eu/justice/fundamental-rights/files/charter_report_2012_en.pdf> (accessed 20 May 2013).

such as education, vocational training, social security, healthcare, and access to goods and services for the public, covering housing.[62] Rules to combat discrimination on the grounds of religion or belief in employment and occupation have also been enacted,[63] while the Framework Decision on combating racism and xenophobia has penalized racist and xenophobic speech and crimes against persons or groups of persons defined by reference to race, colour, religion, descent, or national or ethnic origin.[64] Relevant rules and norms display the EU's firm commitment towards equal treatment and diversity, and are complemented by various financial support instruments targeting civil society and state actors to promote equality.[65] They are supplemented by the information-gathering activities of the EU Agency for Fundamental Rights, which compiles comprehensive data on the situation of fundamental rights in the member states, including with regard to discriminatory practices.

All these instruments and activities are beneficial to cultural diversity and may support the protection of the cultural identity of specific cultural groups and communities in a wide sense.[66] The measures combating discrimination on the ground of ethnic origin, for example, by means of the Race Equality Directive, may correspond to measures combating discrimination based on membership of a cultural or linguistic minority. This is so despite the fact that member states are the key decision-makers on minority policies, minority protection, and the use of minority languages on their territory.[67] Action supportive of cultural diversity and cultural interaction more broadly has also been an integral part of the EU efforts to support

---

[62] Council Directive 2000/43/EC of 29 June 2000 implementing the principle of equal treatment between persons irrespective of racial or ethnic origin, OJ 2000 L 180/22.

[63] Council Directive 2000/78/EC of 27 November 2000 establishing a general framework for equal treatment in employment and occupation, OJ 2000 L 303/16.

[64] Council Framework Decision 2008/913/JHA of 28 November 2008 on combating certain forms and expressions of racism and xenophobia by means of criminal law, OJ 2008 L 328/55. Note also that the Audiovisual Media Services Directive bans incitement to hatred based on race, sex, religion or nationality (Art 6) in audiovisual media services, and the inclusion and promotion of discrimination based on sex, racial or ethnic origin, nationality, religion or belief, disability, age or sexual orientation in audiovisual commercial communications (Art 9(1)). See Directive 2010/13/EU of the European Parliament and of the Council of 10 March 2010 on the coordination of certain provisions laid down by law, regulation, or administrative action in member states concerning the provision of audiovisual media services, OJ 2010 L 95/1.

[65] See, in particular, the Fundamental Rights and Citizenship Programme and the Programme for Employment and Social Solidarity (Council Decision of 19 April 2007 establishing for the period 2007–13 the specific programme Fundamental Rights and Citizenship as part of the general programme Fundamental Rights and Justice, OJ 2009 L 110/33; Decision 1672/2006/EC of the European Parliament and of the Council of 24 October 2006 establishing a Community Programme for Employment and Social Solidarity—Progress, OJ 2006 L 315/1).

[66] On this, see also De Witte, 'The Value of Cultural Diversity in European Union Law', in H. Schneider and P. van den Bossche (eds), *Protection of Cultural Diversity from a European and International Perspective* (2008) 219 at 232–6.

[67] On this, see also European Commission, 2012 Report on the application of the EU Charter of Fundamental Rights, <http://ec.europa.eu/justice/fundamental-rights/files/charter_report_2012_en.pdf> (accessed 20 May 2013), 56–7. Note, however, that in the area of language use, in particular, the Commission has developed a comprehensive strategy to promote national, regional, but also minority and migrant languages in the EU. The strategy calls for the 'mainstreaming' of multilingualism across a series of EU policy areas, including lifelong learning, employment, social inclusion, competitiveness, culture, youth and civil society, research, and the media, with a view to strengthening

EU citizenship, including by eliminating or mitigating the existing restrictions on the right of citizens and their family members to move and reside freely within the territory of the member states,[68] as well as of the EU immigration policy. The latter has rested both on introducing a legislative framework granting migrants specific rights[69] and taking steps to ensure their successful integration in the host country as part of effective migration management.[70]

The EU equality, citizenship, and immigration policies can enhance cultural diversity and stimulate cultural encounters but are not directly concerned with cultural rights. The action of the European institutions pertaining to the EU's largest ethnic minority, the Roma, is enlightening. In 2011, the Commission adopted the EU framework for national Roma integration strategies up to 2020, as a complement to the EU equality legislation.[71] The framework encourages member states to formulate comprehensive integration policies that address the specific needs of Roma regarding equal access to employment, education, housing, and healthcare, including by making EU funds accessible to the community. However, the framework remains silent on matters concerning access to culture, participation in cultural life, or the protection of the Roma cultural identity. A more culture-friendly approach is taken by the 2011 European Agenda for the Integration of Third-Country Nationals.[72] The agenda advocates a positive attitude towards diversity as a driver for economic development and social cohesion, with strong guarantees for fundamental rights and mutual respect for different cultures and traditions. It identifies various measures and areas for action that are recommended to the member states, and specifies the role of the EU in the process, namely to provide a framework for monitoring, benchmarking, and exchanging good practices, while creating incentives through its financial instruments. But while the agenda takes the position that 'integration policies should create favourable conditions for migrants' economic, social, cultural and political participation', at the same time noting that the receiving society must respect migrants' rights and

---

the 'life chances of citizens' through increased employability, better access to services and rights, and enhanced solidarity through intercultural dialogue and social cohesion. See Communication from the Commission to the European Parliament, the Council, the European Economic and Social Committee and the Committee of the Regions: Multilingualism: an asset for Europe and a shared commitment, COM(2008) 566, 18 September 2008.

[68] Directive 2004/38/EC of the European Parliament and of the Council of 29 April 2004 on the right of citizens of the Union and their family members to move and reside freely within the territory of the Member States, OJ 2004 L 158/77.

[69] See Council Directive 2003/86/EC of 22 September 2003 on the right to family reunification, OJ 2003 L 251/12; Council Directive 2003/109/EC of 25 October 2003 concerning the status of third-country nationals who are long-term residents, OJ 2004 L 16/44.

[70] Council of the European Union, Press Release 14615/04, 2618th Council meeting, Justice and Home Affairs, 19 November 2004, 15.

[71] Communication from the Commission to the European Parliament, the Council, the European Economic and Social Committee and the Committee of the Regions: An EU framework for national Roma integration strategies up to 2020, COM(2011) 173, 5 April 2011.

[72] Communication from the Commission to the European Parliament, the Council, the European Economic and Social Committee and the Committee of the Regions: European Agenda for the integration of third-country nationals, COM(2011) 455, 20 July 2011.

cultures,[73] only a limited number of the measures suggested actually have a cultural dimension. The agenda mentions, for instance, that the recruitment of migrants as teachers might be a means to 'open national education systems to other European and non-European cultures'.[74] It also refers to 'culturally adapted health promotion programmes' as part of targeted action to improve migrants' living conditions, and stresses the need to stimulate cultural activity in migrant populated disadvantaged urban areas, in support of urban development.[75] However, no measures are specifically designed to encourage migrants' engagement with cultural activity or to facilitate enjoyment of their own culture.

Perhaps a major drawback for the protection of fundamental rights in the EU, including those with a cultural connotation, is the fragmented, rudimentary monitoring of member states' compliance with fundamental rights. Although the Treaty of Lisbon has rendered the CFR legally binding, the EU still lacks a comprehensive internal human rights policy with effective accountability mechanisms to address human rights failures. This explains the calls of the European Parliament to increase coherence among the various bodies of the EU institutions and the member states responsible for the monitoring and implementation of fundamental rights protection, and to reinforce a cross-EU monitoring mechanism as well as an early warning system with thoughtful *ex ante* examination of breaches or risks of breaches of EU fundamental rights.[76] Scrutiny of the fundamental rights situation in the member states is not systematic, and for the most part rests on the annual Commission reports on the application of the CFR and the annual fundamental rights reports issued by the European Parliament and the EU Agency for Fundamental Rights, without robust interinstitutional cooperation and meaningful follow-up. This denotes institutional reluctance to shape a unified human rights policy intended to promote and ensure alignment of national policies with EU fundamental rights and freedoms. Quite importantly, it also contrasts the EU's approach with developed policies concerning the protection of fundamental rights around the world, disclosing an asymmetry of institutional fundamental rights attention within and outside the EU.[77]

With regard to cultural rights in particular, there is a clear emphasis on monitoring and reporting on other categories of rights, that is, civil, political, economic, and social rights, though the cultural dimension that some of these rights enjoy in a broad sense is generally acknowledged. Interestingly, as part of its tasks 'to provide the relevant institutions, bodies, offices and agencies of the [Union] and its Member States when implementing [Union] law with assistance and expertise',[78] the EU Agency of Fundamental Rights (FRA) has dedicated substantial efforts

---

[73] COM(2011) 455, 20 July 2011, 3 and 4.        [74] COM(2011) 455, 20 July 2011, 6.
[75] COM(2011) 455, 20 July 2011, 6 and 8.
[76] EP Resolution of 15 December 2010 on the situation of fundamental rights in the European Union (2009)—effective implementation after the entry into force of the Treaty of Lisbon (2009/2161(INI)), <http://www.europarl.europa.eu/sides/getDoc.do?pubRef=-//EP//NONSGML+TA+P7-TA-2010-0483+0+DOC+PDF+V0//EN> (accessed 28 May 2012).
[77] For a detailed overview of the EU's human rights 'toolbox' in relation to its external action, see <http://eeas.europa.eu/human_rights/how/index_en.htm> (accessed 28 May 2012).
[78] Article 1 Council Regulation 168/2007/EC of 15 February 2007 establishing a European Union Agency for Fundamental Rights, OJ 2007 L 53/1.

and resources to the development of a reliable data set on the situation of immigrant and ethnic minority groups which are vulnerable to ethnic and racial discrimination in the member states. In 2011, the agency published a lengthy report reviewing the relationship between the EU legal system and minority protection, highlighting relevant EU developments but also looking at minorities' experiences of discrimination across the EU in selected areas of social life, including in relation to religious freedom and the use of minority languages.[79] In 2012, the agency published the findings of a pilot household survey on the socio-economic status of Roma alongside data on the enjoyment of their rights in 11 EU member states, working in parallel with the United Nations Development Programme (UNDP) and the World Bank.[80] Whether the agency's work will feed into specific EU initiatives remains, however, to be seen.

## 5. Cultural Rights and EU Cultural Policy

A variety of tools to stimulate cultural creation, promote access to culture and facilitate enjoyment of a diversified cultural offering—all supportive of the fulfilment of cultural rights—have been gradually developed in the context of the EU's cultural policy. The mechanisms display variance. They consist of creating funding opportunities for engagement in cultural activity, sustaining a process of mutual learning among national administrations, and ensuring that all EU policies with cultural implications strike the right balance between respect for and promotion of cultural diversity and other EU policy objectives.

In terms of funding, Article 167(5) TFEU has given rise to a series of cultural support instruments, aimed at fostering creativity and encouraging diffusion of cultural content. Following a first generation of sectoral programmes providing assistance to cultural cooperation projects in the fields of performing, visual and applied arts; books and reading; and heritage protection, the EU has moved to a single financing and programming instrument as a means to strengthen cooperation between cultural operators in all artistic and cultural disciplines.[81] With a total budget of €400 million, *Culture (2007–2013)* has offered financial assistance

---

[79] FRA, *Respect for and protection of persons belonging to minorities 2008–2010* (2010), <http://fra.europa.eu/fraWebsite/attachments/FRA-Report-Respect-protection-minorities-2011_EN.pdf> (accessed 28 May 2012).

[80] FRA and UNDP, *The situation of Roma in 11 EU Member States. Survey results at a glance* (2012), <http://fra.europa.eu/sites/default/files/fra_uploads/2099-FRA-2012-Roma-at-a-glance_EN.pdf> (accessed 28 May 2012).

[81] Decision 719/96/EC of the European Parliament and of the Council of 29 March 1996 establishing a programme to support artistic and cultural activities having a European dimension (Kaleidoscope), OJ 1996 L 99/20; Decision 2085/97/EC of the European Parliament and of the Council of 6 October 1997 establishing a programme of support, including translation, in the field of books and reading (Ariane), OJ 1997 L 291/26; Decision 2228/97/EC of the European Parliament and of the Council of 13 October 1997 establishing a Community action programme in the field of cultural heritage (Raphael), OJ 1997 L 305/31; Decision 508/2000/EC of the European Parliament and of the Council of 14 February 2000 establishing the Culture 2000 programme, OJ 2000 L 63/1.

to various cultural cooperation projects in the pursuit of three interrelated object-ives: enhancing cross-border mobility of those working in the cultural sector; increasing transnational circulation of cultural and artistic output; and reinforc-ing intercultural dialogue.[82] Three distinct levels of intervention have been estab-lished: support for cultural actions of variable length and scale; support for highly specialized bodies active in the field of culture; and support for research, policy anal-ysis, dissemination activities, and sharing of experience in relation to European cul-tural cooperation and cultural policy development. Other initiatives that have been set up to promote cultural activity and raise awareness of cultural diversity include the European Capitals of Culture,[83] the European Heritage Days (in cooperation with the Council of Europe),[84] and the 2008 European Year of Intercultural Dialogue.[85] By creating opportunities for enhanced mobility of cultural practition-ers, goods, and services, and by facilitating enjoyment of cultural assets, the EU has encouraged cultural exchanges and interaction, contributing to the establishment of alternative platforms to those available at the national level for access to, and participation in culture and cultural life.

Whereas EU cultural policy has for years been a policy primarily dedicated to the granting of financial resources to cultural cooperation projects, mainly due to the constraints imposed on the European institutions by Article 167(5) TFEU (the legal basis for express EU cultural action), the cultural activity of the European institutions seems to have entered a new phase following the publication of the Commission's ambitious 2007 Communication on a European Agenda for Culture in a Globalizing World.[86] The agenda suggested distinct objectives to steer the cultural action of the EU, and envisaged new working methods for the devel-opment of cultural partnerships between the European institutions, the member states and cultural stakeholders. Promotion of cultural diversity and intercultural dialogue, promotion of culture as a catalyst for creativity in the framework of the Lisbon strategy,[87] and promotion of culture as a vital element of the EU's external relations were identified as the overarching goals that should guide the EU's cul-tural endeavours. In terms of working methods, the Commission highlighted the importance of structured dialogue with the cultural sector, evidence-based infor-mation for the development of EU cultural policy, and increased attention afforded to the interface between cultural diversity and other EU policies. Furthermore,

---

[82] Decision 1955/2006/EC of the European Parliament and of the Council of 12 December 2006 establishing the Culture Programme (2007–13), OJ 2006 L 372/1.

[83] Decision 1419/1999/EC of the European Parliament and of the Council of 25 May 1999 estab-lishing a Community action for the European Capital of Culture event for the years 2005 to 2019, OJ 1999 L 166/1.

[84] For detailed information, see <http://ec.europa.eu/culture/our-programmes-and-actions/heritage-days/european-heritage-days_en.htm> (accessed 28 May 2012).

[85] Decision 1983/2006/EC of the European Parliament and of the Council of 18 December 2006 concerning the European Year of Intercultural Dialogue (2008), L 2006 412/44.

[86] Communication from the Commission to the European Parliament, the Council, the European Economic and Social Committee and the Committee of the Regions on a European agenda for culture in a globalizing world, COM(2007) 242, 10 May 2007.

[87] See Presidency Conclusions, Lisbon European Council, 23–24 March 2000, <http://consilium.europa.eu/ueDocs/cms_Data/docs/pressData/en/ec/00100-r1.en0.htm> (accessed 28 May 2012).

the Commission anticipated use of the open method of coordination (OMC)—a means to invigorate member states' cultural cooperation.

Favouring decentralization and flexibility rather than command-and-control modes of regulation, the OMC was considered to be particularly apposite for the area of culture where the EU competences are carefully circumscribed. In its resolution endorsing the agenda, the Council opted for a flexible application of the OMC in the cultural field, with voluntary member state participation in the actions and procedures concerned.[88] The OMC should serve the objectives of the agenda through triennial work plans covering a limited number of priority areas determined by the Council, and specific actions proposed on their basis by the Commission. In terms of reporting obligations, the Commission was required to prepare a report to be submitted to the Council, after having consulted the competent Council body (the Cultural Affairs Committee), drawing, among others, on the information provided by the member states on a voluntary basis.

In line with the Council work plan on culture, five priority themes were identified for the period 2008–10: improving conditions for the mobility of artists and other professionals in the cultural field; promoting access to culture (particularly through the promotion of cultural heritage, multilingualism, digitization, cultural tourism, synergies with education, and greater mobility of collections); developing data, and statistics in the cultural sector; maximizing the potential of cultural and creative industries; and promoting and implementing the UNESCO Convention on the Protection and Promotion of the Diversity of Cultural Expressions.[89] Four working groups (WGs) were then created to exchange experiences and formulate recommendations on some of these priority themes: a WG on mobility of artists and other cultural professionals; a WG on mobility of collections and other museum activities; a WG on synergies between culture and education; and a WG on cultural and creative industries.[90]

The first phase of the cultural OMC offered a mixed picture, as ascertained by the Commission in its first report on the implementation of the agenda.[91] Although the OMC generally provided a useful framework for networking and the exchange of views and opinions, most expert groups concentrated on sharing experiences and developing policy recommendations, without engaging in a systematic collection and analysis of national practices. Moreover, channelling the OMC findings and policy recommendations in EU and national policy-making proved particularly challenging. The revised Council work plan for culture (2011–14) sought to address these deficiencies by better articulating the work of the expert groups with

[88] Resolution of the Council of 16 November 2007 on a European Agenda for Culture, OJ 2007 C 287/1.

[89] Conclusions of the Council and of the Representatives of the Governments of the Member States, meeting within the Council, on the Work Plan for Culture 2008–10, OJ 2008 C 143/9.

[90] Eurostat should in turn work on making better use of available statistics at the EU level, disseminating data and developing a specific methodology for cultural statistics.

[91] Commission report to the European Parliament, the Council, the European Economic and Social Committee and the Committee of the Regions on the implementation of the European Agenda for Culture, COM(2010) 390, 19 July 2010.

that of the Council presidencies, the Commission and the member states.[92] It also revised the principles for the setting up and functioning of the WGs, and adjusted the priority areas for action, focusing on the following: cultural diversity, intercultural dialogue and accessible and inclusive culture; cultural and creative industries; skills and mobility; cultural heritage, including mobility of collections; culture in external relations; and culture statistics.

In relation to the first priority area, a WG has been invited to identify policies and good practices concerning public arts and cultural institutions, with a view to promoting better access to and wider participation in culture, including by disadvantaged groups and groups experiencing poverty and social exclusion. This group has also been required to identify instruments and policy tools allowing public arts and cultural institutions to highlight the intercultural dimension of heritage, strengthen artistic education, and promote intercultural dialogue, so as to facilitate exchanges among cultures and between social groups, and to help develop key 'cultural awareness and expression' competences through education. Another WG has been mandated to examine strategic use of EU support programmes in order to foster the potential of culture for local and regional development and the wider economy; encourage the international presence of European culture industries; and identify good practices on financial engineering for small and medium-sized cultural and creative enterprises. Two WGs have further been requested to identify barriers and good practices on the mobility of collections, the mobility of small-scale operators and young artists, and the development of successful creative partnerships.

Evidently, none of the WGs has been specifically devoted to developing policy strategies for the fulfilment of cultural rights. The OMC could have offered a vehicle for the pursuit of a precise cultural rights agenda, providing a policy space for the promotion of best practices and the shaping of a general frame of reference within which domestic policies could then be formulated and implemented.[93] Linking the OMC to the promotion of cultural rights would have been particularly helpful, bearing in mind that the CFR and its culture-related provisions are addressed to the member states only when these act within the scope of EU law. A cultural rights-focused OMC would have indeed allowed addressing those situations where member states act in autonomous capacity, outside the scope of EU law. While the sensitivity of the member states in the area might explain the non-association of the cultural OMC to a specific cultural rights discourse, it is clear that many aspects of the remit of the WGs are concerned with facilitating access to and participation in cultural life, supporting cultural interaction, and creating the socio-economic conditions necessary for engagement in cultural activity. From this perspective, it could be argued that the cultural OMC may indirectly

---

[92] Conclusions of the Council and of the Representatives of the Governments of the Member States, meeting within the Council, on the Work Plan for Culture 2011–14, OJ 2010 C 325/1.

[93] On the use of the open method of coordination in the pursuit of a social and cultural rights agenda, see Bernard, 'A "New Governance" Approach to Economic, Social and Cultural Rights in the EU', in T.K. Hervey and J. Kenner (eds), *Economic and Social Rights under the EU Charter of Fundamental Rights: A Legal Perspective* (2003) 247.

sustain member states in their efforts to implement cultural rights, provided of course that the OMC output is broadly endorsed by the member states.

Concurrently, through the exercise of the implicit cultural powers set out in Article 167(4) TFEU, the European institutions have developed a broad range of measures and actions that support cultural diversity in the context of EU policies other than the EU cultural policy *stricto sensu*. Certainly, the rigour of incorporating cultural diversity concerns in EU action overall largely depends on the opportunities created to link culture and cultural diversity to other EU policies, effective interinstitutional cooperation, and efficient interservice coordination between the various Commission departments and services, responsible for the preparation of proposals of a regulatory or financial nature. While the Education and Culture Directorate General of the Commission cannot easily be compared to other heavyweight divisions of the Commission, in the wake of the European agenda for culture, its influence seems to have become more pronounced. Accounting for this has not only been the creation of an interservice Commission group, intended to bring various Commission departments together so as to facilitate cultural mainstreaming, but also increased awareness of the role of culture as catalyst of European integration and growth, triggered by the European agenda for culture and the policy attention it has received internally within the Commission.

In July 2010, the Commission published a working document, providing an overview of 'developments in EU policies in which culture is present in one way or another'.[94] The working document discusses the integration of cultural diversity considerations in such diverse EU policies as education and training; active citizenship; cohesion policy; research, enterprise and industry; competition policy; the internal market; employment, social affairs and equal opportunities; freedom, security and justice; development cooperation; trade policy; and so on. The document does not offer an assessment of the depth or level of accommodation of cultural diversity considerations but rather engages in a mapping exercise of the EU policies that enjoy a cultural component, occasionally identifying issue areas for further consideration. The Commission refers, for instance, to the various national and regional support measures for museums and cultural centres, national heritage, theatre and music productions, printed cultural media, and the cinematographic and audiovisual sector that were sanctioned under the EU state aid rules; the important contribution of the funding instruments of the EU cohesion policy to small and medium-sized enterprises (SMEs) operating in the cultural sector, the preservation and promotion of cultural heritage, and the development of cultural infrastructure as part of regional socio-economic development; EU funding schemes and the assistance they provide to research projects focusing on the digitization of cultural heritage, its conservation as well as the use of communication and information technologies to increase access to, and use of, cultural resources;

---

[94] Commission Working Document, The European Agenda for Culture—progress towards shared goals, Accompanying document to the Commission Report to the European Parliament, the Council, the European Economic and Social Committee and the Committee of the Regions on the implementation of the European agenda for culture, SEC(2010) 904, 19 July 2010, 3.

EU support for fostering the competitiveness and innovation of cultural enterprises; the harmonization of intellectual property rights providing a high level of protection for rightholders and creators; and the support offered to partner countries and regions for the emergence and strengthening of cultural industries, the protection of cultural heritage, and the promotion of local access to culture.

## 6. Conclusion

The EU system of fundamental rights protection emanates from distinct, varied sources which are not devoid of cultural effect. The rights guaranteed by the ECHR and the EU Treaties, though not concerned with the protection of cultural rights in the strict sense, include several provisions that enjoy a cultural dimension. The legally binding CFR contains both provisions with a cultural component and provisions that directly address respect of cultural diversity and freedom of the arts. Further, the constitutional traditions common to the member states and major international human rights instruments that enshrine specific cultural rights may advise on, and substantiate fundamental rights protection as a general principle of EU law, subject to interpretation by the CJEU.

The fundamental rights provisions of the EU legal framework, especially as provided by the CFR, disclose that although the EU is not expressly required to promote cultural liberties and develop a fully-fledged cultural rights policy, it is under a duty to respect cultural diversity and prohibit discrimination, including on grounds that could be perceived from a cultural perspective. Such a commitment on behalf of the EU and its member states when operating within the framework of EU law is important, although there has so far been reticence to develop the institutional mechanisms necessary that would have allowed for effective monitoring of compliance with fundamental rights and freedoms (including those of a cultural nature), especially on behalf of the member states. Concurrently, the EU is required to develop a cultural policy centred on promoting cultural cooperation between the member states, and allowing their cultural systems to develop freely while meaningfully complementing their activities in specific issue areas. Also, it is mandated to protect and promote cultural diversity whenever its action entails cultural implications, a requirement that has been reinforced by the accession of the EU to the UNESCO Convention on the Protection and Promotion of the Diversity of Cultural Expressions.

Besides a broad set of instruments adopted to ensure equality and non-discrimination, which are beneficial to the protection of cultural diversity and the distinct cultural identities present in Europe, the EU has developed a wide range of measures as part of its cultural policy, tailored to guaranteeing and encouraging access to cultural activity and widespread diffusion of cultural content. The creation of an open, common cultural area, founded on the acceptance and recognition of diverse cultural patterns and practices, to which the EU is powerfully committed, supports the establishment of an environment that facilitates access for individuals and groups to their own culture as well as other cultures of their choice. This is vital for any regime of cultural rights protection, as it increases chances of engagement in cultural activity and enjoyment of cultural resources via a diversified cultural offering. At the same time, it is true that the EU has refrained from making use of instruments and procedures forming part of its rich policy apparatus that could have made a substantive contribution to, and positively influence the formulation of, member states' strategies for the implementation of cultural rights on their territory. The cultural OMC is a clear example in this respect. The OMC could have been directed towards developing a cultural rights agenda to be used for overall policy orientation for the member states. Premised on consensual approaches that favour the exchange of experiences and the promotion of best practices, it could have served as the bedrock of member states' action to fulfil and implement cultural rights. This is a missed opportunity for the EU to strengthen and qualify its culture-related action that should be widely reconsidered.

# 6

# Culture, Human Rights, and the WTO

*Tania Voon*

## 1. Introduction

The relationship between culture, human rights, and the World Trade Organization (WTO) raises a number of different issues, which arise across several WTO agreements. This relationship is of significant current interest as the number of members of the WTO continues to grow, and the variations in cultural foundations within the WTO membership expand accordingly. At the time of writing, the WTO has 155 members, with Russia set to become the 156th Member on 22 August 2012[1] and Vanuatu set to become the 157th Member on 24 August 2012.[2] The WTO rules are designed, in principle, to be able to accommodate extensive regulatory diversity among members, but their impact on human rights and culture remains open to question.

In this chapter, I consider some of the major areas of interest in examining the overlaps between the law of the WTO, human rights law, and international and domestic laws and norms concerning culture. I begin by outlining two key debates that have arisen in the WTO in connection with culture: first, the application of WTO law to audiovisual products and printed publications (so-called 'cultural products'); and, secondly, the significance in a WTO context of cultural differences in attitudes towards risk arising from food. I then examine some specific concerns relating to culture and human rights that are under consideration in the WTO in connection with intellectual property: traditional knowledge, genetic resources, and geographical indications. Finally, I survey certain United Nations institutional perspectives on the overlap between human rights and international trade.

As questions of culture and human rights are posed in relation to different areas of WTO law, no single conclusion on the relationship between these three fields is possible. However, the case studies examined in this chapter tend to suggest that this relationship remains underexplored, particularly from the perspective of

---

[1] WTO, Press Release, 'Lamy hails Russia's WTO accession ratification', PRESS/668, 23 July 2012.
[2] WTO, Press Release, 'WTO members congratulate Vanuatu for ratifying its accession package', PRESS/669, 25 July 2012.

the WTO. One reason for this may be a reluctance on the part of many WTO members to encourage incorporation of non-WTO public international law such as human rights law into WTO disputes or WTO law more generally. Another may be the general absence of explicit references to 'human rights' in the WTO agreements. In any case, the sometimes fraught interaction between WTO law and human rights may well explain difficulties currently being faced by WTO members in reaching agreement on particular subjects in the Doha Round of negotiations and associated talks.

## 2. The Impact of WTO Rules on Culture: Two Key Issues

### A. Cultural products: audiovisual products and printed publications

WTO rules affect culture in many different ways. The aspect of culture that has generated the most discussion and debate in the context of the WTO since its establishment in 1995 (and well before, in the context of its predecessor the General Agreement on Tariffs and Trade (GATT) of 1947) concerns 'cultural products'. Cultural products in the context of international trade law are most often narrowly defined as audiovisual products (film, video, radio, television) and printed publications (books, magazines, periodicals).[3]

At the end of the Uruguay Round of multilateral trade negotiations that established the WTO, the United States and the European Union (EU; then the European Communities in the WTO context) were unable to agree on how WTO law should treat these products.[4] Put simply, the US position was essentially that a cultural product is no different from any other product and requires no special treatment under WTO rules.[5] In contrast, the EU's position was that the protection of culture is a public policy objective requiring a specific exemption from the usual WTO obligations. The failure of the United States and the EU to agree on this issue meant that the GATT contracting parties as a whole could also not agree. As a result, the WTO rules contain little explicit guidance on how WTO law applies to cultural products.

Two significant questions arise in applying WTO law to cultural products. One is whether a 'cultural' justification is inherently discriminatory; that is, whether a WTO member's desire to protect its cultural products or the industries that create those products is any different from (or more legitimate than) a WTO member's desire to protect its domestic industries generally. The GATT 1994 provides some answer to this question. Article XX(f) of that agreement contains a limited

---

[3] T. Voon, *Cultural Products and the World Trade Organization* (2007) 19.

[4] WTO, Council for Trade in Services, Audiovisual Services: Background Note by the Secretariat, S/C/W/40, 15 June 1998, paras 24, 30; GATT, 'Peter Sutherland Responds to Debate on Audiovisual Sector', NUR 069, 14 October 1993.

[5] J. Croome, *Reshaping the World Trading System: A History of the Uruguay Round* (2nd rev edn, 1999) 328.

exception for measures 'imposed for the protection of national treasures of artistic, historic or archaeological value', but this provision does not obviously encompass most cultural products. Article IV of the GATT 1994 provides a specific exception for certain screen quotas in connection with 'cinematograph films', although the precise scope of this exception remains uncertain.

This leads to the second key question in applying WTO law to cultural products: are cultural products 'goods' or 'services' for the purpose of the WTO agreements? While the GATT 1994 contains little guidance on this question, case law developed under the active WTO dispute settlement system offers meaningful insights in this regard as well as in relation to the treatment of cultural products in the WTO more generally. Two WTO cases relate specifically to cultural products in the WTO: *Canada—Periodicals*[6] and *China—Publications and Audiovisual Products*.[7] Both cases were heard by WTO Panels (three-person bodies selected on an ad hoc basis to hear disputes at first instance) and then the WTO Appellate Body (a seven-person standing body that hears appeals of Panel decisions). Other WTO cases, although not specific to cultural products, explain how the Appellate Body is likely to approach cultural policy objectives in the context of how it has approached other non-trade policy objectives such as the protection of health and the environment.

In *Canada—Periodicals*, the United States brought a WTO complaint against various Canadian measures concerning periodicals. The evidence before the WTO Panel and Appellate Body indicated that the Canadian government regarded the Canadian periodical industry as 'a vital element of Canadian cultural expression' and therefore 'use[d] policy instruments that encourage[d] the flow of advertising revenues to Canadian periodicals, since a viable Canadian periodical industry must have a secure financial base'.[8] Without delving into the complexities of the Canadian measures and WTO provisions at issue in that case, the Appellate Body's reasoning can be read as suggesting that, from the perspective of WTO law, WTO members will generally be unable to justify measures discriminating against imports simply on the basis that domestic and imported products have different cultural significance due to their origins alone.[9] If the relevant domestic and imported products (eg 'Canadian' periodicals in contrast to US periodicals) compete in a commercial sense, they are likely to be regarded as 'like' or 'directly competitive or substitutable' within the meaning of WTO rules requiring 'national

    [6] WTO Panel Report, *Canada—Certain Measures Concerning Periodicals*, WT/DS31/R and Corr 1 (circulated 14 March 1997, adopted 30 July 1997); WTO Appellate Body Report, *Canada—Certain Measures Concerning Periodicals*, WT/DS31/AB/R (circulated 30 June 1997, adopted 30 July 1997).

    [7] WTO Panel Report, *China—Measures Affecting Trading Rights and Distribution Services for Certain Publications and Audiovisual Entertainment Products*, WT/DS363/R and Corr 1 (circulated 12 August 2009, adopted 19 January 2010); WTO Appellate Body Report, *China—Measures Affecting Trading Rights and Distribution Services for Certain Publications and Audiovisual Entertainment Products*, WT/DS363/AB/R (circulated 21 December 2009, adopted 19 January 2010).

    [8] Appellate Body Report, *Canada—Periodicals*, 31.

    [9] See Knight, 'The Dual Nature of Cultural Products: An Analysis of the World Trade Organization's Decision Regarding Canadian Periodicals', 57 *University of Toronto Faculty of Law Review* (1999) 165 at 186; Voon (2007) 75–82.

treatment' (that is, not treating imports less favourably than locally produced products)[10] and 'most-favoured nation treatment' (that is, not treating imports from any WTO member less favourably than imports from any other country).[11]

Similarly, the regulatory purpose of protecting or promoting culture is unlikely to be sufficient per se to explain a measure that distinguishes between domestic and imported products. The Appellate Body has consistently rejected the so-called 'aims-and-effects' test, according to which two products may be deemed not 'like' (and therefore not subject to the same regulatory treatment) on the basis that they differ when the aim and effects of the regulatory measure in question are taken into account. Thus, the fact that protecting Canadian-produced periodicals may support the objective of promoting Canadian culture is not a sufficient basis for treating US-produced periodicals less favourably. However, the regulatory purpose of protecting culture may nevertheless feed into the traditional criteria for assessing likeness[12]—particularly consumer preferences (eg if Canadian consumers regard Canadian periodicals as inherently different from US periodicals, precisely because of their Canadian origins)—and is also likely to affect the assessment of whether a measure is applied 'so as to afford protection' to domestic industry.[13]

The Appellate Body has rejected the aims-and-effects test in the context of the GATT 1994, the General Agreement on Trade in Services (GATS)[14] and, implicitly and more recently, the Agreement on Technical Barriers to Trade (TBT Agreement). In *US—Clove Cigarettes*, the Appellate Body rejected the panel's reliance on regulatory purpose in assessing likeness under Article 2.1 of the TBT Agreement, stating:

[W]e do not consider that the concept of 'like products' in Article 2.1 of the *TBT Agreement* lends itself to distinctions between products that are based on the regulatory objectives of a measure.... Nevertheless,... the regulatory concerns underlying a measure, such as the health risks associated with a given product, may be relevant to an analysis of the 'likeness' criteria under Article III:4 of the GATT 1994, as well as under Article 2.1 of the *TBT Agreement*, to the extent they have an impact on the competitive relationship between and among the products concerned.[15]

These restrictions on the use of regulatory purpose in analysing whether a measure treats imported products less favourably than domestic products should not obscure the fact that a number of exceptions and flexibilities exist in WTO law to enable WTO members to enact cultural policy measures in connection with cultural products. In addition to the specific exceptions mentioned above in relation

---

[10] GATT 1994, Art III:2, III:4.  [11] GATT 1994, Art I:1.
[12] WTO Appellate Body Report, *Japan—Taxes on Alcoholic Beverages*, WT/DS8/AB/R, WT/DS10/AB/R, WT/DS11/AB/R (circulated 4 October 1996, adopted 1 November 1996) 20, 22.
[13] GATT 1994, Art III:1 (as referenced in Art III:2).
[14] WTO Appellate Body Report, *European Communities—Regime for the Importation, Sale and Distribution of Bananas* ('*EC—Bananas III*'), WT/DS27/AB/R (circulated 9 September 1997, adopted 25 September 1997), para 241.
[15] WTO Appellate Body Report, *United States—Measures Affecting the Production and Sale of Clove Cigarettes*, WT/DS406/AB/R (circulated 4 April 2012, adopted 24 April 2012), paras 116, 119.

to national treasures and cinematograph films, the general exceptions for measures 'necessary to protect public morals' in Article XX(a) of the GATT 1994 and Article XIV(a) of the GATS provide considerable scope for members to pursue cultural policies. A measure that would otherwise breach a non-discrimination obligation of the GATT 1994 or the GATS may nevertheless be found WTO-consistent if it falls within the public morals exception. In applying that exception, along with other general exceptions under GATT Article XX and GATS Article XIV, the Appellate Body has shown itself to be open-minded in identifying legitimate policy objectives of members, but strict in scrutinizing the reasons for any associated discrimination.

In *China—Publications and Audiovisual Products*, the panel held, and the Appellate Body did not question, that monitoring the content of cultural products and preventing their importation if they contain prohibited content are measures to protect public morals within the meaning of GATT Article XX(a).[16] China's defence under GATT Article XX(a) nevertheless failed because restricting the importation of reading materials and finished audiovisual products to specified state-owned import entities was not *necessary* for the pursuit of that cultural and moral goal.[17] In reaching this conclusion, the Appellate Body applied the test of necessity that it has developed in the context of GATT Article XX and GATS Article XIV more generally. First, a Panel should assess 'the relative importance of the interests or values further by the challenged measure'. Then, the Panel should weigh and balance 'the contribution of the measure to the realization of the ends pursued by it' and 'the restrictive effect of the measure on international commerce', 'in the light of the importance of the objective pursued'. If this exercise leads to the preliminary conclusion that the measure is necessary, the necessity of the measure is confirmed 'by comparing the measure with possible alternatives, in the light of the importance of the interests or values at stake'.[18]

Returning to the question of how to distinguish goods (generally governed by the GATT 1994 and other multilateral agreements on trade in goods) and services (generally governed by the GATS) in the context of WTO law, *Canada—Periodicals* makes clear that a given product may have both goods and services elements and that the GATT 1994 and the GATS may apply simultaneously to those different elements. For example, as the Appellate Body stated, 'a periodical is a good comprised of two components: editorial content and advertising content. Both components can be viewed as having services attributes, but they combine to form a physical product—the periodical itself'.[19] Thus, while the GATS might apply to a tax on advertising in a periodical, the GATT 1994 applies to a tax on the periodical itself. This approach confirms previous WTO rulings indicating that the GATT 1994 and the GATS are not mutually exclusive.[20] More recently, in

---

[16] Panel Report, *China—Publications and Audiovisual Products*, para 7.766.
[17] Appellate Body Report, *China—Publications and Audiovisual Products*, paras 336–7.
[18] Appellate Body Report, *China—Publications and Audiovisual Products*, paras 240–1.
[19] Appellate Body Report, *Canada—Periodicals*, 17.
[20] Appellate Body Report, *EC—Bananas III*, para 221.

*China—Publications and Audiovisual Products*, China unsuccessfully argued that certain Chinese restrictions on importing films applied not to physical goods (eg film reels) but to film *content*.[21] The Appellate Body held that the relevant restrictions '*inevitably* regulate who may import goods for the plain reason that the content of a film is expressed through, and embedded in, a physical good'.[22]

The intersection of culture and trade within the WTO has had greater relevance for human rights considerations following the 2007 entry into force of the UNESCO Convention on the Protection of the Diversity of Cultural Contents and Artistic Expressions.[23] The preamble to this Convention notes that 'cultural activities, goods and services have both an economic and a cultural nature...and must therefore not be treated as solely having commercial value'. The Convention's guiding principles include the '[p]rinciple of sovereignty', whereby 'States have...the sovereign right to adopt measures and policies to protect and promote the diversity of cultural expressions within their territory'.[24] The Convention's specific provisions include a right of each state party to 'adopt measures aimed at protecting and promoting the diversity of cultural expressions within its territory'.[25] The potential for conflict between the rights accorded under the UNESCO Convention and the obligations imposed by WTO law exemplifies the broader debate concerning the relationship between WTO law and public international law more generally.[26]

## B. Food, drink, and attitudes to risk

A second area in which WTO law overlaps with cultural considerations is in the regulation of food and drink. In particular, although WTO disputes in this field are not typically framed in terms of 'culture', consumers' perception and tolerance of risk in connection with food safety often has cultural foundations. Various authors have explored cultural tendencies in explaining different countries' approaches to food safety regulation,[27] for example in addressing the risks of bovine spongiform encephalopathy (BSE or 'mad cow' disease),[28] growth hormones in meat, and genetically modified organisms.[29] Echols writes:

The culture and attitudes of European citizens have tended to favour traditional foods and minimal processing, while being skeptical of new technologies. This skepticism has slowed the

---

[21] Appellate Body Report, *China—Publications and Audiovisual Products*, para 187.

[22] Appellate Body Report, *China—Publications and Audiovisual Products*, para 188.

[23] CLT-2005/CONVENTION DIVERSITE-CULT REV (adopted 20 October 2005, entered into force 18 March 2007) (UNESCO Convention).

[24] UNESCO Convention, Art 2.2.     [25] UNESCO Convention, Art 6.1.

[26] See eg J. Pauwelyn, *Conflict of Norms in Public International Law: How WTO Law Relates to Other Rules of International Law* (2003); A.D. Mitchell, *Legal Principles in WTO Disputes* (2008).

[27] M.A. Echols, *Food Safety and the WTO: The Interplay of Culture, Science and Technology* (2001).

[28] M. Ferrari, *Risk Perception, Culture, and Legal Change: A Comparative Study on Food Safety in the Wake of the Mad Cow Crisis* (2009).

[29] Winickoff et al, 'Adjudicating the GM Food Wars: Science, Risk, and Democracy in World Trade Law', 30 *Yale Journal of International Law* (2005) 81 at 97–9; Coburn, 'Out of the Petri Dish and Back to the People: A Cultural Approach to GMO Policy', 23 *Wisconsin International Law Journal* (2005) 283 at 294–6.

Community's broader regulatory process as well as particular governmental approvals in the EU. In contrast, Americans have been more willing to accept new technologies, an attitude that supports business innovation and a flexible regulatory system supportive of changing technology but skeptical of some traditional production processes.[30]

As such matters are frequently the subject of WTO disputes, the cultural implications may raise questions as to the 'objectivity' of WTO rules. For example, does the reliance on science in the TBT Agreement and the Agreement on the Application of Sanitary and Phytosanitary Measures (SPS Agreement) mean that WTO law is biased against members with a lower risk tolerance in connection with new technologies?[31] Is the WTO's emphasis on trade liberalization as a means to improve global welfare necessarily consistent with realization of the right to food and global food security?[32]

Recent and long-standing WTO disputes can be seen as playing out cultural differences in approaches to food regulation. Most obviously, some of the most controversial WTO disputes ever have related to European food safety restrictions. In *EC—Approval and Marketing of Biotech Products*[33] (which was not appealed), a WTO Panel found several violations by the EU of the SPS Agreement in connection with restrictions on genetically modified or 'biotech' products. Similarly, in the earlier case of *EC—Hormones*,[34] the WTO Appellate Body held that the EU had violated certain SPS provisions in restricting the sale and importation of meat treated with certain growth hormones. Not surprisingly, given the strength of the EU population's views on the subject, that dispute was followed by an arbitration on the period of time the EU had to comply,[35] another arbitration on the extent to which Canada and the United States could retaliate against the EU for failing to comply,[36] and finally (and more unusually) a separate dispute several years later concerning the legality of Canada and the United States continuing to retaliate against the EU.[37] The parties

---

[30] Echols, 'Food Safety Regulation in the European Union and the United States: Different Cultures, Different Laws', 4 *Columbia Journal of European Law* (1998) 525 at 526.

[31] See Voon (2007) 14–15.

[32] See Echols, 'Paths to Local Food Security: A Right to Food, A Commitment to Trade', 40 *Vanderbilt Journal of Transnational Law* (2007) 1115.

[33] WTO Panel Report, *European Communities—Measures Affecting the Approval and Marketing of Biotech Products*, WT/DS291/R, WT/DS292/R, WT/DS293/R, Add.1 to Add.9, and Corr.1 (circulated 29 September 2006, adopted 21 November 2006).

[34] WTO Appellate Body Report, *EC Measures Concerning Meat and Meat Products (Hormones)*, WT/DS26/AB/R, WT/DS48/AB/R (circulated 16 January 1998, adopted 13 February 1998).

[35] WTO Award of the Arbitrator, *EC Measures Concerning Meat and Meat Products (Hormones): Arbitration under Article 21.3(c) of the Understanding on Rules and Procedures Governing the Settlement of Disputes*, WT/DS26/15, WT/DS48/13 (29 May 1998).

[36] WTO Decision by the Arbitrators, *European Communities—Measures Concerning Meat and Meat Products (Hormones)—Original Complaint by the United States: Recourse to Arbitration by the European Communities under Article 22.6 of the DSU*, WT/DS26/ARB (12 July 1999); WTO Decision by the Arbitrators, *European Communities—Measures Concerning Meat and Meat Products (Hormones)—Original Complaint by Canada: Recourse to Arbitration by the European Communities under Article 22.6 of the DSU*, WT/DS48/ARB (12 July 1999).

[37] WTO Appellate Body Report, *Canada—Continued Suspension of Obligations in the EC—Hormones Dispute*, WT/DS321/AB/R (circulated 16 October 2008, adopted 14 November 2008); WTO Appellate Body Report, *United States—Continued Suspension of Obligations in the EC—Hormones Dispute*, WT/DS320/AB/R (circulated 16 October 2008, adopted 14 November 2008).

eventually settled[38] more than 10 years after the Appellate Body ruled on the original dispute, demonstrating the extreme difficulty involved in resolving conflicts arising from deeply held cultural beliefs.

Cultural factors can also be seen in actual and potential trade disputes concerning food regulation that involve WTO members other than the European Union. For example, institutional culture in China can explain how the 'melamine milk scandal' arose within a setting in which food risk assessment is not separated from risk management.[39] Australia's 'island' mentality may be reflected in its stringent SPS measures, leading to a number of food-related disputes in the WTO, including those concerning Australia's restrictions on imports of salmon[40] and apples,[41] both of which were found to violate certain WTO obligations.

## 3. Human Rights Aspects of Culture in the WTO Context

### A. Culture and human rights under the TRIPS Agreement

Several issues arising under the WTO's Agreement on Trade-Related Aspects of Intellectual Property Rights (TRIPS Agreement) relate to both culture and human rights. Helfer identifies

two distinct conceptual approaches to the human rights-intellectual property interface.... The first approach views human rights and intellectual property as being in fundamental conflict. This framing sees strong intellectual property protection as undermining...a broad spectrum of human rights obligations, especially in the area of economic, social and cultural rights....The second approach...sees both areas of law as concerned with the same fundamental question: defining the appropriate scope of private monopoly power that gives authors and inventors a sufficient incentive to create and innovate, while ensuring that the consuming public has adequate access to the fruits of their efforts.[42]

Turning to the cultural aspects of the intersection between intellectual property and human rights, the TRIPS Agreement requires WTO members to protect copyright, which subsists in cultural products as discussed above. This requirement is consistent with the right of '[e]veryone...to the protection of the moral

---

[38] WTO, *European Communities—Measures Concerning Meat and Meat Products (Hormones): Joint Communication from the European Communities and the United States*, WT/DS26/28 (30 September 2009); WTO, *European Communities—Measures Concerning Meat and Meat Products (Hormones): Joint Communication from the European Union and Canada*, WT/DS48/26 (22 March 2011).

[39] Xiao, 'China's Milk Scandals and Its Food Risk Assessment Institutional Framework', 3 *European Journal of Risk Regulation* (2011) 397 at 397, 399, 406.

[40] WTO Appellate Body Report, *Australia—Measures Affecting Importation of Salmon*, WT/DS18/AB/R (circulated 20 October 1998, adopted 6 November 1998).

[41] WTO Appellate Body Report, *Australia—Measures Affecting the Importation of Apples from New Zealand*, WT/DS367/AB/R (circulated 29 November 2010, adopted 17 December 2010).

[42] Helfer, 'Human Rights and Intellectual Property: Conflict or Coexistence?', 5 *Minnesota Intellectual Property Review* (2003) 47 at 48.

and material interests resulting from any scientific, literary or artistic production of which he is the author'[43] (although the TRIPS Agreement does not provide for moral rights).[44]

## B. Traditional knowledge and genetic resources

In addition, recognition of various forms of intellectual property under the TRIPS Agreement may affect minority and indigenous groups. In this regard, intellectual property protection aligns with the right to benefit from the protection of one's own creations (as just mentioned) as well as other rights of indigenous peoples recognized in the United Nations Declaration on the Rights of Indigenous Peoples,[45] for example:

Indigenous peoples and individuals have the right not to be subjected to forced assimilation or destruction of their culture.[46]

Indigenous peoples have the right to their traditional medicines and to maintain their health practices, including the conservation of their vital medicinal plants, animals and minerals.[47]

Indigenous peoples have the right to maintain, control, protect and develop their cultural heritage, *traditional knowledge* and traditional cultural expressions, as well as the manifestations of their sciences, technologies and cultures, including human and genetic resources, seeds, medicines, knowledge of the properties of fauna and flora, oral traditions, literatures, designs, sports and traditional games and visual and performing arts. They also have the right to maintain, control, protect and develop their *intellectual property* over such cultural heritage, traditional knowledge, and traditional cultural expressions.[48]

Traditional knowledge is also encompassed within the definition of 'intangible cultural heritage' in the Convention for the Safeguarding of Intangible Cultural Heritage,[49] which includes 'the practices, representations, expressions, knowledge, skills...that communities...recognize as part of their cultural heritage'.[50] At the national level, states parties must 'take the necessary measures to ensure the safeguarding of the intangible cultural heritage present in its territory'[51] and 'draw up...inventories of the intangible cultural heritage present in its territory'.[52]

The Convention on Biological Diversity (CBD)[53] includes the objectives of 'the conservation of biological diversity, the sustainable use of its components and the fair and equitable sharing of the benefits arising out of the utilization of

---

[43] Universal Declaration of Human Rights, UNGA Res 217A(III), 10 December 1948, Art 27(2). See also International Covenant on Economic, Social and Cultural Rights, 999 UNTS 3 (adopted 16 December 1966), Art 15(1)(c).

[44] TRIPS Agreement, Art 9.1.

[45] United Nations Declaration on the Rights of Indigenous Peoples, UNGA Res 61/295, 13 September 2007, Annex.

[46] UNGA Res 61/295, 13 September 2007, Art 8(1).

[47] UNGA Res 61/295, 13 September 2007, Art 24(1).

[48] UNGA Res 61/295, 13 September 2007, Art 31(1) (emphasis added).

[49] Entered into force 20 April 2006.     [50] Article 2(1).     [51] Article 11(a).

[52] Article 12(1).         [53] Opened for signature 5 June 1992, entered into force 29 December 1993.

genetic resources,... taking into account all rights over those resources...'.[54] The Convention requires each contracting party, 'as far as possible and as appropriate', to

respect, preserve and maintain knowledge, innovations and practices of indigenous and local communities embodying traditional lifestyles relevant for the conservation and sustainable use of biological diversity and promote their wider application with the approval and involvement of the holders of such knowledge, innovations and practices and encourage the equitable sharing of the benefits arising from the utilization of such knowledge, innovations and practices...[55]

[p]rotect and encourage customary use of biological resources in accordance with traditional cultural practices that are compatible with conservation or sustainable use requirements.[56]

The Nagoya Protocol on Access to Genetic Resources and the Fair and Equitable Sharing of Benefits Arising from their Utilization to the Convention on Biological Diversity was adopted in 2010 and opened for signature from 2 February 2011 to 1 February 2012. It will enter into force 90 days after deposit of the 50th instrument of ratification, acceptance, approval, or accession. At the time of writing, only five countries have deposited such instruments. The Protocol states, for example (in Article 5(5)) that 'Each Party shall take legislative, administrative or policy measures, as appropriate, in order that the benefits arising from the utilization of traditional knowledge associated with genetic resources are shared in a fair and equitable way with indigenous and local communities holding such knowledge'.

Traditional knowledge and genetic resources are currently under discussion in the WTO, pursuant to a review being conducted under Article 27.3(b) of the TRIPS Agreement and certain other provisions. Article 27.3(b) allows WTO members to 'exclude from patentability':

plants and animals other than micro-organisms, and essentially biological processes for the production of plants or animals other than non-biological and microbiological processes. However, Members shall provide for the protection of plant varieties either by patents or by an effective *sui generis* system or by any combination thereof. The provisions of this subparagraph shall be reviewed four years after the date of entry into force of the WTO Agreement.

Upon the launch of the Doha round of multilateral trade negotiations in 2001, WTO members agreed that the review foreseen under Article 27.3(b) of the TRIPS Agreement would extend to an examination of 'the relationship between the TRIPS Agreement and the Convention on Biological Diversity, [and] the protection of traditional knowledge and folklore'.[57] Significantly, the review is to be undertaken with reference to the objectives and principles contained in Articles 7

---

[54] CBD, Art 1.    [55] CBD, Art 8(j).    [56] CBD, Art 10(c).
[57] WTO Ministerial Conference, Ministerial Declaration adopted on 14 November 2001, WT/MIN(01)/DEC/1, 20 November 2001 (Doha Declaration), para 19.

and 8 of the TRIPS Agreement and 'the development dimension'.[58] In 2011, the WTO Director-General Pascal Lamy confirmed that WTO

> Members have consistently voiced support for the principles and objectives of the CBD, including the principle of prior informed consent and the principle of equitable sharing of benefits. They have agreed on the need to take steps to avoid erroneous patents, including through the use of databases, as appropriate, to avoid patents being granted on existing traditional knowledge or genetic resources subject-matter.[59]

However, despite this issue being on the agenda for more than a decade, members have so far been unable to agree on concrete rules or guidelines for how the CBD relates to or should be taken into account in the TRIPS Agreement. In particular, as the Director-General's report explains, members have not agreed on: (i) precise definitions of 'genetic resources', 'traditional knowledge', and 'misappropriation'; (ii) whether databases of traditional knowledge and genetic resources should be established or what form they should take; or (iii) whether patent applicants should be required to disclose underlying genetic resources or traditional knowledge in their application, in order to prevent misappropriation and ensure equitable sharing of benefits. For example, several WTO members have proposed a disclosure requirement as follows:

> Where the subject matter of a patent application involves utilization of genetic resources and/or associated traditional knowledge, Members shall require applicants to disclose: (i) the country providing such resources...(ii) the source in the country providing the genetic resources and/or associated traditional knowledge.[60]

One reason for the difficulty WTO members have found in reaching agreement on the treatment of traditional knowledge and genetic resources under the TRIPS Agreement, may be that 'this subject matter does not mesh easily with the prevailing justification for intellectual property rights: to provide inventors and authors with ex ante incentives to create'.[61] However, protection of traditional knowledge aligns more easily with the intellectual property goals of providing an incentive to disclose and share valuable information.[62] These goals

---

[58] Doha Declaration, para 19.

[59] WTO General Council, Trade Negotiations Committee, Issues Related to the Extension of the Protection of Geographical Indications Provided for in Article 23 of the TRIPS Agreement to Products Other Than Wines and Spirits and Those Related to the Relationship Between the TRIPS Agreement and the Convention on Biological Diversity: Report by the Director-General, WT/GC/W/633, TN/C/W/61, 21 April 2011, para 27.

[60] WTO Trade Negotiations Committee, Draft Decision to Enhance Mutual Supportiveness Between the TRIPS Agreement and the Convention on Biological Diversity: Communication from Brazil, China, Colombia, Ecuador, India, Indonesia, Peru, Thailand, the ACP Group, and the African Group, TN/C/W/59, 19 April 2011. For further discussion see Wager, 'Biodiversity, Traditional Knowledge and Folklore: Work on Related IP Matters in the WTO', 3 *Intercultural Human Rights Law Review* (2008) 215 at 220, 222.

[61] Varadarajan, 'A Trade Secret Approach to Protecting Traditional Knowledge', 36 *Yale Journal of International Law* (2011) 371 at 374.

[62] Varadarajan (2011) 376.

are reflected in the 'Objectives' listed in Article 7 of the TRIPS Agreement as follows:

The protection and enforcement of intellectual property rights should contribute to the promotion of technological innovation and to the transfer and *dissemination* of technology, to the mutual advantage of producers and users of technological knowledge and in a manner conducive to social and economic welfare, and to a balance of rights and obligations.[63]

Fletcher contends that the focus on private ownership in the TRIPS Agreement and the focus on state ownership under the CBD both fail to recognize indigenous people's rights of property, culture and self-determination.[64] Vadarajan suggests that one way of merging the human rights and biodiversity justifications for protecting traditional knowledge with doctrinal aspects of intellectual property law would be to protect at least some forms of traditional knowledge as confidential information in the form of trade secrets. This approach would require broadening and clarifying the existing obligation in Article 39 of the TRIPS Agreement for the protection of undisclosed information.[65]

In the absence of agreement among WTO members as to how to resolve this issue with respect to the TRIPS Agreement, the question arises how the different relevant treaties would apply in the event of a dispute or other scenario requiring a conclusive interpretation. This question forms part of the broader uncertainty regarding the relationship between WTO law and public international law as mentioned above.[66] Starting points for answering the question in relation to a specific treaty obligation or provision may be found in the Vienna Convention on the Law of Treaties[67] and any conflict provision in the relevant treaties. The WTO agreements contain no explicit conflict provision regarding their interaction with non-WTO treaties, which is why this is an uncertain area. However, other treaties routinely address the question of their relationship with other treaties, albeit without always offering a definitive answer. For example, Article 22(1) of the CBD states that '[t]he provisions of this Convention shall not affect the rights and obligations of any Contracting Party deriving from any existing international agreement, except where the exercise of those rights and obligations would cause a serious damage or threat to biological diversity'. As the CBD entered into force in 1993 and the WTO agreements in 1995, this provision sheds little light on the relationship between the CBD and WTO law.

## C. Geographical indications

Article 22.1 of the TRIPS Agreement defines 'geographical indications' as 'indications which identify a good as originating in the territory of a Member, or a region

---

[63] Emphasis added.
[64] Fletcher, 'Indigenous Peoples and the Law—Column 4: Intellectual Property and International Law', 17(4) *ILSA Quarterly* (2009) 66 at 68.
[65] Varadarajan (2011) 408, 416–19.    [66] See note 26 above, and corresponding text.
[67] 1155 UNTS 331 (adopted 22 May 1969), eg Arts 30–2, 41.

or locality in that territory, where a given quality, reputation or other characteristic of the good is essentially attributable to its geographical origin'. The most common example of a geographical indication (GI) is, of course, Champagne.

The purpose of protecting geographical indications in the WTO is reflected in the obligation imposed on WTO members under Article 22.2 of the TRIPS Agreement to 'provide the legal means for interested parties to prevent' goods from being presented in such a way as to mislead consumers as to the true origin of the goods or in a manner that amounts to 'unfair competition'. A secondary purpose of protecting geographical indications, but one that is largely subsumed within these general purposes, may be to preserve culture or cultural values to the extent that these values are encompassed in traditional production methods for food and wine and associated ways of life.[68] However, the extent to which protection of geographical indications pursuant to the TRIPS Agreement contributes to the preservation of culture is debatable. Broude writes: 'market pressures are independently and markedly more influential than legal GI regulation with regard to patterns and practices of production, at least as far as culture is concerned. Where the market demands change, change is enacted, regardless of GI rules'.[69]

If the relevance of culture as a justification for protecting geographical indications is limited, the relevance of human rights is also limited. Some geographical indications may amount to 'cultural expressions' within the meaning of the UNESCO Convention mentioned above, namely 'expressions that result from the creativity of individuals, groups and societies, and that have cultural content'.[70] Similarly, geographical indications may attach to products falling within the definition of cultural goods, being goods that 'embody or convey cultural expressions, irrespective of the commercial value they may have'.[71] Parties to that Convention have the right to adopt measures to promote cultural diversity, such as measures to protect the diversity of cultural expressions and measures providing opportunities for domestic cultural goods to be produced and enjoyed among those available within the national territory.[72] Protecting geographical indications also appears consistent with the obligation on states parties to the International Covenant on Economic, Social and Cultural Rights (ICESCR) to take steps to achieve the realization of the right 'to take part in cultural life', including steps 'necessary for the conservation, the development and the diffusion of . . . culture'.[73] However, the precise nature of steps and measures required in order to fulfil these provisions is uncertain. Members must already protect geographical indications pursuant to the TRIPS Agreement, and this existing level of protection may be sufficient.

---

[68] Voon, 'Geographical Indications, Culture and the WTO', in B. Ubertazzi and E.M. Espada (eds), *Le indicazioni di qualità degli alimenti: Diritto internazionale ed europeo* (2009) 300 at 311.

[69] Broude, 'Taking "Trade and Culture" Seriously: Geographical Indications and Cultural Protection in WTO Law', 26 *University of Pennsylvania Journal of International Economic Law* (2005) 623 at 669.

[70] UNESCO Convention, Art 4(3).　　[71] UNESCO Convention, Art 4(4).

[72] UNESCO Convention, Art 6(2)(a)–(b).　　[73] ICESCR, Arts 15(1)(a), 15(2).

The relationship between protection of geographical indications under the TRIPS Agreement, preservation or promotion of culture, and human rights becomes important in the light of ongoing negotiations concerning the extension of protection. At present, Article 23 of the TRIPS Agreement requires WTO members to provide additional protection for geographical indications for wines and spirits, in particular preventing misuse of a geographical indication for a wine or spirit not originating in the place indicated even where the true origin is indicated, or the geographical indication is translated or used alongside expressions such as 'style' or 'imitation'.[74] In addition to negotiating the creation of a multilateral registration system for geographical indications for wines and spirits, WTO members are currently negotiating the extension of additional protection for geographical indications to products other than wines and spirits.[75] One concern raised is that the current two-tier system, with higher protection for wines and spirits, generally benefits industrialized countries, 'not those developing countries whose GI interests concerned textiles, handicrafts, agricultural products or foodstuffs'.[76]

## 4. Institutional Reflection on Human Rights and the WTO

As discussed in the previous sections of this chapter, various connections exist between WTO law and human rights in connection with cultural products, cultural rights, indigenous rights and related rights. Outside the specific context of culture, the WTO agreements can also be seen as encompassing some limited recognition of human rights, for example in the general exceptions in:

(a) GATT Article XX(a) and GATS Article XIV(a) for measures 'necessary to protect public morals' (as discussed above);

(b) GATT Article XX(b), which includes measures 'necessary to protect human...life or health'; and

(c) GATT Article XX(e) for measures 'relating to the products of prison labour'.

---

[74] TRIPS Agreement, Art 23.1.

[75] Doha Declaration, paras 12, 18; WTO Ministerial Conference, Doha Work Programme: Ministerial Declaration Adopted on 18 December 2005, WT/MIN(05)/DEC, 22 December 2005, para 39.

[76] WTO General Council, Trade Negotiations Committee, Issues Related to the Extension of the Protection of Geographical Indications Provided for in Article 23 of the TRIPS Agreement to Products Other Than Wines and Spirits and Those Related to the Relationship Between the TRIPS Agreement and the Convention on Biological Diversity: Report by the Director-General, WT/GC/W/633, TN/C/W/61, 21 April 2011, para 9.

Reflections of these concepts are also seen in other WTO provisions, such as Article 2.2 of the TBT Agreement, which identifies as a 'legitimate objective' the 'protection of human health or safety', in terms reminiscent of GATT Article XX(b).

Nevertheless, the relationship between human rights and the WTO is rarely scrutinized in a formal way within the WTO. In contrast, this relationship (as well as its relevance to culture) has been the subject of several different reports issued by various United Nations institutions, particularly during the period 2001 to 2005. Several of these relate to the impact of the TRIPS Agreement on human rights. For example, the United Nations High Commissioner for Human Rights reported on this issue in 2001. The High Commissioner noted the absence of an explicit reference in the TRIPS Agreement to 'cultural heritage and technology of local communities and indigenous peoples', suggesting that the TRIPS Agreement needs amendment to resolve tensions between intellectual property and traditional knowledge.[77] More recently, in 2006, the Committee on Economic, Social and Cultural Rights of the United Nations Economic and Social Council issued a general comment elucidating the right to benefit from the protection of interests resulting from scientific, literary, or artistic productions as contained in Article 15(1)(c) of the ICESCR.[78] The Committee distinguished this right (and other human rights) from intellectual property rights as follows:

Human rights are fundamental, inalienable and universal entitlements belonging to individuals and, under certain circumstances, groups of individuals and communities. Human rights are fundamental as they are inherent to the human person as such, whereas intellectual property rights are first and foremost means by which States seek to provide incentives for inventiveness and creativity, encourage the dissemination of creative…productions, as well as the development of cultural identities, and preserve the integrity of scientific, literary and artistic productions for the benefit of society as a whole.[79]

This passage highlights the distinction between a conventional intellectual property approach and a human rights approach to protecting the interests created in inventions and creative works. Although the TRIPS Agreement may assist in realizing the right to benefit from invention and creation, its provisions are not necessarily designed to achieve this objective, and its focus on a balance between producers and users does not necessarily reflect the significance of that right, particularly for indigenous peoples. This discrepancy in the conceptual understanding of intellectual property may help explain why WTO members have so

---

[77] UN ECOSOC, *Economic, Social and Cultural Rights: The Impact of the Agreement on Trade-Related Aspects of Intellectual Property Rights on Human Rights—Report of the High Commissioner*, UN Doc E/CN.4/Sub.2/2001/13, 27 June 2001, para 26.

[78] See note 43 above and corresponding text.

[79] UN ECOSOC, Committee on Economic, Social and Cultural Rights, *General Comment No 17 (2005): The right of everyone to benefit from the protection of the moral and material interests resulting from any scientific, literary or artistic production of which he or she is the author (article 15, paragraph 1(c), of the Covenant)*, UN Doc E/C.12/GC/17, 12 January 2006, para 1.

far been unable to agree on how to deal with traditional knowledge and genetic resources within the framework of the TRIPS Agreement.

Beyond the TRIPS Agreement, several studies have been conducted on the relationship between trade and human rights in connection with issues such as globalization,[80] investment,[81] services,[82] the rights to health[83] and development,[84] the principles of non-discrimination[85] and participation,[86] and the use of general exception clauses to protect human rights.[87] A submission by the Office of the High Commissioner for Human Rights to the WTO Ministerial Conference held in Cancún in 2003 highlighted the impact of the TRIPS Agreement on indigenous peoples' rights, particularly in connection with traditional knowledge, and encouraged the implementation of the earlier Ministerial Declaration requiring the examination of the relationship between the TRIPS Agreement and the CBD.[88]

## 5. Conclusion

The limited reflection on human rights within the WTO and the reluctance by many members to introduce non-WTO public international law into the WTO legal framework (whether implicitly or explicitly) may help explain why WTO members are having such difficulty in agreeing on how to treat subject-matters related to culture such as traditional knowledge and genetic resources in the current negotiations. The failure to reach agreement in the Uruguay Round (or

[80] UN ECOSOC, Commission on Human Rights (CHR), Economic, Social and Cultural Rights: Globalization and its impact on the full enjoyment of human rights—Report of the High Commissioner for Human Rights submitted in accordance with Commission on Human Rights resolution 2001/32, UN Doc E/CN.4/2002/54, 15 January 2002.

[81] UN ECOSOC, CHR, Economic, Social and Cultural Rights: Human rights, trade and investment—Report of the High Commissioner for Human Rights, UN Doc E/CN.4/Sub.2/2003/9, 2 July 2003.

[82] UN ECOSOC, CHR, Economic, Social and Cultural Rights: Liberalization of trade in services and human rights—Report of the High Commissioner, UN Doc E/CN.4/Sub.2/2002/9, 25 June 2002.

[83] UN ECOSOC, CHR, Economic, Social and Cultural Rights: The right of everyone to the enjoyment of the highest attainable standard of physical and mental health—Report of the Special Rapporteur, Paul Hunt, UN Doc E/CN.4/2004/49/Add.1, 1 March 2004.

[84] UN ECOSOC, CHR, Economic, Social and Cultural Rights: Mainstreaming the right to development into international trade law and policy at the World Trade Organization—Note by the Secretariat, UN Doc E/CN.4/Sub.2/2004/17, 9 June 2004.

[85] UN ECOSOC, CHR, Economic, Social and Cultural Rights: Analytical study of the High Commissioner for Human Rights on the fundamental principle of non-discrimination in the context of globalization—Report of the High Commissioner, UN Doc E/CN.4/2004/40, 15 January 2004.

[86] UN ECOSOC, CHR, Economic, Social and Cultural Rights: Analytical study of the High Commissioner for Human Rights on the fundamental principle of participation and its application in the context of globalization—Report of the High Commissioner, UN Doc E/CN.4/2005/41, 23 December 2004.

[87] UN, Office of the High Commissioner for Human Rights (OHCHR), Human Rights and World Trade Agreements: Using General Exception Clauses to Protect Human Rights, UN Doc HR/PUB/05/05 (2005).

[88] UN, OHCHR, 5th WTO Ministerial Conference, Cancún, Mexico, 10–15 September 2003: Human Rights and Trade (2003) 14–16.

subsequently) on the proper approach to audiovisual products and printed publications may also make members wary of opening discussions premised on culture or human rights in a general sense. Instead, members may find themselves focused on technicalities such as the modalities of negotiation and the wording of minor amendments to the existing agreements, even where broader principles (such as adherence to the general objectives of the CBD) are agreed. However, the pragmatic acceptance of a wide range of perspectives on culture and its relationship to trade in the WTO has in some ways been beneficial. Culture is properly a secondary consideration in the formulation of many WTO rules, including some that might appear directly related to culture but that actually have different purposes, such as geographical indications. A healthy disagreement among WTO members about the relationship between the WTO, culture, and human rights may assist in keeping the rules under close examination and encouraging greater contemplation of that relationship within the organization in future.

# PART IV

# 7

# Cultural Pluralism in International Human Rights Law

## The Role of Reservations

*Yvonne Donders*

## 1. Introduction

The link between international human rights law and cultural diversity was clearly expressed in the Universal Declaration on Cultural Diversity, adopted by the member states of UNESCO in 2001, which holds that 'the defence of cultural diversity is...inseparable from respect for human dignity' and that it 'implies a commitment to human rights and fundamental freedoms'. The UNESCO Convention on the Protection and Promotion of the Diversity of Cultural Expressions, adopted in 2005, states that 'cultural diversity can be protected and promoted only if human rights and fundamental freedoms...are guaranteed' (Article 2(1)). International bodies supervising the implementation of human rights treaties have also regularly confirmed the value for human dignity of cultural diversity in a pluralistic society. The precise relationship between cultural diversity and international human rights law, however, leaves room for further exploration from different angles and perspectives.

In the instruments above, the concept of cultural diversity is used. This concept should be distinguished from the concept of cultural pluralism. Cultural diversity is a neutral term to describe the factual situation of the existence of cultural differences between and within states. Cultural pluralism, on the other hand, refers to the way such cultural diversity is valued and translated in laws and policies. The link between cultural diversity and cultural pluralism is explained in the Universal Declaration on Cultural Diversity. In Article 2, called 'From cultural diversity to cultural pluralism', it is stated that 'cultural pluralism gives policy expression to the reality of cultural diversity'. In other words, cultural diversity reflects the factual situation, also termed 'plurality'. There may be different responses to the factual situation of cultural diversity. The response in the sense of the adoption of laws and policies to protect and promote cultural diversity reflects cultural pluralism.

Cultural pluralism implies that cultural diversity is valued as something good, as a desirable and socially and politically beneficial condition. It implies that individuals and communities are given the opportunity to maintain their specific cultural identity, provided that they are consistent with the laws, policies, and values of the wider society. Consequently, although cultural diversity is the term often used in relation to international human rights law, what is often meant is cultural pluralism,[1] which is why this concept is used in this chapter.

This chapter addresses cultural pluralism in international human rights law by analysing one specific aspect of international law, namely the use of reservations to human rights treaties. It has been argued that reservations 'are a legitimate, perhaps even desirable, means of accounting for cultural, religious, or political value diversity across nations'.[2] Others have expressed concern about reservations, in particular those referring to cultural diversity, as they would undermine the universality of human rights and would not be allowed as being against the object and purpose of human rights treaties.[3]

This chapter elaborates on the question whether and to what extent the instrument of reservations is used by states to express cultural pluralism, including religious pluralism, between and among them. Another question is how other states and international supervisory bodies have reacted to such reservations, including to what extent such reservations are accepted as a reflection of cultural pluralism between states.

The first part of the chapter, dealing mainly with the first question, contains an empirical evaluation of how often and in what way reservations to human rights treaties are made that refer to cultural pluralism. Cultural pluralism is taken broadly, to include reservations that refer to the specific culture, religion, customs, or history of or within a state. The second part of the chapter deals with the second question by looking at how these 'cultural reservations' have been received. Sometimes other states explicitly objected to these reservations and the monitoring bodies of these treaties have also expressed their concern about them. Such criticism on cultural reservations gives an idea about the extent to which states are limited in the use of such reservations. In some instances, states have withdrawn or adjusted their reservations. Based on this, conclusions can be drawn reflecting the use of reservations as a tool for states to reaffirm cultural pluralism.

The general regime concerning reservations to treaties is laid down in the Vienna Convention on the Law of Treaties (VCLT).[4] Sometimes human rights treaties

---

[1] The term pluralism in relation to international law is also used to describe differences in legal systems or in institutional structures between and within states. This chapter concerns cultural pluralism in relation to the substantive aspects of international human rights law.

[2] Neumayer, 'Qualified Ratification: Explaining Reservations to International Human Rights Treaties', 36 *Journal of Legal Studies* (2007) 397 at 398.

[3] Neumayer (2007) 398; Pergantis, 'Reservations to Human Rights Treaties, Cultural Relativism and the Universal Protection of Human Rights', in K. Koufa (ed), *Multiculturalism and International Law* (2007) 427 at 433–4, 437, 447.

[4] Vienna Convention on the Law of Treaties, UNTS 1155, 331, done at Vienna on 23 May 1969, entry into force 27 January 1980.

have their own specific provisions on reservations. The fact is that human rights treaties are a special kind of multilateral treaty, which makes the general VCLT rules on reservations not easily applicable. Unlike other multilateral treaties, on for example trade or the law of the sea, human rights treaties involve not only states, but also individuals and communities as main beneficiaries of those treaties. The contractual dimension of human rights treaties, including the important element of reciprocity, is complemented by the moral, broader dimension of fulfilling certain legal obligations not towards the contractual counterparts, but to third parties, being individuals and/or communities. Consequently, the VCLT rules on reservations do not always fit well to reservations in human rights treaties.

The treaty selected for this chapter is the Convention on the Elimination of all Forms of Discrimination against Women (CEDAW).[5] This treaty was selected for several reasons: first, it is one of the human rights treaties that is widely, almost universally, ratified by states, from all regions of the world. Secondly, CEDAW belongs to those treaties regarding which the largest number of states parties have filed one or more reservations.[6] Thirdly, these reservations quite often refer to cultural or religious arguments as justification for the reservation. This has to do with the fact that several provisions in CEDAW, on for instance equality between men and women in family matters, have strong cultural connotations. Most of the reservations are justified with reference to cultural pluralism *between* states, but some also refer to cultural pluralism *within* states. Where the latter is the case, it will be explicitly shown. This chapter focuses on the role of reservations to express and maintain pluralism between states.

## 2. Reservations to International Human Rights Treaties

Reservations allow a state to become party to a treaty, while exempting itself from certain specific obligations in the treaty in question. Reservations find their rationale in two important factors in the international legal system: state sovereignty and diversity between states. States as main subjects of international law are sovereign, which means that they decide for themselves whether, and to what extent, they wish to become parties to international treaties. In other words, states can only be bound to international treaties that they have explicitly consented to and vice versa, they cannot be bound to international standards or norms that they have explicitly objected to. This situation implies that states negotiate and draft treaties and, in doing so, they try to come to a common set of rules, applicable to all

---

[5] Convention on the Elimination of All Forms of Discrimination Against Women, adopted GA Res 34/180, 18 December 1979, entry into force 3 September 1981.

[6] The other treaty widely ratified on which many states parties have filed reservations is the Convention on the Rights of the Child (CRC), adopted GA Res 44/25, 20 November 1989, entry into force 2 September 1990. Early research on the reservations to the CRC shows similar patterns to those to the CEDAW. See also, Harris-Short, 'International Human Rights Law: Imperialist, Inept and Ineffective? Cultural Relativism and the UN Convention on the Rights of the Child', 25 *Human Rights Quarterly* (2003) 130.

of the parties equally. This may lead them to water down or compromise on the provisions, but the end result should reflect an agreement on common norms and standards of behaviour. This is why treaties are, first and foremost, a contractual agreement between states.[7]

At the same time, states across the world vary as regards their cultural, economic, historical, and social setting and, moreover, they often wish to promote and defend this variety. States may therefore during the drafting process disagree on certain issues, for example because of a conflict with their national interest. This may very well be a national interest of a cultural or religious nature, raising the issue of the diversity between states. When states finally adopt and sign a treaty, some of them may feel that their specific interest is not sufficiently reflected in the treaty or they may disagree with certain specific provisions. Some states may decide not to become parties to the treaty at all. A state may also decide to become a party to the treaty, but with the explicit notification, in the form of a reservation, that it does not want or consider itself to be bound to certain parts or provisions of the treaty.[8]

This possibility to opt out has been an important factor in encouraging states to become parties to human rights treaties.[9] Reservations allow states to express that they do not want to be bound to certain elements or provisions of the treaty, without having to reject the treaty as a whole.[10] In this regard, 'reservations carry the promise of reconciling the interests of individual states with those of the international community at large' which is to have the largest amount of states parties possible.[11] Similarly, reservations to human rights treaties have been considered as a possible solution to the 'universality-integrity dilemma'.[12] The universality approach reflects the interest to have as many states as possible ratify the treaty, in particular because of the importance of international and national human rights promotion and protection. The integrity approach relates to the idea that human rights treaties should be seen as a coherent package that states should accept in full. Reservations could be a way to overcome the challenge of balancing universal participation with the integrity of the treaty.[13]

With reservations, states express that they do not want or consider themselves to be bound by certain elements or provisions of the treaty. Sometimes this non-bindingness is meant to be of a temporary nature. A state can maintain that it is not yet ready to implement the treaty in full, because it still has to adjust

---

[7] L. Lijnzaad, *Reservations to UN-Human Rights Treaties: Ratify and Ruin?* (1994) 107; Pergantis (2007) 435.

[8] Interestingly, research shows that these reservations often reflect the same issues as expressed during the drafting of the treaty. See Klabbers, 'On Human Rights Treaties, Contractual Conceptions and Reservations', in I. Ziemele (ed), *Reservations to Human Rights Treaties and the Vienna Convention Regime: Conflict, Harmony or Reconciliation* (2004) 149 at 182.

[9] Lijnzaad, however, argues that the argument that reservations facilitate ratification is not absolutely valid. See Lijnzaad (1994) 107.

[10] Klabbers argues that reservations may also be important for democratic concerns, allowing the legislator to protect itself from some legal consequences of a treaty submitted to it by the executive. See Klabbers (2004) 166.

[11] Klabbers (2004) 150.     [12] This dilemma is described in detail by Lijnzaad (1994) 103–12.

[13] Lijnzaad (1994) 105; Klabbers (2004) 155, 165, 169; Pergantis (2007) 442.

certain national laws and policies. With the reservation, it wants to 'buy time' and make clear to the other states parties that it cannot fulfil certain parts of the treaty. Sometimes the non-bindingness is supposed to be of a more structural nature. In this case, a state finding certain provisions for instance incompatible with its own cultural or religious rules, wishes to remain free to disregard that provision in the treaty and not be bound by it. The reservation is to show other states that there are differences that the state party intends to keep.[14]

The international legal regime for reservations is laid down in the VCLT. According to Article 2(d) of the VCLT, a reservation is 'a unilateral statement, however phrased or named, made by a State, when signing, ratifying, accepting, approving or acceding to a treaty, whereby it purports to exclude or to modify the legal effect of certain provisions of the treaty in their application to that State'. This provision implies that no matter how a state calls its statement, if it is meant to exclude or modify the legal effect of certain provisions, it is considered a reservation.

The possibility for states to make reservations is limited. According to Article 19 VCLT, a state may, when signing, ratifying, accepting, approving, or acceding to a treaty, formulate a reservation unless:

(a)  the reservation is prohibited by the treaty;

(b)  the treaty provides that only specified reservations, which do not include the reservation in question, may be made; or

(c)  in cases not failing under subparagraphs (a) and (b), the reservation is incompatible with the object and purpose of the treaty.

States may not, according to the above, make reservations which are incompatible with the object and purpose of the treaty.[15] The object and purpose of the treaty are, however, not easy to define, which makes the assessment whether certain reservations are compatible or not a difficult matter.[16] This assessment is traditionally done by other states parties. After a reservation is made, other states parties to the treaty may object to this reservation. Such an objection, according to Art 20(4)b VCLT, does, however, 'not preclude the entry into force of the treaty as between the objecting and reserving States unless a contrary intention is definitely expressed by the objecting State'.

Moreover, there is reciprocity: according to Article 21(1) VCLT, the reservation 'modifies for the reserving State in its relations with that other party the provisions of the treaty to which the reservation relates to the extent of the reservation; and ... modifies those provisions to the same extent for that other party in its relations with the reserving State'. This idea is based on the contractual character of

---

[14]  See Neumayer (2007) 403; Klabbers (2004) 167; Seibert-Fohr, 'The Potentials of the Vienna Convention on the Law of Treaties with respect to Reservations to Human Rights Treaties', in I. Ziemele (ed), *Reservations to Human Rights Treaties and the Vienna Convention Regime: Conflict, Harmony or Reconciliation* (2004) 183 at 184.

[15]  According to Lijnzaad, this is something else than stating that the reservation should be in conformity with the object and purpose. See Lijnzaad (1994) 84.

[16]  See, for an extensive analysis of the object and purpose theory, Lijnzaad (1994) 80–102.

treaties, which usually contain reciprocal rights and obligations for the states that become parties to those treaties. Human rights treaties, however, are a special kind of treaties, which begs the question to what extent the regime of the VCLT is appropriate in relation to human rights treaties.[17]

Human rights treaties differ from the strict contractual treaty model, since they regulate states' domestic behaviour more than states' behaviour inter se. The obligations of states in human rights treaties are owed not so much to fellow states parties, but mostly to individuals and communities as beneficiaries. This was indicated by the International Court of Justice (ICJ) in its Advisory Opinion on reservations to the Genocide Convention. According to the ICJ, such treaties do not maintain a 'perfect contractual balance between rights and duties' and states do not have individual advantages or disadvantages nor interest of their own, but merely a common interest.[18] The Human Rights Committee (HRC), supervising the International Covenant on Civil and Political Rights (ICCPR),[19] formulated it as follows: 'Such treaties, and the Covenant specifically, are not a web of inter-state exchanges of mutual obligations. They concern the endowment of individuals with rights. The principle of inter-state reciprocity has no place.'[20] In other words, the important purpose of human rights treaties—the advancement of human rights for individuals and communities—goes beyond the mere contractual model.

This has consequences for the working and effect of reservations to human rights treaties in relation to the acceptance or rejection of reservations by other states. The ICJ in its Advisory Opinion on reservations to the Genocide Convention indicated that it does not think that there is a rule of international law concerning the absolute integrity of a convention. Consequently, it cannot be maintained that the effect of a reservation would be subject to the express or tacit assent of all of the contracting parties. Similarly, a reservation is not merely accepted if none of the other states parties has objected to it.[21] The ICJ concluded that the 'appraisal of a reservation and the effect of objections...depend upon the particular circumstances of each individual case'.[22]

---

[17] This matter has been extensively discussed in academic literature. See eg J.P. Gardner (ed), *Human Rights as General Norms and a State's Right to Opt Out—Reservations and Objections to Human Rights Conventions* (1997); Lijnzaad (1994); I. Ziemele (ed), *Reservations to Human Rights Treaties and the Vienna Convention Regime: Conflict, Harmony or Reconciliation* (2004); Tyagi, 'The Conflict of Law and Policy on Reservations to Human Rights Treaties', 71 *British Yearbook of International Law* (2000) 181; Klabbers, 'Accepting the Unacceptable? A New Nordic Approach to Reservations to Multilateral Treaties', 69 *Nordic Journal of International Law* (2000) 179.

[18] *Reservations to the Convention on the Prevention and Punishment of the Crime of Genocide (Advisory Opinion)*, ICJ Reports (1951) 19, 28 May 1951, 12. See also Lijnzaad (1994) 110–11.

[19] International Covenant on Civil and Political Rights, GA Res 2200 A (XXI), adopted 16 December 1966, entry into force 23 March 1976.

[20] HRC, *General Comment No 24: Issues Relating to Reservations Made Upon Ratification or Accession to the Covenant or the Optional Protocols Thereto, or in Relation to Declarations under Article 41 of the Covenant*, 52nd Session (4 November 1994), UN Doc CCPR/C/21/Rev.1/Add.6, 17. See also Pergantis (2007) 439.

[21] *Reservations to the Convention on the Prevention and Punishment of the Crime of Genocide (Advisory Opinion)*, ICJ Reports (1951) 19, 28 May 1951, 13.

[22] ICJ Reports (1951) 19, 28 May 1951, 15.

The ICJ, in the same Advisory Opinion, confirmed that it is in principle states as contractors that assess the validity of reservations by other states parties. States can object to reservations, for instance if they are considered to be incompatible with the object and purpose of the treaty. However, in relation to human rights treaties, because of their *erga omnes* character and importance for individuals and communities as beneficiaries, not only states, but also international monitoring bodies have increasingly involved themselves in the assessment of the compatibility of reservations with the object and purpose of the treaty. Interestingly, several judges of the ICJ have in a separate opinion in a more recent case concerning the Genocide Convention affirmed the practice of international monitoring bodies, including the ICJ itself, pronouncing on the compatibility of reservations with the object and purpose of the treaty. The judges also emphasized the fact that the majority of states have not taken up the task of scrutinizing reservations.[23] The HRC has formally given itself this role in its *General Comment No 24*, in which it maintained that 'it necessarily falls to the Committee to determine whether a specific reservation is compatible with the object and purpose of the Covenant. This is in part because, as indicated above, it is an inappropriate task for States Parties in relation to human rights treaties, and in part because it is a task that the Committee cannot avoid in the performance of its functions... Because of the special character of a human rights treaty, the compatibility of a reservation with the object and purpose of the Covenant must be established objectively, by reference to legal principles, and the Committee is particularly well placed to perform this task'.[24] In other words, the HRC finds itself the most appropriate body to assess the compatibility of reservations with the object and purpose of the treaty. It should be noted that several states expressed formal objections to this General Comment, disagreeing with this role the Committee gave itself.[25]

Although other treaty bodies have not been so explicit, they also concern themselves with reservations. They ask questions to states parties about their reservations during the reporting procedure and the treaty bodies that have an individual complaint procedure, have dealt with reservations in relation to individual complaints as well.[26] Practice shows that states parties include information on reservations

---

[23] *Armed Activities on the Territory of the Congo (New Application: 2002) (Democratic Republic of the Congo v Rwanda)*, Jurisdiction and Admissibility, ICJ Reports (2006) 6, judgment of 3 February 2006, joint separate opinion of judges Higgins, Kooijmans, Elaraby, Owada, and Simma, 10, 11, and 23.

[24] HRC, *General Comment No 24*, 18.

[25] The United States, the United Kingdom, and France made formal objections. See HRC, Annual Report, GAOR, Supp No 40 (1994–95) in UN Doc A/50/40, Vol I, 126–31, 5–16 and HRC, Annual Report, GAOR, Supp No 40 (1996) in UN Doc A/51/40, Vol I, 104–6, 1–2.

[26] See, for instance, the following cases for the European Court of Human Rights: *Temeltasch v Switzerland* (1983) DR 31, 120; *Belilos v Switzerland*, ECHR (1988) Series A, No 132; *Weber v Switzerland*, ECHR (1990) Series A, No 177; *Chorherr v Austria*, ECHR (1993) Series A, No 266-B. The Inter-American Court of Human Rights took a similar position in its *Advisory Opinion OC-2/82 on the Effect of Reservations on the Entry into Force of the American Convention (Arts 74–75)*, IACtHR (1982) Series A, No 2, 24 September 1982, 29. See, for a discussion, Marks, 'Three Regional Human Rights Treaties and their Experience of Reservations', in J.P. Gardner (ed), *Human Rights as General Norms and a State's Right to Opt Out: Reservations and Objections to Human Rights Conventions* (1997) 37.

in their reports to be discussed by and with the treaty bodies, thereby broadly accepting this role of the treaty body. Most treaty bodies comment on reservations and their (in)compatibility with the object and purpose of the treaty. The treaty bodies also urge states parties to redraft or withdraw certain reservations. However, although the treaty bodies deal with reservations as monitoring bodies of the implementation of their respective treaties, their role remains a complementary one, as the 'control of the permissibility of reservations is the primary responsibility of the States Parties'.[27] The International Law Commission (ILC) has emphasized this primary role of states by stating that although monitoring bodies may be competent to comment upon and make recommendations with regard to the admissibility of reservations, this does not 'affect the traditional modalities of control by the contracting parties' as laid down in the VCLT.[28]

The consequences of an invalid reservation once again show the primacy of the normative character of human rights treaties over their contractual character. International monitoring bodies broadly adhere to the so-called 'severability thesis', whereby a state is bound by the treaty even if a reservation made by that state to the treaty is invalid. The reservation is 'severed' from the rest of the treaty. This approach finds support in the normative character of human rights treaties and the search for universal application. 'Non-severability' would namely oblige a state to withdraw from the treaty and to reenter without the invalid reservation, which might mean that the state does not become a party anymore and remains outside the monitoring by international bodies.[29] The ILC, however, has been critical about the severability approach, emphasizing that it is the responsibility of the reserving state to take action in case of inadmissibility of a reservation, for example by modifying or withdrawing it 'or forgoing becoming a party to the treaty'.[30]

## 3. Cultural Reservations to the Convention on the Elimination of All Forms of Discrimination Against Women

Below first an overview is given of the cultural reservations made by the different states parties to the Convention on the Elimination of All Forms of Discrimination Against Women (CEDAW). Reservations can be categorized in different ways: first, according to the *scope* of the reservation, distinguishing between reservations that concern a particular provision and general reservations

---

[27] CEDAW Committee, Statements on Reservations to the Convention on the Elimination of All Forms of Discrimination Against Women, 18th and 19th Sessions (1998), UN Doc A/53/38/Rev.1, at 22–4. Lijnzaad even calls it the obligation of states parties to respond to reservations that are incompatible with the object and purpose of the treaty. See Lijnzaad (1994) 97.

[28] International Law Commission, Preliminary Conclusions on Reservations to Normative Multilateral Treaties including Human Rights Treaties, *Yearbook of the International Law Commission*, Vol II, Pt 2 (1997), 57, para 6.

[29] Klabbers (2000) 188–90.     [30] International Law Commission (1997) 57, para 10.

that concern the treaty as a whole. Secondly, reservations can be classified according to the *type* of reservation, distinguishing between substantive, procedural, and territorial reservations. And thirdly, reservations can be categorized according to the *source of justification*, for instance national law, international law, religious law, religion, culture, or custom.

The reservations analysed below were firstly selected on the basis of the sources of justification. Only reservations that referred to cultural pluralism, including religion and custom, as justification to make the reservation, were included. Sometimes religion and custom were referred to as a source in themselves, sometimes they were referred to as legal sources, for instance as part of national law. As regards the scope of these cultural reservations, the selection includes broad and general ones, reserving the treaty as a whole, but also those referring to a specific provision in the treaty. As regards the type, the reservations selected are mainly substantive reservations. They concern the substance of the treaty and/or a provision and are not linked to the non-acceptance of a procedure or the limited or specific application of the treaty to a certain territory. It appears that cultural justifications are typically connected to the substance of the norms.

## A. The CEDAW and reservations

The CEDAW has been ratified by 187 states.[31] Of all states parties, 62 currently maintain one or more reservations. Several more made reservations in the past, but withdrew them. The CEDAW itself contains a specific provision on reservations. Article 28 reads:

1. The Secretary-General of the United Nations shall receive and circulate to all states the text of reservations made by states at the time of ratification or accession.
2. A reservation incompatible with the object and purpose of the present Convention shall not be permitted.
3. Reservations may be withdrawn at any time by notification to this effect addressed to the Secretary-General of the United Nations, who shall then inform all states thereof. Such notification shall take effect on the date on which it is received.[32]

In comparison with the general regime on reservations in Articles 19 and 20 VCLT, it should be noted that while the VCLT includes that states may formulate reservations unless they are incompatible with the object and purpose of the treaty, the language of CEDAW is somewhat stronger, stating that such reservations are not permitted. There is, however, no further specification in the CEDAW of the

---

[31] See United Nations Treaty Collection, via <http://www.ohchr.org> (accessed 1 August 2012).

[32] Article 29 CEDAW concerns a dispute settlement procedure. According to Art 29(2): 'Each State Party may at the time of signature or ratification of the present Convention or accession thereto declare that it does not consider itself bound by paragraph I of this article. The other States Parties shall not be bound by that paragraph with respect to any State Party which has made such a reservation.' Several states have made such reservations, which will not be dealt with here.

consequence of an incompatible reservation or of an objection to a reservation by other states parties.[33]

The cultural reservations made by states parties concern mainly Articles 2, 9, 15, and 16 CEDAW. It appears that many states that entered reservations to these provisions were already critical of their content during the drafting process and voted against their adoption.[34]

Article 2 CEDAW is the general provision condemning discrimination of women and containing the obligation of states parties to adopt legislative and other measures and pursue policies to eliminate discrimination against women. It also obliges states parties to embody the principle of the equality of men and women and to integrate this in their national constitution and other legislation. Article 2(f) obliges states parties to 'take all appropriate measures, including legislation, to modify or abolish existing laws, regulations, customs and practices which constitute discrimination against women'. This last paragraph is linked to cultural or religious norms or rules at the national level, which, according to this provision, should be changed if they comprise discrimination against women.

Article 9 concerns equal rights of men and women in relation to nationality, including in relation to family life. Article 9(1) states that states parties should ensure that 'neither marriage to an alien nor change of nationality by the husband during marriage shall automatically change the nationality of the wife, render her stateless or force upon her the nationality of the husband' and Article 9(2) states that states parties should 'grant women equal rights with men with respect to the nationality of their children'.

Article 15 concerns equality between women and men before the law, including identical legal capacity in civil matters. Article 15(4) states that states parties should give women and men equal rights in relation to movement of persons and the freedom to choose residence and domicile.

Article 16 concerns marriage and family life and is the provision on which most cultural reservations have been made. It reads as follows:

1. States Parties shall take all appropriate measures to eliminate discrimination against women in all matters relating to marriage and family relations and in particular shall ensure, on a basis of equality of men and women:

   (a) The same right to enter into marriage;
   (b) The same right freely to choose a spouse and to enter into marriage only with their free and full consent;

---

[33] The Convention on the Elimination of All Forms of Racial Discrimination, adopted 21 December 1965 GA Res 2106 (XX), entry into force 4 January 1969, holds in its Art 20(2) that a reservation shall be regarded as incompatible or inhibitive if it is objected to by two-thirds of the other states parties.

[34] GAOR, 34th Session (18 December 1979), Agenda Item 75, UN Doc A/34/PV.107, in Connors, 'The Women's Convention in the Muslim World', in J.P. Gardner (ed), *Human Rights as General Norms and a State's Right to Opt Out: Reservations and Objections to Human Rights Conventions* (1997) 85 at 88–9.

(c) The same rights and responsibilities during marriage and at its dissolution;

(d) The same rights and responsibilities as parents, irrespective of their marital status, in matters relating to their children; in all cases the interests of the children shall be paramount;

(e) The same rights to decide freely and responsibly on the number and spacing of their children and to have access to the information, education and means to enable them to exercise these rights;

(f) The same rights and responsibilities with regard to guardianship, wardship, trusteeship and adoption of children, or similar institutions where these concepts exist in national legislation; in all cases the interests of the children shall be paramount;

(g) The same personal rights as husband and wife, including the right to choose a family name, a profession and an occupation;

(h) The same rights for both spouses in respect of the ownership, acquisition, management, administration, enjoyment and disposition of property, whether free of charge or for a valuable consideration.

2. The betrothal and the marriage of a child shall have no legal effect, and all necessary action, including legislation, shall be taken to specify a minimum age for marriage and to make the registration of marriages in an official registry compulsory.

Cultural reservations made by states parties to the CEDAW are mostly justified with reference to Islamic law and/or the Sharia. These will be dealt with first. Sometimes, the national constitution or specific national private or family laws are also indicated as sources of justification for reservations. Although these laws may be based on religious prescripts, reservations which only refer to national laws are not included, as the link with cultural or religious pluralism is not as clearly established. In the next section, cultural reservations that are justified with reference to other religions or customs are dealt with.

## B. Cultural reservations with reference to Islamic law and the Sharia

Some of the reservations referring to Islamic Law and the Sharia are of a general nature and have a very broad scope, while others have been made in relation to specific provisions. Some states have made use of both broad and specific reservations.[35]

General and broad reservations were made by Brunei Darussalam, Mauritania, Saudi Arabia, Oman, and Malaysia. These states all made reservations stating that

---

[35] The texts of the reservations were taken from the website of the UN Office of the High Commissioner for Human Rights <http://www.ohchr.org> and the UN treaty collection database, <http://treaties.un.org/Pages/ViewDetails.aspx?src=TREATY&mtdsg_no=IV-8&chapter=4&lang=en> (accessed 1 August 2012).

they do not consider themselves bound by any provisions of the CEDAW that may be or are contrary to Islam or the Sharia.[36]

Several states parties made reservations with reference to Islamic law or the Sharia to specific provisions of the CEDAW. Most of these reservations concern Articles 2, 9, 15, and 16, or parts thereof. Sometimes only a reference to Islam and/ or Sharia was given, sometimes a bit more explanation was provided.

Brunei Darussalam and Saudi Arabia, apart from their general reservations, made specific reservations to Article 9(2) without further justification. Oman and Malaysia also reserved specifically Articles 9(2), 15(4), 16(1)(a), (c), and (f) without further justification.

Reservations to specific provisions of the CEDAW making only a general reference to Islam or Sharia were made by Bahrain, Qatar, Syria, Kuwait, and the Maldives. Bahrain made a reservation to Articles 2, 9, 15(4), and 16, in which it indicated that the reservation to Article 2 was 'in order to ensure its implementation within the bounds of the provisions of the Islamic Shariah' and in relation to Article 16 'in so far as it is incompatible with the provisions of the Islamic Shariah'. Qatar made reservations to Articles 2(a), 9(2), 15(1), and 16(1)(a), (c), and (f), in which it referred to Articles 15 and 16 as being inconsistent with the provisions of Islamic law. Syria made reservations to Article 2, Article 9(2), Article 15(4), Article 16(1)(c), (d), (f), and (g), and Article 16(2) 'inasmuch as this provision is incompatible with the provisions of the Islamic Shariah'. Kuwait made a reservation to Article 16(f) 'inasmuch as it conflicts with the provisions of the *Islamic Shariah*, Islam being the official religion of the State'. The Maldives made a similar reservation, asserting its right to apply Article 16 'without prejudice to the provisions of the Islamic Sharia, which govern all marital and family relations of the 100 percent Muslim population of the Maldives'.

More specific elaboration of the elements of the Islam and/or Sharia that were considered incompatible with the CEDAW was given in the reservations by Egypt, Iraq, Libya, Morocco, and the United Arab Emirates.

Egypt made a reservation to Article 2, stating that it is willing to comply with the content of this provision 'provided that such compliance does not run counter to the Islamic *Sharia*'. Egypt also made a reservation to Article 16 'without prejudice to the Islamic *Sharia*'s provisions whereby women are accorded rights equivalent to those of their spouses so as to ensure a just balance between them'. Egypt

---

[36] Reservation Brunei Darussalam: all provisions that may be contrary to 'the beliefs and principles of Islam, the official religion of Brunei Darussalam'. Reservation Mauritania: approving all parts of the CEDAW 'which are not contrary to Islamic Sharia'. Reservation Saudi Arabia: 'In case of contradiction between any term of the Convention and the norms of Islamic law, the Kingdom is not under obligation to observe the contradictory terms of the Convention.' Reservation Oman: 'all provisions of the Convention not in accordance with the provisions of the Islamic sharia'. Declaration Malaysia: accession is subject 'to the understanding that the provisions of the Convention do not conflict with the provisions of the Islamic Sharia law'.

explained the specific aspects of religious laws concerning marriage that conflict with Article 16 CEDAW, which led to the reservation made.

This is out of respect for the sacrosanct nature of the firm religious beliefs which govern marital relations in Egypt and which may not be called in question and in view of the fact that one of the most important bases of these relations is an equivalency of rights and duties so as to ensure complementary [sic] which guarantees true equality between the spouses. The provisions of the *Sharia* lay down that the husband shall pay bridal money to the wife and maintain her fully and shall also make a payment to her upon divorce, whereas the wife retains full rights over her property and is not obliged to spend anything on her keep. The *Sharia* therefore restricts the wife's rights to divorce by making it contingent on a judge's ruling, whereas no such restriction is laid down in the case of the husband.

Iraq made a reservation to Article 2(f) and (g), Article 9(1) and (2), and Article 16. As regards Article 16, it did so 'without prejudice to the provisions of the Islamic *Shariah* according women rights equivalent to the rights of their spouses so as to ensure a just balance between them'.

Libya made a reservation to Article 2 in that it should be implemented 'with due regard for the peremptory norms of the Islamic *Shariah* relating to determination of the inheritance portions of the estate of a deceased person, whether female or male'. It also made a reservation stating that it would implement Article 16(c) and (d) 'without prejudice to any of the rights guaranteed to women by the Islamic *Shariah*'.

Morocco made a declaration that it would apply Article 2 provided that it does not conflict with the provisions of the Islamic Sharia and that the provisions in the Moroccan Law on Personal Status, which accord women different rights than men, may not be infringed upon because they derive primarily from the Islamic Sharia.

The United Arab Emirates made reservations to Article 2(f), because it 'violates the rules of inheritance established in accordance with the precepts of the Shariah' and Article 15(2) because it is 'in conflict with the precepts of the Shariah'. In relation to other provisions, such as Article 16, it states that it will respect the provisions 'insofar as they are not in conflict with the principles of the Shariah'. The United Arab Emirates further explained in this regard that it

considers that the payment of a dower and of support after divorce is an obligation of the husband, and the husband has the right to divorce, just as the wife has her independent financial security and her full rights to her property and is not required to pay her husband's or her own expenses out of her own property. The Shariah makes a woman's right to divorce conditional on a judicial decision, in a case in which she has been harmed.

It is interesting to see that, although at first sight similar, the reservations are formulated slightly differently. Some states parties state that they consider themselves not to be bound by these provisions, because they are in conflict with Islamic law or the Sharia. Bangladesh, for example, made a reservation that it does not consider 'as binding upon itself the provisions of article 2 ... [and] 16(1)(c) as they conflict with *Sharia* law based on Holy Quran and Sunna'. The State of Bangladesh clearly considers that Articles 2 and 16 *are* in conflict with the Sharia. Qatar made reservations to Articles 15 and 16, because it found them to be inconsistent with the provisions of Islamic law. Other states, however, consider themselves bound to these provisions, *provided that* or *insofar as* they do not conflict with Islamic law and Sharia. For example, Bahrain, Egypt, Iraq, Kuwait, Maldives, Libya, Morocco, and Syria let the Sharia prevail in case of conflict. These states parties do not categorically reject the provisions, only to the extent that they would be in conflict with Islamic law and the Sharia. It depends therefore on the interpretation of the provisions in question. The United Arab Emirates made a mixed reservation: it considers Article 2 and Article 15(2) to be in conflict with the Sharia, but reserves Article 16 only in case of conflict with the Sharia.

Most states parties justify their reservations by simply referring to the (potential) incompatibility of these provisions with Islamic law or the Sharia. Other states parties, including Egypt and United Arab Emirates, not only refer to Islamic law or the Sharia in general, but also elaborate on the specific aspects of Islam or of the Convention that would be incompatible.

## C. Cultural reservations with reference to other religions or customs

Several states parties have made reservations referring to other religions or to local customs or traditions. The latter group of reservations may refer not only to pluralism *between* states, but also *within* states.

References to other religions than Islam were made by Israel and Singapore. Israel made a reservation to Article 7(b) on the rights of women to perform all public functions at all levels of government on equal terms with men. It expressed a reservation in relation to the appointment of women as judges in religious courts 'where this is prohibited by the laws of any of the religious communities in Israel'. It also made a reservation to Article 16 'to the extent that the laws on personal status which are binding on the various religious communities in Israel do not conform with the provisions of that article'. Singapore made reservations to Article 2(a) to (f), and Article 16(1)(a), (c), (h), and 16(2) 'where compliance with these provisions would be contrary to their religious or personal laws'. It justified these reservations by referring to 'Singapore's multiracial and multi-religious society and the need to respect the freedom of minorities to practice their religious and personal laws'.

Custom was referred to by Micronesia, Niger, New Zealand, and India. Micronesia made a reservation reserving the right 'not to apply the provisions of Articles 2(f), 5, and 16 to the succession of certain well-established traditional titles, and to marital customs that divide tasks or decision-making in purely voluntary or consensual private conduct'. Niger made reservations to articles 2(d) and (f), Article 5(a), Article 15(4), Article 16(1)(c), (e), and (g), stating that these provisions cannot be applied immediately, 'as they are contrary to existing customs and practices which, by their nature, can be modified only with the passage of time and the evolution of society and cannot, therefore, be abolished by an act of authority'. It seems that Niger is willing to try and change these customs and practices, but that it needs time to do so.

New Zealand made a reservation not to apply Articles 2(f) and 5(a) where they are inconsistent with 'the customs governing the inheritance of certain Cook Islands chief titles'. India made a declaration in relation to Article 16(2), stating that it supported the principle of compulsory registration of marriages, but that it found this 'not practical in a vast country like India with its variety of customs, religions and level of literacy'. As this declaration is more a general statement and does not seem to specifically refer to the legal effect of this provision, it is not necessarily a reservation.

## D. Reservations to Article 5 CEDAW

An important provision in relation to cultural pluralism between, but also within states, is Article 5 of the CEDAW. It reads:

States Parties shall take all appropriate measures:

(a) To modify the social and cultural patterns of conduct of men and women, with a view to achieving the elimination of prejudices and customary and all other practices which are based on the idea of the inferiority or the superiority of either of the sexes or on stereotyped roles for men and women;

(b) To ensure that family education includes a proper understanding of maternity as a social function and the recognition of the common responsibility of men and women in the upbringing and development of their children, it being understood that the interest of the children is the primordial consideration in all cases.

Several states made declarations, not reservations, on this provision. For instance, France and Niger made a declaration that Article 5 will be applied subject to Article 17 of the International Covenant on Civil and Political Rights (ICCPR), which contains the right to respect for private life and family life.

India declared that it will abide by Article 5 'in conformity with its policy of non-interference in the personal affairs of any Community without its initiative and consent'. Qatar made a more specific statement on this matter, declaring that 'the question of the modification of "patterns" referred to in article 5(a) must not be understood as encouraging women to abandon their role as mothers and their role in child-rearing, thereby undermining the structure of the family'.

In short, most reservations that are made in relation to cultural pluralism between states concern religion or religious laws, mostly Islamic law, which states parties want to prevail over CEDAW provisions. While some of the reservations are very broad in scope and concern the whole of the CEDAW, most concern specific provisions, including Articles 2, 9, 15, and 16 CEDAW. Not surprisingly, these are the provisions on discrimination in family affairs and legal affairs, where the tension with religious laws is most present and therefore states parties decided to make reservations. However, other states parties do not always agree with these reservations, and some have made specific objections to them.

## 4. Objections to Cultural Reservations by Other States Parties

Twenty-four states parties have made objections to one or more reservations by other states parties.[37] Most objections concern the reservations referring to Islamic law or the Sharia. It is worth noting that sometimes states parties object to reservations by certain states parties, but not to similar reservations by other states parties. It is unclear how states select the reservations they object to, but it seems it is not always done systematically and consistently. It is, however, not the intention here to focus on the use, or lack of use, of objections by specific states parties, but to provide a general overview of objections to cultural reservations and, most importantly, the arguments used by states parties for such objections. Broadly, two sorts of arguments were used: (1) reservations were objected to because they raised doubts on the commitment of the other state party, and (2) reservations were objected to because they were considered to be incompatible with the object and purpose of the treaty. This once again reflects the double nature of human rights treaties: they are not only contracts between states, but also standards to be implemented for the benefit of individuals and communities.

Broadly speaking, general and broad reservations are objected to because they raise doubts as to what extent the state party considers itself bound, and reservations to specific provisions are objected to because they are considered to be against the object and purpose of the treaty.

### A. Objections to general reservations—doubts as to the commitment

Several states parties objected to the general reservations made by, inter alia, Saudi Arabia, Brunei, Mauritania, and Oman. They found these reservations to be too general, broad and vague, in the sense of the broadness of the reservation itself, reserving the treaty as a whole, and/or in relation to the justification by reference to Islamic law or the Sharia, which was considered not to be specific enough. Objecting states parties considered such reservations to leave too much uncertainty as to which obligations the other state party actually felt bound to. Sometimes this was linked to the object and purpose of the treaty, either by raising doubts about the commitment of the other state party 'as to the object and purpose of the Convention', or by explicitly maintaining that the reservation in question was considered to be incompatible with the object and purpose of the treaty. States parties broadly use similar language as regards the objections they make to the different reservations.

Poland, for instance, objecting to the general reservations by Oman, Brunei Darussalam, and Qatar, indicated that it found that by making a general reference

---

[37] The texts of the objections were taken from the website of the UN Office of the High Commissioner for Human Rights <http://www.ohchr.org> and the UN treaty collection database, <http://treaties.un.org/Pages/ViewDetails.aspx?src=TREATY&mtdsg_no=IV-8&chapter=4&lang=en> (accessed 1 August 2012).

to the Islamic Sharia without indicating the provisions of the Convention to which the Islamic Sharia applies, these states did not specify the exact extent of the limitations and thus did not define precisely enough the extent to which they accepted the obligations under the Convention. While mentioning Article 28(2) and Article 19(c) VCLT, Poland did not elaborate further on the incompatibility of these reservations with the object and purpose of the treaty.

Belgium expressed objections to the general reservations of Brunei Darussalam, Oman, and Qatar, using similar language in each of them. Belgium considered that making the implementation of the Convention's provisions dependent upon their compatibility with national laws and the beliefs and principles of Islam, created uncertainty as to which obligations under the Convention these states parties intended to observe and raised doubts as to these states parties' respect for the object and purpose of the Convention.

The Czech Republic and Hungary objected to the general reservations by Oman, because they did not 'clearly define for the other States Parties to the Convention the extent to which the Sultanate of Oman has accepted the obligations of the Convention and therefore raises concerns as to its commitment to the object and purpose of the Convention'. The Czech Republic made similar objections to the general reservation by Brunei. The Czech Republic also objected to the general reservation by Qatar, whereby it specifically noted its objection to notions such as 'Islamic law' and 'established practice' being used without specifying its contents.

Romania formulated objections to reservations by Brunei, Oman, and Qatar stating that such general reservations are 'problematic as they raise questions with regard to the actual obligations the respective State Party understood to undertake by acceding to the Convention, and with regard to its commitment to the object and purpose of the Convention'.

Some states objected for similar reasons to the general reservations, but added the argument of the incompatibility of such reservations with the object and purpose of the treaty. Canada, for instance, objected to the general reservation made by Brunei Darussalam, stating that

such general reservation of unlimited scope and undefined character does not clearly define for the other States Parties to the Convention the extent to which Brunei Darussalam has accepted the obligations of the Convention and creates serious doubts as to the commitment of the state to fulfill its obligations under the Convention. Accordingly, the Government of Canada considers this reservation to be incompatible with the object and purpose of the Convention.

Germany made objections to the reservations made by Saudi Arabia, Mauritania, Bahrain, Syria, United Arab Emirates, Oman, and Brunei, all in similar terms. It argued that 'by giving precedence to the beliefs and principles of Islam and its own constitutional law over the application of the provisions of the Convention, Brunei Darussalam has made a reservation which leaves it unclear to what extent it feels bound by the obligations of the Convention and which is incompatible with the object and purpose of the Convention'. The United Kingdom used comparable language in its objections to the general reservations made by Saudi Arabia,

Mauritania, and Oman, as well as in its objections to the reservations to specific provisions by Syria, Bahrain, United Arab Emirates, and Brunei.

Spain objected in similar terms to the general reservation made by Saudi Arabia, pointing at the lack of clarity on the commitment by Saudi Arabia. It also added that it found such a reservation incompatible with the object and purpose of the Convention 'since it refers to the Convention as a whole and seriously restricts or even excludes its application on a basis as ill-defined as the general reference to Islamic law'.

Finland used similar language in its objection to the general reservation by the Maldives. 'The unlimited and undefined character of the said reservations creates serious doubts about the commitment of the reserving state to fulfill its obligations under the Convention. In their extensive formulation, they are clearly contrary to the object and purpose of the Convention.'

Austria objected to the general reservation made by Saudi Arabia in the following terms:

The fact that the reservation concerning any interpretation of the provisions of the Convention that is incompatible with the norms of Islamic law does not clearly specify the provisions of the Convention to which it applies and the extent of the derogation therefrom raises doubts as to the commitment of the Kingdom of Saudi Arabia to the Convention. Given the general character of this reservation a final assessment as to its admissibility under international law cannot be made without further clarification. Until the scope of the legal effects of this reservation is sufficiently specified by the Government of Saudi Arabia, Austria considers the reservation as not affecting any provision the implementation of which is essential to fulfilling the object and purpose of the Convention. In Austria's view, however, the reservation in question is inadmissible to the extent that its application nega-tively affects the compliance by Saudi Arabia with its obligations under the Convention essential for the fulfillment of its object and purpose. Austria does not consider the reser-vation made by the Government of Saudi Arabia as admissible unless the Government of Saudi Arabia, by providing additional information or through subsequent practice, ensures that the reservation is compatible with the provisions essential for the implementation of the object and purpose of the Convention.

This objection shows that Austria basically considers the reservation as non-existent until Saudi Arabia provides additional information, on the basis of which it can better assess the scope of this reservation.

A similar approach was taken by Austria in the objection to another broad res-ervation, the one of Mauritania. Again it was pointed out that 'in the absence of further clarification, this reservation raises doubts as to the degree of commitment assumed by Mauritania in becoming a party to the Convention since it refers to the contents of Islamic Sharia'. The lack of clarity was this time explicitly linked to the incompatibility of the reservation with the object and purpose of the treaty by stating that 'according to art. 28(2) of the Convention as well as customary international law as codified in the Vienna Convention on the Law of Treaties, a reservation incompatible with the object and purpose of a treaty shall not be per-mitted'. Similar objections and remarks were made by Austria to reservations made by Bahrain, Syria, the United Arab Emirates, and Oman.

Some states not only object to the general reservations in terms of commitment or (in)compatibility with the object and purpose of the treaty, they also touch upon the working and effect of such reservations in international law.

Denmark, in its objection to the reservation by Saudi Arabia, stated that 'the general reservation with reference to the provisions of Islamic law are [sic] of unlimited scope and undefined character. Consequently, the Government of Denmark considers the said reservations as being incompatible with the object and purpose of the Convention and accordingly inadmissible and without effect under international law.' Denmark hereby not only objected to the reservation, but also formally declared it invalid. It used the same language in its objection to the reservations by Mauritania, Bahrain, and Oman.

Finland objected to the reservations by Libya, Malaysia, Saudi Arabia, Mauritania, Bahrain, Syria, United Arab Emirates, Oman, Brunei, and Qatar stating that such reservations

consisting of a general reference to religious and national law without specifying the contents thereof and without stating unequivocally the provisions the legal effect of which may be excluded or modified, do not clearly define to the other Parties of the Convention the extent to which the reserving state commits itself to the Convention and therefore creates serious doubts about the commitment of the reserving state to fulfill its obligations under the Convention. Reservations of such unspecified nature may contribute to undermining the basis of international human rights treaties.

Finland hereby expressed a more general concern that general, broad, and unspecified reservations could damage the working of human rights treaties.

France also linked its objection to a more overall concern on general reservations and their impact on human rights treaties. In its objection to the reservation by Saudi Arabia it stated that 'the Kingdom of Saudi Arabia formulates a reservation of general, indeterminate scope that gives the other States Parties absolutely no idea which provisions of the Convention are affected or might be affected in future. The Government of the French Republic believes that the reservation could make the provisions of the Convention completely ineffective'.

Ireland used similar language in its objection to the reservations by Saudi Arabia, Brunei, Oman, and Qatar, stating that 'a reservation which consists of a general reference to religious law without specifying the content thereof and which does not clearly specify the provisions of the Convention to which it applies and the extent of the derogation therefrom, may cast doubts on the commitment of the reserving state to fulfill its obligations under the Convention. The Government of Ireland is furthermore of the view that such a general reservation may undermine the basis of international treaty law.' The Netherlands and Portugal used similar language in their objections to the reservations by Saudi Arabia, Mauritania, Bahrain, Syria, United Arab Emirates, Oman, Brunei, and Qatar.

Norway expressed similar objections to reservations made by Libya, Maldives, Brunei, and Kuwait. Its objection was formulated as follows:

A reservation by which a State Party limits its responsibilities under the Convention by invoking religious law (Shariah), which is subject to interpretation, modification, and selective application in different states adhering to Islamic principles, may create doubts about the commitments of the reserving state to the object and purpose of the Convention. It may also undermine the basis of international treaty law. All states have common interest in securing that all parties respect treaties to which they have chosen to become parties.

## B. Objections to reservations on specific provisions—against the object and purpose of the treaty

Several states parties objected to reservations made by other states parties to specific provisions of the treaty, often with the argument that these reservations were considered to be incompatible with the object and purpose of the treaty. In this respect, some states parties specifically refer to Article 28(2) CEDAW and/or Article 19(c) VCLT, others do not. Sometimes the objections also include a judgment on the validity of the reservation, apart from its permissibility, sometimes not.

Austria, for example, objected to the reservation by Saudi Arabia concerning Article 9(2) as being incompatible with the object and purpose of the treaty. For the same reasons, Austria objected to the reservation by the Maldives to Article 16, which it found inadmissible under Article 19(c) VCLT and Article 28(2) CEDAW. Canada objected for similar reasons to the reservation by the Maldives.

Denmark objected to the reservations by Niger to parts of Articles 2, 5, 15, and 16, because it found these reservations 'not in conformity with the object and purpose of the Convention'. The Netherlands made similar objections to the reservations by Egypt, Iraq, Libya, Kuwait, and Malaysia.

Greece objected to the reservations made by Bahrain, Syria, United Arab Emirates, Oman, and Brunei, arguing that reservations which contain a reference to the provisions of the Islamic Sharia are of unlimited scope and, therefore, incompatible with the object and purpose of the Convention. Spain used similar argumentation to object to the reservations made by Syria, United Arab Emirates, Oman, Brunei, and Qatar.

Latvia objected to the reservations made by United Arab Emirates, Brunei, and Oman with the general argument that they were against the object and purpose of the treaty, whereby it elaborated on the purpose of the provisions in relation to the reservations.

Estonia objected to the reservation by Syria to Article 16(2), because of the general reference to the Islamic Sharia. It stated that 'in the absence of further clarification, this reservation which does not clearly specify the extent of the Syrian Arab Republic's derogation from the provision in question raises serious doubts as to the commitment of the Syrian Arab Republic to the object and purpose of the Convention'. Similar objections were made by Estonia to reservations by Brunei and Oman to Article 16(2).

Again, some states parties, in their objections to reservations to specific provisions, not only referred to the incompatibility of these reservations with the object and purpose of the Convention, but also signalled the risk of such reservations for the working of general international law.

France, for example, in its objection to the reservations by Bahrain, Syria, United Arab Emirates, Oman, and Brunei on (parts of) Articles 2, 9, 15, and 16, stated that such reservations 'would likely be incompatible with the object and purpose of the Convention'. It also stated that such reservations 'could make the provisions of the Convention completely ineffective' (Bahrain), or could deprive 'the provisions of the Convention of any effect' (United Arab Emirates).

Estonia, in its objection to the reservation by the Syrian Arab Republic to Article 2, maintains that 'by making a reservation to this article, the Government of the Syrian Arab Republic is making a reservation of general scope that renders the provisions of the Convention completely ineffective'.

Finland in its objection to the reservation by Kuwait to Article 16(f), stated that 'the unlimited and undefined character of the reservation to article 16(f) leaves open to what extent the reserving state commits itself to the Convention and therefore creates serious doubts about the commitment of the reserving state to fulfil its obligations under the Convention. Reservations of such unspecified nature may contribute to undermining the basis of international human rights treaties.'

Sweden emphasized in this regard the contractual nature of the convention by stating that 'the reason why reservations incompatible with the object and purpose of a treaty are not acceptable is precisely that otherwise they would render a basic international obligation of a contractual nature meaningless. Incompatible reservations...do not only cast doubts on the commitments of the reserving states to the objects and purpose of this Convention, but moreover, contribute to undermine the basis of international contractual law'. Sweden also made objections to reservations to specific provisions by Saudi Arabia, Mauritania, Bahrain, Syria, United Arab Emirates, Oman, Brunei, and Qatar.

## C. Objections against reservations on provisions of a fundamental nature

Some states parties have objected to reservations to specific provisions because of their incompatibility with the object and purpose of the treaty, indicating in the process that the provisions in question are considered to be of a fundamental nature or core provisions of the treaty.

Belgium, for example, in its objections to reservations made by Brunei, Oman, and Qatar, indicated that it considers Articles 9(2), 15(4), and 16 fundamental provisions, making reservations to these provisions incompatible with the object and purpose of the treaty. Canada also indicated that Article 9(2) is a fundamental provision, making reservations incompatible with the object and purpose, in its objection to the reservation by Brunei. Ireland indicated that the reservation by Saudi Arabia to Article 9(2) would be contrary to the essence of the Convention. Slovakia also objected to the reservation by Brunei to Article 9(2), asserting that it undermined one of the key provisions of the Convention and was incompatible with its object and purpose.

Denmark, Sweden, Estonia, and Greece consider the reservation by Syria to Article 2 incompatible with the object and purpose of the Convention, using the term 'core article' in relation to Article 2. In its objection to the reservations by Oman, Estonia also called Article 16 one of the core provisions of the Convention 'to which reservations are incompatible with the Convention and therefore impermissible'. Italy also considered Articles 2 and 16 to be 'core provisions' of the Convention, the observance of which is necessary to achieve its purpose. It added in its objection to the reservations by Qatar that 'neither traditional, religious or cultural practice nor incompatible domestic laws and policies can justify violations of the Convention'.

Finland stated in its objection to reservations by Malaysia and Niger that Article 2(f) and 5(a) were 'fundamental provisions...the implementation of which is essential to fulfilling its object and purpose'. Norway also maintained in its objection to the reservation by Niger that Article 2 is the core provision of the CEDAW. In its objection to the reservation by Syria to Articles 2, 9(2), 15(4), and 16, Norway stated that 'the said reservations, as they relate to core provisions of the Convention, render the provisions of the Convention ineffective. Moreover, and due to the reference to Islamic Sharia, it is not clearly defined for other States Parties to what extent the reserving state has undertaken the obligations of the Convention.'

Another way of formulating the key importance of certain provisions, is by stating that a reservation to this provision would 'inevitably lead to discrimination of women', stopping which is of course the central aim of the CEDAW. Several states parties have used such formulations in their objections to reservations.

Denmark, for example, stated that the reservations to Articles 9(2), 15(4), and 16(1) by Syria, Oman, and Brunei would 'inevitably result in discrimination against women on the basis of sex, which is contrary to the object and purpose of the Convention'. Other states parties, for example the Czech Republic in its objection to reservations by Oman, Brunei, and Qatar, Austria in its objections to the reservations by Bahrain, Qatar, and Malaysia, Germany in its objections to reservations by Mauritania, United Arab Emirates, Oman, and Brunei, Hungary in its objections to reservations by Oman, Brunei, and Qatar, and Slovakia in its objections to reservations by Qatar, instead of calling these provisions 'fundamental', indicate their importance by stating that reservations would automatically lead to violations of the treaty.

### D. Objections by states parties to non-Islamic reservations

Almost no objections have been made to the cultural reservations made by states parties with reference to other arguments than Islamic law or the Sharia.

Sweden objected to the reservation by Micronesia, stating that 'this reservation raises serious doubts as to the commitment of the Government of Micronesia to the object and purpose of the Convention. The reservation would, if put into practice, result in discrimination against women on the basis of sex'. All three arguments—doubts about the commitment, possible incompatibility with the object, and purpose and automatic violation of the treaty—are used here.

Sweden also objected to the reservation by New Zealand to Article 2(f) and 5(a) as being incompatible to the object and purpose of the Convention. Sweden added that 'the reason why reservations incompatible with the object and purpose of a treaty are not acceptable is precisely that otherwise they would render a basic international obligation of a contractual nature meaningless. Incompatible reservations, made in respect of the Convention on the elimination of all forms of discrimination against women, do not only cast doubts on the commitments of the reserving states to the objects and purpose of this Convention, but moreover, contribute to undermine the basis of international contractual law.'

## E. Concluding remarks on the objections by other states parties

Although the practice of objections is rather variable and unpredictable, since states parties do not consistently object to reservations, some concluding remarks can be made.

It appears that most objections concern the reservations justified by references to Islamic law and the Sharia. While states parties avoid a general qualification of the compatibility of these religious laws with the CEDAW, they indicate that general references are too broad and vague, as they do not specify the possible conflict between these religious laws and the CEDAW. Moreover, some states argue that religion is not static and also a matter of interpretation, which makes the concrete consequences of the reservation unclear.

As regards the scope of the reservations, it is no surprise that general reservations, possibly exempting the state party from the treaty as a whole, are firmly objected to by other states parties. Most of the objections contain the lack of clarity on the commitment of the other state party, emphasizing the contractual relationship between states parties to the treaty. This raises the question to what extent reservations based on Islamic law would be accepted by other states parties if they were more specific.

Reservations to specific provisions are also objected to, often with the argument that these reservations are considered to be incompatible with the object and purpose of the treaty. While the object and purpose of the treaty are not defined specifically, the objections show that states parties generally agree that Articles 2, 9, 15, and 16 CEDAW reflect its object and purpose. Would this mean that no reservations to such provisions would be acceptable? Or could very specific reservations to particular parts of these provisions be acceptable? This could be the case, considering that fact that hardly any objections were made to more specific cultural reservations made to the same provisions, but justified by other arguments than Islamic law and the Sharia.

Most states parties that have objected to reservations by other states parties, have clearly indicated that their objection does not preclude the entry into force of the treaty between them. This is in line with Article 20(4)(b) VCLT as outlined above.

Some states indicated that they considered the reservation to be invalid. Some states, notably the Nordic countries but also Estonia, added that the reserving state would not benefit from its reservations.[38]

The above also shows that a large majority of states parties does not object to cultural reservations. This does not necessarily mean that they agree with them. One reason could be that states parties aim for an inclusive approach, preferring to have states on board, allowing for international supervision, even with general or broad reservations, than to have them outside the scope of the treaty.[39] States may also consider objecting as a politically unfriendly act that they do not wish to engage in. Probably the most important reason is that there is not much practical effect in an objection to a reservation. Precisely because the reciprocity between contracting parties is mostly absent in human rights treaties, objections by other states parties have 'primarily symbolic significance'.[40]

## 5. The Committee on the Elimination of Discrimination Against Women

### A. The role of the Committee in relation to reservations

The CEDAW Committee has, since its establishment, expressed its general concern about the large number of reservations to its treaty. It has, however, always been aware of the question as to what extent treaty bodies are formally competent to determine whether a specific reservation was incompatible with the object and purpose of the treaty. In the 1980s, the CEDAW Committee sought legal advice from the UN secretariat on this matter. The reply was that 'the functions of the Committee do not appear to include a determination of the incompatibility of reservations, although reservations undoubtedly affect the application of the Convention and the Committee might have to comment thereon in its reports'.[41]

---

[38] This new approach whereby the reserving state does not get what it wants and cannot profit from its reservation is explained by Klabbers, who doubts that this approach is compatible with the rules on reservations in the VCLT. See Klabbers (2000) 179–93.

[39] Lijnzaad (1994) 105.

[40] Chinkin, 'Reservations and Objections to the Convention on the Elimination of All Forms of Discrimination Against Women', in J.P. Gardner (ed), *Human Rights as General Norms and a State's Right to Opt Out: Reservations and Objections to Human Rights Conventions* (1997) 64 at 76. As the HRC stated in its *General Comment No 24*: 'because the operation of the classic rules on reservations is so inadequate for the Covenant, States have often not seen any legal interest in or need to object to reservations. The absence of protest by States cannot imply that a reservation is either compatible or incompatible with the object and purpose of the Covenant', para 17.

[41] Report of the Secretariat on Ways and Means of Improving the Work of the Committee (30 May 2001), UN Doc CEDAW/C/2001/II/4 Annex VI, 33–4; or UN Doc A/39/45, Vol II, Annex II. See Schöpp-Schilling, 'Reservations to the Convention on the Elimination of All Forms of Discrimination Against Women: An Unresolved Issue or (No) New Developments?', in I. Ziemele (ed), *Reservations to Human Rights Treaties and the Vienna Convention Regime: Conflict, Harmony or Reconciliation* (2004) 3 at 13.

The CEDAW Committee did, however, express its opinion on the issue of reservations in so-called General Recommendations. With these General Recommendations, which are based on its experience with the assessment of periodic state reports and since 2000 with the individual communications, the Committee elaborates on general issues in relation to the Convention or on the normative content and state obligations of specific provisions. These General Recommendations are not legally binding. In its *General Recommendation No 4* of 1987, the Committee stated that many reservations 'appeared to be incompatible with the object and purpose of the Convention', carefully avoiding a final verdict on the issue. It did suggest to states parties to 'reconsider such reservations with a view to withdrawing them'.[42]

On a number of occasions, the Committee asked for more information and study on the relationship between the Convention and Islamic law, which was, however, never carried out by the UN.[43] In the meantime, the Committee formulated a new General Recommendation on reservations in 1992. In this Recommendation, the Committee recommended states parties to reconsider their reservations and consider the introduction of 'a procedure on reservations to the Convention comparable with that of other human rights treaties'. It most likely referred to the procedure in Article 20 of the Convention on the Elimination of All Forms of Racial Discrimination,[44] according to which a reservation shall be regarded as incompatible or inhibitive if it is objected to by two-thirds of the other states parties. States parties, however, did not want such a procedure.[45]

In the beginning of the 1990s, the UN Sub-Commission on Prevention of Discrimination and Protection of Minorities proposed to seek an advisory opinion from the International Court of Justice on the validity and legal effect of reservations to the CEDAW, following the example of the advisory opinion on reservations to the Genocide Convention. The Committee took up this idea, but wanted to do so together with other treaty bodies.[46] As the CEDAW Committee is not competent to seek such an advisory opinion itself, it should have persuaded the ECOSOC or the General Assembly to do so. This idea, however, never materialized.[47]

The CEDAW Committee has dealt with the reservations in its assessment of states parties' reports within the framework of the periodic reporting procedure. According to this procedure, states parties should periodically report on what legal and other measures they have taken to implement the Convention and what

---

[42] CEDAW Committee, *General Recommendation No 4: Reservations*, 6th Session (1987), UN Doc A/42/38.

[43] Report of the Committee on the Elimination of Discrimination Against Women, 7th Session (1988), UN Doc A/43/38, 61, in: Connors (1997) 99; Schöpp-Schilling, (2004) 14.

[44] International Convention on the Elimination of All Forms of Racial Discrimination, General Assembly Resolution 2106 (XX), adopted 21 December 1965, entry into force 4 January 1969.

[45] Schöpp-Schilling (2004) 15.

[46] See Reports of CEDAW: Report of the Committee on the Elimination of Discrimination against Women, 11th Session (1992), UN Doc A/47/38, 106, para 469; Report of the Committee on the Elimination of Discrimination against Women, 12th Session (1993) UN Doc A/48/38, 7, para 4, in Schöpp-Schilling (2004) 16–17.

[47] Chinkin (1997) 81–2; Schöpp-Schilling (2004) 17.

challenges they face in advancing the rights in the Convention. At the beginning of the 1990s, the Committee amended its guidelines for the reporting procedure and required states to include in their reports information on their reservations, the reasons for making them, and their effect.[48] After having received the report, the Committee prepares a so-called list of issues that it wishes to discuss and the state party gets the opportunity to respond to these issues in writing. Then the state party is invited for a dialogue with the Committee, where the issues and other points are discussed in person. Finally, the Committee adopts concluding observations, in which it indicates the positive aspects of the state party's implementation, as well as its concerns, and it provides the state with recommendations. These concluding observations are not legally binding, but should encourage the state party to improve its implementation of the treaty. Not all states which have made cultural reservations have (yet) taken part in the reporting procedure.

As shown above, neither the CEDAW nor the VCLT give the Committee formal powers to rule on the compatibility of reservations with the object and purpose of the CEDAW. However, the Committee has dealt with the issue of reservations in its General Recommendations on specific provisions. In its *General Recommendation No 21 on equality in marriage and family relations*, the Committee addressed reservations to Articles 9, 15, and 16, in particular those based on cultural or religious beliefs. It explains that 'many of these countries hold a belief in the patriarchal structure of the family which places the father, husband or son in a favourable position'. The Committee requires states parties to 'gradually progress to a stage where, by its resolute discouragement of notions of the inequality of women in the home, each country will withdraw its reservation, in particular to articles 9, 15 and 16 of the Convention'. Furthermore, 'states parties should resolutely discourage any notions of inequality of women and men which are affirmed by laws, or by religious or private law or by custom, and progress to the stage where reservations, particularly to article 16, will be withdrawn'.[49] Although the Committee hereby confirms the crucial importance of these provisions and strongly urges states parties to withdraw these reservations, it does not categorically reject them as being against the object and purpose of the treaty.[50]

More recently, the Committee expressed itself in more explicit terms. In its General Recommendation on Article 2, the Committee underlined that it finds Article 2 the very essence of the Convention and therefore 'considers reservations to 2 or to subparagraphs of article 2 to be in principle, incompatible of the

---

[48] Reporting Guidelines adopted at the 27th Session of the CEDAW Committee (1994), UN Doc A/57/38; Report of the Committee on the Elimination of Discrimination against Women, 27th Session (1994), UN Doc A/48/38, at 137; see also Connors (1997) 99–100, Schöpp-Schilling (2004) 29.

[49] CEDAW Committee, *General Recommendation No 21, Equality in Marriage and Family Relations*, 13th Session (1994), UN Doc CEDAW/C/GC/21, paras 41–7.

[50] See also Schöpp-Schilling (2004) 19.

object and purpose of the Convention and thus impermissible under article 28, paragraph 2'.[51]

## B. The assessment of cultural reservations by the Committee in its dialogues with states parties

Reservations, including cultural reservations, have formed a recurrent item in the assessment of state parties' reports. In relation to general reservations, as well as those on specific provisions such as Articles 2, 9, 15, and 16, the Committee has in its list of issues always asked states parties to clarify the scope of the reservations and to describe the impact of the reservations on the practical realization of the principle of equality between women and men.[52] Sometimes states indeed provide additional justification and clarification of their reservations, explaining in more detail why they deem them necessary.

Oman, for example, stated that the 'reservations can in no way be considered discrimination against women within the meaning of the Convention, nor do they detract from the realization of the principle of equality and non-discrimination provided for in article 2 thereof'.[53] It further indicated that the reservation to Article 15(4) was made because the provision was inconsistent with national law, which prescribed that 'a wife must live with her husband in the home that he has prepared and move from it when he moves, unless stipulated otherwise in the marriage contract or unless the husband intends to harm his wife by moving'.[54] Oman also indicated that it was studying the possibility of withdrawing or reducing the reservations.[55]

The United Arab Emirates gave extensive explanations for its reservations. In its response to the list of issues, the United Arab Emirates first explained why it had no reservation with respect to article 2(a): 'because it believes in the importance of making women full partners in the development process, both through participation in that process and by benefiting from the fruits of development projects'. It further gave the reasoning for its reservations on other specific provisions. It argued, for example, that Article 2(f) on the abolishment of laws, customs, and practices which constitute discrimination, conflicts with the provisions of the Islamic Sharia concerning inheritance. With regard to its reservation to Article 9, it argued that it found the acquisition of nationality an internal matter and that national laws

---

[51] CEDAW Committee, *General Recommendation No 28, The Core Obligations of States Parties under Art 2 of the Convention on the Elimination of All Forms of Discrimination against Women*, 47th Session (2010), UN Doc CEDAW/C/GC/28, para 41.

[52] See eg the list of issues for Oman, List of Issues and Questions with Regard to the Consideration of Initial Reports (7 March 2011), UN Doc CEDAW/C/OMN/Q/1, para 3; the United Arab Emirates, List of Issues and Questions with Regard to the Consideration of Initial Reports (13 March 2009), UN Doc CEDAW/C/ARE/Q/1, para 4; Saudi Arabia, List of Issues and Questions with Regard to the Consideration of Periodic Reports (17 August 2007), UN Doc CEDAW/C/SAU/Q2, para 2.

[53] Oman's reply to the List of Issues and Questions with Regard to the Consideration of Initial Reports (18 May 2011), UN Doc CEDAW/C/OMN/Q/1/Add.1, para 12.

[54] UN Doc CEDAW/C/OMN/Q/1/Add.1, para 117.

[55] UN Doc CEDAW/C/OMN/Q/1/Add.1, paras 13, 117.

provided that a child shall acquire nationality through its father. It found Article 15(2) as regards equality to conclude contracts and in procedures in courts and tribunals to be in conflict with the Islamic Sharia, 'with regard to jurisdiction, testimony and the character of a legal contract under the sharia'. As regards Article 16, the United Arab Emirates explained that it 'believes that a husband is obliged to pay dowry and maintenance after divorce; a husband has the right to seek a divorce; and a wife has independent financial security and full rights to her own property. A wife is under no obligation to support her husband or herself from her own funds. The Islamic sharia limits a wife's right to seek divorce, stipulating that it should be at the discretion of a judge, when she has suffered injury.'[56] In its concluding observations, the Committee urged the state party to withdraw or narrow its reservations to Articles 2(f), 9, 15(2), and 16. In particular, it argued that Articles 2 and 16 are central to the object and purpose of the Convention and that 'in accordance with article 28, paragraph 2, reservations to these articles should be withdrawn'.[57] As regards Article 16, it called upon the state party to, inter alia, 'end the practices of dowry and polygamy'.[58]

Libya indicated that it had modified its original general reservation that stated that accession should not conflict with the Islamic Shariah, and changed it into reservations to specific provisions. It made reservations to Article 2, in particular concerning Sharia rules on the determination of the share of the heirs to the estate of a deceased person, male or female, and Article 16(c) and (d). In relation to the latter, Libya stipulated that it maintained its reserving position 'on everything which conflicts with the clear and definitive Koranic texts'.[59] Libya reiterated this in its response to the list of issues, also stating that 'Libyan legislation distinguishes between men and women only in the areas in which the Libyan Arab Jamahiriya has formulated a reservation to the Convention'.[60] In other words, Libya does not consider this discrimination, but distinction based on religious laws.

Bahrain, in its report, dealt extensively with its reservations, trying to explain the reasons for them as well as their scope. For example, the reason for its reservation to Article 2 was 'to ensure that this article is implemented within the framework of the Islamic Sharia... Therefore, Bahrain's reservation stems from its desire not to apply the aforesaid article literally, i.e., in a way that would lead to a conflict with Shariah provisions on the woman's position in the family, particularly regarding inheritance.'[61] Bahrain then elaborated extensively on its interpretation

---

[56] United Arab Emirates reply to the List of Issues and Questions with Regard to the Consideration of Initial Reports (19 October 2009) UN Doc CEDAW/C/ARE/Q/1/Add.1, para 4

[57] CEDAW, Concluding Observations of the CEDAW Committee, United Arab Emirates (5 February 2010), UN Doc CEDAW/C/ARE/CO/1, paras 16, 17, 33, 45, 46.

[58] UN Doc CEDAW/C/ARE/CO/1, para 48.

[59] CEDAW, Consideration of Reports Submitted by States Parties under Article 18 of the Convention on the Elimination of All Forms of Discrimination against Women, Libyan Arab Jamahiriya (4 December 2008), UN Doc CEDAW/C/LBY/5, 13.

[60] Libyan Arab Jamahiriya's reply to the List of Issues and Questions with Regard to the Consideration of the Second Periodic Report (9 January 2009), UN Doc CEDAW/C/LBY/Q/2/Add.1, para 5.

[61] CEDAW, Concluding Observations of the CEDAW Committee, Libyan Arab Jamahiriya (6 February 2009), UN Doc CEDAW/C/LBY/CO/5, paras 83–4.

of inheritance under Islamic laws, explaining that 'a literal interpretation of the Shariah provision that grants a woman one-half of the inheritance of a man might be challenged on the grounds that it discriminates against women'.[62]

Islam does not make a woman's inheritance one-half that of a man as a general rule in inheritance. Rather, this rule applies only in some cases for explicable reasons. A woman sometimes receives one-half the share of a man . . . Sometimes a woman receives more than a man, as in the case where a person dies, leaving behind one daughter and his two parents: The two parents each receive one sixth of the inheritance, whereas the daughter receives one half, which is more than the share or received by her grandfather, a man. Moreover, in the case of a surviving daughter and father, the daughter receives three quarters, whereas her grandfather receives only one quarter.[63]

As regards the reservation made by Bahrain to Article 9 concerning nationality, it explained the national system of patrilineal *jus sanguinis* as the sole basis for the granting of Bahraini nationality. However, Bahrain indicated that it was working on matrilineal *jus sanguinis* to be established as a criterion for determining nationality.[64] As regards Bahrain's reservation to Article 15, it stated that although Islamic law requires a woman to obtain the permission of the husband or guardian to travel and move, this was not applied in practice and that there were no legal impediments to a woman's movement and travel. It stated that the reservation was limited to a married woman's freedom to choose her residence.

In this regard, the Islamic Shariah requires a married woman to live in the matrimonial home. Moreover, religious teachings and social customs require that an unmarried woman live with her family. Consequently, Bahrain's reservation concerning residence is a logical consequence of the necessity entailed by the marriage contract for the wife to actually live in the residence prepared for her by the husband, so that she may assume her responsibilities as a wife and mother in the matrimonial home. The wife's right to maintenance is forfeited if she is found to be disobedient under a judicial judgment, i.e., if she refuses to reside in the matrimonial home without reasonable justification.[65]

Saudi Arabia argued that it considered its reservations to be 'consistent with articles 19–23 of the Vienna Conventions on the Law of Treaties, concerning reservations, especially as they accord with the subject of the Convention and are not incompatible with its purpose'.[66] Saudi Arabia explained that 'it made this reservation on the basis of its conviction that the Islamic sharia is compatible with the obligations contained in the general principles of the Convention, even if there is a small disparity with regard to some of the implementing provisions. Judgements about whether or not such a disparity exists are made on the basis of the texts of the Islamic sharia and the relevant provisions of the Convention on a case-by-case

---

[62] UN Doc CEDAW/C/LBY/CO/5, para 85.
[63] UN Doc CEDAW/C/LBY/CO/5, paras 85–6.
[64] UN Doc CEDAW/C/LBY/CO/5, paras 164–5.
[65] UN Doc CEDAW/C/LBY/CO/5, paras 317–18.
[66] CEDAW, Consideration of Reports Submitted by States Parties under Article 18 of the Convention on the Elimination of All Forms of Discrimination against Women, Saudi Arabia (29 March 2007) UN Doc CEDAW/C/SAU/2, para 6.

basis.'[67] Saudi Arabia further stated that its general reservation did not affect the core of the Convention and that it did not believe 'that the wording of its reservation interferes with its obligations under the Convention'. It was merely 'a precautionary measure at a time when human rights concepts are developing rapidly as a result of interpretations following the entry into force of international human rights instruments such as the Convention'. It seems that Saudi Arabia wanted to emphasize that it wished to retain the final say in the interpretation of the provisions of the Convention.[68] It finally emphasized that its report showed that 'there is no contradiction between the main provisions that form the basis of the Convention and Islamic sharia principles relating to women's rights'.[69]

Niger explained in its report that it had made a reservation to Article 5(a) because it considered that 'social and cultural patterns of conduct that are deeply rooted in the collective consciousness cannot be modified simply by enacting legislation. Modifications can take place only gradually'.[70]

The Committee has generally signalled to states parties its concern about cultural reservations, especially the general ones. It has, however, not always been clear and consistent in its qualification of the various reservations in terms of their (in)compatibility with the object and purpose of the treaty.[71] The Committee has moreover been careful in the language it used; even if it finds certain reservations in conflict with the object and purpose of the treaty and therefore impermissible, it does not declare them inadmissible or invalid. It merely requests states parties to reconsider, modify, narrow, or withdraw them, and to do so within a limited timeframe.[72]

For instance, in relation to Oman, the Committee stated that it was of the opinion that 'a general reservation, as well as the reservation to article 16 are contrary to the object and purpose of the Convention and are thus impermissible under article 28 of the Convention'. In the case of Libya, the Committee expressed its concern at the remaining reservations, which it found to be contrary to the object and purpose of the Convention. It made an interesting link with the ICCPR, noting that 'the state party did not enter any reservations to the International Covenant on Civil and Political Rights, which also requires equality between women and men in these areas'. A similar reference was made in the concluding observations

[67] Saudi Arabia's reply to the List of Issues and Questions with Regard to the Consideration of the Second Reports (18 December 2007), UN Doc CEDAW/C/SAU/Q/2/Add.1, para 2.

[68] According to Lijnzaad, uncertainty and possible disagreement with the (future) interpretation of provisions of human rights treaties is a common argument for making reservations to human rights treaties. See Lijnzaad (1994) 79–80.

[69] Saudi Arabia's reply to the List of Issues and Questions with Regard to the Consideration of the Second Reports (18 December 2007), UN Doc CEDAW/C/SAU/Q/2/Add.1, para 2.

[70] CEDAW, List of Issues and Questions with Regard to the Consideration of Initial Reports, Niger (21 November 2005), UN Doc CEDAW/C/NER/1-2, para 3.3.

[71] Schöpp-Schilling (2004) 34–5.

[72] For example in the case of Oman, List of Issues and Questions with Regard to the Consideration of Initial Reports (7 March 2011), UN Doc CEDAW/C/OMN/Q/1, paras 3, 29; United Arab Emirates, List of Issues and Questions with Regard to the Consideration of Initial Reports (5 February 2010), UN Doc CEDAW/C/ARE/Q/1, paras 17, 33, 45; Concluding observations of the CEDAW Committee, Bahrain (14 November 2008), UN Doc CEDAW/C/BHR/CO/2, paras 17, 31.

of Niger. The Committee expressed its concern on the reservations by Niger and noted that 'reservations to articles 2 and 16 are contrary to the object and purpose of the Convention'. It also noted that Niger had not entered reservations to other human rights treaties, 'which all contain the principle of equality between women and men and the prohibition of discrimination on the basis of sex'.[73] It therefore urged Niger to withdraw the reservations.[74]

In relation to Bahrain, the Committee in its concluding observations took note of the explanations, but was still of the opinion that these reservations were contrary to the object and purpose of the Convention and urged Bahrain to withdraw them.[75] In its Concluding Observations on Saudi Arabia, the Committee stated that it was concerned about this general reservation 'which is drawn so widely that it is contrary to the object and purpose of the Convention'. Here the Committee did not refer to Article 28(2). The Committee also urged Saudi Arabia to consider withdrawing its reservation, 'particularly in light of the fact that the delegation assured that there is no contradiction in substance between the Convention and Islamic Sharia'.[76] It also requested Saudi Arabia to withdraw its reservation to Article 9(2).[77]

Sometimes states parties have indeed decided to withdraw their reservations. Malaysia, for example, decided to withdraw its reservations to Articles 2(f), 9(1), 16(b), (d), (e), and (h), as it did not find them to be in contradiction with Islamic Sharia law. It kept reservations to articles 9(2) and 16(1)(a), (f), and (g), because Malaysia found these to be in conflict with the provisions of the Islamic Sharia law. It further made declarations, sometimes similar to reservations, for Articles 5(a), 7(b), 9(2), 16(1)(a), and 16(2).[78] In its concluding observations, the Committee, while commending Malaysia for the withdrawal of certain reservations, urged Malaysia to remove the remaining ones, 'especially reservations to article 16, which are contrary to the object and purpose of the Convention'. The Committee was particularly concerned about the state party's position that laws based on Sharia interpretation could not be reformed.[79]

The Maldives changed its reservation from a general one to a more specific reservation. Upon accession, the Maldives had made a general reservation that it would not comply with provisions of the Convention that the Government may consider contradictory to the principles of the Islamic Sharia upon which the laws

[73] CEDAW, Concluding Observations of the CEDAW Committee, Niger (11 June 2007), UN Doc CEDAW/C/NER/CO/2, para 9.

[74] UN Doc CEDAW/C/NER/CO/2, para 10.

[75] CEDAW, Concluding Observations of the CEDAW Committee, Bahrain (14 November 2008), UN Doc CEDAW/C/BHR/CO/2, paras 16 and 17.

[76] CEDAW, Concluding Observations of the CEDAW Committee, Saudi Arabia (8 April 2008), UN Doc CEDAW/C/SAU/CO/2, paras 9–10.

[77] UN Doc CEDAW/C/SAU/CO/2, para 28.

[78] CEDAW, Consideration of Reports Submitted by States Parties under Article 18 of the Convention on the Elimination of All Forms of Discrimination against Women, Combined Initial and Second Periodic Reports of States Parties, Malaysia (12 April 2004), UN Doc CEDAW/C/MYS/1-2, para 69.

[79] CEDAW, Concluding Observations of the CEDAW Committee, Malaysia (31 May 2006), UN Doc CEDAW/C/MYS/CO/2, paras 9–10.

and traditions of the Maldives is founded. Its current reservation only concerns Article 16.

Libya also withdrew its general reservation that accession could not conflict with the laws on personal status derived from the Islamic Sharia. It now has a reservation on Articles 2 and 16(c) and (d). Singapore withdrew its reservation to Article 9. And where it had first made a reservation to Articles 2 and 16 as a whole, it later changed that into specific paragraphs of these provisions.

Syria is an example of a state party which had announced the intention to withdraw its reservations, but never really did. Originally, Syria had made cultural reservations to Articles 2, 9, 15(4), 16(1)(c), (g), and (f), and 16(2). In its report, it indicated that after examination and dialogue at the national level, it decided to remove the reservations to Articles 2, 15(4), 16(1)(g), and 16(2), as these were considered not to be incompatible with the Islamic Sharia. It kept its reservations to Articles 9 and 16(1)(c) and (f), because of their incompatibility with the Sharia.[80] In the List of Issues, the Committee asked the Syrian authorities to describe progress made in the removal of the mentioned reservations.[81] In its written replies, Syria indicated that the matter was being considered by the competent ministries.[82] In its concluding observations, the Committee called upon Syria to speed up this process, as well as to 'review and withdraw all remaining reservations, and especially reservations to articles 9 and 16, which are incompatible with the object and purpose of the Convention'.[83] It appears that Syria never went through with the withdrawal of the reservations, as they are still in place.

The above shows that the Committee pays a lot of attention to reservations in its state reporting procedure. It is a valuable addition to the formal objections by other states parties, as this procedure allows for dialogue and discussion on the scope, content, and effect of the reservations as well as their (in)compatibility with provisions of the CEDAW.[84] Sometimes, further study by the state party on the compatibility of the provisions of the Convention and the Sharia—perhaps partially pushed by the Committee —has led to a change in the state's position and revision of the reservations.

---

[80] CEDAW, Consideration of Reports Submitted by States Parties under Article 18 of the Convention on the Elimination of All Forms of Discrimination against Women, Syria (29 August 2005), UN Doc CEDAW/C/SYR/1, Section 2, Introduction, paras 10–15.

[81] CEDAW, Concluding Comments of the Committee on the Elimination of Discrimination against Women: Syrian Arab Republic (5 October 2006), UN Doc CEDAW/C/SYR/Q/1, para 3.

[82] Syrian reply to the List of Issues and Questions with Regard to the Consideration of Initial Reports (2 March 2007), UN Doc CEDAW/C/SYR/Q/1/Add/1, answer to question 3.

[83] CEDAW, Concluding Observations of the CEDAW Committee, Syria (11 June 2007), UN Doc CEDAW/C/SYR/CO/1, paras 11–12.

[84] Reservations to human rights treaties, including those to the CEDAW, are also discussed in the Universal Periodic Review within the Human Rights Council, composed of states' representatives. States mainly urge each other to reconsider or withdraw their reservations, eg in the case of Bahrain, Oman, and Saudi Arabia. See Report of the Working Group on the Universal Periodic Review: Bahrain (22 May 2008), UN Doc A/HRC/8/19, para 9 and Recommendation 2; Report of the Working Group on the Universal Periodic Review: Oman (24 March 2011), UN Doc A/HRC/17/7, paras 90.16 and 90.17; Report of the Working Group on the Universal Periodic Review (4 March 2009), UN Doc A/HRC/11/23, paras 27, 44, 46, 49, 54, and 79.

The CEDAW Committee commonly considers general and broad reservations, as well as reservations to Articles 2 and 16, to be contrary to the object and purpose of the Convention. The Committee, logically, involves itself less with a lack of clarity regarding the exact obligations a state party has bound itself to in light of its reservations. Where states parties in their objections often refer to the lack of clarity concerning the commitment of the other state party, the Committee focuses on the possible lack of respect for and protection of the actual rights. It is interesting that the Committee in this regard also refers to the fact that for similar provisions in other human rights treaties, no reservations were made.

## 6. Concluding Remarks: Cultural Pluralism through Reservations

From the above, it can be concluded that states have indeed made reservations to the CEDAW based on cultural, mostly religious, differences between them. By making such reservations, these states express their will not to be bound by certain provisions of this treaty, because they want their own cultural or religious particularities to prevail. These cultural reservations reflect cultural pluralism between states in relation to this human rights treaty.

The large majority of the cultural reservations to the CEDAW are based on Islamic laws and the Sharia and they concern its provisions on equality in matters of nationality, family affairs, and legal affairs. It is on these issues that, according to the reservations made, Islamic law may be different and should prevail.

Most of these cultural reservations made by states parties were objected to by other states parties and they also met with great concern from the CEDAW Committee. The main problem seems to be that most cultural reservations were formulated too broadly and generally, as regards to their scope of application (the treaty as a whole) and as regards their justification (Islamic law in general without specifying which parts of Islamic law). The vagueness of these reservations leaves too much ambiguity as regards their outcome and thereby the scope of commitment of the state party. Other states parties therefore objected to these reservations, because of doubt as regards the obligations the state party is prepared to respect.

Cultural reservations to specific provisions were also objected to. The argument in these cases was often that the reservations were incompatible with the object and purpose of the CEDAW. The object and purpose of the treaty form a general limitation on the making of acceptable reservations. These objections, based on the incompatibility with the object and purpose, not only concerned contractual considerations; they also reflected disagreement with the cultural or religious arguments underlying the reservation.[85] At the same time, it is not so much the cultural or religious argument per se that is the object of disagreement, but the consequences for the implementation of the CEDAW. In other words, culture or

---

[85] Klabbers (2004) 179.

religion may be accepted as a justification for reservations and cultural reservations are not categorically rejected. This is also shown by the fact that reservations based on other cultural arguments than Islamic law are hardly objected to by other states parties and do not meet as much concern by the Committee. It is merely where cultural or religious arguments undermine the working of the treaty that they are not accepted by other states parties and by the Committee. In other words, relying on cultural or religious arguments to reserve a certain provision is acceptable, as long as this is not contrary to the object and purpose of the treaty and the rights in the treaty are respected and protected.

It should be noted that a minority of states object to reservations. This might mean that other states parties find these reservations acceptable and have no objections to them. There can also be other reasons why states parties do not object, including possible ignorance of the reservations, diplomatic reasons avoiding political or economic problems with another state, but also the lack of effect of an objection. Practice shows that the severability approach is broadly accepted, whereby states remain parties to and are bound by the treaty, despite their reservations being considered invalid.

The two faces of human rights treaties, the one being contracts between states and the other being normative standards for states' behaviour towards individuals and communities, clearly appear in relation to cultural reservations and the objections to them. States parties often emphasize their contractual relationship in their objections by stating that, as contract partners, they want to know to what extent their fellow states parties consider themselves bound by the provisions of the treaty. At the same time, they emphasize the normative importance of the treaty by stating that the objection to the reservation does not preclude the entry into force of the treaty between them.

The monitoring body, not being a contracting party and in its role of supervisor of the implementation of the treaty, links its objection to the protection and promotion of human rights towards the beneficiaries. It emphasizes the possible negative impact of some cultural reservations on the implementation of the rights in the CEDAW. Although the Committee could use the objections by other states parties as an indication of the permissibility of these reservations, it appears to prefer to make its own assessment on the matter.

In conclusion, it can be stated that the principle remains that states parties may make reservations to certain provisions in a human rights treaty with reference to their specific cultural or religious background. Reservations may therefore be a useful or even necessary reflection of cultural pluralism.[86] Such cultural reservations, however, must be formulated in concrete and specific terms. They must state which specific (parts of) provisions of the treaty the state party does not consider itself bound to, and explain the cultural or religious reasons behind the reservation, which determine its scope, content, and consequences.

---

[86] Pergantis (2007) 455.

Moreover, cultural reservations have to be able to pass the object and purpose test, to prevent them from going against the essential parts of the treaty or under-mining the effect of the treaty as a whole. It seems that existing reservations to the CEDAW based on cultural arguments do not often pass that test. In the case of the CEDAW, this also reflects the continuing lack of universal consensus on women's rights. Whereas discrimination based on race is more or less universally objected to, discrimination based on sex is still often justified, exactly with religious, cul-tural, and historical arguments, and reservations are used as a tool in the process.[87] However, as with all tools, they should be used with caution. While reservations may be a means of accounting for cultural diversity, it should be emphasized, as indicated in the UNESCO instruments, that the promotion of cultural diversity always requires that human rights are guaranteed.

---

[87] Chinkin (1997) 77; Neumayer (2007) 404.

# 8

# Suppressing and Remedying Offences against Culture

*Federico Lenzerini*

## 1. Introduction: A Holistic Understanding of 'Culture'

The term 'culture' originates from the Latin verb *colere*, which means 'cultivate'. In his *Tusculanae Disputationes*, written in circa 45 BC, Cicero uses an agricultural metaphor to describe the highest goal pursued by the human being, ie *cultura animi* (cultivation of the soul), the philosophical development of the soul. Culturalization, therefore, represents the supreme enlightenment of the individual, the highest context in which the human person realizes her identity, on an individual basis and in community with others. Culture is hence to be conceived as the complex of intellectual, spiritual, and emotional elements shaping an individual and/or a community. It is consequently self-evident that the meaning of 'culture' is not limited to arts and literature, but includes all social, spiritual, and anthropological values making up the human being from cradle to grave.

In legal terms, such a holistic understanding of culture is well expressed in the 1982 Mexico City Declaration on Cultural Policies, according to which it consists in 'the whole complex of distinctive spiritual, material, intellectual and emotional features that characterize a society or social group. It includes not only the arts and letters, but also modes of life, the fundamental rights of the human being, value systems, traditions and beliefs'.[1] The culture of a people—and, a fortiori, of a person—is conceived by the Declaration as 'a unique and irreplaceable body of values... [representing] its most effective means of demonstrating its presence in the world'.[2] Its cultural heritage includes

the works of its artists, architects, musicians, writers and scientists and also the work of anonymous artists, expressions of the people's spirituality, and the body of values which give

---

[1] See UNESCO, Mexico City Declaration on Cultural Policies (1982), available at <http://portal.unesco.org/culture/en/files/35197/11919410061mexico_en.pdf/mexico_en.pdf> (accessed 2 August 2012).
[2] See <http://portal.unesco.org/culture/en/files/35197/11919410061mexico_en.pdf/mexico_en.pdf> (accessed 2 August 2012), para 1.

meaning to life. It includes both tangible and intangible works through which the creativity of that people finds expression: languages, rites, beliefs, historic places and monuments, literature, works of art, archives and libraries.[3]

Culture is a dynamic concept, which is shaped by a process of continuing renovation and cross-fertilization between the innumerable cultural identities making up the world. The cultural identity of every people is therefore 'renewed and enriched through contact with the traditions and values of others'.[4] This makes cultural identity a value that cannot be considered in isolation, as culture 'withers and dies in isolation'; on the contrary, it is part of the broader universe of 'cultural diversity'.[5] As emphasized by Article 1 of the 2001 UNESCO Universal Declaration on Cultural Diversity,[6] the latter 'is embodied in the uniqueness and plurality of the identities of the groups and societies making up humankind. As a source of exchange, innovation and creativity, cultural diversity is as necessary for humankind as biodiversity is for nature'.

Another decisive feature of culture is that—in its *spiritual* dimension—it is inextricably linked to the very core of human dignity. The enjoyment of one's own culture is indeed an essential prerequisite in order for the person and/or community concerned to benefit from some of her/his/its internationally recognized fundamental human rights. It is for this reason that—as will be explained in the following section—offences against culture may play a profound and negative influence on human rights; this is a circumstance which leads these offences to reach a particularly high degree of intolerability.

Ultimately, offences against culture may have a disruptive impact on intercultural relations. Correct understanding of the complex notion of 'culture' explained in this section would indeed be decisive in order to promote a world order based on tolerance and mutual acceptance among different peoples.

## 2. 'Offences Against Culture': A Multifaceted Concept which May Have Huge Implications for the Integrity of Human Dignity

In the contemporary international legal order, culture is the object of a well-developed body of law specifically aimed at its safeguarding. The relevant legal instruments cover a number of different aspects which may be subsumed within the area covered by the concept of culture, including cultural heritage of

---

[3] See <http://portal.unesco.org/culture/en/files/35197/11919410061mexico_en.pdf/mexico_en.pdf> (accessed 2 August 2012), para 23.

[4] See <http://portal.unesco.org/culture/en/files/35197/11919410061mexico_en.pdf/mexico_en.pdf> (accessed 2 August 2012), para 4.

[5] <http://portal.unesco.org/culture/en/files/35197/11919410061mexico_en.pdf/mexico_en.pdf> (accessed 2 August 2012), para 4.

[6] UNESCO Universal Declaration on Cultural Diversity (2001), 41 ILM (2002) 57.

tangible[7] and intangible[8] character, of movable[9] and immovable[10] nature, as well as cultural diversity. In addition, all these instruments take into consideration the cultural elements on which they are focused from very specific perspectives, in light of the particular purposes pursued: protection of cultural goods in the event of armed conflict, mainly in the interest of the territorial state;[11] protection of the world's most formidable examples of monumental heritage, in the interest of the international community as a whole;[12] protection of the diversity of cultural expressions, in the interest of their stakeholders;[13] etc. As a whole, these instruments represent a relatively comprehensive legal body on the subject of culture. They even take into account the spiritual significance of culture, especially those of more recent adoption. However, the concern for the spiritual side of culture usually translates only into the proclamation of principles, which are usually not accompanied by effective operational legal provisions. For example, the 2003 UNESCO Convention on the Safeguarding of Intangible Cultural Heritage—although proclaiming that the heritage concerned is 'transmitted from generation to generation [and] constantly recreated by communities and groups in response to their environment, their interaction with nature and their history, and provides them with a sense of identity and continuity'[14]—is not properly equipped with adequate operational provisions capable of converting such a principle into a legally enforceable set of rules.[15] This situation epitomizes a reality in the context of which the pertinent international legal instruments offer effective means for suppressing and remedying offences against culture only to a partial extent, as will be explained below in Section 3. Therefore, in order to achieve this goal, it is often necessary to rely on other mechanisms available in international and/or domestic law. However, before undertaking the attempt to ascertain what are the most adequate and effective mechanisms in this respect, it is first of all opportune to endeavour to define the notion of 'offences against culture'.

---

[7] See, inter alia, Convention for the Protection of Cultural Property in the Event of Armed Conflict (1954), 249 UNTS 240, and its two Protocols: First Protocol to the Convention for the Protection of Cultural Property in the Event of Armed Conflict (1954), 249 UNTS 358; Second Protocol to the Convention for the Protection of Cultural Property in the Event of Armed Conflict (1999), 2253 UNTS 172; UNESCO Convention concerning the Protection of the World Cultural and Natural Heritage (1972, World Heritage Convention), 1037 UNTS 151; Convention on the Protection of the Underwater Cultural Heritage (2001), 2562 UNTS 1.

[8] See Convention for the Safeguarding of the Intangible Cultural Heritage (2003), 2368 UNTS 3.

[9] See UNESCO Convention on the Means of Prohibiting and Preventing the Illicit Import, Export and Transfer of Ownership of Cultural Property (1970), 823 UNTS 231; UNIDROIT Convention on Stolen or Illegally Exported Cultural Objects (1995), 34 ILM (1995) 1322.

[10] See, in particular, the World Heritage Convention.

[11] See the 1954 Convention for the Protection of Cultural Property in the Event of Armed Conflict and its two 1954 and 1999 Protocols.

[12] See the World Heritage Convention.

[13] See Convention on the Protection and Promotion of the Diversity of Cultural Expressions (2005), 2440 UNTS 311.

[14] See the definition of intangible cultural heritage in Art 2.

[15] See, on this issue, Lenzerini, 'Intangible Cultural Heritage: The Living Culture of Peoples', 22 *EJIL* (2011) 101.

The concept of 'offences against culture', considered as a whole, is relatively complex. In fact, there are several categories of actions that may be subsumed within such a concept, which differ with each other either for the *mens rea* of the perpetrator and/or for the *values prejudiced* by the offence. At the same time, the *occasio criminis* does not usually represent a distinctive element of the different categories of offences against culture, as all of them may take place both in peacetime and in the event of armed conflict. At a preliminary stage, it is important to emphasize that it is extremely unlikely that offences against culture may be inspired by the *mens rea* of purely damaging culture as such (ie committed only because the perpetrator hates culture *in itself*), without being moved by a different purpose; this kind of approach could only be imagined by a mentally unstable person. Having said this, in this writer's opinion, offences against culture may be divided into three main categories.

## A. The first category of offences against culture: damaging culture in order to pursue different legitimate interests

One first category of offences against culture relates to cases in which cultural heritage is sacrificed to an interest—*legitimate in itself*—considered by the perpetrator of the offence as preponderant over the cultural interest. With respect to this category, the *mens rea* is represented by the will of pursuing the said interest (in antithesis with the cultural one). One could assert that, in this case, the offence against culture is an 'unavoidable side effect' of a different activity which the perpetrator considers indispensable to his/her/its interests.

This category may be divided into two subcategories, differing with each other in light of the diversity of the values prejudiced by the relevant offences.

The first subcategory is represented by the cases in which the value sacrificed to the interest considered as predominant is a general interest—of a state or of the international community as a whole—to the protection of cultural heritage *only*. This may happen, for example, in the event of armed conflict, when a cultural property is destroyed during an armed attack, such a destruction being considered unavoidable to allow the attacking faction to achieve the goals pursued through the armed attack.[16] In this case, according to international law, the offence against

---

[16] Among the countless examples in which, throughout history, cultural properties were destroyed or damaged in time of war, one may refer to the recent occupation of Iraq, also known as 'Second Gulf War' or 'Operation Iraqi Freedom', which lasted from 2003 to 2011. Since the beginning of the war, huge damage was caused to some of the world's most important archaeological sites—including the ancient cities of Babylon and Ur—as a consequence of the presence of the Coalition Forces. For example, the ancient city of Babylon, situated 90 kilometres south of Baghdad, was used as military field by the Coalition Forces, leading to a huge amount of irreparable damage to the archaeological area, including excavation of trenches, demolitions, construction of barriers and military facilities, as well as levelling of the ground; see Moussa, 'The Damages Sustained to the Ancient City of Babel as a Consequence of the Military Presence of Coalition Forces in 2003', in P.G. Stone and J.F. Bajjaly (eds), *The Destruction of Cultural Heritage in Iraq* (Boydell Press, 2008) 143. The information included in this footnote has been taken from the graduation thesis written by Mr Claudio Guardì for his final exam to obtain the MA at the Faculty of Literature and Philosophy of the University of Siena (Italy), supervised by the present writer and discussed on 15 September 2009; the thesis is entitled 'I beni

culture may even be considered as lawful, provided that the conditions for the application of the excuse of *imperative military necessity* are met.[17] One further example of cases belonging to this subcategory is provided by the situation in which a project of exploitation is performed in a culturally valuable area, as a consequence of which the value of such an area is impaired. Even in these cases, it would be very hard to assert—*as a general rule*—that a breach of international law took place, except in the event that the heritage prejudiced is of special value. This happens, for example, when the integrity of a property inscribed on the World Heritage List[18] is prejudiced;[19] in this instance, in principle there is a breach of the World Heritage Convention, irrespective of the importance of the interest pursued by the state concerned, because such a state, through requesting the inscription of the relevant property on the List, had accepted the obligation to ensure that its integrity was preserved to the benefit of the international community as a whole, including future generations.

The second subcategory is qualified by the fact that the prejudice produced by the relevant offences is not limited to a damage to the value of culture as such, but goes much beyond, translating into serious breaches of the fundamental human rights of the person(s) and/or community identifying her-/him-/them-/itself with the affected culture. This subcategory is of special importance, because the foremost

---

culturali sotto assedio. Il caso iracheno' (Cultural Heritage under Attack. The Iraqi Case), and is on file with the author (the information concerning Babylon is available at 90–9).

[17] The concept of 'imperative military necessity' is contemplated, inter alia, by Art 4(2) of Convention for the Protection of Cultural Property in the Event of Armed Conflict, which, however, does not define its meaning. Such a definition is offered by Art 6 of the Second Protocol to the said Convention of 1999, according to which imperative military necessity may only be invoked if 'i. [the] cultural property [concerned] has, by its function, been made into a military objective; and ii. there is no feasible alternative available to obtain a similar military advantage to that offered by directing an act of hostility against that objective'.

[18] The World Heritage List is established by Art 11 of the World Heritage Convention; the List can be consulted at <http://whc.unesco.org/en/list> (accessed 2 August 2012).

[19] In the practice of the World Heritage Convention there are several examples of state misconduct threatening the integrity of World Heritage sites. When these cases occur, the property concerned may be inscribed on the List of World Heritage in Danger established by Art 11(4) of the Convention, reserved for property previously inscribed on the World Heritage List 'threatened by serious and specific dangers, such as the threat of disappearance caused by accelerated deterioration, large-scale public or private projects or rapid urban or tourist development projects; destruction caused by changes in the use or ownership of the land; major alterations due to unknown causes; abandonment for any reason whatsoever; the outbreak or the threat of an armed conflict; calamities and cataclysms; serious fires, earthquakes, landslides; volcanic eruptions; changes in water level, floods, and tidal waves'. In most cases, however, the simple intimidation by the World Heritage Committee to inscribe the property potentially in danger on the said List persuades the state concerned to remove the cause threatening such a property. Nevertheless, in two cases, so far, particularly serious threats to the integrity of a World Heritage site led the World Heritage Committee to remove the relevant property from the World Heritage List. This happened in 2007, with respect to the Arabian Oryx Sanctuary, located in Oman—following a decision by the national government to reduce the area of the site by 90% in order to proceed with hydrocarbon prospection (see <http://whc.unesco.org/en/news/362>, accessed 2 August 2012)—and in 2009, following the building by Germany of a four-lane bridge in the heart of the cultural landscape of Dresden Elbe Valley (see <http://whc.unesco.org/en/news/522>, accessed 2 August 2012). In both cases, the World Heritage Committee considered that, following the said events, the sites had lost their 'outstanding universal value', which is an essential prerequisite for inscribing (as well as for keeping) a property on the World Heritage List.

significance of culture lies exactly in its role as essential prerequisite for the enjoyment of a remarkable range of internationally recognized human rights. The most obvious example of the symbiosis between culture and human rights is represented by Article 27 of the 1966 International Covenant on Civil and Political Rights (ICCPR),[20] proclaiming the right of persons belonging to ethnic, religious, or linguistic minorities to enjoy their own culture, to profess and practise their own religion, or to use their own language, in community with the other members of their group. Although this provision defends individual rights, their actual enjoyment depends 'in turn on the ability of the minority group to maintain its culture, language or religion. Accordingly, positive measures by States may also be necessary *to protect the identity of a minority* and the rights of its members to enjoy and develop their culture and language and to practise their religion, in community with the other members of the group'.[21] The very—although implicit—purpose of Article 27 is therefore that of 'ensuring the survival and continued development of the cultural, religious and social identity of the minorities concerned, thus enriching the fabric of society as a whole'.[22] In this way, the relationship between the explicit and the implicit constituents of Article 27 is reversed and—in the complex dynamic produced by the provision in point—they become mutually supportive to each other: on the one hand, protection of the cultural identity of a minority (implicit constituent) plays the role of essential prerequisite to ensure the actual enjoyment of its members to enjoy their own culture, profess and practise their own religion, or use their own language (explicit constituent); on the other hand—and contextually—the *collective* right to cultural identity becomes the primary prerogative to be safeguarded, the actual realization of which presupposes that the members of the community concerned are allowed to enjoy their own culture, profess and practise their own religion, or use their own language. In order for the right in point to be fully protected, it is necessary that states take all 'positive legal measures' necessary with respect to a given minority, including for example allowing an indigenous community to fish or hunt in its ancestral territories or 'ensur[ing] the effective participation of members of minority communities in decisions which affect them'.[23] In the case of Article 27 ICCPR, therefore, an offence against the culture of a minority (a concept interpreted by the Human Rights Committee in a very broad sense, so as to include, inter alia, indigenous peoples)[24] translates into a breach of certain internationally recognized human rights of its members. At the same time, due to the relationship of 'circularity' existing between culture and human rights in the case concerned, a violation of those rights produces an offence against culture.

The dynamic process just described with respect to Article 27 ICCPR applies to several other human rights. The best illustration of such a reality is undoubtedly

---

[20] 999 UNTS 171.

[21] Human Rights Committee (HRC), *General Comment No 23: The Rights of Minorities (Art 27)*, UN Doc CCPR/C/21/Rev.1/Add.5, 8 April 1994, para 6.2 (emphasis added).

[22] UN Doc CCPR/C/21/Rev.1/Add.5, 8 April 1994, para 9.

[23] UN Doc CCPR/C/21/Rev.1/Add.5, 8 April 1994, para 7.

[24] See UN Doc CCPR/C/21/Rev.1/Add.5, 8 April 1994, paras 3.2 and 7.

offered by the practice of the Inter-American Court of Human Rights (IACtHR). For example, in a judgment of 2005, concerning the N'djuka community of Moiwana, in the state of Suriname,[25] the Court found that the lack of judicial guarantees in favour of the said community following an attack perpetrated against its village by members of the armed forces of Suriname (in the context of which more than 40 men were massacred and the village was razed to the ground) did not give rise to a breach of the rights to a fair trial and to judicial protection only. On the contrary, it also reached the threshold of inhuman treatment, for the reason that 'the ongoing impunity [had caused] a particularly severe impact upon the Moiwana villagers... [because] *justice and collective responsibility are central precepts within traditional N'djuka society*'.[26] The Court continued by stressing that, when

a community member is wronged, the next of kin—which includes all members of his or her matrilineage—are obligated to avenge the offense committed. If that relative has been killed, the N'djuka believe that his or her spirit will not be able to rest until justice has been accomplished. While the offense goes unpunished, the affronted spirit—and perhaps other ancestral spirits—may torment their living next of kin.[27]

Therefore, 'not only must the Moiwana community members endure the indignation and shame of having been abandoned by Suriname's criminal justice system—despite the grave actions perpetrated upon their village—they also must *suffer the wrath of those deceased family members who were unjustly killed* during the attack'.[28]

In a more recent case, relating to another community living in Suriname (the Saramaka people), the Court emphasized—reiterating the position already taken in a number of previous cases[29]—that the right of ownership by indigenous and tribal peoples of their traditional lands needs to be safeguarded in light of 'the special relationship that members of [the said] peoples have with their territory, and on the need to protect their right to that territory in order to safeguard the physical and cultural survival of such peoples'.[30] As a consequence,

environmental damage and destruction of lands and resources traditionally used by the Saramaka people... [constitutes an offence] not just as it pertains to its subsistence

---

[25] See *Case of the Moiwana Community v Suriname* (IACtHR) Series C, No 124, judgment of 15 June 2005, para 3.

[26] *Case of the Moiwana Community v Suriname*, para 95 (emphasis added).

[27] *Case of the Moiwana Community v Suriname*, para 95.

[28] *Case of the Moiwana Community v Suriname*, para 96 (emphasis added).

[29] See *Case of The Mayagna (Sumo) Awas Tingni Community* (IACtHR) Series C, No 27, judgment of 31 August 2001, para 149; *Case of the Plan de Sánchez Massacre v Guatemala* (IACtHR) Series C, No 116, judgment of 19 November 2004, para 85; *Case of the Indigenous Community Yakye Axa* (IACtHR) Series C, No 125, judgment of 17 June 2005, para 131; *Case of the Indigenous Community Sawhoyamaxa* (IACtHR) Series C, No 146, judgment of 29 March 2006, para 118.

[30] See *Case of the Saramaka People v Suriname* (IACtHR) Series C, No 172, judgment of 28 November 2007, para 90. This position is also shared, inter alia, by the HRC (see *General Comment No 23*, para 7), as well as by the Committee on the Rights of the Child (CRC), according to which '[i]n the case of indigenous children whose communities retain a traditional lifestyle, the use of traditional land is of significant importance to their development and enjoyment of culture' (see *General Comment No 11 (2009), Indigenous Children and their Rights under the Convention*, UN Doc CRC/C/GC/11, 12 February 2009, para 35).

resources, but also with regards to the spiritual connection the Saramaka people have with their territory... [and to] the suffering and distress that the members of the Saramaka people have endured as a result of the long and ongoing struggle for the legal recognition of their right to the territory they have traditionally used and occupied for centuries... as well as their frustration with a domestic legal system that does not protect them against violations of said right.[31]

All these prejudices suffered by the Saramaka people were considered by the Court as constituting a 'denigration of their basic cultural and spiritual values', as well as 'alterations to the very fabric of their society'.[32]

Following the same approach, in a case decided in 2010, the Court stressed that the forced displacement of an indigenous family from its traditional lands implicates 'the loss of [the] culture, traditions, language and ancestral past [of the people concerned] which had an "even more dramatic effect given the fact that they are indigenous, as a result of the cultural value that the lands have from the point of view of [their] culture"'.[33] In other words, 'the forced displacement of the indigenous peoples out of their community or from their members' produces a huge 'cultural and spiritual loss', and places the persons concerned

in a special situation of vulnerability, that for its destructive consequences regarding their ethnic and cultural fabric, generates a clear risk of extinction and cultural or physical rootlessness of the indigenous groups, for which it is indispensable that the States adopt specific measures of protection considering the particularities of the indigenous peoples, as well as their customary law, values, uses, and customs, in order to prevent and revert the effects of said situation.[34]

In addition, in light of the fact that indigenous children were among the victims, the Court found that they were deprived of their right to cultural life. In fact, according to the Court—'for the full and harmonious development of their personality, the indigenous children in agreement with their world vision, preferably require to grow and be raised within their natural and cultural environment, particularly because they possess a distinctive identity that roots them with their land, culture, religion, and language'.[35]

---

[31] See *Case of the Saramaka People v Suriname*, para 200.

[32] See *Case of the Saramaka People v Suriname*, para 200.

[33] See *Case of Chitay Nech et al v Guatemala* (IACtHR) Series C, No 212, judgment of 25 May 2010, para 135.

[34] *Case of Chitay Nech et al v Guatemala*, paras 145ff.

[35] *Case of Chitay Nech et al v Guatemala*, para 169f. See also—to a similar extent—the *Case of Xákmok Kásek Indigenous Community v Paraguay* (IACtHR) Series C, No 214, judgment of 24 August 2010, with respect to which the Court emphasized the detrimental impact on an indigenous community's cultural identity resulting from the failure to restore its traditional lands; the Court, in particular, noted that the cultural practices of the community concerned—including 'their own language...', their shaman rituals, their male and female initiation rituals, their ancestral shamanic knowledge, their ways of commemorating the dead, and their relationship with the land [which] are essential for developing their cosmology and unique way of existing' were affected by the lack of access to their traditional lands (*Case of Xákmok Kásek Indigenous Community v Paraguay*, paras 176–7), as well as that 'the loss of traditional practices, such as male and female initiation rites and the Community's

In all these cases—which have been illustrated for purely descriptive purposes and without any pretension of exhaustiveness with respect to the existing practice in the field—the relationship of circularity between culture and human rights referred to above is crystal clear. Particularly, what is important for the purposes of the present chapter is that we are looking at a type of offence against culture which—in addition to the *mens rea* of the first subcategory described above, consisting in the will of pursuing an interest in antithesis with the cultural one—clearly presents an additional element. This additional element, as previously said, consists in the fact that the mutilations determined by such crimes are not limited to damage to the value of cultural heritage as such, but extend to serious breaches of fundamental human rights.

## B. The second category of offences against culture: damaging culture in order to pursue different unlawful interests

The second category of offences against culture (according to a taxonomy personally elaborated by the present writer, which finds no correspondence in any legal instrument) is given by the cases in which the executor aims at achieving an *unlawful* goal—usually for reasons of personal convenience—and accepts that certain elements of culture are damaged in consequence of his/her/its conduct. This second category is apparently similar to the first, but a significant difference may be found in the *mens rea* of the executor, who acts in the pursuit of a purpose which is unlawful, while, with respect to the first category, the goal pursued is per se legitimate.

In the context of the category in point, the *unlawfulness* of the purpose of the executor may well be qualified by the fact that the target of his/her/its action *is actually cultural heritage*. To make this clearer, one may use the example of theft of cultural objects—which indeed represents one of the most evident cases of offences belonging to the second category. While robbery is usually unlawful in itself, irrespective of the object of the pillage, it attains an especially high degree of gravity when its target is cultural heritage, the significance of which is given not only by its economic cost, but also by its spiritual and cultural value.

The example of theft of cultural objects, which, as just noted, represents one of the main instances of offences against culture fitting in the category concerned, is a subcategory of the wider category of unlawful movement of cultural property, also including illicit import, export and transfer of ownership. A very unfortunate

languages, as well as the harm arising from the lack of territory, particularly affect the cultural identity and development of the children of the Community, who will not be able to develop that special relationship with their traditional territory and that particular way of life unique to their culture if the necessary measures are not implemented to guarantee the enjoyment of these rights' (*Case of Xákmok Kásek Indigenous Community v Paraguay*, para 263). According to the Court, 'the sorrow that [the individuals concerned] and the other members of the Community feel owing to the failure to restore their traditional lands, the gradual loss of their culture … give rise to suffering that necessarily violate the mental and moral integrity of all the members of the Community' (*Case of Xákmok Kásek Indigenous Community v Paraguay*, para 244).

example in this respect is represented by the well-known case of the looting of the National Museum of Iraq, in Baghdad, which took place in April 2003, during the Second Gulf War.[36] More generally, cases of unlawful movement of cultural property virtually occur on a daily basis. The values affected by the cases falling in the category in object may be of a different kind. First, it is possible that the general interest of humanity in the enjoyment of culture is affected, when a theft is perpetrated in order to clandestinely add a cultural object to a private collection, keeping it out of public enjoyment. Secondly, the affected entity may be a national[37] or a minority community, when a cultural property is unlawfully exported to a state or territory different than the one of origin and publicly displayed; in this case, the property concerned continues to be available to humanity in general, but its usability by the community specially concerned—the said property being part of its cultural identity—is impaired. Finally, in the event of an unlawful transfer of ownership of a cultural object between two private persons, the affected interest is the one of the legitimate individual proprietor to retain ownership of such an object; although in this case an offence against culture may hardly be detectable— the right of ownership usually being the only infringed value—it is nevertheless possible that the lawful owner of the object has a special interest of cultural nature in retaining its ownership, for example if its ancestors had established a spiritual connection with the object concerned.

In addition to cases of unlawful movement of cultural property, other examples of offences against culture belonging to the second category may be mentioned. For instance, one may think of the case of an edifice built abusively inside or in the vicinity of a culturally valuable area, leading to the impairment of the cultural significance of the site; also in this case the *mens rea* is to use the cultural element in order to achieve a personal goal (eg to possess a house inside a fascinating cultural site, or to have an hotel which will be especially attractive to tourists for its vicinity to a cultural area) contrary to applicable law.

## C. The third category of offences against culture: hitting culture to discriminate against a cultural group

The third category of offences against culture combines the effects already detected with respect to the second subcategory of the first category[38]—ie perpetration of an offence against the value of the *fundamental human rights* of individuals and/ or communities—with a deliberately criminally-oriented *mens rea*. The most blatant cases of offences against culture—*rectius*: *crimes against culture*—fall within

---

[36] See note 16 above. On the the looting of the National Museum of Iraq, see Phuong, 'The Protection of Iraqi Cultural Property', 53 *ICLQ* (2004) 985; Francioni and Lenzerini, 'The Obligation to Prevent and Avoid Destruction of Cultural Heritage: From Bamiyan to Iraq', in B.T. Hoffman (ed), *Art and Cultural Heritage. Law, Policy and Practice* (2006) 28 at 38–9.

[37] See eg the renowned case of the Elgin Marbles, the famous Parthenon marbles currently displayed in the British Museum in London, of which Greece claims return.

[38] See Section A above.

this category, as perpetrators act with the specific intent of destroying the cultural identity of certain individuals or (more often) communities.

The most renowned example of offences belonging to the category in point is probably represented by the blatant destruction of the two giant Buddha statues located in the valley of Bamiyan, in Afghanistan, perpetrated by the Taliban regime in March 2001,[39] for the shock it provoked to the whole international community. In that case, the demolition of the two irreplaceable statues—real masterpieces of the human artistic genius—was committed as part of a systematic and discriminatory campaign aimed at deleting all traces of non-Muslim cultural heritage from the Afghan territory.[40] It was carefully planned, scrupulously announced to the media all over the world, and cynically documented in all its phases, in absolute defiance of the protests raised by governments, international organizations, and representatives of civil society. The Afghan case, however, is not the only one of its kind which has occurred throughout history. On the contrary, countless cases of destruction of cultural heritage may be detected throughout history—since the notorious case of the demolition of the Temple of Serapis, in Alexandria of Egypt, ordered in AD 391 by the Roman Emperor Theodosius to obliterate the last refuge of non-Christians—especially in the event of armed conflict.[41]

The outrageous practice of destroying cultural heritage for discriminatory purposes attained a systematic character—and, probably, reached its peak so far—during the Balkan civil wars which took place in the 1990s. The

---

[39] See, on this case, Francioni and Lenzerini, 'The Destruction of the Buddhas of Bamiyan and International Law', 14 *EJIL* (2003) 619.

[40] The demolition of the two giant Buddhas was indeed the tip of the iceberg of this discriminatory campaign, as it was accompanied by the destruction of many other cultural objects; see Francioni and Lenzerini (2003) 627.

[41] Unfortunately, at the moment of revising the present chapter, another extraordinary heritage of humanity came under attack. Starting from 29 June 2012, the members of the extremist Islamic group Ansar Dine began to deliberately destroy the cultural heritage of the ancient city of Timbuktu, in Northern Mali, of which they had obtained control a few days earlier; the destructive acts involved in particular the tombs and mausoleums dedicated to Islamic saints, which, according to the members of Ansar Dine, would be idolatrous as contrary to Islam because God is unique and only God—and not men, albeit saints—may be the object of veneration. The international community reacted harshly; among others, the Chief Prosecutor of the International Criminal Court (ICC), Fatou Bensouda, on 16 January 2013 opened investigation into war crimes in Mali, including the crime of intentionally directing attacks against protected objects, the legal requirements for a possible breach of Art 8 ICC Statute (see note 44 below) having been fulfilled; see Nossiter, 'Mali Islamists Exert Control, Attacking Door to a Mosque', *The New York Times*, 2 July 2012, available at <http://www.nytimes.com/2012/07/03/world/africa/mali-islamists-exert-control-with-attacks-on-mosques.html> (accessed 2 August 2012); 'Timbuktu's Sidi Yahia mosque "attacked by Mali militants"', *BBC News*, 2 July 2012, available at <http://www.bbc.co.uk/news/world-africa-18675539> (accessed 2 August 2012); 'ICC Prosecutor opens investigation into war crimes in Mali: "The legal requirements have been met. We will investigate"', ICC Press Release, 16 January 2013, available at <http://www.icc-cpi.int/en_menus/icc/press%20and%20media/press%20releases/news%20and%20highlights/Pages/pr869.aspx> (accessed 20 March 2013). Generally on the issue of destruction of cultural property see Francioni and Lenzerini (2003); Lenzerini, 'The UNESCO Declaration Concerning the Intentional Destruction of Cultural Heritage: One Step Forward and Two Steps Back', 14 *Italian Yearbook of International Law* (2004) 131; O'Keefe, 'World Cultural Heritage Obligations to the International Community as a Whole?', 53 *ICLQ* (2004) 189; Vrdoljak, 'Intentional Destruction of Cultural Heritage and International Law', XXXV *Thesaurus Acroasium* (2007) 377.

destruction of cultural heritage was part of a deliberate strategy aimed at anni-
hilating the enemy, through the humiliation of its pride and self-esteem and
mortification of its culture, in light of its special spiritual and cultural relationship with the heritage concerned. Religious heritage, in particular, was systematically destroyed or heavily damaged without, in most cases, any direct utility
in order to favour the military victory of the destroyers. Just to have an idea,
it is sufficient to consider that, from March 1992 to November 1995, of 277
mosques located in Bosnia and Herzegovina which were the object of an ad hoc
study, 255 were destroyed (136) or heavily damaged (119)—for a total of 92
per cent—by the Serb forces as a result of shelling. Also, 75 per cent of the 57
Catholic churches which were the object of the same study were seriously damaged (30) or destroyed (13).[42]

Another very unfortunate example of destruction of cultural heritage occurring
during the Balkan wars is offered by the Stari Most, the world famous Mostar
bridge. It was demolished, 427 years after its construction, on 9 November 1993
(the day of the fourth anniversary of the fall of the Berlin Wall), in order to remove
the only existing physical connection uniting the Croat and Muslim communities
living in the town, which were linked by the bridge 'in spite of their religious differences and the circumstances of the present war'.[43]

Pursuant to a well-established rule of international criminal law, the act of
'[i]ntentionally directing attacks against buildings dedicated to religion, education,
art, science or charitable purposes, historic monuments, hospitals and places where
the sick and wounded are collected, provided they are not military objectives'
amounts to a war crime.[44] Such an offence, therefore, is considered per se as one
of the most awful crimes against peace and security of mankind. However, when
it is committed with a discriminatory intent, in order to annihilate a community
which reflects its cultural identity on the heritage concerned, it attains an even
higher degree of gravity. According to the International Criminal Tribunal for the
Former Yugoslavia (ICTY), when perpetrated with discriminatory purposes, the
plunder and wilful destruction of institutions dedicated to religion or education
*upgrades* to a modality of perpetration of the crime against humanity of persecution, which 'may take forms other than injury to the human person, in particular
those acts rendered serious not by their apparent cruelty but by the discrimination

---

[42] See Riedlmayer, 'Destruction of Cultural Heritage in Bosnia-Herzegovina, 1992–
1996: A Post-war Survey of Selected Municipalities' (2002), available at <http://hague.bard.edu/
reports/BosHeritageReport-AR.pdf> (accessed 2 August 2012), 10.

[43] See Final Report of the Commission of Experts Established Pursuant to Security Council
Resolution 780 (1992), UN Doc S/1994/674, 27 May 1994, IV.J.

[44] See Art 8(2)(b)(ix) and 8(2)(e)(iv) of the Rome Statute of the International Criminal Court
(1998), 2187 UNTS 90. See also, inter alia, Protocol Additional to the Geneva Conventions of 12
August 1949, and relating to the Protection of Victims of International Armed Conflicts (Protocol I)
(1977) 1125 UNTS 3, Art 53; Protocol Additional to the Geneva Conventions of 12 August 1949,
and Relating to the Protection of Victims of Non-International Armed Conflicts (Protocol II) (1977),
1125 UNTS 609, Art 16; Statute of the International Criminal Tribunal for the Former Yugoslavia
(1993), SC Res 827 (1993), 25 May 1993, Art 3(d).

they seek to instil within humankind'.[45] In the words of the ICTY, destruction of cultural property, 'when perpetrated with the requisite discriminatory intent, amounts to an attack on the very religious identity of a people. As such, it manifests a nearly pure expression of the notion of "crimes against humanity", for all of humanity is indeed injured by the destruction of a unique religious culture and its concomitant cultural objects'.[46]

In the end, the element qualifying the present category of offences against humanity is the *mens rea* of hitting the community for the cultural identity of which the heritage in point represents an essential element. This intention may assume different degrees, possibly reaching the level of aiming at the total obliteration of the community concerned from the earth's surface. In the latter instance, the *mens rea* of the perpetrator meets the requirements of the subjective element of the crime of genocide. In this respect, although according to the predominant view intentional destruction of cultural heritage may not be considered—as such—as an act of genocide,[47] it nevertheless may represent an 'evidence of an intent to physically destroy the group', on the condition that it is accompanied by the 'physical or biological destruction' of members of the group to whom the heritage concerned belongs.[48] In other words, deliberate destruction of cultural heritage of particular significance for a living community may represent, if the latter condition is met, evidence of the intent to commit genocide.

---

[45] See *Prosecutor v Blaskić*, Case IT-95-14-T, Trial Chamber, judgment of 3 March 2000, paras 227 and 421.

[46] See *Prosecutor v Kordić & Cerkez*, Case IT-95-14/2-T, Trial Chamber, judgment of 26 February 2001, para 207. See also, among others, *Prosecutor v Blaskić*, Case IT-95-14-A, Appeals Chamber, judgment of 29 July 2004, paras 144–9; *Prosecutor v Brđanin*, Case IT-99-36-T, Trial Chamber, judgment of 1 September 2004, para 1050; *Prosecutor v Krajišnik*, Case IT-00-39-T, Trial Chamber, judgment of 27 September 2006, paras 180–3; *Prosecutor v Martić*, Case IT-95-11-T, judgment of 12 June 2007, para 399; *Prosecutor v Milutinović, Šainović, Ojdanić, Pavković, Lazarević, Lukić*, Case IT-05-87-T, judgment of 26 February 2009, para 205; *Prosecutor v Đorđević*, Case IT-05-87/1-T, Trial Chamber, judgment of 23 February 2011, para 1771.

[47] See *Application of the Convention on the Prevention and Punishment of the Crime of Genocide (Bosnia and Herzegovina v Serbia and Montenegro)*, ICJ Reports (2007) 43, para 344, according to which '[t]he destruction of historical, cultural and religious heritage cannot be considered to constitute the deliberate infliction of conditions of life calculated to bring about the physical destruction of the group. Although such destruction may be highly significant inasmuch as it is directed to the elimination of all traces of the cultural or religious presence of a group, and contrary to other legal norms, it does not fall within the categories of acts of genocide'; International Law Commission, Commentary on the International Law Commission Draft Code of Crimes against the Peace and Security of Mankind, Report of the International Law Commission on the work of its 48th session, 6 May–26 July 1996, Official Documents of the United Nations General Assembly's 51st Session, Supplement No 10 (UN Doc A/51/10), 90–1 (stating that the notion of genocide only refers to 'the material destruction of a group either by physical or by biological means, not the destruction of the national, linguistic, religious, cultural or other identity of a particular group. The national or religious element and the racial or ethnic element are not taken into consideration in the definition of the word "destruction", which must be taken only in its material sense, its physical or biological sense').

[48] See ICTY, *Prosecutor v Krstić*, Case IT-98-33-T, Trial Chamber, judgment of 2 August 2001, para 580; *Application of the Convention on the Prevention and Punishment of the Crime of Genocide (Bosnia and Herzegovina v Serbia and Montenegro)*, para 344.

## D. Offences against culture as breaches of collective rights

The preceding analysis shows that offences against culture assume a peculiar characterization when their perpetration constitutes a violation of fundamental human rights. The instances in which this situation occurs probably represent the majority of cases of offences against culture, and, for sure, the most awful ones. The symbiosis between culture and human rights may assume countless shades of colour: as emphasized by the HRC, 'culture manifests itself in many forms';[49] it therefore translates into an innumerable amount of specific prerogatives, the infringement of any of which produces an offence against culture. This is the reason why offences against culture may also take innumerable forms, the majority of which affect social dynamics in which cultural rights are conceived, practised, and enjoyed in the context of a community, individual cultural rights being subsumed within the rights of the collectivity. To use again the words of the HRC, in order to protect certain human rights 'positive measures by States may also be necessary *to protect the identity of a minority*'.[50] In most cases, therefore, offences against culture affect a community as a whole, and it is consequently essential—when this happens—that they are treated as such. This presupposes that the measures to be adopted in view of suppressing and remedying the said offences must be conceived as measures taken in favour of a *community*—and not simply of a sum of individuals—in light of the specific needs and expectations of the community concerned.

## 3. Preventing Offences against Culture through Cultural Heritage-Related International Legal Norms

Suppressing and remedying represent two distinct moments of the action for the safeguarding of culture as well as of the rights related to it. According to the *Oxford English Dictionary*, the term 'suppress' means '[t]o put down by force or authority', but also '[t]o prevent or inhibit (an action or phenomenon)'. Therefore, the action of suppressing may be intended as both keeping something from happening and putting something to an end. Suppression may therefore refer to two different moments: first, the phase of *prevention*, aimed at avoiding, *ex ante*, that something will happen; secondly, the stage of *repression*, that is the action aimed at bringing an act already performed—in total or in part—to an end. Differently, the verb *remedy* means '[t]o put right, reform (a state of things); to rectify, make good', as well as to 'provide redress to'. It refers to an action carried out *ex post*, ie after the event (in our case, the offence against culture) has taken place, an action which is aimed at restoring the pre-existing situation and reinstating—to the maximum extent possible—the correct order in the society. It is important to stress that in some cases the phase of repression is strictly linked to that of remedying, as—especially in the mind of the victims—an offence may not be really repressed until justice is

---

[49] See HRC, *General Comment No. 23*, para 7.
[50] See note 21 above (and corresponding text, emphasis added).

done through establishing and operating effective remedies. Needless to say, while in the event that the phase of prevention is successful no further step is needed (as the offensive event does not occur at all), when the offence is 'simply' repressed the phase of remedy usually remains necessary, for the reason that the negative effects of the offence have actually been produced and reparation is consequentially needed.

There are several methods which may potentially be used in order to suppress and remedy offences against culture, the most significant of which are reliance on international conventions, use of judicial enforcement, as well as international cooperation. Each of them, however, present different potentialities with respect to the different actions of suppressing and remedying offences against culture.

As regards reliance on cultural heritage-related treaties, while it could prima facie appear the most direct avenue to act against the offences in point—as they have been created with the specific purpose of safeguarding culture—in the real world they usually exhaust their utility in the context of the stage of *prevention* of the said offences, as they generally offer very little perspective in terms of *ex-post* suppression and remedying.

In addition, when thinking about international conventions on cultural heritage, one could assert provocatively that most of them resemble—more than real treaties—declarations of principles. Indeed, such a provocation is not too far from reality, particularly with respect to the conventions aimed at safeguarding the intangible aspects of culture, namely the 2003 Convention for the Safeguarding of the Intangible Cultural Heritage and the 2005 Convention on the Protection and Promotion of the Diversity of Cultural Expressions. This is particularly unfortunate, in light of the fact that a huge part of offences against culture which translate into breaches of the fundamental human rights of the victims—probably the majority—affect immaterial aspects of culture. In this respect, the two conventions just quoted are of virtually no use in terms of suppression and remedying, while they are of relatively little use when it comes to preventing the offences in point. As a matter of fact, it is likely that the Convention for the Safeguarding of the Intangible Cultural Heritage may help to prevent offences related to elements of such an heritage inscribed on the Representative List of the Intangible Cultural Heritage of Humanity or in the List of Intangible Cultural Heritage in Need of Urgent Safeguarding, established respectively by Articles 16 and 17 of the Convention. Inscription on one of these two lists may indeed allow the cultural element concerned to attain wide international visibility, which may usually persuade the territorial state to ensure the safeguarding of such an element if it wants to avoid being attributed a negative profile in the eyes of the international community.

This process has worked efficiently for the World Heritage Convention—concerning tangible immovable heritage inscribed on the World Heritage List—since the 1970s, as in many instances states have given up their intention to make world heritage properties the object of activities (usually of economic character) which could potentially threaten their integrity due to the fear of achieving bad international visibility as a consequence of such behaviour. However, the cases of Oman's

Arabian Oryx Sanctuary and Germany's Dresden Elbe Valley[51] demonstrate that, when a state considers an interest at odds with the protection of world heritage really predominant over the latter, there is virtually no way to prevent the offence against the property concerned. At this point, the only 'penalty' available against the responsible state is to delete such a property from the World Heritage List. However, considering that the very 'philosophical' purpose of the World Heritage Convention is to protect the heritage concerned in the interest of the international community as a whole, in the end it is not really the territorial state which is going to be damaged by the deletion of its property from the List, but rather all of humanity. Therefore, not only does the offence against culture remain, but (paradoxically) in a way it is doubled: indeed, the first offence is the one committed by the territorial state through not complying with its duties under the World Heritage Convention and affecting the cultural value of the property concerned; the second offence occurs when such a property is taken out from the World Heritage List and, for this reason, in the future will no longer enjoy the qualified protection reserved to world heritage properties. As for possible reactions by the other states parties to the Convention when a situation of this kind takes place, in practice, so far, they have been limited to very soft statements of sorrow.[52]

Apart from the World Heritage Convention, the best conventional regime in the field of cultural heritage protection—in terms of prevention of offences against culture—is undoubtedly represented by the 1954 Hague Convention for the Protection of Cultural Property in the Event of Armed Conflict and its two Protocols. It is a well-consolidated regime that has been notably improved by the Second Protocol of 1999, which has already been ratified by 64 states.[53] It establishes a well-balanced system characterized by the circumstance that the same state interested in ensuring the protection of cultural properties that may be the object of belligerent acts—ie the territorial state—is the first to be bound to make such properties the object of protective measures.[54] The relative success of the system of

---

[51] See note 19 above.

[52] See, for instance, the declaration by the Ambassador and Permanent Delegate of Spain to UNESCO, María Jesús San Segundo—who was chairing the 33rd Session of the World Heritage Committee in Seville, in 2009, when the site of Dresden Elbe Valley was removed from the World Heritage List—saying that '[e]very time we fail to preserve a site, we share the pain of the State Party' (see <http://whc.unesco.org/en/news/522>); more than a statement of condemnation of the misconduct of Germany, this seems to be an expression of solidarity with the German government, as if it would have been forced by somebody else to build a four-lane bridge in the middle of the cultural landscape...

[53] See <http://portal.unesco.org/la/convention.asp?KO=15207&language=E> (accessed 30 July 2013). Although this ratification rate may appear quite limited in comparison with that of the Convention for the Safeguarding of the Intangible Cultural Heritage (154 parties at the moment of this writing; see <http://portal.unesco.org/la/convention.asp?language=E&KO=17116>) and the Convention on the Protection and Promotion of the Diversity of Cultural Expressions (ratified by 130 states and by the European Union; see <http://portal.unesco.org/la/convention.asp?KO=31038&language=E>), it is to be noted that the 1999 Protocol—contrary to the two conventions just quoted—includes a number of real obligations in the technical sense of the term.

[54] See eg Art 3 of the Convention, according to which '[t]he High Contracting Parties undertake to prepare in time of peace for the safeguarding of cultural property situated within their own territory against the foreseeable effects of an armed conflict, by taking such measures as they consider appropriate'.

the 1954 Hague Convention is attested by the fact that the principal rule arising from it, ie the prohibition of acts of violence against cultural heritage in the event of armed conflicts, has reached the status of customary international law, and has been applied as such by several states not parties to the Convention,[55] in addition to the ratifying ones. In the end, therefore, the system in point has proven to be relatively effective in preventing offences against culture in the event of armed conflict, even though violations to its rules are frequent (but this is a reality which is intrinsic to virtually all international law instruments).

With respect to the conventions concerning the regulation of international movement of cultural objects, the picture is not as (relatively) optimistic as the one depicted with respect to the systems of the World Heritage Convention and of the 1954 Hague Convention. Indeed, the main relevant treaties—ie the UNESCO Convention on the Means of Prohibiting and Preventing the Illicit Import, Export and Transfer of Ownership of Cultural Property of 1970 and the 1995 UNIDROIT Convention on Stolen or Illegally Exported Cultural Objects—are obviously inapplicable retroactively, and therefore only apply to the situations originated after their entry into force for both (or all) the states involved in the controversy. In addition, the 1970 Convention is quite ineffective both in preventing the exit of cultural properties from their state of origin in violation of its law and in ensuring their return thereafter. At the same time, the UNIDROIT Convention, although much more effective in legal terms, has been ratified by a quite limited number of states, not including the countries which traditionally represent the most important importers of cultural objects.[56] In practice, states which make a claim for the return of illegally exported cultural properties may rely on the conventions in point only in very limited cases, and are usually forced to find alternative means in order to achieve their goal, in particular through contracts of private law with foreign museums and other institutions.[57]

Similar considerations may be developed with respect to the field of underwater cultural heritage. In this writer's opinion, the principal convention in this field, that is the 2001 Convention on the Protection of the Underwater Cultural Heritage, is indeed the result of an unpersuasive compromise between the opposite and hardly reconcilable views of different groups of states. On the one hand, certain countries support the idea that the right of property over the heritage concerned should be recognized in favour of the state having a cultural, historical, or archaeological link with it, or—at least—that the preservation of underwater cultural heritage should be ensured *in situ*. On the other hand, other states defend a relatively unconditioned freedom of search and occupation of the heritage concerned—of course provided that it is located outside the territorial

---

[55] See Francioni and Lenzerini (2003) 635–7; Francioni, 'Beyond State Sovereignty: The Protection of Cultural Heritage as a Shared Interest of Humanity', 25 *Michigan Journal of International Law* (2004) 1 at 6.

[56] See <http://www.unidroit.org/english/implement/i-95.pdf> (accessed 2 August 2012). At the time of writing, the Convention had 33 states parties.

[57] See eg the 2006 Agreement between the Italian government and the Metropolitan Museum of New York (on file with the author).

sea of whatever state—in favour of everybody, including private treasure hunt-
ers. In addition, although the Convention tries to limit—to the maximum extent
possible—the effects of the law of salvage or law of finds, obviously the countries
promoting and recognizing these laws in their own domestic legal orders carefully
avoid ratifying the treaty in point, which, at the moment of this writing, has 44
states parties only.[58]

The category of 'international legal norms' is not limited to international treaties,
even though the latter usually represent the most effective tools—among the said
norms—in terms of prevention of violations and enforcement of state obligations.
However, one should not ignore the possible role that may be played in this respect—
depending on the circumstances—by customary international law, on the one hand,
and by soft law instruments on the other.

With respect to the former, a few principles of customary international law exist in
the field of cultural heritage protection which may play a more or less effective role
in preventing offences against culture. The first of these customary rules is the general principle according to which cultural heritage must be safeguarded in the interest of the international community as a whole;[59] although this principle is relatively
vague in terms of its reach and the specific duties arising from it, it has nevertheless
contributed to the development and progressive strengthening of a global awareness
that at least the most exceptional elements of cultural heritage must be protected as
a matter of legal and moral responsibility. This awareness, for example, led the whole
international community, in 2001, to react harshly against the destruction of the two
Buddha statues in the valley of Bamiyan by the Taliban regime,[60] and in some cases
may persuade a state to refrain from performing acts of hostility against cultural heritage, especially with respect to elements of this heritage which are particularly visible
internationally.

The general rule just referred to is complemented by a more specific principle—
also of a customary character—prohibiting acts of violence against cultural property
in the event of armed conflict, with the only exception of acts determined by imperative military necessity.[61] This principle has been expressed, inter alia, by the ICTY,
according to which 'destruction or wilful damage done to institutions dedicated to
religion...has...already been criminalised under customary international law'.[62]
Such a customary rule, in some cases, has actually proven effective in convincing states
to spare cultural property when carrying out belligerent activities, as demonstrated
by the example of the United States, which, well before ratifying the 1954 Hague
Convention for the Protection of Cultural Property in the Event of Armed Conflict,[63]

---

[58] See <http://portal.unesco.org/la/convention.asp?KO=13520&language=E> (accessed 30 June 2013).
[59] See Francioni and Lenzerini (2003) 633–5.
[60] See Francioni and Lenzerini (2003) 621. The same happened with respect to the destruction of
the cultural heritage of Timbuktu; see note 41 above.
[61] Francioni and Lenzerini (2003) 635–7. See also note 55 above and corresponding text.
[62] See *Prosecutor v Kordić & Cerkez*, para 206.
[63] The United States deposited its instrument of ratification of the Convention on 13 March 2009;
see <http://portal.unesco.org/la/convention.asp?KO=13637&language=E> (accessed 2 August 2012).

included in its military manuals the instruction of respecting cultural property during military operations.[64]

While the existence of the provision of customary law just described is reasonably undisputed, more controversy exists with respect to the actual existence of another related principle, also of customary international law, that is the rule dictating the prohibition of intentional destruction of cultural heritage also in time of peace, supported by the present and other authors.[65] Although the existence of such a rule seems to be confirmed by relevant practice and supported by logical arguments, the negative position would appear to be corroborated by the 2003 UNESCO Declaration concerning the Intentional Destruction of Cultural Heritage,[66] conceived and adopted in reaction to the wanton destruction of the Buddhas of Bamiyan of March 2001: first, the *travaux préparatoires* of the Declaration explicitly affirm that 'uncertainties [are] still evident in customary international law on the existence of rules providing clear obligations to protect cultural heritage from intentional destruction both in time of peace and in time of armed conflict';[67] secondly, the adopted text shows particular obsequiousness to state sovereignty, expressing all duties contemplated by its articles in the conditional form 'should' and not including a strong and explicit prohibition for states to perpetrate acts of hostility against cultural heritage located in their own territory.[68] In this writer's opinion, however, the inadequacy of the 2003 Declaration cannot be taken as a decisive element to deny the existence of a customary rule in the field, especially if one takes into account the politically driven context in which the negotiations leading to the adoption of the Declaration took place.[69] Apart from the problem of whether or not the provision of customary international law in point exists, it is not to be excluded a priori that the Declaration may play some role in preventing offences against culture, even though—due to its soft law status—it cannot produce state obligations per se.

Finally, a very specific rule—which may also be considered as having reached the status of customary international law[70]—is represented by the right of indigenous peoples to recognition and preservation of their cultural identity, in light

---

[64] See eg *Operational Law Handbook* (2007), available at <http://www.loc.gov/rr/frd/Military_Law/pdf/operational-law-handbook_2007.pdf> (accessed 2 August 2012), at VII.D.2 (affirming, with reference to the 1954 Hague Convention, that '[a]lthough the United States has not ratified the treaty, it regards its provisions as relevant to the targeting process').

[65] See Francioni and Lenzerini (2003) 638; Lenzerini (2004) 132–5 and 139–40. See contra, O'Keefe (2004). See also the comprehensive and lucid assessment on this issue by Vrdoljak (2007) 382–5.

[66] The full text of the Declaration is available at <http://portal.unesco.org/en/ev.php-URL_ID=17718&URL_DO=DO_TOPIC&URL_SECTION=201.html> (accessed 2 August 2012).

[67] See Draft UNESCO Declaration concerning the Intentional Destruction of Cultural Heritage, UNESCO Doc 32C/25, 17 July 2003, Annex II, 3, para 9.

[68] For a more detailed comment on the 2003 Declaration, see Lenzerini (2004).

[69] The present writer participated in the whole course of the formation of the Declaration, first as an independent expert and then as member of the Italian delegation during the diplomatic negotiations.

[70] See International Law Association, Committee on the Rights of Indigenous Peoples, 'The Hague Conference (2010): Interim Report' (2010), available at <http://www.ila-hq.org/en/committees/index.cfm/cid/1024> (accessed 2 August 2012), 51.

of the decisive importance of culture as an essential prerequisite to allowing said peoples to survive as distinct human communities. The right in point presupposes that all prerogatives which are essential to the cultural identity of indigenous peoples, including some elements of their own cultural heritage, are adequately safeguarded. The existence of the obligation in point—in conjunction with other obligations pertaining to indigenous peoples' rights—is today generally perceived by the international community, as demonstrated, inter alia, by the almost universal support manifested in favour of the 2007 United Nations Declaration on the Rights of Indigenous Peoples.[71] Such an obligation may actually have an important impact, in contemporary international law, on the prevention of offences against indigenous peoples' cultural heritage.

In sum, international legal norms on cultural heritage may actually play a significant role in the prevention of offences against culture. In particular, they may have an important impact especially with respect to those, among the said offences, which are suitable of infringing state interests (eg in the case of the prohibition of carrying out acts of hostility against cultural property in the event of armed conflict), the relevant international norms having in most cases the purpose of defending such interests. In addition, in consideration of the special philosophy of the World Heritage Convention—inspired by the aspiration to protect cultural heritage of outstanding universal value in the interest of the international community as a whole—also the general interest of humanity may benefit from the norms in point in terms of prevention of offences against culture. Furthermore, the interest of specific human groups—particularly indigenous peoples—that their own cultural heritage is not offended may also be defended by the said norms. However, in light of the relatively weak preventive force of international law in general, and international cultural heritage law in particular, the shield construed by international legal norms against offences against culture is inherently characterized by notable gaps and weaknesses, making the actual perpetration of such offences a daily reality all over the world. Action of the international community in this field therefore needs to rely on additional means which, once the preventive phase has been unsuccessful, concentrate on the stages of repression and remedying, in order to ensure the realization of justice in favour of victims.

## 4. Repressing Offences against Culture

As emphasized at the beginning of the previous section, the phase of suppression may be split into two different moments, ie prevention and repression. In principle, repression is an activity usually carried out through the use of force by some kind of authority—*de jure* or de facto—and expressed in operational action. In the reality of contemporary international law on cultural heritage, repression is

---

[71] The full text of the Declaration is available at <http://www.un.org/esa/socdev/unpfii/documents/DRIPS_en.pdf> (accessed 2 August 2012).

in most cases an exclusive task of national authorities, as the pertinent multilateral instruments do not obviously contemplate any mechanism of intervention by states (or international organizations) in territories outside their territorial sovereignty. In carrying out this task, the competent national authority should act not only in conformity with its own domestic law, but also with international obligations binding the state of which it is an organ.

In exceptional cases, however, it is possible that the stage of repression is carried out through means established by international law and in conformity with international legal rules. This may happen in a number of situations, for example in the event that the UN Security Council includes the task of protecting cultural property in the mandate of peacekeeping missions.[72] Another instance may occur in the case of possible bilateral agreements establishing a right to visit in favour of warships of each state party with respect to vessels having the nationality of the other party in order to repress illegal trade in underwater cultural heritage. One further example is offered by the case of military occupation, in the context of which the occupying power may have the responsibility (by treaty or as a matter of customary international law) to prevent the export of cultural heritage from the occupied territory[73] and/or, more in general, that of generally repressing offences against culture in such a territory.

In the specific event of offences prejudicing an interest of the international community as a whole, the possible activities of repression may be carried out by the competent bodies of the international organizations which represent the said interest (usually, in the field of culture, UNESCO). For example, when a (potential or actual) breach of the World Heritage Convention takes place, the World Heritage Committee may use all weapons at its disposal in order to bring such an offence to an end, particularly through threatening to inscribe the property concerned on

---

[72] See, in this respect, UNESCO, 9th Meeting of the High Contracting Parties to the 1954 Hague Convention for the Protection of Cultural Property in the Event of Armed Conflict, 12 December 2011, UNESCO Doc CLT-11/CONF/209/INF.1, 28 November 2011, 2.c (in which it is recommended to advance the request for the inclusion of a mention to 'the need to protect cultural property in the mandate of peace-keeping missions'); Secretary-General's Bulletin on the Observance by UN Forces of International Humanitarian Law, UN Doc ST/SGB/1999/13, 6 August 1999, para 6.6 (stating that '[t]he United Nations force is prohibited from attacking monuments of art, architecture or history, archaeological sites, works of art, places of worship and museums and libraries which constitute the cultural or spiritual heritage of peoples. In its area of operation, the United Nations force shall not use such cultural property or their immediate surroundings for purposes which might expose them to destruction or damage. Theft, pillage, misappropriation and any act of vandalism directed against cultural property is strictly prohibited').

[73] This obligation is contemplated, for example, in Art I.1 of the First Protocol to the Convention for the Protection of Cultural Property in the Event of Armed Conflict. See also UNSC Res 1483 (2003), 22 May 2003, adopted by a vote of 14-0, with Syria not present. It is notable that the United Kingdom and the United States, which were not parties to the 1954 Convention for the Protection of Cultural Property in the Event of Armed Conflict, supported the resolution. In particular, the Security Council decided that 'all Member States shall take appropriate steps to facilitate the safe return to Iraqi institutions of Iraqi cultural property and other items of archaeological, historical, cultural, rare scientific, and religious importance illegally removed from the Iraq National Museum, the National Library, and other locations in Iraq...and calls upon the United Nations Educational, Scientific, and Cultural Organization, Interpol, and other international organizations, as appropriate, to assist in the implementation of this paragraph' (para 7).

the List of World Heritage in Danger or to delete it from the World Heritage List. In these cases, however, the term 'repression' assumes a softer meaning than in the other cases, as, rather than an exercise of authoritative force, it takes the form of diplomatic or political effort.

## 5. Remedying Offences against Culture through Judicial Enforcement

Once an offence against culture has been perpetrated, the main quest is represented by the need of finding a remedy capable of removing—to the extent possible—the effects produced by such an offence. Available remedies vary depending on the characteristics of the offence, particularly on the identity of the affected entity. While no remedy is usually granted when the offence is only directed towards the international community as a whole, in the event that the affected body is a state (for instance in the case of a cultural property destroyed as a consequence of a bombing carried out during an armed conflict) it will be possible to rely on the usual methods for the resolution of international disputes, ranging from diplomatic means to the recourse to arbitration.

However, certainly the most interesting cases—as well as those with respect to which a remedy is most needed—are those in the context of which an offence against culture hits the value of individual and/or collective human rights. In this instance, the traditional remedy of diplomatic protection is of very little use, as it may play some role only in the event of offences of transnational character. This may happen, for instance, in consequence of an armed conflict, in the event that a cultural property destroyed by the attacking state had a special significance for specific persons and/or groups, to the extent that the destruction of the said property has led to the infringement of their human rights. Another case in which diplomatic protection may be useful to remedy an offence against culture suffered by specific persons is when such an offence is of 'symbolic' character, for example a statement of denigration, a racist declaration or a similar kind of offence made by a state official against a cultural group living in the territory of another country. As we will see in Section 8 below, the symbolic element has a huge significance when it comes to remedying offences against culture. Therefore, in the case just described, it may be necessary that adequate restoration takes place, and the state of nationality of the offended cultural group could well act in diplomatic protection on behalf of that group to pursue such a goal.

In any event, there is little doubt about the fact that, when an offence against culture translates into a prejudice against the human rights of specific communities and/or individuals, judicial enforcement—*where available*—represents the most immediate, direct, and effective means of remedying it. There are two main situations in the context of which the victims of offences against culture may have recourse to judicial protection, depending on the characteristic of the offence.

The first of these situations refers to cases in which the relevant offence is included in the second subcategory of the first category as resulting from the taxonomy developed above in Section 2, ie when cultural heritage is sacrificed to an interest legitimate in principle, but the realization of which produces a breach of human rights.[74] This situation may obviously concern rights expressly related to the enjoyment of cultural life—including, in particular, Article 27 ICCPR[75] and Article 15 of the 1966 International Covenant on Economic, Social and Cultural Rights (ICESCR)[76]—but also rights of a different kind, the realization of which requires, in light of the specific circumstances of the instant case, that certain cultural elements pertaining to the person(s) and/or community concerned are adequately safeguarded. In particular, as explained above in Section 2A, offences against culture may translate into breaches of the right of ownership by a community of its traditional lands and even of the prohibition of inhuman treatment (corresponding to a principle of *jus cogens*). Also, offences against culture may give rise to violations of the prohibition of racial discrimination.[77]

---

[74] See the examples described above, Section 2A.     [75] See above, Section 2A.

[76] 993 UNTS 3. Article 15 provides for, inter alia, the right of everyone to take part in cultural life. In its *General Comment No 21: Right of Everyone to Take Part in Cultural Life (Art 15, para 1 (a), of the International Covenant on Economic, Social and Cultural Rights)*, UN Doc. E/C.12/GC/21, 21 December 2009, the Committee on Economic, Social and Cultural Rights (CESCR) stressed that, in order for the right in point 'to be ensured, it requires from the State party both abstention (i.e., non-interference with the exercise of cultural practices and with access to cultural goods and services) and positive action (ensuring preconditions for participation, facilitation and promotion of cultural life, and access to and preservation of cultural goods)' (para 6); among the obligations of states in this respect, the following are included: '(a) Respect and protect cultural heritage in all its forms, in times of war and peace, and natural disasters; Cultural heritage must be preserved, developed, enriched and transmitted to future generations as a record of human experience and aspirations, in order to encourage creativity in all its diversity and to inspire a genuine dialogue between cultures. Such obligations include the care, preservation and restoration of historical sites, monuments, works of art and literary works, among others. (b) Respect and protect cultural heritage of all groups and communities, in particular the most disadvantaged and marginalized individuals and groups, in economic development and environmental policies and programmes;...(c) Respect and protect the cultural productions of indigenous peoples, including their traditional knowledge, natural medicines, folklore, rituals and other forms of expression; This includes protection from illegal or unjust exploitation of their lands, territories and resources by State entities or private or transnational enterprises and corporations' (para 50).

[77] The need to safeguard culture as a prerequisite for the enjoyment of the right not to be racially discriminated has been affirmed by the Committee on the Elimination of Racial Discrimination (CERD) on several occasions. The Committee, for example, in 1996 stressed that 'Governments should be sensitive towards the rights of persons belonging to ethnic groups, particularly their right to lead lives of dignity, to preserve their culture'; see *General Recommendation No 21: Right to Self-determination*, 23 August 1996, available at <http://www.unhchr.ch/tbs/doc.nsf/(Symbol)/dc59 8941c9e68a1a8025651e004d31d0?Opendocument> (accessed 2 August 2012), para 5. On another occasion, with respect to indigenous peoples, the CERD pointed out that states are required to '(a) Recognize and respect indigenous distinct culture, history, language and way of life as an enrichment of the State's cultural identity and to promote its preservation;...(e) Ensure that indigenous communities can exercise their rights to practise and revitalize their cultural traditions and customs and to preserve and to practise their languages'; see *General Recommendation No 23: Indigenous Peoples*, 18 August 1997, available at <http://www.unhchr.ch/tbs/doc.nsf/(Symbol)/73984290dfea022b802565 160056fe1c?Opendocument>, para 4. Finally, with regard to people of African descent, the CERD stated that they are entitled to, inter alia, '(a) The right to property and to the use, conservation and protection of lands traditionally occupied by them and to natural resources in cases where their ways of life and culture are linked to their utilization of lands and resources; (b) The right to their cultural identity, to keep, maintain and foster their mode of life and forms of organization, culture, languages

This reality is the result of the evolutionary interpretation of human rights standards included in international conventions of universal and regional application; it is perfectly consistent with general rules of treaty interpretation[78] and is generally shared by human rights monitoring bodies. For example, the African Commission on Human and Peoples' Rights recently manifested its view that

protecting human rights goes beyond the duty not to destroy or deliberately weaken minority groups, but requires respect for, and protection of, their religious and cultural heritage essential to their group identity, including buildings and sites such as libraries, churches, mosques, temples and synagogues... [The Commission]... understands culture to mean that complex whole which includes a spiritual and physical association with one's ancestral land, knowledge, belief, art, law, morals, customs, and any other capabilities and habits acquired by humankind as a member of society—the sum total of the material and spiritual activities and products of a given social group that distinguish it from other similar groups.[79]

In the instant case, concerning an indigenous people living in Kenya, the Commission found that the right to preserve the community's cultural identity is closely connected to the possibility to live in its own traditional lands. States have the duty to 'tolerate diversity and to introduce measures that protect identity groups different from those of the majority/dominant group',[80] as well as 'to promote cultural rights including the creation of opportunities, policies, institutions, or other mechanisms that allow for different cultures and ways of life to exist, develop in view of the challenges' faced by the group concerned.[81] As a consequence, the forced eviction of the community concerned from its ancestral lands led the state to infringe a number of rights of both the community as a whole and its members individually, namely the right to freedom of conscience, profession, and free practice of religion, the right to property, the right to take part in the cultural life of the community, the right of peoples to freely dispose of their wealth and natural resources, as well as the right to their economic, social, and cultural development.

One notable feature of the said evolutionary interpretation is represented by the fact that—although the rights contemplated by the relevant treaties are

---

and religious expressions; (c) The right to the protection of their traditional knowledge and their cultural and artistic heritage'. See *General Recommendation No 34. Racial Discrimination Against People of African Descent*, UN Doc CERD/C/GC/34, 3 October 2011, para 4.

[78] See, in particular, Art 31(3)(c) Vienna Convention on the Law of Treaties (1969), 1155 UNTS 331, according to which, in interpreting a treaty, there shall be taken into account, together with the context, '[a]ny relevant rules of international law applicable in the relations between the parties'. This rule corresponds to a well-established principle of customary international law.

[79] See *Centre for Minority Rights Development (Kenya) and Minority Rights Group International on behalf of Endorois Welfare Council v Kenya* (ACHPR) Communication No 276/2003, 4 February 2010, available at <http://www.unhcr.org/refworld/publisher,ACHPR,,,4b8275a12,0.html> (accessed 2 August 2012), para 241.

[80] See <http://www.unhcr.org/refworld/publisher,ACHPR,,,4b8275a12,0.html> (accessed 2 August 2012), para 246.

[81] See <http://www.unhcr.org/refworld/publisher,ACHPR,,,4b8275a12,0.html> (accessed 2 August 2012), para 248.

in most cases reserved to individuals (with the only exceptions of the right to self-determination of peoples contemplated by common Article 1 of the two UN Covenants of 1966 and a few rights included in the 1981 African Charter on Human and Peoples' Rights[82])—they have been 'adapted' to cover in practice collective rights; indeed, when it comes to cultural rights, they may hardly be conceived as prerogatives that the individual may enjoy in isolation. As emphasized by the Committee on Economic, Social and Cultural Rights (CESCR), the right of everyone to take part in cultural life 'may denote the individual or the collective; in other words, cultural rights may be exercised by a person (a) as an individual, (b) in association with others, or (c) within a community or group, as such'.[83] As already noted in Section 2D above, this circumstance is to be taken into account adequately—as it is actually taken in the practice of human rights monitoring bodies—when remedying offences against culture. This aspect attains special significance with respect to the issue of reparation, and will therefore be the object of further assessment in Section 8 below.

A different kind of judicial remedy to offences against culture is offered by the courts having the task of enforcing international criminal law. The foremost example in this respect—with regard to the specific object of the present enquiry—is offered by the ICTY,[84] but other international or mixed tribunals have the competence to deal with crimes against cultural heritage, particularly the ICC[85] and the Extraordinary Chambers in the Courts of Cambodia (ECCC), established in 2003 to prosecute members of the Khmer Rouge for serious violations of Cambodian criminal law and international law perpetrated during the period between 17 April 1975 and 6 January 1979.[86] These tribunals, however, usually bear with themselves two problems, which make their action—in terms of *remedying*—much less effective than human rights courts: (a) their competence is typically very limited both in time and in space; (b) the purpose of the tribunals in point is to secure the persons responsible for international crimes to justice—as *hostis humani generi*—rather than providing redress in favour of victims; they therefore give realization to the phase of remedying only to a limited extent.[87] These problems, though, have been remarkably eased as regards the ICC; indeed, this Court is of a permanent character, is in principle competent to exercise its jurisdiction over the crimes perpetrated in the territory of, or

---

[82] 21 ILM (1992) 58.      [83] See CESCR, *General Comment No 21*, para 9.

[84] See above, Section 2C.      [85] See note 44 above (and corresponding text).

[86] According to Art 6 of the Amended Cambodian Law on the Establishment of the Extraordinary Chambers in the Courts of Cambodia for the Prosecution of Crimes Committed During the Period of Democratic Kampuchea (2004), available at <http://www.eccc.gov.kh/sites/default/files/legal-documents/KR_Law_as_amended_27_Oct_2004_Eng.pdf> (accessed 2 August 2012), the Extraordinary Chambers have the power to bring to trial all suspects who committed or ordered the commission of, inter alia, 'destruction and serious damage to property, not justified by military necessity and carried out unlawfully and wantonly'. In addition, in light of Art 7 of the same Law, the Chambers 'have the power to bring to trial all Suspects most responsible for the destruction of cultural property during armed conflict pursuant to the 1954 Hague Convention for Protection of Cultural Property in the Event of Armed Conflict'.

[87] For additional reflections on this point, see Section 8 below.

elsewhere by a national of, all states which have ratified its Statute,[88] and, as will be explained in Section 8 below, has the competence to order reparations in favour of victims.

The action of international criminal law tribunals may be complemented by domestic courts, not only through applying their own national law. These courts, by virtue of the principle of *universal jurisdiction*, could indeed try persons responsible for international crimes subject only to the condition that they are present in their national territory. However, domestic courts are usually very reluctant to use the opportunity in point if it is not expressly contemplated by their national law on criminal procedure. For this reason, it is very unusual that they actually rely on universal jurisdiction, even in the event that the person concerned is responsible for particularly awful crimes.[89] The situation may be different when an obligation to prosecute—or, as it is usually the case, an alternative between two options, ie extradite or prosecute *(aut dedere aut judicare)*—is included in an international treaty. With respect to offences against culture, specifically those occurring in the event of armed conflict, the Second Protocol to the Hague Convention of 1954 for the Protection of Cultural Property in the Event of Armed Conflict of 1999[90] devotes an entire chapter (Chapter 4) to this topic. Article 16, in particular, requires states parties to 'take the necessary legislative measures to establish its jurisdiction' with respect to individuals responsible for serious violations of the Protocol itself.[91] What is especially notable about this article is that, while as a general rule jurisdiction must be established only with respect to offences committed in the territory of the state concerned or allegedly perpetrated by a national of the said state, in the event of particularly serious crimes against cultural property, the only condition to be met in order to make prosecution possible *(rectius: mandatory)* is that the alleged offender is *present* in its territory.[92] The Protocol, therefore, transposes the principle of universal jurisdiction in its text, at least with respect to the most intolerable offences against cultural property taking place in the event of armed conflict. This rule is complemented by the principle *aut dedere aut judicare*,

---

[88] See Art 12 of the Rome Statute of the International Criminal Court. At the time of writing, 122 states were parties to the Statute; see <http://treaties.un.org/pages/ViewDetails.aspx?src=TREATY&mtdsg_no=XVIII-10&chapter=18&lang=en> (accessed 30 March 2013).

[89] Among the few exceptions to this trend one may recall the renowned case of the former Chilean dictator Augusto Pinochet, tried in United Kingdom and Spain at the end of 1990s; on this case, with a focus on the principle of universal jurisdiction, see Roht-Arriaza, 'The Pinochet Precedent and Universal Jurisdiction', 35 *New England Law Review* (2001) 311.

[90] See note 7 above.

[91] According to Art 15(1), the following are serious violations of the Protocol: 'a. making cultural property under enhanced protection the object of attack; b. using cultural property under enhanced protection or its immediate surroundings in support of military action; c. extensive destruction or appropriation of cultural property protected under the Convention and this Protocol; d. making cultural property protected under the [1954 Hague] Convention and this Protocol the object of attack; e. theft, pillage or misappropriation of, or acts of vandalism directed against cultural property protected under the Convention.'

[92] The offences with respect to which this rule applies are those set forth in Art 15, sub-paras (a) to (c); see previous note.

also contemplated by the Protocol, as clearly shown by the combination of Articles 17(1)[93] and 18.[94]

## 6. A Cooperative Approach to Remedying and Preventing Offences Against Culture

According to the above-mentioned Mexico City Declaration on Cultural Policies, the assertion of 'cultural identity...contributes to the liberation of peoples'.[95] This sentence expresses a very delicate concept, open to different understandings (even misunderstandings) and interpretations. It is not a mystery that an egocentric and blind assertion of one's own cultural identity may lead to prejudice, hatred, discrimination, intolerance, persecution and, eventually, to ethnic conflicts, as well as that the reference to the term *liberation* may be misinterpreted as 'emancipation' from, and 'victory' over, different cultural models. The sentence quoted above is therefore like a big flame, which, if handled in the right way may enlighten humanity and promote shared understanding of cultural diversity; at the same time, if managed incorrectly, it may lead the world to burn in the ashes of hatred and fanaticism. Therefore, it is particularly important to spread an education of multiculturalism—allowing people to realize that the assertion of one's own culture stops exactly where the expectations of another's culture begin—for the purpose of construing a stable social environment of solidarity and mutual understanding among people that is effectively capable of preventing offences against culture on a long-lasting basis.

Offences against culture usually represent a very complex reality, as they are often like a deep cut in the soul of the victims which is not easy to treat, and its effects may continue to be conveyed from generation to generation for a very long time, as is demonstrated by a number of unfortunate events which have occurred

---

[93] According to Art 17(1), '[t]he Party in whose territory the alleged offender of an offence set forth in Article 15 sub-paragraphs 1 (a) to (c) is found to be present shall, *if it does not extradite that person*, submit, without exception whatsoever and without undue delay, the case to its competent authorities, for the purpose of prosecution, through proceedings in accordance with its domestic law or with, if applicable, the relevant rules of international law' (emphasis added).

[94] Article 18 states as follows: '1. The offences set forth in Article 15 sub-paragraphs 1 (a) to (c) shall be deemed to be included as extraditable offences in any extradition treaty existing between any of the Parties before the entry into force of this Protocol. Parties undertake to include such offences in every extradition treaty to be subsequently concluded between them. 2. When a Party which makes extradition conditional on the existence of a treaty receives a request for extradition from another Party with which it has no extradition treaty, the requested Party may, at its option, consider the present Protocol as the legal basis for extradition in respect of offences as set forth in Article 15 sub-paragraphs 1 (a) to (c). 3. Parties which do not make extradition conditional on the existence of a treaty shall recognise the offences set forth in Article 15 sub-paragraphs 1 (a) to (c) as extraditable offences between them, subject to the conditions provided by the law of the requested Party. 4. If necessary, offences set forth in Article 15 sub-paragraphs 1 (a) to (c) shall be treated, for the purposes of extradition between Parties, as if they had been committed not only in the place in which they occurred but also in the territory of the Parties that have established jurisdiction in accordance with Article 16 paragraph 1.'

[95] Mexico City Declaration on Cultural Policies, para 2.

in recent times, like the Balkan and Rwandan civil wars. It is for this reason that suppressing and remedying these offences through authoritative means (including judicial action) may sometimes not be enough to remove the effects of the offence from the mind of people, and may even produce the opposite result and instil new resentment in those who feel victimized as a result of the outcome of the controversy originated by the offence itself.

In light of the foregoing, an alternative method for remedying offences against culture rests in what the 1976 UNESCO Recommendation on Participation by the People at Large in Cultural Life and their Contribution to It[96] calls 'communication', ie 'relations between groups or individuals desirous of freely exchanging or pooling information, ideas and knowledge with a view to promoting dialogue, concerted action, understanding and a sense of community while respecting their originality and their differences, in order to strengthen mutual understanding and peace'.[97] When offences against culture are of such a kind to affect the rights and cultural identity of a community, communication, or dialogue, is exactly the path to be taken in order to (re)build a culture of harmony and reconciliation. Certainly it is a difficult path, but past experience shows that it may actually work. Indeed, on a number of occasions, especially in the aftermath of armed conflicts, UNESCO has developed programmes aimed at reopening a dialogue between the communities involved in the conflict, usually through the reconstruction of local cultural heritage. For instance, on 25 June 1999 UNESCO launched the reconstruction of the old Stari Most, the Mostar Bridge, in Bosnia and Herzegovina,[98] after it was able to find a point of convergence between the formerly enemy Muslim and Croat communities living in the town. On that day, in the presence of the UNESCO Director General, the mayors of the Eastern and Western parts of Mostar met and shook hands again, for the first time in several years.[99] Of course it is essential that, in promoting and carrying out these initiatives, the communities concerned are adequately involved, taking into account and balancing the respective grievances and expectations in order to find a mutually satisfactory and stable solution.[100]

Although the method described in this section is aimed at *remedying* offences against culture, it ultimately produces the effect of *preventing* the recurrence of such offences, exactly through building a stable, harmonic relationship between the communities concerned. For this reason, it is a method with a double value, and should therefore be promoted to the maximum extent possible.

---

[96] The full text of the Declaration is available at <http://portal.unesco.org/en/ev.php-URL_ID=13097&URL_DO=DO_TOPIC&URL_SECTION=201.html> (accessed 2 August 2012).

[97] See para 2(c).     [98] See Section 2C above.

[99] See Lévi-Strauss, 'The Action of UNESCO in Bosnia and Herzegovina to Restore Respect and Mutual Understanding Among Local Communities through the Preservation of Cultural Heritage', in F. Maniscalco (ed), *La Tutela del Patrimonio Culturale in caso di conflitto* (2002) 143.

[100] More comprehensively on this issue, see Lenzerini, 'Fostering Tolerance and Mutual Understanding among Peoples', in A.A. Yusuf (ed), *Standard-setting in UNESCO. Volume I: Normative Action in Education, Science and Culture* (2007) 187 at 200–1.

### 7. Combining Different Methods: Prosecution followed by Reconciliation as the Most Effective Means for Remedying and Preventing Offences Against Culture

It is clear that, in an *ideal world*, the method for remedying (and preventing) offences against culture described in the previous section would represent in itself the perfect option to rely on. In the *real world*, however, certain problems may arise making it hardly usable, especially if the right conditions for it to work properly are not created. In particular, it is certainly possible that the victims of an offence against culture are not willing to establish a constructive dialogue with the offender(s), especially when they continue to sense a strong feeling of injustice. In this kind of situation, people may be unable to leave the past behind, and any attempt to promote dialogue would therefore be destined to fail.

In these cases it is consequently necessary to remove the said feeling of injustice, and the best (probably the only) way to achieve this goal is to actually take injustices away. As will be elaborated in the following section, sometimes punishment of perpetrators or—at least—official recognition of the wrong by a court represents an essential step in order not only to allow the victims to have a sense of redress, but also to reconstitute the correct social and spiritual order within the society. Pending fulfilment of this condition, it is obviously impossible for the community concerned to agree to any kind of reconciliation with the perpetrators. It is for this reason that, when this situation exists, in order for any cooperative approach to function adequately, it is necessary to have it preceded by an investigation of the facts and prosecution of the perpetrators before a court. Once the correct state of justice has been reestablished, then the victims will actually have the mental predisposition to negotiate reconciliation with the perpetrators.

One apparent obstacle to the functioning of the process just described could be represented by the circumstance that, once they have been tried and found guilty by a court, perpetrators themselves may be no longer willing to develop any reconciliation programme in conjunction with the victims. It is certainly natural that, for example, once a person has been sentenced to several years in jail, he/she develops some rancour towards the victims and is therefore unwilling to cooperate with them in whatever respect. In most cases, however, this may be a false problem. Indeed, the programmes of reconciliation in point usually make sense in cases in which the offence against culture to be remedied was the result of some kind of intolerance existing between two different communities, even though the material executor(s) of the offence necessarily were one or more persons. As a consequence, the two phases of judicial enforcement and reconciliation have—at least from the side of the offender(s)—two different addressees, ie the person(s) who materially perpetrated the offence with respect to the former, and the community as a whole with respect to the latter. Even when reconciliation is to be achieved directly with the person(s) responsible for the offence—who have been found guilty and sentenced following the judicial phase—the above obstacle could anyway be overcome by offering adequate incentives to the said person(s), for example a reduction in the length of the sentence, on the condition that they agree to cooperate in good faith with the victim(s).

## 8. Leaving the Past Behind: The Decisive Role of Reparations

As emphasized at the beginning of Section 3, one meaning of the term 'remedy' is 'provide redress to'. Indeed, with respect to the present topic, the aspect of redress may be decisive in order to make a remedy effective. Irrespective of the method that one intends to use in order to remedy offences against culture, reparation remains the best—if not *the only*—way through which the victim may be led to feel that the situation existing before the perpetration of the offence has actually been restored.

As regards offences against culture entailing a violation of human rights, reparation is usually indispensable. In this respect, it is necessary that a very flexible understanding of the term 'reparation' is applied, in the sense that it cannot be understood according to a predetermined catalogue of measures established in light of a static vision of law. On the contrary, it is essential that reparatory measures are tailored to the specific expectations and needs of the victims, or—that is the same—to what is effectively necessary to make it possible that the prejudice produced through the offence that must be repaired is actually restored. In other words, reparation must be effective and adequate to re-establish the situation which would have existed if the offence had not been produced.[101] To this end, when a specific reparatory measure is chosen, it is necessary to assess the *actual* damage suffered by the victims of the offence and ascertain what kind of measure they would consider adequate in order to feel *effectively* repaired. In a gross approximation, this may be realized through ensuring *restitutio in integrum*—when possible—*plus* pecuniary and non-pecuniary damage. The most delicate operation in this respect is represented by the determination of what is adequate in order to effectively repair the non-pecuniary damage, as well as, when *restitutio in integrum* is not possible, of what the most appropriate reparation is per equivalent in light of the specificities of the instant case.

Excellent guidance on how to manage the problem of reparation for culture-related human rights breaches (ie offences against culture determining human rights violations) is offered by the practice of the I/ACtHR, probably the most advanced international body in this respect. This practice is epitomized by the reparatory measures established by the Court in the *Xákmok Kásek* case,[102] a controversy concerning the denial of land rights to an indigenous community living in Paraguay. In this case, the Court first of all ordered that return to the said community of their traditional land was ensured, as 'the measure of reparation

---

[101] On this issue see the assessment in Lenzerini, 'Reparations for Indigenous Peoples in International and Comparative Law: An Introduction', in F. Lenzerini (ed), *Reparations for Indigenous Peoples: International and Comparative Perspectives* (2008) 3 at 13–15.
[102] See *Case of Xákmok Kásek Indigenous Community v Paraguay*.

that comes closest to *restitutio in integrum*'; this implied that the state had to take 'all the necessary legislative, administrative and any other measures to ensure the Community members' right to ownership of their traditional land, and, consequently, to the use and enjoyment of those lands'.[103] In determining reparation for non-pecuniary damage, the I/ACtHR adopted a marked culturally-driven approach, stressing the need to

assess the special meaning that land has for indigenous peoples in general and for the Xákmok Kásek Community in particular… This means that all denial of the enjoyment or exercise of property rights harms values that are very significant to the members of those peoples, who run the risk of losing or suffering irreparable harm to their life and identity and to the cultural heritage to be passed on to future generations.[104]

Furthermore, the Court established a number of measures of reparation of symbolic nature, which may have a fundamental significance in the context of violations affecting the culture of the community concerned. First of all, the Court considered the judgment as constituting per se a form of reparation;[105] establishment of the truth and of perpetrators' responsibility may indeed represent a decisive step in order to re-establish the pre-existing situation, ie to ensure effective reparation. Additionally—among the other reparatory measures ordered by the I/ACtHR—the state was recommended to conduct a public act of acknowledgment of its responsibility with respect to the violations found in the judgment, to be held at a public ceremony with the participation of senior state officials and community members, with the additional duty for the state to provide the means necessary to facilitate their transportation to the place of the ceremony.[106] Furthermore, the Court established the obligation of the state to ensure publication and broadcasting by radio of the most significant excerpts of the judgment, as well as publication of the entire judgment on an official web page.[107] These forms of reparations, which represent only a part of the totality of those ordered by the I/ACtHR in the case in point, were deemed by the Court as being the most appropriate in light of the circumstances of the case itself. It is important to emphasize that—consistent with what has been stressed at the beginning of this section—the I/ACtHR uses a very dynamic approach in establishing the forms of reparation to be applied, which are shaped in accordance with the specific needs of the victims in each case. Hence, in other judgments the Court ordered reparatory measures of a different kind than those considered appropriate for the *Xákmok Kásek* case, including, for example, building of monuments in memory of the wrong suffered by the victims[108] or naming a recognized street with the name of the victim, including a commemorative plaque making reference to his/her activities.[109] Part of these

[103] See *Case of Xákmok Kásek Indigenous Community v Paraguay*, para 281.
[104] See *Case of Xákmok Kásek Indigenous Community v Paraguay*, para 321.
[105] See *Case of Xákmok Kásek Indigenous Community v Paraguay*, operative para 11.
[106] See *Case of Xákmok Kásek Indigenous Community v Paraguay*, para 297.
[107] See *Case of Xákmok Kásek Indigenous Community v Paraguay*, paras 298–9.
[108] See eg *Case of the Moiwana Community v Suriname*, para 218.
[109] See *Case of Chitay Nech et al v Guatemala*, para 251. For a more comprehensive assessment of the measures of reparation applied by the IACtHR in cases concerning indigenous peoples, see

measures have a markedly psychosocial nature, pursuing the aim of restoring the collective social structure of the affected community.[110]

Another point to be stressed is that, when an offence against culture translates into a human rights breach, it most likely affects a community as a whole rather than one or a few single individuals. As mentioned above in Section 5, this circumstance is to be duly considered when establishing the measures of reparation to be applied in a specific case. These measures must therefore be modelled in light of the peculiar needs of the community as a collective rather than of—or in addition to—those of its members who are authors of the relevant claim, as persons individually damaged by the offence.[111] Indeed, as previously mentioned, the ultimate purpose of cultural rights—even though formally recognized on an individual basis—consists in 'ensuring the survival and continued development of the cultural, religious and social identity' of the communities to which the individuals concerned belong.[112] It follows that, once the 'survival and continued development' of the cultural identity of the relevant community has been affected, reparation must pursue the goal of restoring such a value. Reparatory measures must therefore be selected so as to ensure that they are capable of fulfilling this purpose.

Human rights regional courts undoubtedly represent the most efficient international bodies in terms of effectiveness of reparation. Less effective are international criminal law courts; indeed, as noted above in Section 5, their main purpose consists in ensuring punishment of perpetrators of international crimes, and therefore they are usually not equipped with adequate competence to order reparatory measures in favour of victims. The most notable exception in this respect is represented by the ICC, as its Statute,[113] for the first time as regards international criminal tribunals, contemplates the possibility for the Court to order a perpetrator to pay reparation in favour of the victim(s) of his/her action. In particular, Article 75 of the Statute states that reparation may take the forms of restitution, compensation, and rehabilitation, on the basis of the principles established by the Court. The Court may make an order directly against a convicted person specifying appropriate reparations due to the victim(s) or, where appropriate, may also order that the award for reparations be made through the Trust Fund provided for by Article 79 of the Statute.[114] Such a Trust Fund was established in 2002 and is funded by

Citroni-Quintana Osuna, 'Reparations for Indigenous Peoples in the Case Law of the Interamerican Court of Human Rights', in Lenzerini (2008) 317; see also Vrdoljak, 'Reparations for Cultural Loss', in Lenzerini (2008) 197.

[110] See Gomez, 'Indigenous Peoples and Psychosocial Reparation: The Experience with Latin American Indigenous Communities', in Lenzerini (2008) 143.

[111] It may be useful to recall that—with only the exception of the African regional system—cases concerning violations of human rights may be formally brought before international monitoring bodies only by, or on behalf of, individuals, in consequence of the fact that the main human rights treaties (with the important exception of the African Charter of Human and Peoples' Rights) conceive and attribute such rights as individual prerogatives.

[112] See note 22 above and corresponding text.     [113] See note 44 above.

[114] On the legal foundations of the ICC Trust Fund, see Mégret, 'Justifying Compensation by the International Criminal Court's Victims Trust Fund: Lessons from Domestic Compensation Schemes', 5 November 2009, available at <http://papers.ssrn.com/sol3/papers.cfm?abstract_id=1501295> (accessed 2 August 2012).

voluntary contributions, money, and other property collected through fines or for-feiture transferred to the Fund by order of the Court, resources collected through awards for reparations, and all other resources that the Assembly of states parties decides to allocate to the Trust Fund.[115] The Court may grant not only individual, but also collective reparation to the benefit of a whole group or community.[116]

Apart from the ICC, the opportunity to receive redress from international criminal law courts is limited to the symbolic forms of reparation represented by the official recognition—in a judgment—of the wrong suffered as well as by the punishment of perpetrators. However, the significance of these forms of reparation should not be underestimated, as they often represent extremely important steps in re-establishing the social order in the community upset by the offence suffered and, in many cases, are felt by victims as being much more rewarding than economic compensation and other reparatory measures.

## 9. Conclusion

Offences against culture represent a quite intricate reality, with huge implications from a number of perspectives, culture being the 'spiritual genetic code' of persons individually and communities collectively. As can be concluded from the foregoing assessment, the offences in point may bring with themselves countless implications, all of which must be duly taken into account when managing the delicate problem of suppressing and remedying the said offences. In many occasions suppressing and remedying an offence against culture does not simply mean resolving only the specific offence in itself; sometimes it also means redressing serious wrongs committed against the supreme value of human dignity, or allowing a community to preserve and transmit its cultural identity to future generations, or even creating fertile ground for a better future, based on tolerance and understanding rather than on hatred and prejudice. It is therefore essential that an holistic understanding of 'culture' is nurtured, in the context of which all the innumerable shades of colour and meanings subsumed within such a simple word are accurately understood, as well as that all of them are reinstated in their correct place when trying to eliminate the effects of an offence against culture. Only in this way, the action of suppressing and remedying offences against culture will be tantamount to doing justice, and culture will be allowed to effectively play its role in the world, to the benefit of the whole of humanity.

---

[115] See Resolution ICC-ASP/1/Res.6 of the Assembly of States Parties to the ICC Statute of 9 September 2002, available at <http://www.icc-cpi.int/iccdocs/asp_docs/Resolutions/ICC-ASP-ASP1-Res-06-ENG.pdf> (accessed 2 August 2012), para 2.

[116] See Resolution ICC-ASP/4/Res.3 of the Assembly of States Parties to the ICC Statute of 3 December 2005, available at <http://www.icc-cpi.int/iccdocs/asp_docs/Resolutions/ICC-ASP-ASP4-Res-03-ENG.pdf> (accessed 2 August 2012), Annex, Pt III, Ch IV.

# Bibliography

## BOOKS

Ahmed, T., *The Impact of EU Law on Minority Rights* (Hart Publishing, 2011)

Ahrén, M., Scheinin, M., and Henriksen, J.B., *The Nordic Sami Convention: International Human Rights, Self-Determination and Other Central Provisions* (Resource Centre for the Rights of Indigenous Peoples, 2007)

Aikio, P. and Scheinin, M. (eds), *Operationalizing the Right of Indigenous Peoples to Self-Determination* (Åbo Akademi University, Institute for Human Rights, 2000)

Anaya, S.J., *Indigenous Peoples in International Law* (2nd edn, Oxford University Press, 2004)

Anderson, B., *Imagined Communities: Reflections on the Origin and Spread of Nationalism* (2nd edn, Verso, 1991)

Beck, P.V., Walters, A.L., and Francisco, N., *The Sacred: Ways of Knowledge, Sources of Life* (Navajo Community College, 1977)

Benhabib, S., *The Claims of Culture: Equality and Diversity in the Global Era* (Princeton University Press, 2002)

Berger, T.R., *A Long and Terrible Shadow: White Values, Native Rights in the Americas 1492–1992* (Douglas & McIntyre, 1991)

Bernhardt, R. et al (eds), *Völkerrecht als Rechtsordnung—Internationale Gerichtsbarkeit—Menschenrechte. Festschrift für Hermann Mosler* (Springer, 1983)

Bouchard, G. and Taylor, C., *Building the Future: A Time for Reconciliation. Report of the Commission on Accommodation of Practices Related to Cultural Differences* (Gouvernement du Québec, 2008)

Charters, C. and Stavenhagen, R. (eds), *Making the Declaration Work: The United Nations Declaration on the Rights of Indigenous Peoples* (IWGIA, 2009)

Claude, I.L., *National Minorities: An International Problem* (Harvard University Press, 1955)

Coates, K.S., *A Global History of Indigenous Peoples: Struggle and Survival* (Palgrave Macmillan, 2004)

Cohen, F.S., *Handbook of Federal Indian Law* (US Government Printing Office, 1942)

Craig, P. and de Búrca, G., *EU Law: Text, Cases and Materials* (4th edn, Oxford University Press, 2008)

Craig, P. and de Búrca, G. (eds), *The Evolution of EU Law* (2nd edn, Oxford University Press, 2011)

Croome, J., *Reshaping the World Trading System: A History of the Uruguay Round* (2nd rev edn, Kluwer Law International, 1999)

Curry, S., *Indigenous Sovereignty and the Democratic Project* (Ashgate Publishing, 2004)

Daes, E.-I., *Indigenous Peoples: Keepers of Our Past, Custodians of Our Future* (IWGIA, 2008)

Deloria, V. Jr, *Custer Died For Your Sins: An Indian Manifesto* (Macmillan, 1969)

Donders, Y.M., *Towards a Right to Cultural Identity?* (Intersentia, 2002)

Durkheim, E., *The Division of Labour in Society* (Free Press, 1933)

Echols, M.A., *Food Safety and the WTO: The Interplay of Culture, Science and Technology* (Kluwer Law International, 2001)

Edmunds, R.D., Hoxie, F.E., and Salisbury, N., *The People: A History of Native America* (Houghton Mifflin Harcourt Publishing Co, 2006)

Eliade, M., *The Sacred and the Profane* (Harcourt, Inc, 1959)

Ferrari, M., *Risk Perception, Culture, and Legal Change: A Comparative Study on Food Safety in the Wake of the Mad Cow Crisis* (Ashgate Publishing, 2009)

Gardner, J.P. (ed), *Human Rights as General Norms and a State's Right to Opt Out: Reservations and Objections to Human Rights Conventions* (British Institute of International and Comparative Law, 1997)

Getches, D.H., Wilkinson, C.F., and Williams, R.A. Jr (eds), *Cases and Materials on Federal Indian Law* (5th edn, Thomson/West, 2005)

Glendon, M.A., *Rights Talk: The Impoverishment of Political Discourse* (Free Press, 1991)

Glendon, M.A., *A World Made New: Eleanor Roosevelt and the Universal Declaration of Human Rights* (Random House, 2001)

Hertzke, A.D., *Freeing God's Children: The Unlikely Alliance for Global Human Rights* (Rowman & Littlefield, 2004)

Jaimes, M.A. (ed), *The State of Native America: Genocide, Colonization, and Resistance* (South End Press, 1992)

Jaulin, R., *La Paix Blanche: Introduction à l'ethnocide* (Éditions du Seuil, 1970)

Jennings, F., *The Invasion of America: Indians, Colonialism, and the Cant of Conquest* (University of North Carolina Press, 1975)

Joas, H., *The Sacredness of the Person: A New Genealogy of Human Rights* (Georgetown University Press, 2013)

Kant, I., *Grounding for the Metaphysics of Morals* (J.W. Ellington trans, 3rd edn, Hackett Publishing Company, 1993)

Kickingbird, K., et al, *Indian Sovereignty* (The Institute, 1977)

Knapp, A. and Wright, V., *The Government and Politics of France* (5th edn, Routledge, 2006)

Koselleck, R., *The Practice of Conceptual History: Timing History, Spacing Concepts* (Stanford University Press, 2002)

Kretzmer, D. and Klein, E. (eds), *The Concept of Human Dignity in Human Rights Discourse* (Kluwer Law International, 2002)

Kymlicka, W., *Liberalism, Community and Culture* (Clarendon Press, 1989)

Kymlicka, W., *Multicultural Citizenship: A Liberal Theory of Minority Rights* (Clarendon Press, 1995)

Kymlicka, W., *Multicultural Odysseeys: Navigating the New International Politics of Diversity* (Oxford University Press, 2007)

Lasswell, H.D. and Kaplan, A., *Power and Society: A Framework for Political Inquiry* (Yale University Press, 1950)

Lasswell, H.D. and McDougal, M.S., *Jurisprudence for a Free Society: Studies in Law, Science and Policy* (Martinus Nijhoff Publishers, 1992)

Lauterpacht, H., *International Law and Human Rights* (Stevens, 1950)

Lenzerini, F. (ed), *Reparations for Indigenous Peoples: International and Comparative Perspectives* (Oxford University Press, 2008)

Lévi-Strauss, C., *Race et Histoire: Suivi de l' Œuvre de Claude Lévi-Strauss* (Gonthier, 1967)

Lijnzaad, L., *Reservations to UN-Human Rights Treaties: Ratify and Ruin?* (Martinus Nijhoff Publishers, 1994)

Lillich, R.B., *The Human Rights of Aliens in Contemporary International Law* (Manchester University Press, 1984)

Locke, J., *Locke on Toleration*, R. Vernon (ed) (Cambridge University Press, 2010)

MacCormick, N., *Legal Rights and Social Democracy: Essays in Legal and Political Philosophy* (Clarendon Press, 1982)

MacPherson, C.B., *The Political Theory of Possessive Individualism: Hobbes to Locke* (Clarendon Press, 1962)

Mazzola, R. (ed), *Diritto e religione in Europa. Rapporto sulla giurisprudenza della Corte europea dei diritti dell'uomo in materia di liberta religiosa* (Il Mulino, 2012)

Merlini, C. and Roy O. (eds), *Arab Society in Revolt. The West's Mediterranean Challenge* (Brookings Institution Press, 2012)

Mitchell, A.D., *Legal Principles in WTO Disputes* (Cambridge University Press, 2008)

Morris, C.W. (ed), *George Herbert Mead, Mind, Self and Society: From the Standpoint of a Social Behavioralist* (University of Chicago Press, 1934)

Muir, R., *Modern Political Geography* (Wiley, 1975)

Ndahinda, F.M., *Indigenousness in Africa: A Contested Legal Framework for Empowerment of 'Marginalized' Communities* (T.M.C. Asser Press, 2011)

Newman, D., *Community and Collective Rights: A Theoretical Framework for Rights Held by Groups* (Hart Publishing, 2011)

Pauwelyn, J., *Conflict of Norms in Public International Law: How WTO Law Relates to Other Rules of International Law* (Cambridge University Press, 2003)

Pentassuglia, G., *Minorities in International Law: An Introductory Study* (Council of Europe, 2002)

Perry, M.J., *The Idea of Human Rights: Four Inquiries* (Oxford University Press, 1998)

Posner, E.A., *The Perils of Global Legalism* (University of Chicago Press, 2009)

Psychogiopoulou, E., *The Integration of Cultural Considerations in EU Law and Policies* (Martinus Nijhoff Publishers, 2008)

Rawls, J., *Political Liberalism* (Columbia University Press, 1993)

Raz, J., *Ethics in the Public Domain: Essays in the Morality of Law and Politics* (Clarendon Press, 1994)

Rosas, A. and Armati, L., *EU Constitutional Law: An Introduction* (Hart Publishing, 2010)

Roy, O., *Secularism Confronts Islam* (Columbia University Press, 2009)

Roy, O., *Holy Ignorance: When Religion and Culture Part Ways* (Columbia University Press, 2010)

Schneider, H. and van den Bossche, P. (eds), *Protection of Cultural Diversity from a European and International Perspective* (Intersentia, 2008)

Slaughter, A.-M., *A New World Order* (Princeton University Press, 2004)

Strauss, A. (ed), *George Herbert Mead, On Social Psychology: Selected Papers* (University of Chicago Press, 1964)

Sunder, M., *From Goods to a Good Life: Intellectual Property and Global Justice* (Yale University Press, 2012)

Torbisco Casals, N., *Group Rights as Human Rights: A Liberal Approach to Multiculturalism* (Springer, 2006)

Vaïsse, J., *Neoconservatism: The Biography of a Movement* (Belknap Press of Harvard University Press, 2010)

Voltaire, *Treatise on Tolerance*, Harvey, S. (ed), (Cambridge University Press, 2000)

Voon, T., *Cultural Products and the World Trade Organization* (Cambridge University Press, 2007)

Wenzel, N., *Das Spannungsverhältnis zwischen Gruppenschutz und Individualschutz im Völkerrecht* (Springer, 2008)

Wiessner, S., *Die Funktion der Staatsangehörigkeit* (Attempto, 1989)

Wilmer, F., *The Indigenous Voice in World Politics: Since Time Immemorial* (Sage, 1993)

Witte, Jr, J. and Alexander, F.S. (eds), *Christianity and Human Rights: An Introduction* (Cambridge University Press, 2010)

Xanthaki, A., *Indigenous Rights and United Nations Standards: Self-Determination, Culture and Land* (Cambridge University Press, 2007)

Ziemele, I. (ed), *Reservations to Human Rights Treaties and the Vienna Convention Regime: Conflict, Harmony or Reconciliation* (Martinus Nijhoff Publishers, 2004)

## ARTICLES, CHAPTERS, AND REPORTS

Addis, 'Individualism, Communitarianism, and the Rights of Ethnic Minorities', 67 *Notre Dame L Rev* (1992) 615

Addis, 'On Human Diversity and the Limits of Toleration', in I. Shapiro and W. Kymlicka (eds), *Ethnicity and Group Rights* (New York University Press, 1997)

Åhren, 'Protecting Peoples' Cultural Rights: A Question of Properly Understanding the Notion of States and Nations?', in F. Francioni and M. Scheinin (eds), *Cultural Human Rights* (Martinus Nijhoff Publishers, 2008)

Allott, 'On First Understanding Plato's *Republic*', 22 *EJIL* (2011) 1165

Anaya and Grossman, 'The Case of Awas Tingni v. Nicaragua: A New Step in the International Law of Indigenous Peoples', 19 *Arizona J Int'l & Comp L* (2002) 1

Anaya and Wiessner, 'The UN Declaration on the Rights of Indigenous Peoples: Towards Re-empowerment', *JURIST Forum*, 3 October 2007, available at <http://jurist.law.pitt.edu/forumy/2007/10/un-declaration-on-rights-of-indigenous.php>

Anaya and Williams, 'The Protection of Indigenous Peoples' Rights Over Lands and Natural Resources under the Inter-American Human Rights System', 14 *Harvard Human Rights J* (2001) 33

Annicchino, 'Winning the Battle by Losing the War: The Lautsi Case and the Holy Alliance between American Conservative Evangelicals, the Russian Orthodox Church and the Vatican to Reshape European Identity', 6 *Religion and Human Rights* (2011) 213

Annicchino, 'Osservazioni sul conflitto tra il principio di autonomia dei gruppi religiosi ed altri diritti fondamentali: a proposito di alcune recenti pronunce della Corte Suprema degli Stati Uniti e della Corte europea dei diritti dell'uomo', 1 *Quaderni di diritto e politica ecclesiastica* (2013) 55

Annicchino, 'Tra margine di apprezzamento e neutralità: il caso "Lautsi" e i nuovi equilibri della tutela europea della libertà religiosa', in R. Mazzola (ed), *Diritto e religione in Europa. Rapporto sulla giurisprudenza della Corte europea dei diritti dell'uomo in materia di libertà religiosa* (Il Mulino, 2012)

Balibar, 'Possessive Individualism Reversed: From Locke to Derrida', 9 *Constellations* (2002) 299

Barelli, 'The Role of Soft Law in the International Legal System: The Case of the United Nations Declaration on the Rights of Indigenous Peoples', 58 *Int'l & Comp LQ* (2009) 957

Bay, 'From Contract to Community: Thoughts on Liberalism and Postindustrial Society', in F.R. Dallmayr (ed), *From Contract to Community* (M. Dekker, 1978)

Bernard, 'A "New Governance" Approach to Economic, Social and Cultural Rights in the EU', in T.K. Hervey and J. Kenner (eds), *Economic and Social Rights under the EU Charter of Fundamental Rights: A Legal Perspective* (Hart Publishing, 2003)

Broude, 'Taking "Trade and Culture" Seriously: Geographical Indications and Cultural Protection in WTO Law', 26 *University of Pennsylvania Journal of International Economic Law* (2005) 623

Burger, 'Making the Declaration Work for Human Rights in the UN System', in C. Charters and R. Stavenhagen (eds), *Making the Declaration Work: The United Nations Declaration on the Rights of Indigenous Peoples* (IWGIA, 2009)

Calderwood, 'The Protection of Minorities by the League of Nations', 2 *Geneva Research Information Committee Special Studies* (1931) 17

Calo, 'Religion, Human Rights, and Post-Secular Legal Theory', 85 *St John's Law Review* (2011) 495

Capotorti, 'The Protection of Minorities under Multilateral Agreements on Human Rights', 2 *Italian Yearbook of International Law* (1976) 3

Carlson, 'Premature Predictions of Multiculturalism?', 100 *Michigan L Rev* (2002) 1470

Charters, 'The Legitimacy of the UN Declaration on the Rights of Indigenous Peoples', in C. Charters and R. Stavenhagen (eds), *Making the Declaration Work: The United Nations Declaration on the Rights of Indigenous Peoples* (IWGIA, 2009) 280

Chávez, 'The Declaration on the Rights of Indigenous Peoples Breaking the Impasse: The Middle Ground', in C. Charters and R. Stavenhagen (eds), *Making the Declaration Work: The United Nations Declaration on the Rights of Indigenous Peoples* (IWGIA, 2009)

Chinkin, 'Reservations and Objections to the Convention on the Elimination of All Forms of Discrimination Against Women', in J.P. Gardner (ed), *Human Rights as General Norms and a State's Right to Opt Out: Reservations and Objections to Human Rights Conventions* (British Institute of International and Comparative Law, 1997)

Christie, 'Indigeneity and Sovereignty in Canada's Far North: The Arctic and Inuit Sovereignty', 110 *South Atlantic Q* (2011) 329

Christoffersen, 'Impact on General Principles of Treaty Interpretation', in M.T. Kamminga and M. Scheinin (eds), *The Impact of Human Rights Law on General International Law* (Oxford University Press, 2009)

Citroni and Quintana Osuna, 'Reparations for Indigenous Peoples in the Case Law of the Interamerican Court of Human Rights', in F. Lenzerini (ed), *Reparations for Indigenous Peoples: International and Comparative Perspectives* (Oxford University Press, 2008)

Coburn, 'Out of the Petri Dish and Back to the People: A Cultural Approach to GMO Policy', 23 *Wisconsin International Law Journal* (2005) 283

Connors, 'The Women's Convention in the Muslim World', in J.P. Gardner (ed), *Human Rights as General Norms and a State's Right to Opt Out: Reservations and Objections to Human Rights Conventions* (British Institute of International and Comparative Law, 1997)

Corntassel and Hopkins Primeau, 'Indigenous "Sovereignty" and International Law: Revised Strategies for Pursuing "Self-Determination"', 17 *Human Rts Q* (1995) 343

Courtis, 'Notes on the Implementation by Latin American Courts of the ILO Convention 169 on Indigenous Peoples', 18 *Int'l Journal on Minority and Group Rights* (2011) 433

Craufurd Smith, 'The Evolution of Cultural Policy in the European Union', in P. Craig and G. de Búrca (eds), *The Evolution of EU Law* (2nd edn, Oxford University Press, 2011)

Daes, 'The Contribution of the Working Group on Indigenous Populations to the Genesis and Evolution of the UN Declaration on the Rights of Indigenous Peoples', in C. Charters and R. Stavenhagen (eds), *Making the Declaration Work: The United Nations Declaration on the Rights of Indigenous Peoples* (IWGIA, 2009)

De Búrca, 'The Evolution of EU Human Rights Law', in P. Craig and G. de Búrca (eds), *The Evolution of EU Law* (2nd edn, Oxford University Press, 2011)

Deloria, 'Self-Determination and the Concept of Sovereignty', in J.R. Wunder (ed), *Native American Sovereignty* (Garland Publishing, 1996)

De Witte, 'The Cultural Dimension of Community Law', IV-1 *Collected Courses of the Academy of European Law* (Kluwer Law International, 1993)

De Witte, 'The Value of Cultural Diversity in European Union Law', in H. Schneider and P. van den Bossche (eds), *Protection of Cultural Diversity from a European and International Perspective* (Intersentia, 2008)

Donders, 'A Right to Cultural Identity in UNESCO', in F. Francioni and M. Scheinin (eds), *Cultural Human Rights* (Martinus Nijhoff Publishers, 2008)

Donders, 'The Protection of Cultural Rights in Europe: None of the EU's Business?', 10 *Maastricht Journal of European and Comparative Law* (2003) 117

Dorough, 'The Significance of the Declaration on the Rights of Indigenous Peoples and Its Future Implementation', in C. Charters and R. Stavenhagen (eds), *Making the Declaration Work: The United Nations Declaration on the Rights of Indigenous Peoples* (IWGIA, 2009)

Dussias, 'Indigenous Languages under Siege: The Native American Experience', 3 *Intercultural Human Rights L Rev* (2008) 5

Dworkin, 'Foreword', in I. Hare and J. Weinstein (eds), *Extreme Speech and Democracy* (Oxford University Press, 2009)

Echols, 'Food Safety Regulation in the European Union and the United States: Different Cultures, Different Laws', 4 *Columbia Journal of European Law* (1998) 525

Echols, 'Paths to Local Food Security: A Right to Food, A Commitment to Trade', 40 *Vanderbilt Journal of Transnational Law* (2007) 1115

Erueti, 'The International Labour Organization and the Internationalization of the Concept of Indigenous Peoples', in S. Allen and A. Xanthaki (eds), *Reflections on the UN Declaration on the Rights of Indigenous Peoples* (Hart Publishing, 2011)

Estevez, 'Beyond Education', in L. Meyer and B.M. Alvarado (eds), *New World of Indigenous Resistance* (City Lights Books, 2010)

Firestone, Lilley, and Torres de Noronha, 'Cultural Diversity, Human Rights, and the Emergence of Indigenous Peoples in International and Comparative Environmental Law', 20 *American University Int'l L Rev* (2005) 219

Fletcher, 'Indigenous Peoples and the Law—Column 4: Intellectual Property and International Law', 17 *ILSA Quarterly* (2009) 66

FRA, *Respect for and Protection of Persons Belonging to Minorities 2008–2010* (2010), available at <http://fra.europa.eu/fraWebsite/attachments/FRA-Report-Respect-protection-minorities-2011_EN.pdf>

FRA and UNDP, *The Situation of Roma in 11 EU Member States. Survey Results at a Glance* (2012), available at <http://fra.europa.eu/sites/default/files/fra_uploads/2099-FRA-2012-Roma-at-a-glance_EN.pdf>

Francioni, 'Beyond State Sovereignty: The Protection of Cultural Heritage as a Shared Interest of Humanity', 25 *Michigan Journal of International Law* (2004) 1

Francioni, 'Culture, Heritage and Human Rights: An Introduction', in F. Francioni and M. Scheinin (eds), *Cultural Human Rights* (Martinus Nijhoff Publishers, 2008)

Francioni, 'International Human Rights in an Environmental Horizon', 21 *EJIL* (2010) 41

Francioni and Lenzerini, 'The Destruction of the Buddhas of Bamiyan and International Law', 14 *EJIL* (2003) 619

Francioni and Lenzerini, 'The Obligation to Prevent and Avoid Destruction of Cultural Heritage: From Bamiyan to Iraq', in B.T. Hoffman (ed), *Art and Cultural Heritage. Law, Policy and Practice* (Cambridge University Press, 2006)

Franck, 'Are Human Rights Universal?', 80 *Foreign Affairs* (2001) 191

Garet, 'Communality and Existence: The Rights of Groups', 56 *S Cal L Rev* (1982–83) 1001

Germain, 'La religion dans l'espace public en context multiethnique: des accommodements raisonnables au zonage', *Plan Canada*, 11 January 2010, available at <http://www.inrs.ca/sites/default/files/u62/PlanCanada_AnnickGermain_f.pdf>

Goldman, 'The Need for an Independent International Mechanism to Protect Group Rights: A Case Study of the Kurds', 2 *Tulsa J Comp & Int'l L* (1994) 45

Gomez, 'Indigenous Peoples and Psychosocial Reparation: The Experience with Latin American Indigenous Communities', in F. Lenzerini (ed), *Reparations for Indigenous Peoples: International and Comparative Perspectives* (Oxford University Press, 2008)

Harris, 'Race and Essentialism in Feminist Legal Theory', 42 *Stanford Law Review* (1990) 584

Harris-Short, 'International Human Rights Law: Imperialist, Inept and Ineffective? Cultural Relativism and the UN Convention on the Rights of the Child', 25 *Human Rights Quarterly* (2003) 130

Helfer, 'Human Rights and Intellectual Property: Conflict or Coexistence?', 5 *Minnesota Intellectual Property Review* (2003) 47

Higgins, 'A Babel of Judicial Voices? Ruminations from the Bench', 55 *ICLQ* (2006) 791

Hitchcock, 'The Plight of Indigenous Peoples', 49 *Soc Educ* (1985) 457

International Law Association, Committee on the Rights of Indigenous Peoples, 'The Hague Conference (2010): Interim Report' (2010), available at <http://www.ila-hq.org/en/committees/index.cfm/cid/1024>

International Law Association, Committee on the Rights of Indigenous Peoples, 'Sofia Conference (2012): Final Report' (2012), available at <http://www.ila-hq.org/en/committees/index.cfm/cid/1024>

Kahn, 'The Legal Framework Surrounding Maori Claims to Water Resources in New Zealand: In Contrast to the American Indian Experience', 35 *Stanford J Int'l L* (1999) 49

Kibbee, 'Minority Language Rights: Historical and Comparative Perspectives', 3 *Intercultural Human Rights L Rev* (2008) 79

Kingsbury, '"Indigenous Peoples" in International Law: A Constructivist Approach to the Controversy', 92 *American Journal of Int'l Law* (1998) 414

Kiper, 'Do Human Rights Have Religious Foundations?', 7 *Religion and Human Rights* (2012) 109

Klabbers, 'Accepting the Unacceptable? A New Nordic Approach to Reservations to Multilateral Treaties', 69 *Nordic Journal of International Law* (2000) 179

Klabbers, 'On Human Rights Treaties, Contractual Conceptions and Reservations', in I. Ziemele (ed), *Reservations to Human Rights Treaties and the Vienna Convention Regime: Conflict, Harmony or Reconciliation* (Martinus Nijhoff Publishers, 2004)

Klein, 'Minderheitenschutz im Völkerrecht', 123 *Schriftenreihe Kirche und Gesellschaft* (1994)

Klein, 'Menschenwürde und Sprache', in K. Grözinger (ed), *Sprache und Identität im Judentum* (Harrassowitz, 1998)

Klein, 'Minderheiten', 'Minderheitenrechte', 'Minderheitenschutz', in M. Honecker et al (eds), *Evangelisches Soziallexikon* (Kohlammer, 2001)

Knight, 'The Dual Nature of Cultural Products: An Analysis of the World Trade Organization's Decision Regarding Canadian Periodicals', 57 *University of Toronto Faculty of Law Review* (1999) 165

Koivurova, 'Jurisprudence of the European Court of Human Rights Regarding Indigenous Peoples: Retrospect and Prospects', 18 *Int'l Journal on Minority and Group Rights* (2011) 1

Kullmann, 'Der Mensch als politisches Lebewesen bei Aristoteles', 108 *Hermes* (1980) 419

Kymlicka, 'Beyond the Indigenous/Minority Dichotomy?', in S. Allen and A. Xanthaki (eds), *Reflections on the UN Declaration on the Rights of Indigenous Peoples* (Hart Publishing, 2011)

Lenzerini, 'The UNESCO Declaration Concerning the Intentional Destruction of Cultural Heritage: One Step Forward and Two Steps Back', 14 *Italian Yearbook of International Law* (2004) 131

Lenzerini, 'Fostering Tolerance and Mutual Understanding among Peoples', in A.A. Yusuf (ed), *Standard-setting in UNESCO. Volume I: Normative Action in Education, Science and Culture* (Martinus Nijhoff Publishers, 2007)

Lenzerini, 'Reparations for Indigenous Peoples in International and Comparative Law: An Introduction', in F. Lenzerini (ed), *Reparations for Indigenous Peoples: International and Comparative Perspectives* (Oxford University Press, 2008)

Lenzerini, 'Intangible Cultural Heritage: The Living Culture of Peoples', 22 *EJIL* (2011) 101

Lenzerini, 'The Tension between Communities' Cultural Rights and Global Interests: The Case of the Māori *Mokomokai*', in S. Borelli and F. Lenzerini (eds), *Cultural Heritage, Cultural Rights, Cultural Diversity: New Developments in International Law* (Martinus Nijhoff Publishers, 2012)

Letsas, 'The Truth in Autonomous Concepts: How to Interpret the ECHR', 15 *EJIL* (2004) 279

Lévi-Strauss, 'The Action of UNESCO in Bosnia and Herzegovina to Restore Respect and Mutual Understanding among Local Communities through the Preservation of Cultural Heritage', in F. Maniscalco (ed), *La Tutela del patrimonio culturale in caso di conflitto* (Massa Editore, 2002)

Lixinski, 'Treaty Interpretation by the Inter-American Court of Human Rights: Expansionism at the Service of the Unity of International Law', 21 *EJIL* (2010) 585

Lixinski, 'Selecting Heritage: The Interplay of Art, Politics and Identity', 22 *EJIL* (2011) 81

Macklem, 'Minority Rights in International Law', 6 *Int'l Journal of Constitutional Law* (2008) 531

Macklem, 'Indigenous Recognition in International Law: Theoretical Observations', 30 *Michigan Journal of International Law* (2008–09) 177

Mancini and De Witte, 'Language Rights as Cultural Rights: A European Perspective', in F. Francioni and M. Scheinin (eds), *Cultural Human Rights* (Martinus Nijhoff Publishers, 2008)

Margalit and Halbertal, 'Liberalism and the Right to Culture', 61 *Social Research* (1994) 491

Marks, 'Three Regional Human Rights Treaties and Their Experience of Reservations', in J.P. Gardner (ed), *Human Rights as General Norms and a State's Right to Opt Out: Reservations and Objections to Human Rights Conventions* (British Institute of International and Comparative Law, 1997)

Martínez Luna, 'The Fourth Principle', in L. Meyer and B.M. Alvarado (eds), *New World of Indigenous Resistance* (City Lights Books, 2010)

McCorquodale and Simons, 'Responsibility Beyond Borders: State Responsibility for Extraterritorial Violations by Corporations of International Human Rights Law', 70 *Modern Law Review* (2007) 598

McDonald, 'Should Communities Have Rights? Reflections on Liberal Individualism', 4 *Can J L & Juris* (1991) 217

Mégret, 'Justifying Compensation by the International Criminal Court's Victims Trust Fund: Lessons from Domestic Compensation Schemes', 5 November 2009, available at <http://papers.ssrn.com/sol3/papers.cfm?abstract_id=1501295>

Milbank, 'Against Human Rights: Liberty in the Western Tradition', 1 *Oxford Journal of Law and Religion* (2012) 203

Modood, '2011 *Paul Hanly Furfey Lecture*: Is There a Crisis of Secularism in Western Europe?', 73 *Sociology of Religion* (2012) 130

Morse, 'A View from the North: Aboriginal and Treaty Issues in Canada', 7 *St Thomas L Rev* (1995) 671

Moussa, 'The Damages Sustained to the Ancient City of Babel as a Consequence of the Military Presence of Coalition Forces in 2003', in P.G. Stone and J.F. Bajjaly (eds), *The Destruction of Cultural Heritage in Iraq* (Boydell Press, 2008)

Mowbray, 'The Creativity of the European Court of Human Rights', 5 *Human Rts L Rev* (2005) 57

Neumayer, 'Qualified Ratification: Explaining Reservations to International Human Rights Treaties', 36 *Journal of Legal Studies* (2007) 397

Nikken, 'Balancing of Human Rights and Investment Law in the Inter-American System of Human Rights', in P.M. Dupuy, F. Francioni, and E.U. Petersmann (eds), *Human Rights in International Investment Law and Arbitration* (Oxford University Press, 2009)

Oguamanam, 'Indigenous Peoples and International Law: The Making of a Regime', 30 *Queen's LJ* (2004) 348

O'Keefe, 'The "Right to Take Part in Cultural Life" under Article 15 of the ICESCR', 47 *ICLQ* (1998) 904

O'Keefe, 'World Cultural Heritage Obligations to the International Community as a Whole?', 53 *ICLQ* (2004) 189

Otto, 'A Question of Law or Politics? Indigenous Claims to Sovereignty in Australia', 21 *Syracuse J Int'l L & Commerce* (1995) 65

Otto, 'Rethinking the "Universality" of Human Rights Law', 29 *Columbia Human Rights Law Review* (1997) 29

Palermo, 'Domestic Enforcement and Direct Effect of the Framework Convention for the Protection of National Minorities: On the Judicial Implementation of the (Soft?) Law of Integration', in A. Verstichel et al (eds), *The Framework Convention for the Protection of National Minorities: A Useful Pan-European Instrument?* (Intersentia, 2008)

Patten, 'Beyond the Dichotomy of Universalism and Difference: Four Responses to Cultural Diversity', in S. Choudhry (ed), *Constitutional Design for Divided Societies: Integration or Accommodation?* (Oxford University Press, 2008)

Pentassuglia, 'Towards a Jurisprudential Articulation of Indigenous Land Rights', 22 *EJIL* (2011) 165

Pergantis, 'Reservations to Human Rights Treaties, Cultural Relativism and the Universal Protection of Human Rights', in K. Koufa (ed), *Multiculturalism and International Law* (Sakkoulas Publications, 2007)

Phuong, 'The Protection of Iraqi Cultural Property', 53 *ICLQ* (2004) 985

Psychogiopoulou, 'The Cultural Mainstreaming Clause of Article 151(4) EC: Protection and Promotion of Cultural Diversity or Hidden Cultural Agenda?', 12 *European Law Journal* (2006) 575

Raz, 'Free Expression and Personal Identification', 11 *Oxford Journal of Legal Studies* (1991) 303

Réaume, 'Individuals, Groups, and Rights to Public Goods', 38 *U Toronto LJ* (1988) 1

Reisman, 'International Law and the Inner Worlds of Others', 9 *St Thomas L Rev* (1996) 25

Reisman, 'International Lawmaking: A Process of Communication', 75 *Proc Am Soc'y Int'l L* (1981) 101

Reisman, 'The View from the New Haven School of International Law', 86 *Proc Am Soc'y Int'l L* (1992) 118

Reisman, 'Designing and Managing the Future of the State', 8 *EJIL* (1997) 409

Reisman, Wiessner, and Willard, 'The New Haven School: A Brief Introduction', 32 *Yale J Int'l L* (2007) 575

Riedlmayer, 'Destruction of Cultural Heritage in Bosnia-Herzegovina, 1992–1996: A Post-war Survey of Selected Municipalities' (2002), available at <http://hague.bard.edu/ reports/BosHeritageReport-AR.pdf>

Robinson, 'International Protection of Minorities: A Global View', 1 *Israeli YB Human Rts* (1971) 61

Rodley, 'Conceptual Problems in the Protection of Minorities: International Legal Developments', 17 *HRQ* (1995) 48

Rodríguez-Piñero Royo, ' "Where Appropriate": Monitoring/Implementing of Indigenous Peoples' Rights under the Declaration', in C. Charters and R. Stavenhagen (eds), *Making the Declaration Work: The United Nations Declaration on the Rights of Indigenous Peoples* (IWGIA, 2009)

Roht-Arriaza, 'The Pinochet Precedent and Universal Jurisdiction', 35 *New England Law Review* (2001) 311

Scheinin, 'The Right of a People to Enjoy Its Culture: Towards a Nordic Saami Rights Convention', in F. Francioni and M. Scheinin (eds), *Cultural Human Rights* (Martinus Nijhoff Publishers, 2008)

Scheinin, 'The Right to Self-Determination under the Covenant on Civil and Political Rights', in P. Aikio and M. Scheinin (eds), *Operationalizing the Right of Indigenous Peoples to Self-Determination* (Åbo Akademi University, Institute for Human Rights, 2000)

Scheinin, 'The Rights of an Individual and a People: Towards a Nordic Sámi Convention', in M. Åhrén, M. Scheinin, and J.B. Henriksen (eds), *The Nordic Sami Convention: International Human Rights, Self-Determination and Other Central Provisions* (Resource Centre for the Rights of Indigenous Peoples, 2007)

Schöpp-Schilling, 'Reservations to the Convention on the Elimination of All Forms of Discrimination against Women: An Unresolved Issue or (No) New Developments?', in I. Ziemele (ed), *Reservations to Human Rights Treaties and the Vienna Convention Regime: Conflict, Harmony or Reconciliation* (Martinus Nijhoff Publishers, 2004)

Seibert-Fohr, 'The Potentials of the Vienna Convention on the Law of Treaties with respect to Reservations to Human Rights Treaties', in I. Ziemele (ed), *Reservations to Human Rights Treaties and the Vienna Convention Regime: Conflict, Harmony or Reconciliation* (Martinus Nijhoff Publishers, 2004)

Simma, 'Foreign Investment Arbitration: A Place for Human Rights?', 60 *ICLQ* (2011) 573

Simma, 'Universality of International Law from the Perspective of a Practitioner', 20 *EJIL* (2009) 265

Simma and Kill, 'Harmonizing Investment Protection and International Human Rights: First Steps Towards a Methodology', in C. Binder et al, *International Investment Law for the 21st Century: Essays in Honour of Christoph Schreuer* (Oxford University Press, 2009)

Slaughter, 'A Global Community of Courts', 44 *Harvard International Law Journal* (2003) 191

Stamatopoulou, 'Taking Cultural Rights Seriously: The Vision of the UN Declaration on the Rights of Indigenous Peoples', in S. Allen and A. Xanthaki (eds), *Reflections on the UN Declaration on the Rights of Indigenous Peoples* (Hart Publishing, 2011)

Stavenhagen, 'Cultural Rights: A Social Science Perspective', in A. Eide, C. Krause, and A. Rosas (eds), *Economic, Social and Cultural Rights: A Textbook* (Martinus Nijhoff Publishers, 2001)

Stavenhagen, 'Making the Declaration Work', in C. Charters and R. Stavenhagen (eds), *Making the Declaration Work: The United Nations Declaration on the Rights of Indigenous Peoples* (IWGIA, 2009)

Stevenson, 'Indigenous Land Rights and the Declaration on the Rights of Indigenous Peoples: Implications for Maori Land Claims in New Zealand', 32 *Fordham Int'l LJ* (2008) 298

Suksi, 'Personal Autonomy as Institutional Form—Focus on Europe Against the Background to Article 27 of the ICCPR', 15 *Int'l Journal on Minority and Group Rights* (2008) 157

Suksi, 'Functional Autonomy: The Case of Finland with Some Notes on the Basis of International Human Rights Law and Comparisons with Other Cases', 15 *Int'l Journal on Minority and Group Rights* (2008) 195

Symonides, 'Cultural Rights', in J. Symonides (ed), *Human Rights: Concepts and Standards* (Ashgate, 2000)

Taylor, 'The Politics of Recognition', in A. Gutmann (ed), *Multiculturalism: Examining the Politics of Recognition* (Princeton University Press, 1994)

Thames, 'Making Freedom of Religion of Belief a True EU Priority', EUI Working Paper, RSCAS 2012/41 (July 2012), available at <http://www.eui.eu/Projects/ReligioWest/Documents/workingpaper/RSCAS2012-41.pdf>

Tomuschat, 'Protection of Minorities under Article 27 of the International Covenant on Civil and Political Rights', in R. Bernhardt et al (eds), *Völkerrecht als Rechtsordnung, Internationale Gerichtsbarkeit, Menschenrechte: Festschrift für Hermann Mosler* (Springer, 1983)

Torres, 'Indigenous Education and "Living Well": An Alternative in the Midst of Crisis', in L. Meyer and B.M. Alvarado (eds), *New World of Indigenous Resistance* (City Lights Books, 2010)

Tyagi, 'The Conflict of Law and Policy on Reservations to Human Rights Treaties', 71 *British Yearbook of International Law* (2000) 181

Underkuffler, 'Human Genetics Studies: The Case for Group Rights', 35 *J L Med & Ethics* (2007) 383

Vadi, 'When Cultures Collide: Foreign Direct Investment, Natural Resources, and Indigenous Heritage in International Investment Law', 42 *Columbia Human Rights L Rev* (2011) 797

Van Genugten, 'Protection of Indigenous Peoples on the African Continent: Concepts, Position Seeking, and the Interaction of Legal Systems', 104 *AJIL* (2010) 29

Varadarajan, 'A Trade Secret Approach to Protecting Traditional Knowledge', 36 *Yale Journal of International Law* (2011) 371

Vezzani, 'Il Primo Protocollo alla Convenzione europea dei diritti umani e la tutela della proprietà intellettuale di popoli indigeni e comunità locali', 1 *Diritti umani e diritto internazionale* (2007) 305

Vitzthum, 'Begriff, Geschichte und Quellen des Völkerrechts', in W. Graf Vitzthum (ed), *Völkerrecht* (3rd edn, De Gruyter, 2004)

Voon, 'Geographical Indications, Culture and the WTO', in B. Ubertazzi and E.M. Espada (eds), *Le indicazioni di qualità degli alimenti: Diritto internazionale ed europeo* (Giuffrè, 2009)

Voyiakis, 'Access to Court v State Immunity', 52 *ICLQ* (2003) 297

Vrdoljak, 'Intentional Destruction of Cultural Heritage and International Law', XXXV *Thesaurus Acroasium* (2007) 377

Vrdoljak, 'Reparations for Cultural Loss', in F. Lenzerini (ed), *Reparations for Indigenous Peoples: International and Comparative Perspectives* (Oxford University Press, 2008)

Vrdoljak, 'Self-Determination and Cultural Rights', in F. Francioni and M. Scheinin (eds), *Cultural Human Rights* (Martinus Nijhoff Publishers, 2008)

Vrdoljak, 'Genocide and Restitution: Ensuring Each Group's Contribution to Humanity', 22 *EJIL* (2011) 17

Vrdoljak, 'Human Rights and Illicit Trade in Cultural Objects', in S. Borelli and F. Lenzerini (eds), *Cultural Heritage, Cultural Rights, Cultural Diversity: New Developments in International Law* (Martinus Nijhoff Publishers, 2012)

Wager, 'Biodiversity, Traditional Knowledge and Folklore: Work on Related IP Matters in the WTO', 3 *Intercultural Human Rights Law Review* (2008) 215

Waldron, 'Dignity and Defamation: The Visibility of Hate', 123 *Harvard Law Review* (2010) 1569

Warren and Jackson, 'Introduction: Studying Indigenous Activism in Latin America', in K.B. Warren and J.E. Jackson (eds), *Indigenous Movements, Self-Representation and the State in Latin America* (University of Texas Press, 2003)

Weller, 'Settling Self-Determination Conflicts: Recent Developments', 20 *EJIL* (2009) 111

Wiessner, 'Faces of Vulnerability: Protecting Individuals in Organic and Non-Organic Groups', in G. Alfredsson and P. Macalister-Smith (eds), *The Living Law of Nations: Essays on Refugees, Minorities, Indigenous Peoples and the Human Rights of Other Vulnerable Groups in Memory of Atle Grahl-Madsen* (N.P. Engel, 1996)

Wiessner, 'International Law in the 21st Century: Decisionmaking in Institutionalized and Non-Institutionalized Settings', 26 *Thesaurus Acroasium* (1997) 129

Wiessner, 'Indigenous Peoples: General Report', 10 *Y.B. Int'l Envtl L* (2000) 193

Wiessner, 'Indigenous Sovereignty: A Reassessment in Light of the UN Declaration on the Rights of Indigenous Peoples', 41 *Vanderbilt J Transnat'l L* (2008) 1141

Wiessner, 'Law as a Means to a Public Order of Human Dignity: The Jurisprudence of Michael Reisman', 34 *Yale J Int'l L* (2009) 525

Wiessner, 'Re-Enchanting the World: Indigenous Peoples' Rights as Essential Parts of a Holistic Human Rights Regime', 15 *UCLA J Int'l L & Foreign Affairs* (2010) 239

Wiessner, 'Rights and Status of Indigenous Peoples: A Global Comparative and International Legal Analysis', 12 *Harvard Human Rts J* (1999) 57

Wiessner, 'The Cultural Rights of Indigenous Peoples: Achievements and Continuing Challenges', 22 *EJIL* (2011) 121

Wiessner, 'The New Haven School of Jurisprudence: A Universal Toolkit for Understanding and Shaping the Law', 18 *Asia Pacific L Rev* (2010) 45

Wiessner, 'The United Nations Declaration on the Rights of Indigenous Peoples: Selected Issues', in A. Constantinides and N. Zaikos (eds), *The Diversity of International Law: Essays in Honour of Professor Kalliopi K. Koufa* (Martinus Nijhoff Publishers, 2009)

Wiessner and Battiste, 'The 2000 Revision of the United Nations Draft Principles and Guidelines on the Protection of the Heritage of Indigenous People', 13 *St Thomas L Rev* (2000) 383

Wiessner and Willard, 'Policy-Oriented Jurisprudence and Human Rights Abuses in Internal Conflict: Toward a World Public Order of Human Dignity', 93 *AJIL* (1999) 316

Wildhaber, 'The Execution of Judgments of the ECtHR: Recent Developments', in P. M. Dupuy et al (eds), *Common Values in International Law: Essays in Honour of Christian Tomuschat* (Engel, 2006)

Willemsen-Díaz, 'How Indigenous Peoples' Rights Reached the UN', in C. Charters and R. Stavenhagen (eds), *Making the Declaration Work: The United Nations Declaration on the Rights of Indigenous Peoples* (IWGIA, 2009)

Winickoff et al, 'Adjudicating the GM Food Wars: Science, Risk, and Democracy in World Trade Law', 30 *Yale Journal of International Law* (2005) 81

Witte, Jr, 'Law, Religion and Human Rights', 28 *Columbia Human Rights Law Review* (1996) 1

Woehrling, ' "Droits", "liberté" et "accommodements" linguistiques dans la jurisprudence de la Cour suprême du Canada', in *Humanisme et Droit: Ouvrage en Hommage au Professeur Jean Dhommeaux* (Éditions A. Pedone, 2013)

Woehrling, 'Les trois dimensions de la protection des minorités en droit constitutionnel comparé', 34 *Revue de droit de l'Université de Sherbrooke* (2003–04) 93

Woehrling, 'L'obligation d'accommodement raisonnable et l'adaptation de la société à la diversité religieuse', 43 *McGill Law Journal* (1998) 325

Xanthaki, 'Indigenous Rights in International Law Over the Last 10 Years and Future Developments', 10 *Melbourne J Int'l L* (2009) 27

Xiao, 'China's Milk Scandals and Its Food Risk Assessment Institutional Framework', 3 *European Journal of Risk Regulation* (2011) 397

# Index